D0787644

ROBERT DE COTTE

ROBERT NEUMAN

ROBERT DE COTTE

and the Perfection of Architecture in Eighteenth-Century France

THE UNIVERSITY OF CHICAGO PRESS · CHICAGO AND LONDON

ROBERT NEUMAN is associate professor of
art history at Florida State University.

*Publication of this book has been aided
by a grant from the Millard Meiss Publication Fund
of the College Art Association.*

The University of Chicago Press, Chicago 60637
The University of Chicago Press, Ltd., London
© 1994 by The University of Chicago
All rights reserved. Published 1994
Printed in the United States of America

03 02 01 00 99 98 97 96 95 94   1 2 3 4 5

ISBN: 0-226-57437-7 (cloth)

Library of Congress Cataloging-in-Publication Data
Neuman, Robert.
  Robert de Cotte and the perfection of architecture in
eighteenth-century France / Robert Neuman.
        p.   cm.
  Includes bibliographical references and index.
    1. Cotte, Robert de, 1656–1735—Criticism and
interpretation.   2. Architecture, Baroque—
France.   3. Architecture and society—France—
History—18th century.   I. Cotte, Robert de,
1656–1735.   II. Title.
NA1053.C64N48   1994
720′.92—dc20   93-30046

CAL
NA
1053
C64
N48
1994

*For my parents
and for
Jeanne, Mitsy, and Skip*

Contents

Illustrations

Abbreviations

DOCUMENTS

Archives nationales, Paris

		Bibliothèque nationale, Paris	
E	Conseil d'état du roi	Ha, Hc, Hd	Cabinet des estampes
H⁵	Etablissements religieux	Va, Vb, Vc, Vd, Ye	
N II Seine	Cartes et plans	Ms. fr.	Cabinet des manuscrits
N III Seine			
O¹	Maison du roi		

Bibliothèque de l'Institut, Paris

MS 1037–1043   Papiers de Robert de Cotte
MS 1604–1606   Plans divers

PUBLICATIONS

BSHAF   *Bulletin de la Société de l'histoire de l'art français*
GBA   *Gazette des beaux-arts*
JSAH   *Journal of the Society of Architectural Historians*
Marcel   Pierre Marcel, *Inventaire des papiers manuscrits du cabinet de Robert de Cotte* (Paris: Champion, 1906)

NOTE ON MEASUREMENTS AND TRANSCRIPTIONS

Dimensions are normally given in *toises*, the unit of measure employed on plans and in documents during the ancien régime:

    1 *toise* = 6 *pieds* = 1.949 meters = 6.39 feet.

Transcriptions from documents and published sources in the text and notes follow the spelling and diacritical marks of the originals.

Preface

T HIS MONOGRAPH unites for the first time and examines as a coherent whole the major architectural designs of Robert de Cotte. Despite the scope and impact of his career, writings on de Cotte have tended to be fragmentary until now. It is my goal to provide a basic study of his artistic personality and thereby delineate his position in French architectural history.

As head of a governmental agency responsible for international building operations, de Cotte accomplished a considerable quantity of work. My task has been to impose a sense of order upon his wide-ranging activities. I have limited the projects discussed to those for which he took complete credit or in which he played a key role. The major extant buildings with which his name is connected are emphasized here: the Palais Rohan, Strasbourg; Schloss Poppelsdorf, Bonn; the Palais Episcopal, Verdun; the Abbey of Saint-Denis, north of Paris; the Hôtel d'Estrées, Paris; the Hôtel de Réauville, Aix-en-Provence; and the church of Saint-Roch, Paris.

This book focuses on design histories—the germination and growth of projects as indicated by surviving documents, correspondence, and drawings. My text only minimally considers construction histories, which have been outlined by other historians for some of de Cotte's buildings. The unusually large number of drawings from his atelier, many introduced here for the first time, form an intimate record of his professional experiences and, equally, of the requirements of his clients. In discussing the designs, I have attempted to reconstruct the major steps in their evolution, reconstituting lost or abandoned ideas when possible. Analysis of the projects is keyed to several themes outlined in the first three chapters: the process of architectural creation in the Service des bâtiments du roi; de Cotte's formative years in Paris and his study trip to Italy; the various functions of drawings; and the theoretical concepts governing considerations of decorum and use.

In de Cotte's world, architecture comprised a symbolic vehicle that projected the beliefs of contemporary society. The layout of buildings was determined by social, economic, cultural, and political forces, as well as by artistic considerations. Appropriately, therefore, the design histories are accompanied by contextual investigation. Evidence in this realm consists of a variety of primary resources. Letters, diaries, and memoranda serve to illuminate the tastes and contributing roles of de Cotte and his patrons, while contemporary printed sources, such as guidebooks, newspapers, and handbooks on etiquette and court protocol, provide a broad background. Direct quotations allow the participants to speak for themselves.

Several essential studies have provided the foundation for this monograph. In 1906 Pierre Marcel catalogued all of the written papers in the Fonds de Cotte at the Bibliothèque nationale,

Paris, and published concise résumés of their contents, listing the drawings specifically related to each document. In a dissertation on Jules Hardouin-Mansart, Bertrand Jestaz detailed de Cotte's relationship to his mentor (Ecole des chartes, 1962); similarly, in a dissertation based on resources in the Archives nationales, Paris, José-Luc d'Iberville-Moreau produced the first extensive biography of de Cotte (University of London, 1972). For an account of de Cotte's personal history, the reader should consult both of these unpublished works.

Jestaz has also published a transcription of de Cotte's notebooks from his Italian journey of 1689–90. The most zealous champion of de Cotte as a creative designer has been Wend Graf Kalnein, first in a study of Schloss Poppelsdorf, and second, in a volume in the Pelican History of Art series (1972). Most recently, a group of books and articles by Jean-Daniel Ludmann and Bruno Pons have touched on many aspects of de Cotte's output, particularly interior design, a problematic area that I do not discuss except to summarize their findings.

My interest in de Cotte began with my doctoral dissertation, overseen by Nathan T. Whitman (University of Michigan, 1978). I wish to record my indebtedness to the many scholars who have assisted me over the years through conversation, correspondence, and published works, notably the following: in France, Michel Gallet and Danielle Gallet-Guerne, Bertrand Jestaz, Colette Lamy-Lasalle, Jean-Daniel Ludmann, and Bruno Pons; elsewhere in Europe, Christiane Andersson, Rosalys Coope, Jörg Garms, Börje Magnusson, and Roswitha Neu-Kock; in North America, Hilary Ballon, Robert W. Berger, Richard Cleary, George L. Hersey, Steven N. Orso, Christian F. Otto, Myra Nan Rosenfeld, John Rule, Barry Shifman, Patricia Waddy, and Guy Walton. At the Cabinet des estampes, Bibliothèque nationale, Marianne Grivel and Françoise Jestaz graciously accommodated my needs.

Generous financial assistance facilitating research abroad was awarded by the French government, the Kress Foundation, the University of Michigan, and Florida State University. John Jakobson, Patricia Rose, and Suzanne Sutton kindly checked my translations. Thanks are also due to Susan Baldino, my research assistant of some four years, and to Jeannette Hanisee, who provided skillful editing help. Paris was made all the more pleasant across many seasons through the abundant hospitality of Sue and John Love, Suzanne Sutton, and Kate and Martyn Chandler.

ROBERT DE COTTE

Chapter One

Origins and Career

Robert de Cotte was the most influential architect practicing in France during the first half of the eighteenth century.[1] His career spanned the transitional period of Louis XIV's late years as sovereign (1690–1715), the regency government of Philippe, duc d'Orléans (1715–23), and the opening phase of Louis XV's rule (1723–35). As Premier Architecte du Roi from 1708 to 1734, de Cotte executed designs for the French monarch and his court, while acting as consultant to numerous princes, nobles, and urban governors throughout the Continent, all of whom were eager to adopt the formal and iconographic devices associated with the Sun King.

De Cotte's Background and Character

Since de Cotte's written correspondence was carried out in an official capacity, his letters offer little insight into his personality, although they do reveal a certain degree of aristocratic *hauteur* befitting his status. One of the few surviving contemporary summations of de Cotte's abilities appeared in the official journal, the *Mercure galant*, upon his appointment in 1708 as head of the Service des bâtiments du roi, the governmental agency devoted to architecture: "He is an energetic, intelligent, and hard-working man—capable of conceiving grandiose schemes and of carrying them out; and all who have some knowledge of the fine arts speak of him in these terms.

Accordingly, the choice of the king has been universally applauded."[2]

It is tempting to inspect portraits of de Cotte for some revelation about his character. We might presume to detect the vigor and alertness cited by the *Mercure galant* in the sculpted bust by Antoine Coysevox (c. 1707; Frick Collection, New York; fig. 1) or the painting by Hyacinthe Rigaud (1713; Louvre, Paris; fig. 2), were it not for the fact that these works employ the typically flattering conventions of state portraiture.[3] The likenesses are useful, nevertheless, for situating de Cotte within a broad context. The lives of these three major figures—Coysevox (1640–1720), Rigaud (1659–1743), and de Cotte (1656/7–1735)—extended across the years when many French artists absorbed and humanized the styles of the seventeenth century. Two other painters in the vanguard, Antoine Watteau (1684–1721) and the portraitist Nicolas de Largillierre (1656–1746), were also de Cotte's contemporaries. Partly as a result of the international influence wielded by these masters, Paris had firmly replaced Rome as the center of artistic and cultural fashion in Europe by the time of de Cotte's death in 1735.

De Cotte was born into a family of architects.[4] His grandfather, Fremin de Cotte (d. 1666), was architect and engineer to Louis XIII and author of a short treatise on the classical orders (1644).[5] Robert's father and uncle, Charles and Louis,

1. (*Above*) Antoine Coysevox, *Robert de Cotte*, c. 1707 (Frick Collection, New York).

2. (*Right*) Hyacinthe Rigaud, *Robert de Cotte*, 1713 (Musée du Louvre, Paris).

were both architects, and his brother Louis received the post of Contrôleur (supervisor) of the Château Royal de Fontainebleau in 1699.[6] In 1682, Robert married Catherine Bodin, whose sister Anne was the wife of Jules Hardouin-Mansart, de Cotte's predecessor as Premier Architecte. In a tradition stemming from medieval practice, the de Cottes were thus linked through family ties to several closely related architectural dynasties that monopolized the royal building trade from the sixteenth through the eighteenth century—the Mansarts, the Gabriels, and the Delespines.[7] The status of the de Cotte family rose considerably on 21 March 1702, when Robert received *lettres de noblesse* from Louis XIV.[8]

Throughout most of his career de Cotte held several appointments simultaneously in the Bâtiments. As a member of the Académie royale d'architecture, he was theoretically barred from acting as an entrepreneur (contractors were hired independently outside the Bâtiments). However, from the mid-seventeenth century onward numerous government architects engaged in the activity of acquiring land, building on it speculatively, and selling the completed house to a buyer.[9] In this way de Cotte, Hardouin-Mansart, Germain Boffrand, Jacques V Gabriel, and others reaped enormous fortunes outside their official duties. De Cotte rapidly achieved a substantial revenue that permitted him to live like a *grand*

4

seigneur; on his death he left a sizeable estate. The extent of his wealth is suggested by surviving correspondence with the bishopric of Châlons-sur-Marne. In 1719 the bishop of Châlons, Jean-Baptiste-Louis-Gaston de Noailles, wrote to de Cotte indicating that property for a country house was available in the neighboring region. Later, in 1720, following the bishop's death, de Cotte sought to obtain a large four-wheeled carriage from the estate.[10]

Likewise, de Cotte's descendants were social climbers, developing political and legal contacts throughout the eighteenth century. In particular, his architect-son, Jules-Robert (1683–1767), purchased the estate and title of baron de Réveillon from the marquis d'Argenson.

In the instance of princely commissions, de Cotte offered "his services without compensation," as the German architect Balthasar Neumann remarked in 1723 concerning de Cotte's willingness to work on the drawings for the Würzburg Residenz.[11] But letters and documents also reveal de Cotte's desire to receive luxurious gifts from his clients in lieu of payment. For example, his tastes are mentioned in a letter of 26 May 1699 addressed to the prior of the Abbey of Saint-Denis from the supervisor of building operations there, Dom François Quenet, who hoped to pay the architect for designing the new monastery. De Cotte had refused remuneration, insisting that it was his pleasure to serve the abbey, but he offered an alternative, according to Quenet: "'Well,' [de Cotte] said to me, 'if you would like to make me a present of some silver, I will accept that,'" and the architect proceeded to recommend "Monsieur [Nicolas] de Launay, silversmith, who resides at the Louvre gallery; . . . 'But always remember,' [de Cotte] told me, 'that I will accept it only as a gift that you have given to me, not as something that I consider to be my due.'"[12] The Louvre workshops were famous for exquisite and pricey *objets de vertu*.

Similar circumstances further suggest the tenor of de Cotte's relationships with his clients. Along with an itemized list of expenses incurred while in the service of Philip V of Spain (1712–15), the Premier Architecte included a note to the effect that the patron could present to the architect whatever gift was deemed appropriate thanks for the work.[13] He declined payment from the town council of Lyon for services rendered during a visit there in 1700, but Louis XIV granted him permission to accept from the city, renowned for its textile production, the gift of a gold brocaded coat and an article made of crimson damask.[14] For the same reason, the elector of Bavaria, Max Emanuel, gave de Cotte a diamond ring valued at 6000 *livres* in gratitude for a suite of architectural projects (March 1715).[15] In autumn 1725 the Premier Architecte took the elector, who was visiting Paris, on a buying excursion to the Louvre gallery workshops.[16]

Jules-Robert also owned expensive objects. Several extant items that have been traced to his collection were likely handed down from his father: Watteau's painting, *Assembly in a Park* (1716–17; Louvre, Paris), and a pair of medal cabinets with brass-and-tortoise-shell marquetry, attributed to André-Charles Boulle (both first quarter of the century; J. Paul Getty Museum, Malibu, and Hermitage, Leningrad).[17]

The Sun King and His Chief Architect, Jules Hardouin-Mansart

In every respect de Cotte was a product as well as a representative of the Age of Louis XIV, a period when France became the most populous and the most powerful nation in Western Europe. For this reason, before outlining de Cotte's career, it will be useful to survey briefly the principal political events and architectural accomplishments of the Sun King's reign—particularly the buildings designed by the chief architect, Jules Hardouin-Mansart, in whose office de Cotte spent his formative years and whose artistic vocabulary he absorbed.

It was in 1661, some four years after de Cotte's birth, that Louis XIV announced his decision to rule independently without a prime minister. This was the year of the spectacular fête given in honor of the king by his finance minister, Nicolas Fouquet, at the Château de Vaux-le-Vicomte (1657–61; fig. 3). Although the sumptuous building, famous for the domed oval *salon* that swells outward from the garden façade, was in part the cause of Fouquet's disgrace, it became one of the prototypes for the design of country houses and palaces throughout Europe until the end of the eighteenth century. The collaborative team working there, composed of architect Louis Le Vau, decorator Charles Le Brun, and landscape architect André Le Nostre, was called by the monarch to recreate and magnify the splendor of Vaux in the enlargement of the royal retreat at Versailles (the Enveloppe surrounding the earlier Petit Château, 1668–69).

Erecting monumental edifices and waging war proved to be the two chief preoccupations of Louis XIV, usually in alternating sequence on account of the vast sums required for each. Jean-Baptiste Colbert, the minister of commerce and internal affairs who successfully organized the various centralized bureaus of the state, proclaimed in 1663, the year before he became Surintendant des Bâtiments du Roi (financial administrator for royal buildings), "Your Majesty realizes that failing brilliant military actions, nothing establishes the grandeur and spirit of princes better than buildings; and that all of posterity takes the measure of princes by the standard of the superb residences they erected during their lifetime."[18] Out of the old royal architectural office, which dated back to the reign of Charles V (1364–80), Colbert fashioned the new Service des bâtiments du roi. The Premier Architecte acted as administrator, coordinating teams

of architects, draftsmen, building supervisors, and craftsmen, all of whom were on the annual payroll of the agency. Colbert's institution of the Académie royale d'architecture in 1671 had as its purpose the further centralization of the profession, thus ensuring that the principal goal of the building arts was to glorify the king.

Jules Hardouin-Mansart (1646–1708) descended from a dynasty of painters, architects, and sculptors working for the Crown.[19] He was trained by his great-uncle, François Mansart (1598–1666), whose name he took and many of whose drawings he inherited. Having initiated his career around 1667 as a builder of private houses in Paris and Versailles, he rose rapidly in the Bâtiments. Hardouin-Mansart entered the Académie in 1675, became Premier Architecte in 1681, was ennobled in 1682, was named Surintendant in 1699, and received the title of comte de Sagonne in 1702. In his work he proved himself the heir to the two geniuses of mid-seventeenth-century French architecture: his great-uncle, who was widely recognized for having superimposed a monumental and cerebral classicism onto traditional French forms; and Le Vau (1612–70), in whose work dynamic, fluid volumes complemented a theatrical command of space. For example, Hardouin-Mansart deftly combined two motifs favored by Le Vau, the square dome and the three-bay, two-story pedimented frontispiece, with simple but stylish Mansartian elevations in the low wings of one of his earliest royal commissions, the enlargement of the Château de Clagny for the king's mistress, Madame de Montespan (1675–82; fig. 4, bottom right; fig. 5). To this he added his own imprint: an insistent horizontality that resulted from exaggerating the length of the wings and lowering the tall roofs commonly employed by the elder Mansart and Le Vau.

In 1676 Hardouin-Mansart began working at the Hôtel des Invalides, the military hospice lo-

3. Louis Le Vau, garden front, Château de Vaux-le-Vicomte, 1657–61.

cated in Paris on the Left Bank, where he replaced the architect Libéral Bruant. In designing the Eglise du Dôme, he borrowed the central-plan layout from François Mansart's unexecuted plan for the Bourbon funerary chapel at Saint-Denis and modeled the pyramidal south elevation on the elder Mansart's composition for the Minimes church façade, Paris (fig. 6). The result was a daringly original masterpiece, whose soaring vertical lines, crescendo of relief surfaces toward the central axis, and unprecedented height impart a feeling of noble triumph (constructed 1677–91, inaugurated 1706).

Following the peace settlements of the Dutch War in 1678, Louis XIV put into operation the expansion of the palace and park of Versailles on a grand scale; the seat of government was transferred from Paris to the new capital in 1682. On the Garden Front of the palace Hardouin-Mansart filled in the terrace of Le Vau's Enveloppe with the Galerie des Glaces and prolonged the new elevation along two vast wings set back from the Garden Front and extending north and south (figs. 4, 7). The sweeping horizontality of the ensemble is made all the more emphatic by its overwhelming length and the absence of the standard French roof. At the same time, in the newly created town of Versailles Hardouin-Mansart utilized the French basilican form in his design for the church of Notre-Dame, whose columnar frontispiece articulates the street façade (1684–86; fig. 4, lower right, "Paroisse"; fig. 8).

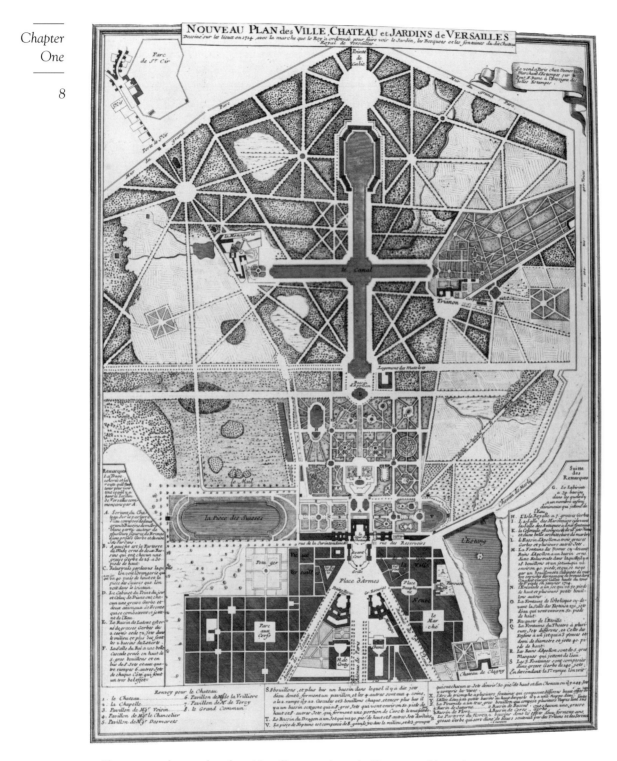

4. Plan, town, palace, and gardens, Versailles, 1714 (print by Demortain, Va 442).

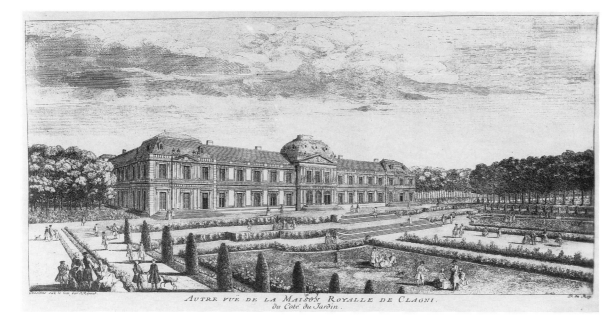

AUTRE VUË DE LA MAISON ROYALLE DE CLAGNI.
du Coté du Jardin.

5. Jules Hardouin-Mansart, garden front, Château de Clagny, 1675–82 (destroyed; print by Rigaud, Va 78h, t. 4).

6. Jules Hardouin-Mansart, façade, Dôme des Invalides, Paris, designed 1676–77, constructed 1677–91, inaugurated 1706.

7. Garden Front, Palace of Versailles, central wing constructed by Louis Le Vau from 1669 and remodeled by Jules Hardouin-Mansart from 1679; Aisle du Midi, 1678–82; below, the Orangerie, 1684–86.

8. (*Left*) Jules Hardouin-Mansart, façade, Notre-Dame de Versailles, 1684–86.

From 1679 to 1686 Hardouin-Mansart worked on the Château de Marly, a garden retreat for the king located north of Versailles. Here two symmetrical files of six guest pavilions faced the main axis of the complex, which was dominated by the Pavillon du Roi, a two-story, freestanding block (fig. 9). The latter was an extraordinary exercise in Italianate planning: the cross-in-square layout, with its central domed *salon,* altered the sixteenth-century prototype, Palladio's Villa Rotonda near Vicenza, through the felicitous insertion of independent apartments in the angles between the vestibules.

The later wars of the Sun King, especially the War of the League of Augsburg (1688–97), increasingly drained the financial resources of the Crown, rendering further large-scale projects impossible and stifling completion of the big undertakings in progress. Ultimately, however, the Treaty of Ryswick in 1697 led to a partial resurgence within the Bâtiments. In Paris construction commenced on the Place Louis-le-Grand, where wealthy financiers built huge town houses behind Hardouin-Mansart's façades bordering the open rectangle of space and focusing on François Girardon's *Equestrian Louis XIV* (Place Vendôme; fig. 10). The elevations resemble the Versailles Garden Front in the emphatic horizontality and seemingly limitless repetition of bays. Mansart introduced greater variety, however, by employing giant Corinthian pilasters to frame the bays and columnar pedimented frontispieces to emphasize the cross axis and the canted corners. The ensemble set the standard for urban squares throughout France during the eighteenth century.

In his final works, Hardouin-Mansart proved to be an innovator by striving for simplicity and habitability in domestic structures. For instance, his plan for the Château Neuf at Meudon, the guest house on the grounds of the Grand Dauphin's château, stressed the commodious arrangement of apartments through extensive use of central connecting corridors (1706–9).[20] He

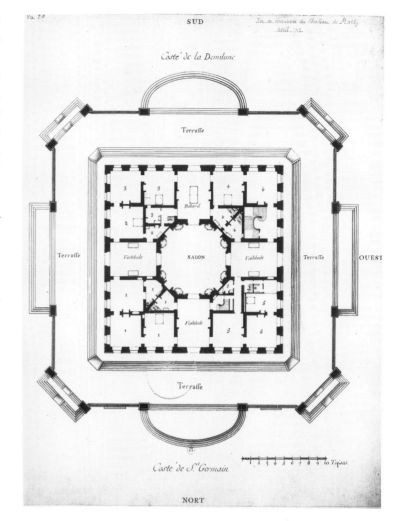

9. Jules Hardouin-Mansart, plan, Pavillon du Roi, Château de Marly, 1679–86 (destroyed; Va 78a, t.3).

10. Jules Hardouin-Mansart, west flank, Place Louis-le-Grand (Place Vendôme), Paris, 1699.

LE CHATEAU NEUF DE MEUDON *est bâty à l'endroit qu'occupoit anciennement la Grotte, c'étoit un bâtiment qui avoit esté fait avec magnificence, mais comme il n'étoit d'aucun usage et qu'il commençoit même à tomber en ruine, Monseigneur le Dauphin fils de Louis XIV voulant profiter de son heureuse situation le fit démolir et bâtir en place ce grand corps de bâtiment qui renferme un nombre d'appartemens très commodes, Ry l'on découvre une vaste fort riche et fort étendue, au dessous de la terrasse qui est au devant du bâtiment est le commencement de l'orangerie qui est une des plus belles qu'on connoisse en France. Mariette excu....*
P. le Pautre Sculp.

11. Jules Hardouin-Mansart, garden front, Château Neuf de Meudon, 1706–9 (partially destroyed; print by Mariette).

concentrated the visual interest of the façade fronting the Parterre de la Grotte not on architectonic motifs, such as columns or horizontal bands defining divisions between floors, but rather on decorative devices, like elegant window surrounds and wrought-iron balconies supported on sculpted brackets (fig. 11).

The eighteenth-century writer Antoine-Nicolas Dezallier d'Argenville aptly characterized Hardouin-Mansart as "the architect most capable of executing the vast projects of Louis XIV. His vivid and brilliant imagination adapted itself equally to different genres—the simple, the gallant, the magnificent, the majestic, or the sublime. Almost all of his works offer up models."[21]

We shall see that the latter judgment was true enough in the case of de Cotte and other architects of the following generation.

De Cotte's Early Years in the Bâtiments

It was in the period of Hardouin-Mansart's ascendancy that de Cotte managed through marriage and professional services to become one of his mentor's valued associates.[22] Having begun his career as an entrepreneur, by 1676 de Cotte was supervising the execution of designs issuing primarily from Mansart's office.[23] Between 1679 and 1687 he received payments, sometimes in partnership with another contractor, for construction at the following royal sites: the château and parish church of Saint-Germain-en-Laye, the château and parish church of Marly, the Machine de Marly, which pumped water from the Seine to Versailles, and reservoirs and stables at the Palace of Versailles.[24]

In his unpublished dissertation on Mansart and his circle, Bertrand Jestaz has shown that de Cotte, unlike the mediocre draftsmen available to Mansart, was the only figure in the late seventies who appears to have assisted in making creative decisions regarding various projects. Moreover, he probably began working in the capacity of draftsman on such buildings as the Eglise des Soldats des Invalides, Paris (under construction 1676–79), and the Château de Clagny. Beginning in 1678 he helped Mansart with domestic commissions in Paris and at the palace and town of Versailles.[25] De Cotte's activities as contractor diminished as his association with Mansart grew, until in 1685 his name appears as Architecte in the building accounts, with the considerable salary of 2,400 *livres*.[26] Thus it was in the late seventies and the early eighties that de Cotte learned the principles of structure and design through direct practical experience.

As Premier Architecte, Mansart organized a new wing of the Bâtiments, the Bureau des plans et dessins, housed in the Surintendance at Versailles. Boffrand and Pierre Cailleteau, called Lassurance, were among the Dessinateurs (draftsmen) employed to develop projects supervised by Mansart. In the years 1685–89 de Cotte played an important role, often through his presence on the site, in such projects as the remodeling of the Château de Fontainebleau and alterations to the Châteaux de Maintenon and d'Ancy-le-Franc; the latter had been purchased by François-Michel Le Tellier, marquis de Louvois, Colbert's successor as Surintendant.[27]

The Trianon de Marbre, Versailles

Dezallier d'Argenville connects de Cotte's rise to fame with an amusing and possibly apocryphal incident (undated) that reveals his repartee with the king:

One day [Mansart] was occupied with laying out *allées* at a royal house in order to procure fine views for Louis XIV. When these [vistas] offered little, he knew how to embellish them. His student [de Cotte] wished to imitate him, but unfortunately he encountered a windmill at the end of an *allée*. The king was taken aback by this. "Sire," said de Cotte to him, "rest assured: Mansart will gild it." To this incident is attributed de Cotte's success, which in turn was responsible for that of his son.[28]

In any case, it is certain that Louis XIV was aware of de Cotte's abilities by 10 January 1687, when Louvois nominated the architect for the chair vacated by Daniel Gittard at the Académie d'architecture.[29] In July of that year the monarch determined to replace the Trianon de Porcelaine, a small retreat set in a luxurious flower garden at the northwestern end of the Petit Parc, Versailles (Le Vau, 1670–72), with the opulent pink and gold Trianon de Marbre that rose on the site in the remarkably short period of seven months. De Cotte's participation in the design of the second Trianon signals his prominence as a member of the Hardouin-Mansart team. In particular, he was involved in the creation of the most innovative part of the building, the peristyle that binds the two halves of the structure together (figs. 4, 12). The king had specifically requested this feature.[30] The peristyle was originally intended to form an open loggia on the colonnaded garden side of the Trianon and a glazed enclosure on the court side.

Letters from Louvois to Mansart, who was ill and thus absent from court in September and October 1687, reveal that the design of the building changed several times during the course of construction and that lesser members of the Bâtiments were called upon to contribute creative solutions. On 18 September the king requested drawings for the peristyle from Mansart, who was taking the cure at Vichy. Impatient for the architect's return, Louis asked de Cotte to propose a solution for the peristyle, as a letter of 22 September 1687 from Louvois to Mansart informs us:

The king, having realized that if he waits until your return, it will not be possible this year to build the wing separating the court of the Trianon from the garden, commanded that I have de Cotte draw up different designs in the style that His Majesty desires. . . . The above-mentioned Monsieur de Cotte presented several projects to His Majesty, who chose the one marked A among the pair in this packet, having found it appropriate to reject the other because of the number of columns it would have been necessary to make. At the same time, he gave the order to begin the foundation and erection of the arcade that will close this gallery-like room on the courtyard side

12. Jules Hardouin-Mansart and collaborators, garden front, Trianon de Marbre (Grand Trianon), Versailles, 1687–88.

of the Trianon. He also commanded that I send the attached plan and elevations to you, so that you may give him your opinion on the decoration necessary to add to the garden front, where His Majesty wishes to have only columns, so that the architecture will be less heavy; since this "room" would remain completely open on the garden side, from within one could enjoy the view of the canal and the entire garden.[31]

Instead of approving de Cotte's project, Mansart sent his own design for the peristyle, but it did not meet with the king's favor.

On 19 October Louvois reported that work on the building was proceeding with such rapidity that further prolongation of Mansart's absence would require more drawings from de Cotte: "Monsieur Mansart, who must not delay his return any longer, will determine the profile of the balusters; but if he does not arrive next week, it will be necessary for de Cotte to design them, so that work can continue without stopping."[32] De Cotte also assisted Le Nostre in drafting plans that coordinated the layout of the structure with that of the new gardens.

In a later retelling of these events, de Cotte's

brother Louis, who presumably knew the details firsthand, spoke of Mansart's jealous reaction to de Cotte's success with the king. In Louis's version of the story, he increased his family's honor by giving his brother the creative edge, as reported by the duc de Luynes in his memoirs:

At this time Monsieur Mansart went to take the cure; meanwhile the king requested a drawing from Monsieur de Cotte, who provided the design of the peristyle as it appears today. (It is from his brother, who is Contrôleur at Fontainebleau, that I know this detail.) The king directed Monsieur de Cotte to execute this drawing at once; Monsieur de Cotte requested the king's permission to send it first to Monsieur Mansart. The king said that he was willing to do so, but that he would commence the work anyway. Monsieur Mansart wrote to the king that this drawing was without value, but his opinions and reasons made no impression on His Majesty, and the project was carried out just as it is today.[33]

The truth is that the design of the peristyle underwent further development at the Bâtiments following the exchange of drawings, with specific authorship remaining uncertain. De Cotte's initial proposals are not extant. Although not documented as being from de Cotte's hand, a cross section of the peristyle bears the stylistic hallmarks associated with him: thin tonal washes to suggest planes of depth, delicate outlines clarifying the forms, edges of shadow brushed without the use of a rule, and brisk hatching (fig. 13; and see chap. 3).[34]

Clearly, de Cotte was an important member of the collaborative group working on the Trianon. His participation at this moment of his career impressed later generations: the peristyle heads the list of de Cotte's works published by the *Mercure de France* upon his death—an attribution repeated by several eighteenth-century biographers.[35]

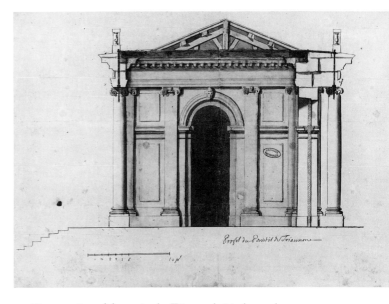

13. Cross section of the peristyle, Trianon de Marbre, colonnade at left, glazed arcade at right, 1687–88 (O¹ 1884¹, no. 2).

Hardouin-Mansart's Reorganization of the Bâtiments in 1699

Despite the architectural successes of the 1680s, the War of the League of Augsburg, begun in 1688, paralyzed activity in the Bâtiments. Although salaries were not affected, Mansart and the other Architectes du Roi turned their attention to private commissions as a means of gaining work.[36] The hiatus in activity offered a welcome opportunity for de Cotte to take a belated study trip to Italy in the company of Jacques V Gabriel between August 1689 and February 1690. Only later did the Treaty of Ryswick usher in a revival of royal projects, notably construction of the Chapelle Royale at Versailles. By 1699 large-scale work, mostly on interiors, was underway at Marly, Meudon, the Trianon, and the King's Apartment, Versailles.

The year 1699 was a crucial one for the Bâti-ments. Mansart, while retaining the post of Pre-mier Architecte, was named Surintendant, the sole time that the important job of financial liai-son with the king was given to an architect instead of a member of the nobility or court bu-reaucracy (7 January).[37] Simultaneously, Mansart instituted changes in the structure of the Bâti-ments and elevated those who had worked faith-fully under him, such as Lassurance. In a lengthy memorandum, he wrote detailed job descriptions for his immediate staff.[38] Furthermore, he en-larged the Bureau des dessins to form three offices located at the main centers of activity—Ver-sailles, Paris, and Marly. The staff of each bureau fluctuated according to the amount of work in progress at each site. Finally, he instituted changes in the Académie d'architecture, particu-larly by increasing the number of academicians from six to seventeen, in addition to the *profes-seur* and *secrétaire*.[39]

Hardouin-Mansart appointed de Cotte direc-tor of the Département de Paris,[40] the most stra-tegic spot in the organization by virtue of the work to be done: the decoration of the Dôme des Invalides,[41] construction of the Place Vendôme, and remodeling of the choir of Notre-Dame de Paris. Although this post removed de Cotte from the king's primary seat at Versailles, the Départe-ment de Paris involved supervision and mainte-nance of such royal dwellings as the Louvre, the Tuileries, the Palais du Luxembourg, and the Châteaux de Vincennes and de Madrid, in addi-tion to such royal foundations as the Manufac-ture des Gobelins, the Jardin Royal, and the Observatoire.[42] Corresponding to this elevated charge, de Cotte's base salary rose to 9000 *livres*.[43] For the first time, certain projects, such as the de-sign of the new Abbey of Saint-Denis (1699), were his responsibility rather than Mansart's.

Mansart described de Cotte's new position as follows:

Duties of Monsieur de Cotte, in the office he directs near me, following my orders:

First, he will be entrusted with the administration of the office where all of the plans for the king's ser-vice will be made; he will have these drawn on the basis of those that I have approved; [he] will main-tain the originals of all these drawings in organized fashion in portfolios divided by royal house, and he will record them consecutively in a register with the date drawn, which will also be inscribed on the sheet; [he] will be charged equally with all of the drawings that were in the office before the resigna-tion of Monsieur de Villacerf [Surintendant follow-ing Louvois], of which an inventory will be made and carefully maintained.[44]

In addition, de Cotte's responsibilities con-sisted of overseeing the royal collection of copper plates and engravings; maintaining the king's warehouses of marble and glass, as well as sup-plies of iron and lead in the magazines of the Dé-partement; keeping track of materials used by the royal factories, such as the Gobelins and Savon-nerie; supervising the use of royal funds allotted to the Académie de peinture et sculpture; and last, but not least, preparing specifications for Mansart's commissions. Small wonder that in May 1699 Quenet described the difficulty of gaining access to de Cotte at the bureau for the purpose of discussing the Saint-Denis project: "Since there was a large crowd waiting to see him, and for a very long time I lacked permission to approach him, I went [instead] to one of the men who had worked on our plans."[45]

De Cotte received another appointment in the form of a royal *brevet:* "Today, 1 March 1699, at Versailles, the king, acknowledging the capa-bility and experience in architecture that Mon-sieur de Cotte has acquired during the twenty-five years he has served in the Bâtiments [i.e., since 1674], has engaged him as his Architecte Ordinaire and Directeur of the Académie d'ar-chitecture established in Paris."[46] With the title of Architecte Ordinaire, de Cotte was clearly designated second in command within the hierarchy of the Bâtiments. As Hardouin-Mansart's right-hand man he journeyed to Lyon in 1700 to present to the city fathers Mansart's drawings for renovating the Hôtel de Ville and the design for the pedestal of Desjardins's *Equestrian Louis XIV*. Traveling with a draftsman, de Cotte prepared plans of the city's squares and bridges as a means of determining the best location for the statue.[47]

With de Cotte thus acting as head of the Paris office, the normal process of collaboration became even more systematized, as the architects and draftsmen contributed at various levels to the overall realization of each project.[48] Jacques V Gabriel, whose mother was Hardouin-Mansart's cousin, was appointed "autre Architecte" after de Cotte. He, too, held extensive administrative responsibilities involving preparation of memoranda and account books and supervision of warehouses not under de Cotte's control.[49]

The Académie royale d'architecture

De Cotte's appointment in 1699 as director of the Académie d'architecture grew out of his role as general overseer of the Département de Paris. He also received the honorary positions of Conseiller Honoraire (7 March 1699) and Vice-Protecteur (30 June 1705) in the Académie de peinture et sculpture.[50] Although François Blondel had acted as director of the Académie d'architecture upon its inception in 1671, de Cotte was the first architect to receive the title officially; after 1717 it was automatically given to the Premier Architecte. The post was strictly honorific, requiring no specific duties. On ceremonial occasions de Cotte presided over the group: for example, on 22 February 1717 he presented the institution's statutes and rules to the company; on 2 August 1719 he welcomed the young Louis XV to the Académie's quarters in the Louvre.[51]

As intended by the king, the purpose of the Académie was to formulate and teach official doctrine. Whatever theoretical training de Cotte may have had was probably the result of the meetings of the academicians, which consisted primarily of readings and discussions of Vitruvius and French and Italian Renaissance theorists (e.g., the year 1695 was devoted to reviewing Alberti's *De re aedificatoria*). Ancient and Renaissance buildings also formed the basis for analysis (the Château de Chambord and the Escorial ranked among the subjects). The minutes show that de Cotte attended meetings sporadically in the late eighties, took a more active part in the early nineties, and then appeared very infrequently until 1717, when he began to attend on a regular basis. Since the meetings were usually conducted by the *professeur*, mention of de Cotte's participation is rare in the minutes of the Académie. In March 1690 he discussed the problem of designing impost blocks in conjunction with pilasters, and in June that year he was charged with presentation of a drawing explaining relative widths between superimposed columns.[52] In April 1693 he gave an illustrated lecture on the principal churches of Venice and Bologna, which he had seen on his Italian trip.[53] In February 1726 he and son Jules-Robert reported on the principle of the steam engine, an interest shared with Boffrand.[54]

De Cotte as Premier Architecte du Roi

With the death of Mansart on 11 May 1708, de Cotte at age fifty-one became Premier Architecte, a position he maintained for twenty-six years.[55] The *Mercure de France* announced the appointment as follows: "Since the work carried out in the royal houses must be very noble, it being more than just a matter of maintaining them, it was necessary to name a successor as soon as possible after the death of Monsieur Mansart, who was a responsible man in filling the position of Premier Architecte. His Majesty did not hesitate to name Monsieur de Cotte, who was appointed to the post of Intendant des Bâtiments, having long worked under the late Monsieur Mansart, whose brother-in-law he was."[56] De Cotte's base salary jumped to 12,000 *livres* per year, to which was added income from other official posts, such as the Académie.[57] More than ever de Cotte consulted directly with the monarch, as contemporaries testified: "The king was at work with de Cotte, his Premier Architecte" (marquis de Dangeau, 23 May 1708); "I have to wait, because Monsieur de Cotte's time is very precious, as he is constantly with the king" (Balthasar Neumann, 24 February 1723).[58]

De Cotte did not, however, become Surintendant. That position was temporarily suppressed, and Louis XIV claimed immediate responsibility for financial decisions. A new post, Directeur Général des Bâtiments, in other respects similar to that of Surintendant, was created and awarded to the son of Madame de Montespan, the duc d'Antin (10 June 1708).[59] Only after the death of Louis XIV was the Surintendance reinstated, with d'Antin acting as financial liaison with the king (1716).[60]

The hierarchical system of the Bâtiments, modeled on that of the monarchy itself and inherited from Mansart, allowed de Cotte to accomplish a great deal of work through the participation of many minds and hands in the conception and elaboration of each project.[61] In brief, the system worked as follows. The Premier Architecte took responsibility for all royal projects, as well as for upkeep and outfitting of royal residences in collaboration with their respective Contrôleurs. Through active supervision on all levels he managed to give his personal stamp to every scheme. He normally worked on the initial ideas in drawings and rough sketches handed over to draftsmen to copy in finished form, and he drew up the accompanying *devis* (specifica-

tions list). He was also responsible for the execution by his assistants of wood, plaster, or wax models and of detailed construction drawings to be used on the site. The *devis* for a royal project was presented to the Conseil des bâtiments for approval, that for a commission outside royal jurisdiction to the individual patron. The *devis* then went to contractors, who presented their bids at a specified meeting at the Hôtel de la Surintendance. A private patron would sign a *marché* (contract) with an entrepreneur before a notary, specifying the price and nature of the work. The Premier Architecte made regular visits to ascertain the progress of construction. Payment was made upon completion of the work and its inspection (*toisé*), with a *mémoire* provided by the contractor.

The assistant to the Premier Architecte was the Architecte Ordinaire (the post held under de Cotte by Jacques V Gabriel), to whom lesser projects were often delegated and who stood in during the absence of the former.[62] They were both responsible to the Directeur Général or Surintendant, who controlled the budget and was accountable to the king. The Surintendant in turn watched over the Contrôleurs of the royal buildings. These Contrôleurs and the Dessinateurs responsible for all of the finished drawings held positions that were creative to varying degrees: for example, Balthasar Neumann wrote to his patron in 1723, "I have talked with [de Cotte's] staff, consisting of very fine architects who help with the work."[63] Depending on the talent they showed and the number of years they served, they might become Architectes du Roi and members of the Académie, *première* or *seconde classe*. As in today's big corporate firms, the head architect received all public credit.

However, despite his position as Premier Architecte, de Cotte faced little prospect of large-scale commissions from the Crown. The costly War of the Spanish Succession (1702–11) forced

France to the brink of bankruptcy. In 1714, one year prior to his death, Louis XIV decreed that the Premier Architecte and members of the Bâtiments should visit all royal properties where work was under way or in preparation so that, on the basis of current prices for labor and materials, the king could determine which programs should continue.[64] Although relatively few new jobs came from the monarch, the repair and remodeling of royal buildings was a continual task for the Premier Architecte and the roughly three hundred employees within various ranks of the Bâtiments.[65]

At Versailles there were no new architectural additions in the years of de Cotte's tenure, with the exception of interiors, of which the chief rooms were the Chapelle Royale (1708–10), the Salon d'Hercule (1712–15, 1729–35), and the Chambre de la Reine (1725–30).[66] It was in his official capacity that de Cotte also supervised the radical transformation of the choir of Notre-Dame de Paris.[67] Nevertheless, compared to the late seventeenth century, when Louis XIV had monopolized building resources, most of the first half of the eighteenth century saw the Crown lose its position as arbiter of the architectural scene. Nor could de Cotte expect jobs from Philippe d'Orléans, Louis XIV's nephew and ruler of France during the minority of Louis XV (1715–23).[68] The regent immediately moved the court from Versailles to Paris and installed the young king in the Palais des Tuileries. Philippe resided in the Palais Royal, where he had his own architect, Gilles-Marie Oppenordt. Although upon coming to power Louis XV eventually requested from de Cotte projects for the Château de Fontainebleau and Château de Compiègne, these were not executed.[69] Only after de Cotte's retirement in 1734 did Louis XV take a more active interest in architecture.

With so few opportunities for major projects, de Cotte responded to requests from other members of the royal family, such as the comte de Toulouse and the duchesse de Bourbon, illegitimate children of the Sun King, who required magnificent dwellings in Paris. The exodus of courtiers from Versailles, which commenced even before the Regency, initiated a widespread revival of private construction in Paris, in which de Cotte participated. Furthermore, the city fathers of both the capital and various provincial towns requested plans for urban projects from the Premier Architecte. The clergy went about the business of completing the basilicas of France. All of Europe may have feared and despised Louis XIV at the time of his death in 1715, but the example he set as absolutist ruler and patron of the arts survived him and flourished. Thus as Premier Architecte de Cotte was much sought after by European sovereigns for palace and villa designs evoking the *Style Louis XIV*.

Since de Cotte rarely traveled to sites beyond the Ile-de-France, he made use of assistants sent out from Paris or of local architects as intermediaries between himself and the patron. Some clients, like Joseph Clemens, elector of Cologne, realized that their chances of conferring with the Premier Architecte were greater if they went to see him in Paris; the elector requested at least an audience with Jules-Robert.[70] In fact, the latter did occasionally act on his father's behalf, as when he traveled to Spain bearing the Buen Retiro Palace projects to Philip V.

De Cotte normally employed assistants to prepare site plans and to advise him on the local terrain. The elector of Cologne, noting a discrepancy between the projects for the Palace of Bonn and the size of the site, wrote to de Cotte: "You have put it well, Monsieur, that in designing a building one cannot make sound judgments without being on the site and seeing for oneself the effect it has."[71] In one particular instance, de Cotte reprimanded an aide. René Carlier, working in Madrid, had failed to inform him about the slope of the terrain around the Palace of Buen Retiro, and as a result the king's agent, Jean Orry, was critical of the excavations necessitated by de Cotte's initial project.[72] Two artists working under de Cotte at the Château de Saverne, Charles Le Bouteux and Charles Carbonnet, turned to their master for advice on the slightest difficulties pertaining to buildings or gardens.[73]

The most important function of these assistants was to oversee execution of the work, especially in foreign countries, where local building traditions threatened to corrupt the designs. Writing to de Cotte from Bonn, Guillaume Hauberat explained the hiatus in the flow of reports concerning construction with this excuse: "It has been a long time since I had the honor of writing to you, because during the entire winter nothing meriting your attention has been accomplished."[74] Hauberat also worked for de Cotte in Frankfurt. In addition to these architects, there were others, some of whom we shall meet in the following chapters: Benoît de Fortier and Michel Leveilly at Bonn; Joseph Massol and Le Chevalier at Strasbourg; a certain Meusnier at Châlons-sur-Marne; Denis Jossenay and Guillain at Verdun; Pierre de Vigny at Constantinople; Martin de Noinville at Dijon; and Claude Simon at Montauban.[75] Wend Graf Kalnein has summarized the situation as follows: "The extension of such a network of building operations right across Europe as far as Turkey from one single central office was remarkable: it was unparalleled in the eighteenth century."[76]

Besides de Cotte there were several other architects who appropriated and extended the Hardouin-Mansart style in the first third of the century. Their relationship to de Cotte and to the Bâtiments varied. Jacques V Gabriel (1667–1742) grew up in an architectural dynasty that by the 1690s was connected through marriage to the

Mansart, de Cotte, Delisle, and Delespine families, all at work in Paris for the Bourbon court.[77] As we have seen, he traveled with de Cotte to Italy in 1689–90. He became an academician and Contrôleur of the Département des dehors de Versailles in 1699, was promoted to Architecte Ordinaire upon de Cotte's advancement to the office of Premier Architecte in 1708, and received control of the Département des dedans de Versailles in 1709. Lassurance (1655–1724) served as Mansart's chief draftsman in the Bâtiments between 1684 and 1699, was promoted to Architecte et Dessinateur in 1700, and received the position of Contrôleur at the Hôtel des Invalides in 1702.

Germain Boffrand (1667–1754) was de Cotte's only serious rival in the scale of his talents and variety of commissions.[78] Beginning in 1686 he was in the service of Hardouin-Mansart, overseeing execution of the Place Vendôme and curating the drawing collection (after 1690). Between 1699 and 1709 he was not employed at the Bâtiments; in this period he designed for the duke of Lorraine and the elector of Bavaria. In de Cotte's administration Boffrand worked again for the Crown and entered the Académie. However, the strained relationship between the two in the 1720s was apparent to Balthasar Neumann, who journeyed to Paris to obtain their opinions of plans for the Würzburg Residenz. Wrote Neumann, "Neither knows anything of [my dealings with] the other, so that I may remain in good standing with both and not arouse jealousy; whenever the subject [of my trip] came up in the company of friends of one or the other, I repeatedly said that I had come to hear the opinion of that particular architect."[79]

De Cotte's bitterest enemy was Pierre-Alexis Delamaire (1676–1745), architect of the twin Hôtels de Rohan and de Soubise, Paris (1704–9). In the manuscript "La pure verité" he claimed that de Cotte owed his fortune as much to connections as to talent and that by means of unjust gossip he ruined Delamaire's hopes of gaining commissions. Furthermore, he asserted that Mansart and "his creatures" undermined his relationship with the prince de Soubise, with the result that de Cotte and Boffrand took over work at the *hôtel* during construction.[80]

Theory

The building designs of de Cotte and his colleagues reflect the ideals expounded by a rising number of contemporary theorists, according to whom it was not strict adherence to the rules of the Ancients and of Renaissance masters that achieved *la belle architecture* but the exercise of good judgment and taste.[81] Three related principles require definition here.

Bienséance was a term that originated among the theoreticians. It signified decorum, the close relationship between a building's form and purpose, and respect for tradition in its design.[82] J. L. de Cordemoy stated, "*Bienséance* is that [rule] which assures that [a particular] layout is such that one can find nothing contrary to nature, custom, or use."[83] The word also denoted harmony between the various parts of a structure.

The word *convenance*, from Alberti's use of *convenienza* (suitability, decorum), was first employed in France by professional architects.[84] Similar to *bienséance*, it meant that all parts of a building—the exterior elevations, the location of rooms, the choice of materials, and the decoration of the interior—should suit its purpose and the social status and wealth of the patron. The lay critic Michel de Frémin wrote in 1702, "*Convenance* in buildings is one of the principal concerns of the architect; it is an art that regulates the entire structure, for in every part the placement of each detail must be suitable, natural, and necessary."[85] This was crucial in a world governed by rules of protocol and public display. By extension, *convenance* required the rapport, both formal and iconographic, between exterior and interior.

Distribution (from the Vitruvian *distributio*), the art of planning, or in de Cordemoy's words, "the suitable arrangement of all the parts of a building," was considered by the architect Jean Courtonne "the principal and most essential" element of architecture.[86] Jacques-François Blondel, defining its broader implications, wrote in 1737, "In addition to consisting of arranging well all of the rooms composing a building, there is another sort of *distribution*, which concerns decoration, both interior and exterior."[87]

The importance accorded these principals resulted in a sharp awareness of building types and the requirement that the function of a building be immediately evident from its appearance. The classification of buildings into types reached its apogee in Blondel's *Cours d'architecture*, where numerous subcategories are grouped under three major headings: private dwellings, public buildings and monuments, and ecclesiastical edifices (vol. 2, 1771). For example, in the first category, under the rubric of city dwellings, Blondel discusses palaces, *hôtels particuliers* (luxurious town houses for those of noble blood and for wealthy bourgeois), and apartment buildings for merchants and shopkeepers.

To de Cotte and his contemporaries, it was clear that every building type had its own tradition of planning, wall articulation, and iconography of architectural and decorative forms. Thus de Cotte treated each commission as a typological problem. At the start of the design process he consulted the established models bequeathed by the great figures of the seventeenth century—above all, François Mansart, Le Vau, and Hardouin-Mansart. We will see that in a period stressing synthesis and resolution, de Cotte's goal was to bring to perfection the repertory of French architectural motifs that these and other architects had developed during the Renaissance and Baroque periods.

The traditional manner of studying an artist's oeuvre is to consider the works chronologically. However, the lack of consistent stylistic evolution in de Cotte's designs allows an alternative method. Given the century's interest in classification, it seems appropriate that a typological survey should form the basis for the discussion of his work, beginning with international princely commissions for palaces and country houses, proceeding to urban structures, including public squares and private houses, and finishing with ecclesiastical designs. The buildings discussed here date from the years 1699–1734, that is, from de Cotte's accession as Architecte Ordinaire to his retirement from the post of Premier Architecte.

Chapter Two

The Italian Sojourn

B<small>Y</small> 1689 <small>DE</small> C<small>OTTE</small> was the chief rising star in the Bâtiments. Surely, it was clear to both Louis XIV and Hardouin-Mansart that he might one day assume a position of leadership. Thus the suspension of building operations caused by the War of the League of Augsburg provided a welcome opportunity for de Cotte to complete his artistic education by traveling abroad. That the king encouraged the trip is suggested by a letter of introduction addressed by the marquis de Louvois, Surintendant des Bâtiments, to La Teulière, Directeur of the Académie de France in Rome: "Monsieur de Cotte, one of the king's architects, [is] going to Rome by order of His Majesty to instruct himself; please help him in every way that you can."[1] De Cotte opened his travel diary with a reference to the royal indulgence: "The king having consented to my taking the Italian voyage, I left Paris 29 August 1689."[2] No doubt the trip was in some measure intended to make up for the fact that Hardouin-Mansart had not been to Italy. De Cotte, then in his early thirties, toured in the company of Jacques V Gabriel, who was ten years his junior.

Upon arrival on the peninsula, de Cotte moved southward from Genoa to Florence, where he stayed a few days. From there he journeyed to Rome, "the goal of my trip," as he put it.[3] The first of thirty-seven days in the Eternal City was spent walking from one end to the other without stopping, in order to get a general pic-

ture of the whole and to decide on which monuments to concentrate. It was not Ancient Rome of the pagan emperors that most impressed him; rather, he stated, "I found this city filled with an infinite number of churches, each as magnificent as the others, and in a different style, and a great quantity of palaces of considerable breadth and height"[4]

He returned northward by moving to the Adriatic coast, first to Ancona and Rimini, and subsequently inland to Bologna. From there he traveled to Venice, where he remained twenty-five days, savoring the delights of the city in painting and sculpture as well as in architecture. Next he moved westward to Padua and Vicenza, proclaiming of the latter,

This town is one of Italy's most beautiful; there are many fine buildings erected after the designs of Palladio, all adorned with classical elements; he discussed them in the book he wrote [*I quattro libri dell'architettura*]; nevertheless, I drew plans of the best things as a reminder; the exterior loggias of the palace [Basilica] and the Théatre de la Comédie [Teatro Olimpico] are the principal works.[5]

Finally, from Verona de Cotte returned to Genoa via Modena and Parma, arriving in Lyon by 17 February 1690. He had spent about five and one-half months abroad.

De Cotte's travel diary consists principally of two small notebooks hastily scribbled in his hand. The numerous misspellings and illegible phrases betray a minimal education in writing skills. He composed the entries during the course of the trip, if not on a daily basis, at least city by city, using notes and drawings made at various sites. Most of the text is devoted to listing, describing, and critiquing the buildings he saw, some in more detail than others. By sampling his comments, arranged here according to building

14. Jacopo Sansovino, Library of St. Mark's, Venice, begun 1537 (left), and Vincenzo Scamozzi, Procuratie Nuove, 1582 (right), detail of northeast elevation and section of ground floor loggia drawn by Robert de Cotte, 1689 (Vb 30, 1140).

type, we may gain some insight into his tastes and ideals before surveying his designs in subsequent chapters.

Occasionally de Cotte refers to other experiences enjoyed during the trip—for example, the splendid fireworks and illuminations accompanying the election of Pope Alexander VIII, or an operatic performance at the Teatro Farnese, Parma, judged admirable for its voices and music but lengthy and wanting in dance compared with French opera. A glimpse of the arduous nature of seventeenth-century travel is allowed when, during the leg of the journey between Genoa and Turin, he complains about difficult mountain roads, unfavorable weather, uncomfortable lodgings, and highway bandits.

One of de Cotte's goals was to compile a visual record that might later yield ideas for his own projects ("qui peut donner des ide").[6] In addition to a few sketches in the diary itself, he recorded more than eighty monuments in plans, elevations, and sections, some possibly with the aid of Gabriel. Drawings were frequently made during the course of a visit to a site, to judge from comments in the notebooks: for example, "I took down plan and elevations" (SS. Annunziata, Florence); "I made a drawing to serve my memory" (altar tabernacle, Cappella dei Principi, S. Lorenzo, Florence); "I felt that drawings would be more valuable than a long report, which is why I drew plans and elevations" (St. Peter's, Rome).[7] Architectural prints, abundant in this period, probably provided models for many of the drawings. Several of the finished renderings that have come down to us may have been carried out following his return to Paris—for example, in preparation for his presentation in 1693 at the Académie on Venetian and Bolognese churches. The drafting technique principally combines pen-and-ink outline with diagonal hatching and brushed washes for tonal modeling, as may be seen in the elevation and section of Sansovino's

Library (begun 1537) and Scamozzi's Procuratie Nuove (1582) in the Piazza S. Marco, Venice (fig. 14).

It is clear from the notebooks that throughout the trip de Cotte exercised a strong and individual sensibility regarding classical architecture. He did not hesitate to denounce Ancient structures that failed to live up to his expectations, including such august examples as the Pantheon, Rome ("Having examined [it] well, I realized that this church is without proportions"), and the Temple of Vesta, Tivoli ("This temple is not good architecture").[8] The degree of critical self-assuredness formed prior to the journey is likewise evident in his reactions to modern buildings; for example, in the lengthy commentary that accompanies the drawings of the Piazza S. Marco, he meticulously evaluated every element in the juxtaposed façades, in particular the use of the orders. He found fault with many details, such as the design of the balusters below the windows and the incorporation of small oval apertures in the Ionic frieze, intended "to illuminate the mezzanine, but serving, I believe, little purpose."[9] In retrospect, it appears from the highly personal nature of his criticisms that as a practicing architect he embraced the ideal of flexibility with respect to rules of proportion and use of the orders. In so doing, de Cotte was following the tenets set forth by such figures as Claude Perrault in the *Ordonnance des cinq espèces de colonnes* (1683) and the expanded second edition of Vitruvius (1684), where he argued that an architect's individual eye and developed sense of taste were the proper determinants of beauty, albeit within certain limits. We shall see in the following chapters that de Cotte's own handling of the orders was at times surprisingly unorthodox. Often he allowed other considerations, such as restraints imposed by the site or conditions arising from the plan, to influence his design of elevations.

The Palazzo

In describing urban dwellings, de Cotte did not distinguish between the palazzo for the *principe assoluto* and the palazzo for the *gentiluomo privato*. This is because in Italy the building types of the palace and the town house were not as strongly differentiated as in France. Nevertheless, he recognized that the imposing blocky grandeur of Italian urban residences, whether of the nobility or the commercial oligarchy, possessed greater monumentality than the French *hôtel particulier*, with its slender wings surrounding a large courtyard. At the same time, he proudly declared his belief that the Palace of Versailles exceeded the dwellings of Italian dukes and princes by virtue of its extraordinary vastness and imposing grounds.

De Cotte's notes on *palazzi* focus on both *distribution* and *circulation*, the control of the visitor's movement through the plan. He does not consider rooms to be independent, inactive units: in his parlance, a vestibule "leads," an enfilade "conducts," a stair "arrives," or a gallery "directs" along a predetermined path. Most of his comments on plans are purely descriptive, intended as an *aide-mémoire* for the future. For example, the elevations of the Palazzo Ducale, Venice, offered de Cotte little visual excitement ("le viel pallais"), but the layout of the rooms, their variety of shapes and functions, and the method of proceeding through the building fascinated him; he sketched plans of the doge's apartment on the second floor and the council chambers on the third floor (fig. 15), and surveyed the palace in a characteristic passage:

One enters by several means of approach into a great courtyard where there are many stairs; within the block is located a stair called the Scala dei Giganti, which projects into the court, facing the principal entry from the square [Piazzetta S. Marco]. This stair is very large and easy to ascend, there being about fif-

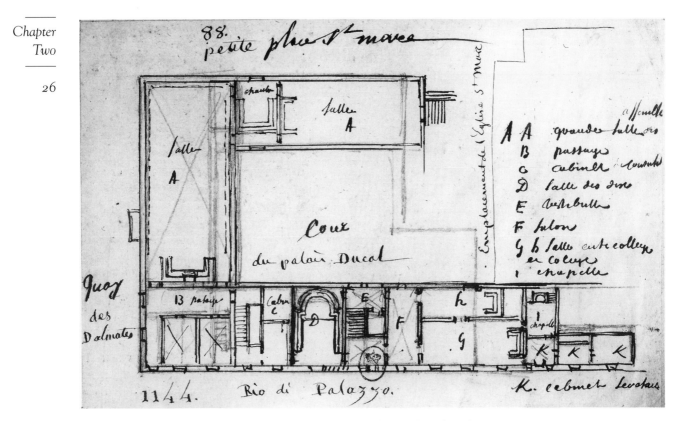

15. Plan, third-floor council chambers, Palazzo Ducale, Venice, drawing by Robert de Cotte
with his handwriting in the legend at right, 1689 (Vb 30, 1144).

teen feet of steps. This leads to a gallery [loggia]
above that on the ground floor, facing the courtyard
while providing access to several rooms that serve as
offices. One comes upon several staircases leading to
the floor above, among them one staircase larger
than the others, whose vaults and walls are decorated
with stucco and paintings in a very good style, being
by Sansovino [Scala d'Oro; 1555–58]; a vestibule on
the third floor leads to all of the audience and assembly rooms and the apartment of the doge. This entire
floor is filled with paintings by the best masters.[10]

The degree of commodious entry into a palazzo was one of de Cotte's concerns. In the case
of the Palazzo Balbi-Senarega, Genoa (Bartolomeo Bianco, after 1620), he believed that the
hilly site imposed severe limitations in this regard: the *cortile*, he said, is inaccessible to carriages, being on higher ground than the street
portal, which must therefore be entered on foot.

Being familiar with the more spacious *hôtel* courtyards in Paris, he found the central *cortile* of Italian palazzi generally to be too constricted. Although he called the Palazzo Farnese (1517–50)
"the most beautiful, most perfect and regular that
is in Rome,"[11] attributing the building to Michelangelo alone (as opposed to Antonio da Sangallo
the Younger, the initial designer), he felt claustrophobic in the court, judging it too high and
too enclosed for a plan of its size. Similarly,
he disapproved of the use of rustication for the
courtyard of the Palazzo Pitti, claiming that the
space was too small for so aggressive an articulation. Even so, what he liked about such interior
courts was the usual presence of loggias. He delighted in rows of arcades and columns, often superimposed, for which there was no equivalent in
French *hôtel* courtyards.

As in the case of the Doge's Palace, staircases of unusual size or shape, particularly when designed to impress the viewer and quicken the sense of anticipation, usually elicited a special response. For example, at the Palazzo Doria-Tursi, Genoa (begun 1551), he described in detail the visitor's movement up a single flight of steps from the vestibule to a colonnaded courtyard, and from there to a "grand escailler" whose single ramp arrives at a landing where two branching stairs rise to opposing loggias on the main floor. Although the play of convex and concave bays in the street elevation of Guarini's Palazzo Carignano, Turin (1679), was too vigorous for de Cotte's taste, he was sufficiently impressed by the pair of curving staircases behind the façade to draw a plan of the central block, "extraordinary and bizarre in style and form."[12]

Once within a private suite of rooms, de Cotte cast about a careful eye in consideration of *commodité*. Describing the arrangement of the rooms at the Palazzo Balbi-Senarega, he noted critically, "I did not see a single room that would properly accommodate a bed. . . . In the apartments on each floor I noticed that there were no fireplaces, since apparently they are concealed."[13]

No element of Italian interior decor amazed him more than the quantity of superb paintings and sculpture. In the Planetary Rooms of the Palazzo Pitti he was overwhelmed by Pietro da Cortona's lush decoration (1641–45), which from the standpoint of *convenance* he perceived to be perfectly suited to the status of the patron: "This is of great magnificence; I have never seen anything more beautiful or impressive—the placement of the pictures, the perfect adaptation of the decoration, and the well-designed cornices. This apartment is furnished very well, serving the grand duke, who gives audience here."[14]

The Villa

The open air and fine prospects of many villas were a source of delight to de Cotte. He had no difficulty in gaining access to major estates, since owners willingly made them quasi-public in order to assert their power and taste through the display of paintings and classical statuary. De Cotte inspected the major villas in and around Rome, including those at Frascati and Tivoli, took in the Medici Villa de Poggio Imperiale on the outskirts of Florence, and went out to Sanpierdarena, "which is next to the city [of Genoa], where all the inhabitants have *maisons de plaisance* entirely painted on the outside with all sorts of frescoes."[15]

As in the case of the palazzo, the ground plan attracted de Cotte's attention first, receiving a brief description in his journal. The classic villa layout had influenced French château design from the early sixteenth century onward, and so de Cotte was familiar with the standard type—a blocklike structure frequently square in plan, with a centrally located two-story *salone* flanked by a pair of identical apartments. The passages in his diary describing such buildings as the Villa Borghese, Rome, and the Villas Mondragone and Aldobrandini, Frascati, stress the simplicity and symmetry of their ground plans.

Despite the Albertian dictum that "the allures of licence and delight are allowed" on exterior elevations of country houses,[16] de Cotte disapproved of the abundance of sculpture adorning such Roman buildings as the Villa Medici and the Villa Borghese. Of the latter he judged, "The building is decorated with figures and marble bas-reliefs, all antique, some fine but the greater part disagreeable, encrusted on the walls more or less symmetrically; however, the number visible have the effect of confusing the good with the bad."[17]

The trip on the Brenta Canal from Venice to Padua offered views of many villas:

The riverbanks are bordered by many palaces and country houses of Venetian *signori*, most ornamented with columns and classical details. They all share virtually the same layout, having a vestibule [portico-loggia] projecting from or receding into the building, thus marking the center and the entry. One ascends by a stair as wide as the vestibule, or by two ramps, to the [main] level or ground floor [see fig. 16]. The *salone* is located behind the vestibule; to left and right are several rooms separated by this *salone*. Above this floor is an attic. Many of these palaces have a forecourt and service courts on the sides, as well as gardens; others have their chief façade toward the river. Several of these palaces are by Palladio, which is to say, the best ones.[18]

Although many of the villas along the Brenta are indeed Palladian in style, the only house designed by the master himself is the Villa Foscari at Malcontenta (c. 1558–60; fig. 16). This villa provided de Cotte with one of his most important firsthand experiences of Palladio's com-

positional ideals. The insistently cubic nature of the structure, the great portico raised on an unusually high base and reflected in the water, and the refined channeled rustication discreetly texturing the wall (actually, stucco over brick) together provided a powerful exemplar to an architect in whose native country Palladian design, in the strictest sense, was still rare around 1690.[19] In this connection, it should be noted that although de Cotte does not specifically mention visiting Palladio's Villa Rotonda while touring Vicenza, he certainly knew the building from the *Quattro libri* and from Hardouin-Mansart, whose plan for the Pavillon du Roi at Marly (begun 1679; fig. 9) is based on that of the Rotonda.

De Cotte had many opportunities to see examples of Italian central-plan villas. From his boat on the Brenta he viewed the Palazzo Contarini (now destroyed), where an octagonal dome towered over a two-story X-shaped plan (un-

16. Andrea Palladio, Villa Foscari, Malcontenta, c. 1558–60 (G. F. Costa, *Delle delicie del fiume Brenta*, Venice, 1750–62).

Veduta del Palazzo del N.H. Foscari alla Malcontenta.

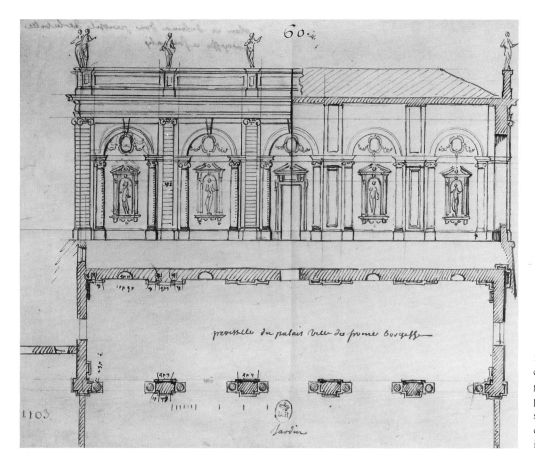

17. Giovanni Vasanzio, garden loggia, Villa Mondragone, Frascati, 1614–21, plan, half elevation and half section drawn by Robert de Cotte, with his handwriting, 1689 (Vb 59, 1103).

documented; c. 1630s, attributed to Baldassare Longhena).[20] He recorded his visit to the Casino dell'Aurora of the Villa Ludovisi, Rome (Giacomo della Porta[?], built before 1577), whose plan is based on the figure of a Greek cross; its two-story arms project from a central core that rises an additional story to form a belvedere. These experiences were of great importance for de Cotte's later participation in the resurgence of ideal planning in France, and particularly in the Palladian Revival, as evidenced by his designs for palaces and *maisons de plaisance*.

De Cotte also recorded the smaller wings and independent garden structures of the villas, such as Giovanni Vasanzio's rusticated loggia built for Cardinal Scipione Borghese at the Villa Mondragone, Frascati (1614–21; fig. 17). His interest in this façade stemmed partly from his admiration for Michelangelo, whom he incorrectly believed to be the loggia's designer.

Compared with the more rigorous effects of the French formal garden, most of the villa gardens visited by de Cotte seemed too simple or casual in composition. The unkempt and deserted air of some, such as those at the Villa Ludovisi and Villa Mattei, Rome, was not to his liking. Nonetheless, having found the fountains at the Villa d'Este to be a good source of ideas, he obtained prints of the garden. To judge from the length of his description, the waterworks at the Villa Aldobrandini pleased him the most. "The view from this house is charming," he wrote, describing the axial alignment of fountains on the hill that rises behind the *palazzino*.[21]

The Italian City

In the journal de Cotte jotted down his reactions to specific aspects of Italian urban planning and to the various metropolitan environments he encountered. His arrival in a city prompted notes on the subject of municipal gates and encircling walls, the particular character of the streets, the lay of the terrain, and the nature of vistas as one moves through a town. Thus, in describing Lucca, he contrasted the long avenue of approach, bordered by trees and splendid gardens on either side, with the crowded narrow streets of the city itself. The Piazza del Popolo, the northern entry into Rome, he called "the most beautiful entrance, forming a great triangular piazza." "This entry gives a superb idea of this city," he exclaimed, describing the obelisk erected by Sixtus V, the twin church façades of S. Maria di Montesanto and S. Maria de' Miracoli, and the trident-shaped configuration of avenues that lead the visitor from the piazza to a network of thoroughfares: "The streets are perfectly beautiful, lying on several hills or knolls creating ups and downs, thus providing variety, which is pleasurable to behold."[22]

De Cotte acknowledged the importance of city gates as impressive frontispieces to the riches contained within the walls. He paid particular attention to the Porta Venezia, Padua, and the Porta del Popolo, Rome, although he criticized minor features of both. This interest was paralleled by his attention to Roman triumphal arches, which had provided many motifs for the design of modern city portals. The connection was made explicit in Ancona, where he spotted "on the city gate a fragment of an ancient arch."[23] He discussed and drew the antique Roman arches he saw in Ancona, Rome, and Verona, often criticizing the incorporation of older sculptural pieces into the framework: "This is

why part of the work is good and part ugly" (Arch of Constantine, Rome).[24]

The contrasting character of Italian cities surprised and delighted de Cotte, who could not resist comparative analysis. Having been charmed by the watery ambience of Venice, he was less enthusiastic about Padua: "This town is not otherwise agreeable after one has seen Venice; the streets are very irregular and poorly paved."[25] The broad avenues of Modena, with their frescoed façades, he characterized in terms very different from those describing the steep, narrow streets of Genoa, where buildings stand six or seven stories tall. In the latter city he experienced one of the most harmonious of Italian urban ensembles, in which the height, width, and alignment of many city palaces had been prescribed when the sector was laid out in the late sixteenth century: "We went to see the Strada Nuova, which is perfectly beautiful, being filled with a great quantity of *palazzi*, all painted on the exterior, with columns, loggias, and marble balconies, the whole forming a very fine prospect."[26] His reaction to the streets of Turin was comparable: "We visited the whole city, half of which is newly built in a regular manner, the streets at right angles, broad, and adorned with buildings whose façades are symmetrical and tastefully ornamented with the classical orders."[27]

Even when monumental structures were lacking, the singularly Italian features of the smaller towns appealed to him, as in the case of the arcaded streets of Faenza and Imola, which allow movement "almost completely under cover."[28] Similarly, the unique quality of Bologna was perceived to be the result of its long stretches of porticoed avenues: "They are both beautiful and of great public utility."[29] De Cotte was impressed by the quantity of paved thoroughfares in Italian towns, praising those that were broad, straight, and laid with sheets of stone, as in Florence, while criticizing others, such as the streets of

Rome, "durable, but difficult to walk on," being comprised of mortared pebbles.[30]

De Cotte recognized the piazza as the principal public space within the Italian townscape. He admired the harmonious and symmetrical grouping of identical façades around a square, such as in the Piazza SS. Annunziata, Florence, and the Piazza S. Carlo, Turin. The Piazza di S. Pietro, Rome (Gianlorenzo Bernini, begun in 1656), although based on an oval plan, he perceived as circular, objecting that "this quantity of columns in the plan is not pleasing—this confusion that resembles a forest." He noted several liberties taken by Bernini in the design of the colonnade, but found acceptable the visual adjustment of the columns to the sloping ground level ("That is quite against the rules, but it is not bad"). Even so, he objected to the method of vaulting the peripheral galleries ("This is poorly designed and unattractive").[31]

Regularity was not a necessary factor in his appreciation of piazzas. The unusual layout and strongly contrasting façades bordering such squares as the Piazza del Duomo, Loreto, and the Piazza Navona, Rome, exerted their own attraction. The Piazza S. Marco, Venice, called forth a detailed description of the various façades, in addition to drawings: "This square is not regular, but that does not keep it from being very beautiful" (figs. 14, 18).[32]

Since water constitutes one of the primary physical components of Italian cities, de Cotte commented extensively on the rivers and canals providing a transportation network. Bridges and quays were described, especially in Venice, whose small bridges he characterized as "very numerous and dangerous, having only a parapet on the side."[33] Roman aqueducts, such as the Aqua Claudia and Aqua Felice, he interpreted as testaments to the engineering skill of the Ancients. The distribution of water throughout Rome was a subject of great interest: "All Rome is filled with

public fountains, much frequented, and in addition almost all of the private houses have water within. Water comes from several sources, from [Lago di] Braccianno, Tivoli, and Trevi, entirely by aqueducts part below and part above ground."[34] The journal also contains descriptions of numerous public fountains he admired, such as those in the Piazza Navona, Rome, and the Piazza del Duomo, Loreto. Taken as a whole, de Cotte's comments on Italian cities demon-

18. Piazza S. Marco, Venice, plan by Robert de Cotte, 1689 (Vb 30, 1139).

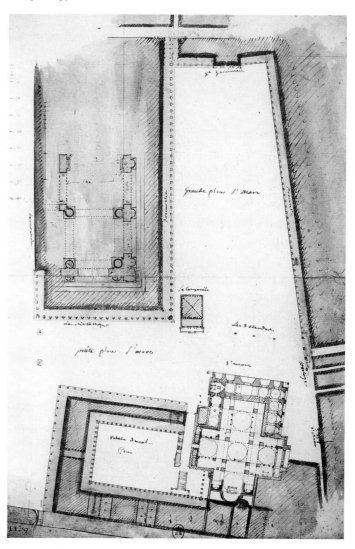

strate that he was a keen observer of the urban scene.

The Church

The majority of drawings and notes from the trip are related to religious monuments. Although de Cotte systematically visited the great Roman Baroque basilicas, dutifully recording plans and interior sections, his verbal descriptions of them tend to lack strong positive comments, and frequently he is very critical. The Gesù he found magnificent, especially its decor, but he objected to certain elements, such as the dome, which he deemed "most unattractive on the outside."[35] Similarly, upon inspecting the basilica of S. Andrea della Valle, he remarked on its size and decoration but disapproved of the bundled pilasters lining the nave walls and the concomitant rippling of the entablature (Fabrizio Grimaldi and Giacomo della Porta, begun in 1591).

Yet certain Northern Italian variations of the Gesù type held great appeal for him, particularly Giuseppe Valeriani's Gesù in Genoa (1589–1606), which he described as "a very beautiful church done with superb taste, small to be sure, but magnificent and correct, in an extremely fine style." He further noted, "What struck me as appearing beautiful is the decoration of the high altar with the same order of pilasters and columns as those used throughout the church; this makes the work more magnificent." In short, the use of a heterogeneous set of elements to provide continuity throughout the interior caused him to exclaim, "This church is one of the best works to be seen. I regretted not having the time to draw a plan."[36] Another modification of the Gesù type, Giovanni Magenta's church of S. Pietro, Bologna (1605), which incorporates two pseudo-crossings within the nave, prompted de Cotte to write, "I found there an extraordinary grandeur and height, treated differently from the other [churches], which is why I drew the plan as a reminder. The architecture [of the elevations] is not treated as well, but the plan is very well done."[37]

De Cotte's reaction to Venetian basilicas was entirely favorable. As usual he had high praise for Palladio, ranking S. Giorgio Maggiore (1564–80) and the Redentore (1576/7–80) among the most superb churches in Venice. He opened a passage on the Redentore by saying, "This church from the designs of Palladio is [one] of the most [beautiful] things"; his admiration for the structure is equally evident in a meticulously rendered sheet of interior and exterior elevations (fig. 19).[38] The appeal of such a building to de Cotte derived in part from qualities shared by Palladian and French ecclesiastical interiors: simplicity, solemnity, and bright, uniform illumination, despite differences in materials (Italian stucco over brick versus French stone masonry). In both traditions, the sculptural density of the orders enlivens the neutral ground of the walls; thus in the margins of the Redentore drawing de Cotte squiggled profiles of entablatures, bases, and plinths. This element of tonal as opposed to polychromatic richness was probably the characteristic that also made Magenta's S. Salvatore in Bologna seem "very beautiful."[39] Its robust Corinthian columns decorating the monochromatic nave, which never received the customary mid-seventeenth-century veneer of paint and gold leaf, are impressive in their subdued grandeur (designed 1605). A connoisseur of Palladio's buildings, de Cotte was not afraid of rejecting an attribution: concerning S. Salvatore, Venice, he stated, "This church is spacious and handsome; they tell me that it was from the designs of Palladio; as for [myself], I believe it to be in the manner of Serlio, but it matters not" (the church was designed by Giorgio Spavento, 1507–34).[40]

In addition to Latin-cross basilicas, central-plan churches and their antique precedents, such

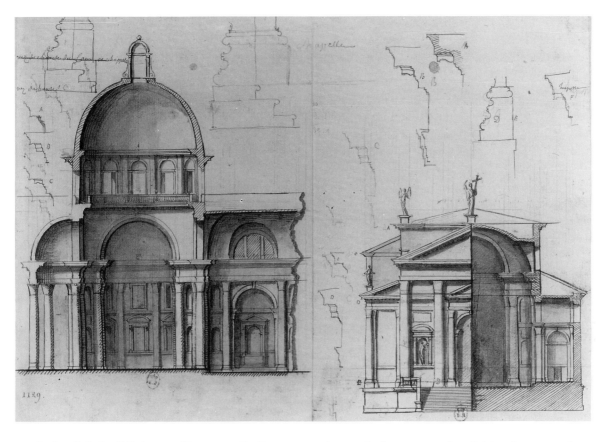

19. Andrea Palladio, Il Redentore, Venice, 1576/7–80, partial longitudinal section, half elevation of façade, and half section of transept drawn by Robert de Cotte, 1689 (Vb 25, 1129).

as the two circular temples of Vesta in Rome and Tivoli, were objects of study. Wandering through the Roman Forum, he drew the plan of the circular Temple of Romulus, incorporated as an entryway and vestibule into the sixth-century church of SS. Cosma e Damiano; in his notes he remarked that the "rotunda" has "in front of the portal two semicircular walls that form a *place*."[41] At the SS. Annunziata, Florence, de Cotte admired the large rotunda attached by Michelozzo to the older Latin-cross basilica and serving as the choir and Gonzaga memorial (begun in 1444, decorated by Giambologna, late sixteenth century); he considered the axial chapel "perfectly beautiful and architecturally fine," drawing the

plan and elevation as he did in the case of numerous chapels.[42]

Several domed octagonal rotundas were also the subject of drawings: S. Maria della Pace and S. Maria di Loreto in Rome, the Madonna di Campagna outside Verona, and Longhena's S. Maria della Salute, Venice. The Salute, while thoroughly Baroque in its grandiosity and scenographic richness, probably appealed to de Cotte on account of its classical restraint and Palladian lucidity (fig. 20). His drawing stresses Longhena's unification of interior and exterior elevations through consonant systems of height, proportion, and the orders (1630–87). However, he did not view the centralized designs of the Roman High Baroque as favorably. Bernini's S. Andrea al Quirinale he deemed "very splendid and decorous, but hardly correct," Borromini's S. Ivo della Sapienza he castigated as "one of the worst things

I have seen," and the same architect's S. Carlo alle Quattro Fontane he left unmentioned.[43]

De Cotte's remarks on ecclesiastical façades show that while on the one hand he appreciated severely planar design and classical harmony, on the other he responded to intrinsically sinewy compositions in which a controlling armature of columns juts dramatically from the wall. On the more classical side he held the rigorously mathematical designs of Palladio in high regard. Bal-

20. Baldassare Longhena, S. Maria della Salute, Venice, 1630–87, half section and half elevation of the façade drawn by Robert de Cotte, 1689 (Vb 33, 1137).

ance, control, and correct handling of the orders are prominent features of the front of the Church of the Redentore, as seen in de Cotte's elevation (fig. 19). Even so static a composition as the portal of the Basilica of Loreto (Giovanni Boccalini et al., 1571–87), with its finely developed equilibrium of parts, elegantly drooping volutes, and paired pilasters dispersed evenly over a planar façade, appealed to de Cotte's more chaste, academic side, and was therefore recorded in a drawing.[44]

De Cotte was less fond of Roman Early Baroque façades with their subtly overlapping surfaces in low relief. Concerning the Gesù (Giacomo della Porta, 1571–77) he wrote, "The portal is not as magnificent [as the interior], being however decorated with pilasters and pediments."[45] He preferred Roman High Baroque works displaying the orders fully in the round, such as Pietro da Cortona's S. Maria in Via Lata (1658–62) and the matching fronts of S. Maria di Montesanto and S. Maria de' Miracoli in the Piazza del Popolo. The scenographic effects of Cortona's S. Maria della Pace (1656–57) aroused his admiration, and he described Carlo Rainaldi's rich façade for S. Andrea della Valle as "grand, ornamented with columns, pilasters, niches, the whole of Tiburtine [Travertine] stone."[46] As a rule he found Borromini's elastic spatial effects too extreme, but he allowed an exception in the case of S. Agnese in Piazza Navona, perhaps on account of the classicizing revisions made by Bernini and Rainaldi during construction (1653–67): "The portal of this church is from the designs of Borromini; it is one of his better works, and is located roughly in the middle of one side of this piazza."[47] Finally, the more daring variants of the Roman aedicular façade also attracted de Cotte's attention. At SS. Vincenzo ed Anastasio, of which he executed a plan, he doubtless enjoyed the dramatic contrast between large planar fields and bold clusters of freestanding col-

21. Martino Longhi the Younger, façade, SS. Vincenzo ed Anastasio, Rome, 1646–50.

umns (Martino Longhi the Younger, 1646–50; fig. 21). As we shall see in chapter 9, de Cotte's experience of Italian church fronts had an impact on his own ecclesiastical designs in France.

The Monastery

The Italian journey provided ample opportunity to see yet another building type, the monastery. At the Abbey of S. Giorgio Maggiore, Venice, de Cotte experienced two works by Palladio, the Refectory (1560–63) and the Cloister of the Cypresses (built 1579–1613), as well as Lon-

ghena's revolutionary double-branch stair, in which parallel flights rise along the walls of the staircage (1643–45):

We entered the convent, which is very harmonious, having two cloisters, one perfectly beautiful, from the designs of Palladio, ornamented with slender coupled columns bearing arcades that buttress the wall. The great stair is located in the middle of one of these elevations: [the visitor] ascends by means of two ramps, one to the left and the other to the right, arriving at a corridor that leads to the dormitories. . . . One also sees on the ground floor a beautiful refectory, long, very wide, and high, at the back of which is a large painting representing *The Marriage at Cana* from the hand of Paolo Veronese.[48]

For de Cotte there were two principal treasures in Bologna, the first being the quantity of paintings by local Baroque masters, which he listed with locations in his journal; the second, the monasteries, about which he jotted notes: for example, the Convent of S. Salvatore, "more gothic than modern," but possessing a superb library and very large monks' cells; and the Monastery of S. Domenico, "extremely grand."[49]

Indeed, more than anything else, it was the large scale of these buildings and the capaciousness of their chambers that impressed de Cotte, as revealed by a characteristic passage describing S. Francesco, Bologna:

I entered the monastery, which proved to be of immense grandeur, having several large two-storied cloisters embellished with columns and vaults. This monastery is magnificent. . . . The professed friars are lodged splendidly and in a free manner, more like private individuals than monks. Curiosity led us to view one of their lodgings, and I was surprised by their spaciousness. . . . This form of solitude is nothing but extremely agreeable."[50]

In sum, de Cotte's Italian sojourn was an important learning experience that provided ideas for later commissions while affirming his sense of the French tradition. Not only did the trip form the basis for a presentation at the Académie, but in what was probably a common incident, in 1705 he summoned his knowledge of Italian architecture when naming prototypes for Nicodème Tessin's Louvre project (see chap. 5). As part of our attempt to understand de Cotte's designs, we shall find it helpful to recall the pronouncements recorded in his Italian journal as well as the drawings that resulted from the voyage.

Drawings

Nearly three thousand numbered sheets comprise the bulk of the Fonds de Cotte, one of the largest collections of architectural drawings to survive from the eighteenth century. Not all of the designs date from the years of de Cotte's tenure as Architect Ordinaire and Premier Architecte. For example, one of the most celebrated series is that by François Mansart, including projects for the Louvre and the Château de Blois, which he apparently willed to Jacques IV Gabriel, who passed them to Jacques V, de Cotte's associate; the latter must have seen their usefulness as part of the collection formed under de Cotte.[1] Following de Cotte's death, the drawings and related documents assembled during his directorship remained in the hands of his family rather than in the Bâtiments. Transferred to M. Delaporte in 1810, they were purchased by the Bibliothèque impériale, now the Bibliothèque nationale, where they remained, not as a whole, but divided among several departments.[2] The drawings entered the Topographie section of the Cabinet des estampes to be dispersed according to geographical location and pasted into large albums.[3] Small groups of drawings from de Cotte's studio exist elsewhere, notably, a suite of portfolios in the Bibliothèque de l'Institut, Paris, and scattered sheets in the Archives nationales.[4]

The written documents in the Fonds de Cotte for the most part stayed together in the Estampes.[5] These include letters to de Cotte from his patrons, particularly numerous in the area of foreign correspondence, his responses, usually in draft form, *devis*, *mémoires* (memoranda), copies of contracts, royal letters patent, and records of visits to numerous sites. Pierre Marcel catalogued these in 1906, summarizing their contents and listing those drawings specifically related to each item; in his publication he did not cite the large number of drawings for which there are no corresponding documents.

The production of sets of measured drawings within the bureaucratic system of the Bâtiments permitted the coordination of efforts between collaborating artists and ensured accurate calculation of time, materials, and labor for construction. Extant drawings range from thumbnail sketches by the master himself to huge rolled plans executed by professional draftsmen. The drawings are neither dated nor signed except in instances where a project was approved for construction, usually with the signature of de Cotte, the duc d'Antin, or another official (e.g., figs. 75, 87, 151). Buildings are rendered to scale, with the customary Parisian unit of the *toise* placed prominently. In the instance of foreign commissions, a scale bearing the local unit of measure is also included (figs. 46, 58). The plan was resolved first. Elevations and sections followed, although not every project developed to that stage. In long-distance projects the rooms are keyed by numbers or letters to memoranda, some of which survive. For example, in August 1715 the elector of Cologne wrote to de Cotte to request that the plans for the Bonn Residenz be copied in Paris with the room identification system previously established (fig. 40).[6]

Although there are obvious gaps among the surviving suites of designs, for each commission we may attempt to order extant drawings in a sequence from initial sketch to approved project by interpreting ink and graphite corrections and superimposed swatches of paper indicating alternatives. The design histories thus told, often with the help of written documents, constitute the principal narratives in the chapters that follow.

The drawings generally belong to one of five categories.[7] A site plan is a measured drawing of existing buildings in and around the terrain to be built upon, often with a summary indication of the project superimposed (figs. 39, 132, 177). A process drawing aids in the development of a design and may range from a rough sketch in charcoal, graphite, or ink (fig. 36) to a large detailed study, usually in graphite, incorporating alternative solutions on different levels in an effort to work out several problems simultaneously (figs. 31–32). Many such drawings show evidence of more than one hand or technique, with details either quickly scribbled or carefully indicated with a rule and compass (fig. 169).

A presentation drawing is a finished plan or elevation done by one of the draftsmen under de Cotte's supervision, and usually intended to help the client visualize the building (figs. 27, 46). These were often attached to contracts filed with a notary. In the plans the colors red and black normally differentiate new construction from old (fig. 47). Elevations may employ several media, being constructed initially in graphite or charcoal and completed in pen with ink wash and sparing use of color. Hinged flaps offer the possibility of alternative solutions (figs. 48–49). Perspectival and bird's-eye views are rare (fig. 78);[8] elevations commonly appear as orthogonal

projections, so that the dimensions of every part are accurately represented. The *dessinateurs* employed the full vocabulary of painterly effects developed in the Bâtiments in the second half of the seventeenth century to suggest light and shade and the projecting planes of the wall.[9]

A construction drawing is a plan or an elevation showing all or part of a structure, usually with measurements indicated, to be used on the site as the basis for building operations, sometimes in connection with a scale model (figs. 121, 185). These are infrequent in the case of the de Cotte files, since so many projects were never approved; drawings that did serve this purpose were normally discarded.

Finally, a record drawing is executed after a building is completed. This type is also scarce, but examples likely do exist—often indistinguishable from presentation drawings—notably as references for etchers preparing reproductive prints (figs. 96, 159). Throughout these five stages, which involved a team of interacting individuals, de Cotte supervised the development of a project.

How capable a draftsman was de Cotte? In a famous diatribe of 1708, the duc de Saint-Simon questioned whether de Cotte did any drawing himself and whether he was even capable of artistic invention: Hardouin-Mansart "was ignorant of his métier; de Cotte, his brother-in-law, whom he appointed Premier Architecte [i.e., his successor], was no more knowledgeable. They stole their plans, their designs, and their ideas from a draftsman in the Bâtiments called Lassurance, whom they kept under lock and key as much as possible."[10] However, later in the century three of de Cotte's biographers—Roland Le Virloys, Pingeron, and Lempereur—claimed that he drew and composed with considerable agility.[11] More recently Bertrand Jestaz has convincingly refuted Saint-Simon's statement through systematic study of Mansart's career in the Bâtiments and his circle of assistants.[12]

We may gauge the extent of de Cotte's abilities by considering certain key drawings and documents. His role as draftsman changed throughout the course of his career. Jestaz has demonstrated that during the early years of service to Mansart, 1676–99, de Cotte often acted as *dessinateur*, both in interpreting Mansart's ideas and in visualizing his own. As seen in chapter 1, Louvois's correspondence of 1687 concerning the Trianon de Marbre states expressly that de Cotte and others were drafting in response to Louis XIV's requests (the cross section of the peristyle of the Trianon was part of this collaborative effort; fig. 13). Also, minutes of the Académie for 5 June 1690 indicate that he prepared a drawing to be used in clarifying a discussion.

One of the purposes of the Italian sojourn of 1689–90 was to compile a folio of study drawings; in his notebook de Cotte specifically mentions drafting many of them (see chap. 2; figs. 14–15, 17–20). Some historians claim to recognize more than one hand in these drawings, but the problem of attribution is complicated by the fact that renderings by a single artist can vary in style depending on medium, purpose, and degree of finish.[13] The presence of de Cotte's handwriting on some sheets promotes but by no means confirms his authorship. Some drawings may have been started on the site and finished subsequently; likewise, relatively simple images sketched during a visit may have been supplemented at a later time with more finished renderings copied from architectural prints, thus composing a suite of drawings devoted to a particular monument. It is also conceivable that de Cotte's travel companion, Gabriel, helped to produce the drawings, one of the pair measuring and conveying information while the other was seated and drafting. In any case, a stylistically coherent group of Italian drawings bears the following traits: the considerable presence of freehand drawing, the use of pen-and-ink outline to define essential features, brisk hatching and ink wash to suggest volume and shading, and careful description of small details. These drawings are the work of an artist comfortable with both a fine-pointed brush and a pen, capable of delicate tonal modulations, and interested in lively visual effects achieved by rapid, quirky gestures and idiosyncratic features, such as puffs of smoke rising from chimneys.

From the time of his promotion to Architecte Ordinaire, de Cotte had assistants who could execute his ideas on paper, including concepts expressed to them verbally. He took a draftsman with him to Lyon to prepare site plans for a *place royale* in 1700. Later, in his bill of expenses for the king of Spain, he listed charges of 1,800 *livres* for five *dessinateurs* (1715). Nevertheless, as Premier Architecte de Cotte continued to do preliminary sketches, as is testified by a suite of brushed studies of chimneypieces and overmantle mirrors for his own apartment in Paris, bearing captions specifying "mon cabinet," "ma garderobe," and so forth, with other samples of his handwriting (1722; fig. 22).[14] In 1723, when Balthasar Neumann journeyed to Paris to solicit de Cotte's opinion of the project for the Würzburg Residenz, the Premier Architecte requested a plan drawn in pencil so that he could superimpose his own ideas on it. The corrections on the right-hand side of the extant sheet are in his hand (fig. 44).

Two drawings are useful in understanding de Cotte's relationship with his subordinates, particularly in the area of decoration. The first, a project for the shrine of Saint-Marcel in Notre-Dame de Paris, was initially prepared by an assistant who carefully delineated in ocher chalk the existing surrounding architecture (1710[?]; fig. 23). Jestaz recognized that it was de Cotte who then brushed freely the essential elements of the shrine in ink over a light charcoal and graphite underdrawing. He wrote instructions on the back for both the collaborating draftsman and the sculptor responsible for adding the details: "au sr aubrat [Guillaume Hauberat] pour tracer l'architecture et le s vassé [François-Antoine Vassé] les ornements."[15] The second drawing, a gallery project for the prince of Hesse-Kassel, similarly consists of an armature of ruled graphite lines drawn by a *dessinateur* to block in the system of bays lining the wall; Jean-Daniel Ludmann and Bruno Pons identified the hand of de Cotte in the summary indications of areas to be carved in low relief on the wood paneling (undated; fig. 24).[16] These sheets suggest that de Cotte's role in the creation of interior detailing normally consisted of determining the design of the architectural framework, the subdivision of the wall panels or other components, and the location of relief carving, paintings, and mirrors.[17] This broad conception was then handed over either to a *dessinateur* in the Bâtiments or to a sculptor in an independent workshop, both of whom were responsible for refining the design and determin-

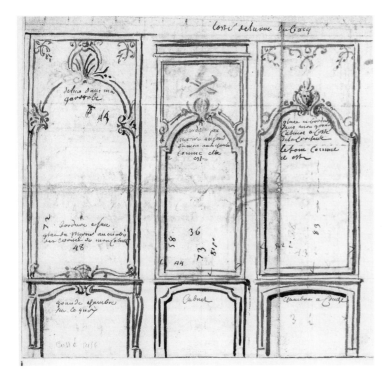

22. Designs for chimneypieces and mirrors, with notes in de Cotte's hand, project, Maisons de Robert de Cotte, 28 July 1722 (Va 270a, 2754–2757).

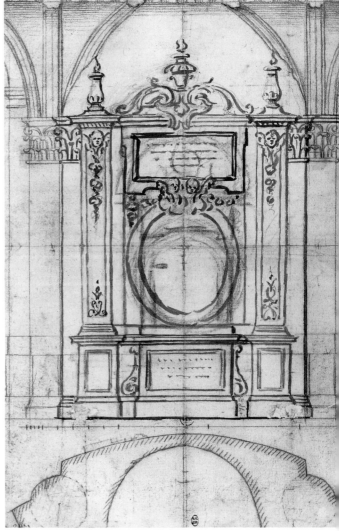

23. Shrine of Saint-Marcel, Notre-Dame de Paris, 1710(?) (Va 78h, t. 3, 2676).

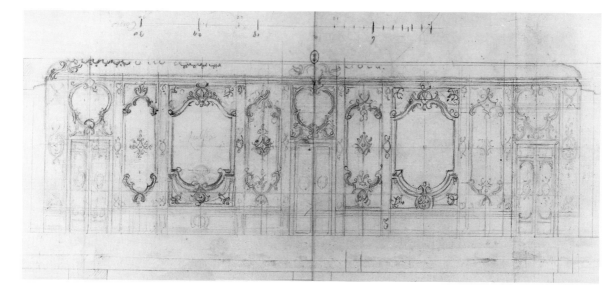

24. Gallery project for the Prince of Hesse-Kassel, n.d. (Ha 18a, 1203).

ing the decorative details in a full-scale drawing.[18] In the case of rococo wall decoration, a sculptor undertook the actual carving of the panels provided by a *menuisier* (woodworker).

The bold reworking with charcoal, brush, scissors, and glue visible in various parts of many process drawings and even presentation drawings in the Fonds de Cotte doubtless represents the mind and the hand of de Cotte (fig. 126). Certain drawings from the twenties that feature deftly brushed ink over a pencil armature share the same formal characteristics found in the Italian drawings: strong plasticity by means of tonal modeling, irregular freehand outlines, and such naturalistic details as foliage and smoking chimneys (figs. 158, 162). Of course, de Cotte may have imposed this technique as a house style on the *dessinateurs,* and indeed, many presentation drawings display elegant refinements of it.

To summarize: while it may be difficult to identify drawings by de Cotte in his capacity as Premier Architecte, it is certain that he drew and sketched throughout his career, and that a particular style of draftsmanship was associated with his studio. In the present study I have defined relatively few drawings as autograph. All of the drawings are "by de Cotte" to the extent that they were created under his direction. Together with his correspondence, they make it clear that, despite the burden of his official duties, he was an active participant in the design process.

Chapter Four

The Palace

THE ESTABLISHMENT of Robert de Cotte at the helm of the Service des Bâtiments coincided with the expansion of the French court style throughout Europe in all areas of culture, from painting and architecture to costume and dance. In every part of the Continent a plethora of crowned heads, including many German princes, each with his independent court, sought to create palaces, *maisons de plaisance*, gardens, and richly appointed interiors modeled after Versailles, the Trianon, and Marly.[1] German rulers visited France on the *Kavaliertour* and sent their architects abroad to familiarize themselves with the latest fashions, to buy furnishings, and to engage Parisian craftsmen. Among the distinguished court architects taking study-sojourns in Paris were Matthäus Daniel Pöppelmann, François de Cuvilliés, and Balthasar Neumann. The influx of French designers into Central and Eastern Europe depended largely on the Treaty of Rastatt and the end of the War of the Spanish Succession in 1714. The host of Frenchmen seeking employment abroad included Boffrand (Lorraine, Bavaria), Nicolas de Pigage (the Palatinate), P.-L.-P. de la Guépière (Württemburg), J.-B.-A. Le Blond, and Nicolas Pineau (Russia).

Several European sovereigns engaged the services of de Cotte in planning palatial residences and garden retreats. The king of Spain, the elector of Bavaria, the elector of Cologne, and the duke of Savoy all had political or dynastic connections with Louis XIV. The prince of Hesse-Kassel enjoyed French artistic affiliations through his family's Protestant sympathies, while the prince-bishop of Würzburg was anxious for Parisian representation on a team of German, imperial, and Italian advisors. In accepting international commissions, the Premier Architecte worked essentially as a consultant, whose role was that of chief representative of French tradition. He participated in various ways—by supplying plans for wholly new structures, by criticizing designs prepared by local architects, or by offering solutions to problematic buildings already under construction. He did not travel abroad to inspect the sites personally. Rather, he met in Paris with the patron or his representative, or he sent an assistant to act as intermediary on foreign soil.

De Cotte made it clear that his clients could utilize as much or as little of a design as they wished. For example, concerning the plan for the Würzburg Residenz, Neumann informed his patron, "As Monsieur de Cotte said, it doesn't matter to him whether Your Highness adopts many or very few" of his recommendations.[2] Frequently the ambition of princely patrons outstripped available means. As a result, not one of de Cotte's palace projects was fully realized, although his proposals for Madrid, Würzburg, and Bonn were influential in various ways, as we shall see.

Close scrutiny of extant drawings and letters

reveals not only de Cotte's approach to the palace as a building type but also the social and political values that underlay court society at the beginning of the eighteenth century. In Western Europe during the Baroque age the most persuasive architectural symbol of power and taste was the palace. To theorists it represented the principal and largest type of *bâtiment d'habitation*.[3] According to de Cordemoy, "With respect to the palaces of princes and sovereigns, nothing must be omitted that art, nature, grandeur, and magnificence can provide that is most rich, beautiful, and superb."[4] Thus the rules of *convenance* required that no effort be spared in the construction and decoration of palaces, because magnificence and wealth were regarded as attributes of a prince. Courtonne put it this way: "In palaces of importance [the architect] must design vestibules, staircases, *salons*, antechambers, state bedrooms, *grands cabinets*, and many other comparable rooms with a degree of grandeur that is above the ordinary and is scaled to the proportions of such a building."[5]

An instrument for the policy of absolutism, the palace provided a compartmentalized stage on which the monarch, his family, administrators, foreign dignitaries, visitors of varying social rank, and servants all had their assigned places. Although the sovereign's palace, properly speaking, was his seat of power within the capital, his country houses, called *maisons royales* in France, also required palatial forms and accoutrements to a greater or lesser extent depending on the administrative and ceremonial functions performed in them.[6]

For most of the seventeenth century the Italian palazzo had provided the standard for international palace design, but by the beginning of the eighteenth century the example of Ludovican absolutism brought French ideals to the fore. In addressing Louis XV before the Académie in 1719, de Cotte acknowledged the widespread emulation of Bourbon architecture: "These magnificent palaces [of the French monarch], with their gardens, fountains, and canals, the result of so much inspiration and hard work, . . . are the admiration of all foreigners, who come from everywhere to gaze upon them and to study them, so that they might serve as models."[7] Versailles was the supreme example of the garden palace because of its form and siting (figs. 4, 7, 25). To the east of the structure lay the town, focusing on the palace by means of trident-shaped avenues; to the west the mathematical arrangement of the garden extended the vista into infinity. The state bedroom of Louis XIV, situated symbolically on the main axis between the town and the park—between the realm of man and that of nature—was the controlling center.

Yet because Versailles was the result of many successive building campaigns by different architects, having originated as a country retreat and grown into a sprawling capital, its rambling plan and early elevations (especially those on the Cour de Marbre) increasingly became objects of vilification. "The beautiful and the ugly were sewn together, the vast and the suffocating," wrote Saint-Simon in a scathing critique.[8] Indeed, the princess Palatine commented in 1699, "The king himself acknowledges that there are faults in the architecture of Versailles."[9] Thus, when imitating Versailles in their designs, eighteenth-century architects improved upon the model while adopting its favorable points. In a similar way the Louvre in Paris, with its immense square plan and long spindly wings linking with the Palais des Tuileries, was also considered old-fashioned, but its exterior elevations provided a vocabulary of suitable architectural motifs.

In general, foreign royalty desired French forms above all in façades and interior decoration; the corridors of power within were subject to the specific requirements of local etiquette,

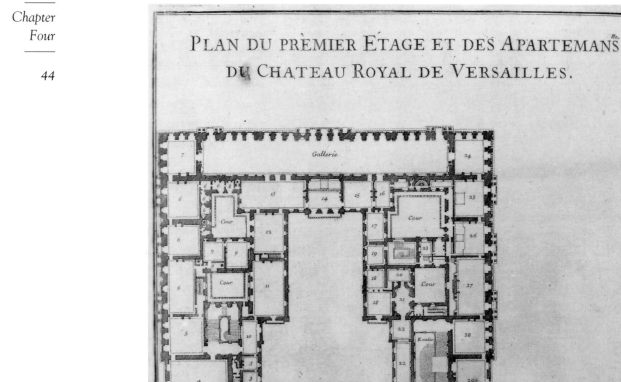

PLAN DU PREMIER ÉTAGE ET DES APARTEMANS
DU CHATEAU ROYAL DE VERSAILLES.

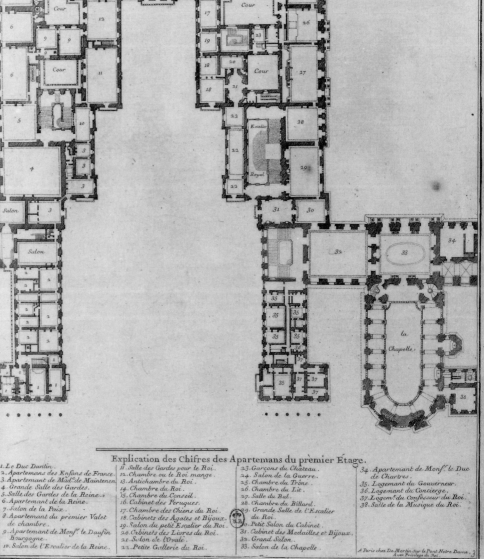

Explication des Chifres des Apartemans du premier Étage.

1. Le Duc Danlin.
2. Apartemans des Enfans de France.
3. Apartemant de Mad.e de Maintenon.
4. Grande Salle des Gardes.
5. Salle des Gardes de la Reine.
6. Apartemant de la Reine.
7. Salon de la Paix.
8. Apartemant du premier Valet de chambre.
9. Apartemant de Monf.r le Daufin Bourgogne.
10. Salon de l'Escalier de la Reine.

11. Salle des Gardes pour le Roi.
12. Chambre ou le Roi mange.
13. Antichambre du Roi.
14. Chambre du Roi.
15. Chambre du Conseil.
16. Cabinet des Peruques.
17. Chambre des Chiens du Roi.
18. Cabinets des Agates et Bijoux.
19. Salon du petit Escalier du Roi.
20. Cabinets des Livres du Roi.
21. Salon de l'Ovale.
22. Petite Gallerie du Roi.

23. Garçons du Chateau.
24. Salon de la Guerre.
25. Chambre du Trône.
26. Chambre du Lit.
27. Salle du Bal.
28. Chambre du Billard.
29. Grande Salle de l'Escalier du Roi.
30. Petit Salon du Cabinet.
31. Cabinet des Medailles et Bijoux.
32. Grand Salon.
33. Salon de la Chapelle.

34. Apartemant de Monf.r le Duc de Chartres.
35. Logemant du Gouverneur.
36. Logemant du Concierge.
37. Logem.t du Confesseur du Roi.
38. Salle de la Musique du Roi.

A Paris chez De Mortin sur le Pont Notre Dame.
Avec Privilege du Roi.

25. Plan, *premier étage*, Palace of Versailles, after 1702 (print by Demortain).

which emphasized the relative status of the participants. In working out his designs, de Cotte showed a concern for the same theoretical ideals that he used in judging Italian *palazzi*, namely, *convenance, commodité,* and logical *distribution.* Additionally, the delight he took in viewing monumental stairs in Italy reappeared in his own drawings of staircases for palatial residences.

Buen Retiro, Madrid

When Philip V (1683–1746), the sixteen-year-old grandson of Louis XIV, journeyed across the Pyrenees in 1700 to assume the throne of Spain, he set about achieving the bureaucratic efficiency and economic prosperity that were won in France through centralized rule at Versailles. Throughout the period of the War of the Spanish Succession (1702–14) he enlisted the aid of two compatriots who took firm grasp of the reins of government, economist Jean Orry and chief lady-in-waiting to the queen, the princesse des Ursins. Like his grandfather, Philip embarked on an ambitious architectural program that focused first of all on the remodeling and eventual reconstruction of his permanent residence, the medieval fortress of the Alcázar in Madrid.[10] Philip also determined to renovate the royal *villa suburbana* located on the eastern outskirts of the capital—the Buen Retiro, whose gardens and fresh air were a source of delight to the king and his bride, Maria Luisa of Savoy.

Originally built as a pious retreat adjoining the royal monastery of San Jeronimo, the Retiro had been enlarged without preestablished plan in 1632–40 by Philip IV and Count-Duke Olivares into a sprawling pleasure palace complete with ballroom and theater.[11] In its size, room layout, and decoration, the Retiro was more extensive than Louis XIV's villas at Trianon and Marly; it was a palace insofar as its use, combined with its physical attributes, exceeded the function of a place of retreat. Royal obsequies and oaths of fe-

alty were staged there, and it was the point of origin for ceremonial entries into Madrid. During construction the name of the building was specifically upgraded from the Royal Apartments of San Jeronimo to the Royal House of the Buen Retiro, and then further reclassified as the Palace of the Buen Retiro in recognition of its heightened status.[12] Nevertheless, owing to cheap materials and hasty construction, by the early eighteenth century the fabric had deteriorated considerably. On 23 June 1708 Madame de Maintenon wrote to the princesse des Ursins that Louis XIV had the plans of the old Retiro in hand and would ask "the most accomplished of our architects"—de Cotte—to work on revisions (Hardouin-Mansart had died the previous month).[13] There are no extant projects from 1708; war and economic pressures precluded their realization.

By 1712, when peace negotiations were underway in Utrecht, de Cotte proposed concealing the old group of ramshackle wings behind new symmetrical façades, a solution that Philip IV had briefly considered a century earlier.[14] Typically, the Premier Architecte had neither the time nor inclination to go to Madrid himself. He sent an assistant, René Carlier, to work at the Retiro as well as at the Alcázar, for which new interiors were being planned in Paris.

The remodeling schemes were rejected, and de Cotte then produced a pair of alternative proposals for a grandiose monument to the new Bourbon dynasty (1714–15). The palace was to be constructed on the hill to the east of the old Retiro, which would remain untouched, being linked to the new building by means of a communicating gallery. On 12 February 1715 de Cotte wrote to Orry,

My son will have the honor of delivering to you the two projects that I have made for the palace of Their Catholic Majesties at Buen Retiro, following the instructions that you have given me concerning the level of the terrain, to which I have conformed as much as possible. You are right to think big. . . . One should not be timid about cost when it is a question of building for great princes: it is necessary that the conception be worthy of those who wish to arouse the admiration of their subjects during their reign and leave to posterity eternal monuments to the grandeur and loftiness of their genius.[15]

He cited his current palace projects for the electors of Bavaria and Cologne, and continued:

Before sending the different projects, I showed them to Louis XIV in order to receive advice and counsel

26. Plan, palace and gardens, first proposal, Buen Retiro, Madrid, 1714–15 (Ha 20, 1003).

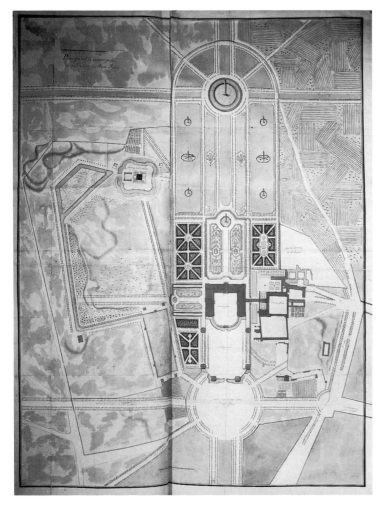

from this great king: no one is more wise than he. I owe this testimony to his good taste and just decisions. He examined the plans with attention, even with pleasure, and applauded them benevolently. For all I know, he may have regretted not having undertaken a project of equal grandeur.[16]

The first of the two proposals calls for a three-wing building set between entry squares and French formal gardens in the manner of the inevitable model for a Bourbon palace, Louis XIV's Versailles (figs. 4, 26).[17] A great circular plaza, surrounded by an *allée* of trees, lies before the palace, serving as a focal point for radiating avenues, including the Alcála road from Madrid (lower right). The forecourt is separated from the square by a moat. Six pavilions for guards and ministers, located symmetrically around the forecourt, bring to mind the guest pavilions of Louis XIV's retreat at Marly in their disposition and design.

The *cour d'honneur* is closed by a roofed corridor whose semicircular shape is repeated by the moat (figs. 26–27). The elevations of this corridor are based on the peristyle of the Trianon de Marbre at Versailles: an arcaded wall faces the exterior court, while a colonnade allows views of the courtyard (compare figs. 12–13).

The disposition of rooms within the palace is identical on both floors of the first proposal (fig. 27). However, the presence of large staircases presupposes an emphasis on the *premier étage* (upper story), as is typical in palace architecture. The symmetry of the plan mirrors the underlying division of palace life into two households governed by the king (on the right) and queen (on the left), each with its own corps of servants. De Cotte described the visitor's path into the building in a *Mémoire instructif*:

From either side of the [courtyard] in the center of the wings, one approaches each apartment by a columnar vestibule that leads to a staircase with triple ramps, whose steps are broad and low, with landings; these lead to a vestibule on the main floor that gives

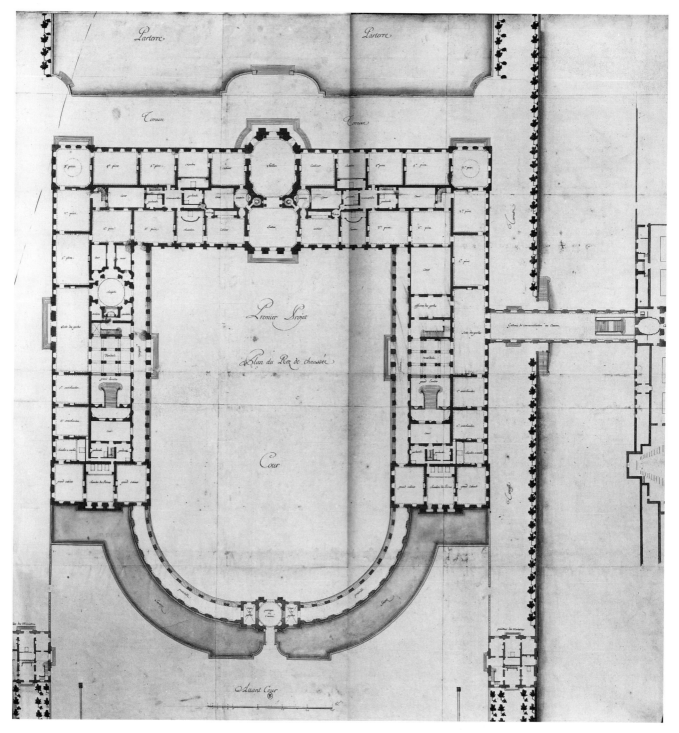

Parterre   Parterre

Terrasse   Terrasse

Premier Projet

Plan du Rez de chaussée

Cour

Auant Cour

27. Plan, *rez-de-chaussée*, first proposal, Buen Retiro (Ha 20, 1005)

access to the apartments of Their Majesties, each composed of a guard room, seven great rooms *en enfilade* serving as *salles* and antechambers, arriving at the bedchambers of Their Catholic Majesties, two large *cabinets*, an oratory, a space for the *chaise de commodité* [close-stool] and several closets, all having their exits via minor stairs.[18]

In other words, each apartment consists of the standard rooms in the normal sequence for European royalty: a guard room for liveried servants (*salle des gardes* on the plan), followed by a series of *antichambres* (the word literally means "before the *chambre*") for waiting, the *chambre* or royal bedroom, and finally the *cabinet*, the sovereign's inner sanctum. The sequence progresses from the most public to the most private rooms. In the Buen Retiro plan the bedrooms are doubled in the main wing, two for each sovereign on both floors if desired. In each case the bed is shown on the plan behind a balustrade. Between the paired *enfilades* a string of small service rooms is accessible to the apartments from either side—two *garde-robes*, a *lieu d'aisance* (loo) with the *chaise* clearly indicated,[19] service stairs, corridors, light wells, and an oratory. A domed chapel appears in the left wing.

The three-wing layout of the first proposal was intended to evoke the plan of the archetypal Bourbon palace. The main block of Versailles was the source for the location of entrance vestibules and staircases in the center of the side wings, and the symmetrical *enfilades* of state rooms facing the gardens to left and right (fig. 25). Even so, there are major differences. As noted earlier, the long history of Versailles had resulted in an incoherent plan and irregular elevations much criticized in the eighteenth century. Awkwardly sharing the left-hand wing are the apartment of Louis XIV (facing the courtyard) and that of the queen (facing the garden along the left of the plan), with the result that both are reached via the same staircase (the Es-

calier de la Reine, center left). The right-hand wing is composed of the Appartement Intérieur, a cluster of small private rooms housing the king's collections and library (along the courtyard), and the Grand Appartement with its Planetary Rooms for ceremonies and court socializing (facing the garden along the right side of the plan).

In contrast, De Cotte's layout is more rigorously organized, clarifying through its insistent symmetry the circulatory paths open to the visitor. In lieu of the newel and double-branched staircases at Versailles (Escalier de la Reine and Escalier des Ambassadeurs; fig. 25, left and right wings, respectively), de Cotte inserted the more modern and visually breathtaking type of the imperial staircase—a single ramp rising to a landing, from which two parallel ramps ascend in the opposite direction. In France the imperial type was strongly associated with royal dwellings.[20] Antoine Le Pautre used such a stair in one of his published designs for palaces (fifth design, 1562), and François Mansart incorporated altogether some twenty-two imperial staircases, singly or paired and in a variety of positions, in five of his six series of projects for the Louvre (c. 1662–66).[21] Le Vau constructed a stair of this type that led to the apartment of Louis XIV on the *premier étage* at the Palais des Tuileries, remodeled as the royal residence in Paris (1664–67) during construction of the Louvre and before the permanent removal to Versailles.[22] Hardouin-Mansart also proposed an imperial stair based on a triangular plan for the Château Vieux de Chantilly (1687, unexecuted) and built a widely admired variant at the Château de Saint-Cloud (1688).[23]

Significantly, in the Buen Retiro plan de Cotte rejected the symbolic placement of the king's bedchamber on the main axis at Versailles, as well as the extravagantly huge space of the Galerie des Glaces. Instead, in the Retiro plan he formed the climax to the paired suites of rooms by joining on the main longitudinal axis two public rooms for large court gatherings: a rectangular hall and a *salon à l'italienne*, the latter being a type of two-story domed room normally oval in plan and projecting from the garden front. De Cotte borrowed this motif from Le Vau, who had introduced and developed it in a series of remarkable designs, particularly the Château de Vaux-le-Vicomte (fig. 3).[24]

The most unexpected feature of the first proposal is the doubling of *antichambres*, *chambres*, and *cabinets* in the central wing on both the ground and main floors, yielding four apartments each for the king and queen. This layout was in response to information de Cotte had sought concerning living arrangements at the Spanish court. On 7 January 1715 Orry wrote,

You asked me whether Their Catholic Majesties lodge on the ground floor or the floor above; I leave it to you to determine [how to proceed], observing that the practice in Spain is to live on the *rez-de-chaussée* during summer in order to find some cool air, and on the floors overhead in winter; . . . however, you must strive to make the palace suitable for all seasons, because I have seen the late queen [d. 1714] frequently unhappy, being obliged to leave the Retiro at the first signs of heat or cold. Moreover, in your layout you should orient the apartments since, besides differentiating between upper and lower floors in this country, they are very careful to live on the north side in the summer and the south side in the winter, and it seems to me that you could easily suppose that your palace is double, . . . so that one might live on the north in summer, the entire southern part serving as state rooms, and one could winter in these same state rooms, leaving those on the north for ceremony in this season.[25]

Further comparison of the plans of Versailles and the Buen Retiro reveals another important difference. At Versailles the king's bedchamber (fig. 25, no. 14) is preceded by a single place of waiting, the Grande Antichambre (no. 13, Salon de l'Oeil de Boeuf),[26] whereas de Cotte, mindful of *convenance*, provided for the Buen Retiro, by

his own count, seven antechambers in each pair of suites. The number of anterooms is significant, because it reveals striking differences between French and Spanish practices in the realm of etiquette. At the court of Louis XIV no distinctions of rank were made among those waiting to see him. Therefore, virtually all visitors shared the same waiting room before being received in the bedchamber. The state bedroom was the ceremonial center of the palace, where Louis not only slept, but dressed and undressed publicly and held his principal audiences. The Grand Cabinet beyond was Louis's office, where he met his councils. Hence there was no private area in the Appartement du Roi. In contrast, the Spanish court based its etiquette on the exceptionally formal Burgundian model, which Charles V had introduced in 1548. This involved the practice of dividing courtiers into groups according to rank, and assigning specific places of waiting along a sequence of antechambers, with access to the bedroom and *cabinet* denied to all but the family and a few high court officials.[27] Louis XIV summarized these differences as follows:

There are some nations where the majesty of kings consists mostly of not letting themselves be seen, and this may have its reasons among spirits accustomed to servitude who can only be governed by fear and by terror; but this is not the character of our French, and as far back as we can go in our history, if there is any unique characteristic about this monarchy, it is the free and easy access of the subjects to the prince.[28]

Despite Louis XIV's orders that Spanish etiquette be abolished entirely from the court of Madrid, Philip accommodated himself to the barrier of protocol, since it served his preference for solitude.

Although Orry did not specify particular room requirements for the Spanish monarchs, de Cotte was certainly informed regarding comparative court practices. Plans of the old Retiro

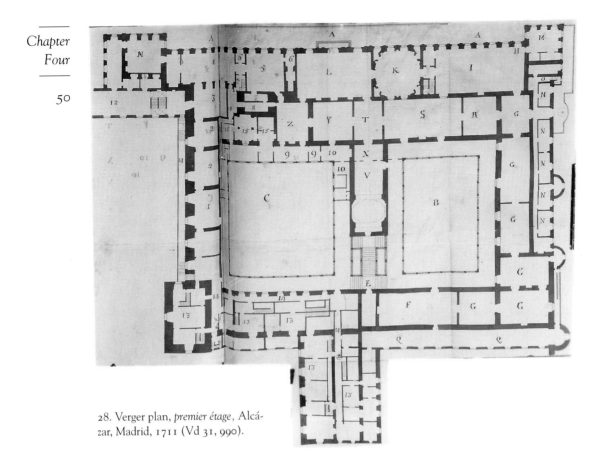

28. Verger plan, *premier étage*, Alcázar, Madrid, 1711 (Vd 31, 990).

and the Alcázar had been sent to him from Madrid. The so-called Verger plan of the Alcázar
had formed the basis for the program of redeco-
rating *à la française* (1711; fig. 28).[29] According
to the plan and accompanying list of rooms, the
visitor entered by the principal or south front
(letter A, top), and made his way to the center
of the building, where the courtyards of the king
and queen (B, C) were separated by a wing containing the chapel (V) and grand staircase (E)
leading to the main floor. Here the king's apartment commenced on the western side at the
guard room (F) and continued through six antechambers (G) that led to the great state rooms on
the south (I, K, L). In sharp contrast, the private
apartments of the king and queen faced inward
toward the courts (R, S, T, Y, Z). As indicated on
the list, they were intended "for the private use

of Their Majesties, being not at all destined for
public usage."[30]

Allowing for the often multiple and changing
functions of rooms in palaces, we may conclude
that on the whole de Cotte was attempting to
satisfy the needs of his patrons by incorporating
an abundance of antechambers, by isolating private rooms at the back of each sequence, and by
providing numerous apartments in various locations to accommodate seasonal changes.

The elevations for the first proposal contain
deliberate references to the palaces of Louis XIV,
although de Cotte strove to improve upon his
sources (figs. 29–30). The scale and sweep are
reminiscent of the Garden Front of Versailles,
with its rusticated base supporting the *piano no-
bile* and attic (fig. 7). On the other hand, the
giant order, window surrounds, and pavilions

conceived for the Retiro owe a debt to the East and South Fronts of the Louvre (1667–68). While in buildings of lesser stature de Cotte reserved the classical orders for central emphasis, in concert with the rule of *convenance* he adopted for the Buen Retiro Palace a giant order all around the building, employing engaged columns for the vigorously projecting court elevation, and flat pilasters for the low-relief garden façade.[31]

The most conspicuous element in these elevations is the dome, a prominent motif in French royal dwellings, noticeably the Louvre (Jacques Lemercier, Pavillon de l'Horloge, from 1639; Le Vau, original South Front, 1661) and the Palais des Tuileries (Le Vau, c. 1664); although lacking at Versailles, a dome was proposed in a remodeling scheme for the Cour de Marbre (Hardouin-Mansart, Grand Dessein, c. 1678). However, these domes were of the square type, the *comble en dôme*, or *dôme à l'impériale*, whereas here the oval *salon* was to carry an oval dome— terminated in the drawing by a crown, a motif

29. (*Below*) Elevation, court façade, first proposal, Buen Retiro (Ha 20, 1008).

30. (*Bottom*) Elevation, garden façade, first proposal, Buen Retiro (Ha 20, 1007).

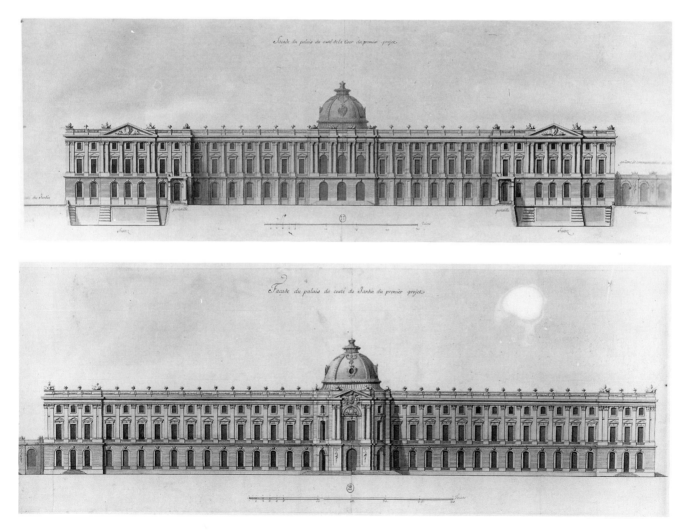

31. Plan, process drawing, *premier étage* of
the central-plan dwelling (with some details
of the *rez-de-chaussée*) and ground floor of
the one-story forecourt wings, second proposal, Buen Retiro, 1714–15 (Ha 20, 1010,
redrawn from the graphite original by Claire
Zimmerman).

often used as a finial in French palatial designs.[32]

The second of the two proposals for the Buen Retiro is comparable in orientation and layout. The visitor arriving from the Grand Place would traverse an immense forecourt bordered by stable courts and lodgings for ministers and nobles. One would then cross a moat, pass through the entry pavilion, and proceed down the main axis of the *cour d'honneur*; alternatively, one could follow covered walkways around the court (fig. 31). The central plan, a huge cross inscribed in a square, again allows the flexibility of paired apartments to the north and south on both stories. De Cotte described the layout in his *Mémoire instructif*:

The body of the palace is a perfect square of fifty-eight *toises* on each side. One enters on axis by means of a vestibule, a hall, and an octagonal *salon* that marks the very center. The grand staircase appears opposite the entry, rising gradually through three ramps and leading to a comparable octagonal *salon* above. This opens to the right and left onto the four Grand Apartments of Their Majesties, two joined on the south by a *salon*, and two others similarly on the north.[33]

De Cotte situated a palatine (two-storied) chapel directly behind the imperial stair and separate from it on the upper level. Large formal rooms face outward to the garden, while a ring of *garde-robes*, *lieux d'aisance*, light wells, and minor stairs faces the inner courts. The lateral oval chambers function as guard rooms, opening onto three antechambers preceding the bedroom in each suite.

The main axis of the building is visible in a pair of extant sketches of the longitudinal cross section, of which one is reproduced here (fig. 32). It shows the domed octagon, illuminated by a gigantic lantern sporting a royal crown, and followed by the staircase and the palatine chapel, which has a balcony on the upper level for the royal couple.

De Cotte sent a copy of the courtyard elevation (not extant) of the second proposal to Madrid, indicating that all four exterior façades were to be identical, and that the style was comparable to that of the first proposal.

While the first proposal clearly suggests the image of a Bourbon palace, the rigorously geometric second proposal is rooted in the tradition of country-house architecture. A typical histori-

32. Section, Second Proposal, Buen Retiro, showing oval and octagonal *salons*, imperial stair, and chapel (Ha 20, 10).

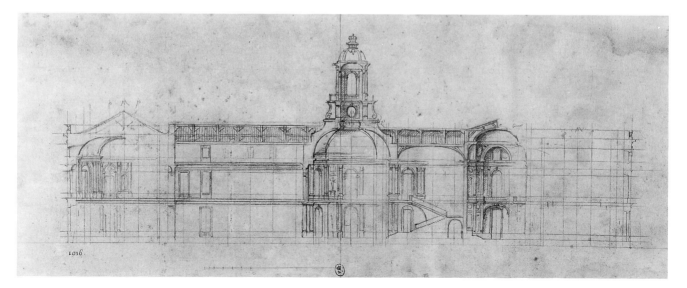

cal precedent for the second proposal is the Château de Chambord, begun in 1519 for François I. In this *maison royale* the motifs of a centrally located stair and a superimposed lantern are combined with a terrace for viewing that towers above the central plan, a cross-in-square. That Chambord embodied monarchical myths in the Baroque period is evident from its association with Louis XIV, who installed a royal apartment

33. Plan, Villa for a King, pl. XL, Sebastiano Serlio on Domestic Architecture, the Sixteenth-Century Manuscript of Book VI in the Avery Library of Columbia University, New York.

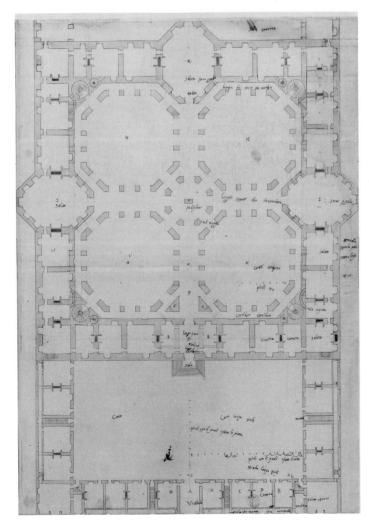

there and ordered the restoration and completion of the building in 1682. Chambord was the subject of discussions at the Académie d'architecture on 30 September 1697 and 1 February 1700.[34] Appropriately enough, Philip V stopped at Chambord en route to Spain in 1700.

The plan of the second project is also analogous to Serlio's design for a villa for a king from the unpublished Sixth Book, *Delle habitationi di tutti li gradi degli uomini* [On Domestic Architecture] (project XL; composed 1540s; fig. 33). The Avery manuscript and Vienna proofs remained in France in the early eighteenth century and were widely known among architects.[35] Serlio's plan comprises a three-story building based on a cross-in-square plan set behind a rectangular courtyard enclosed by one-story wings. Like de Cotte's plan, it features a chapel on the longitudinal axis (in this case at the crossing), diagonally canted corners within the interior courts, and three octagonal *salons* projecting from the outer walls. Serlio's design was the source for a similar though more conservatively medieval cross-in-square project for a château published by Jacques Androuet du Cerceau in the *Premier livre d'architecture* (project XXXVI; 1559). In designing the second proposal for the Buen Retiro (and certain *maisons de plaisance*; see chap. 5), de Cotte participated in a revival of the Italianate central plan that was stimulated by discussions on Renaissance theory at the Académie and by such exceptional designs as Hardouin-Mansart's central plan for the Pavillon du Roi, Marly (fig. 9).

At the same time, the second proposal is in other respects an updated version of the traditional Spanish fortress-palace, with its symmetrical layout, angle towers, and multiple interior courts. For example, the grid plan and the sequence of pavilions, wings, dome, and church are comparable to those of the sixteenth-century royal palace-monastery of the Escorial, a building well known in France, having influenced Libéral

Bruant's conception of the Hôtel Royal des Invalides in Paris (begun 1671) and François Mansart's plans for the Val-de-Grâce convent (1645–46). Engraved plans of the Escorial had been the subject of six meetings of the Académie in July and August 1703. We can only wonder to what extent de Cotte's choice of an imperial stair for the Buen Retiro was influenced by the presence of such a staircase on the longitudinal axis of the monastic sector of the Escorial—the first instance of the type in European architecture (Juan de Herrera, 1571).[36]

Also influential on the layout of the second proposal was the Madrid Alcázar, a scheme known to de Cotte, as we have seen, through the Verger plan (fig. 28). Not only are the basic elements of the Spanish fortress-palace present here, but the unusual juxtaposition of the stair and chapel, isolated in the central wing, was a motif used by de Cotte for the Retiro.

Notwithstanding the pedigree of de Cotte's proposals, the possibility of constructing either scheme never became a reality, due to financial constraints and the remarriage of Philip V to the strong-willed Isabel Farnese of Parma. The queen banished the princesse des Ursins from Spain in December 1714 and arranged for Italian architects to work for the Crown. Orry was relieved of his post early in 1715.

Even so, de Cotte's unexecuted proposals for the Buen Retiro had a significant impact on architectural design in Italy: they were the starting point for Luigi Vanvitelli's conception of the Royal Palace of Caserta, north of Naples (1751–74). The palace was built by Charles III, Philip V's eldest son by his second wife. Although Charles was born a year after the Retiro drawings were prepared, he evidently knew them—he practiced architectural drawing and took an active interest in building commissions. Vanvitelli's first sketch-plan of Caserta is close to de Cotte's second proposal in its use of several el-

ements: cross-shaped arms within a square (as opposed to the definitive rectangular plan), an octagon-stair complex on the main axis, and a file of secondary rooms around the inner courts, whose corners are canted. Similarly, de Cotte's elevations offered schemata for Vanvitelli's elevations.[37]

Schloss Schleissheim

Having embarked upon his reign as elector of Bavaria in 1681, Max Emanuel of Wittelsbach (1662–1736) broke from the austere court life of his forebears and introduced the more lively social atmosphere of the French court.[38] He had been imbued with a love of things Gallic by his mother, Henriette Adelaide, who was the granddaughter of Henri IV and had grown up in the frenchified atmosphere of the Savoyard court. Furthermore, his sister, Marie-Anne, had married Louis XIV's son, the grand dauphin. Even so, during the first half of Max Emanuel's reign, he allied himself with the Holy Roman Empire, fighting several campaigns against the French, marrying Emperor Leopold's daughter Maria Antonia, and working to obtain some part of the Spanish inheritance upon the death of the heirless Charles II.

These political aspirations were paralleled by an ambitious building program that was Italianate in style, like the architecture of the Empire. With his court architect, Enrico Zuccalli, Max Emanuel set about remodeling the electoral apartment (Alexanderzimmer) in the Palace of Munich, his principal seat of power, and expanding Henriette Adelaide's villa at Nymphenburg.[39] For Schleissheim, his country residence six miles north of Munich, he commissioned designs for new structures to be aligned axially with the large rectangular Altes Schloss of Maximilian I (built 1616–28). Max Emanuel's earliest addition to Schleissheim was the little villa of Lustheim, erected at the east end of a huge formal garden, where it was framed by a pair of cubic pavilions (1684–88). Next, in the years 1693–1701, Zuccalli produced a series of projects for a palatial structure to be erected between the Altes Schloss and Lustheim.[40] The proposals ranged from a three-wing building connecting with the Altes Schloss, to the clearing away of the latter to provide room for a quadrangular scheme based on Bernini's Louvre projects. In 1701 work began on the east wing or main block (roofed by 1704), and a decision was taken to delay if not altogether abandon construction of the side wings.

In the second half of his reign, Max Emanuel deserted the Empire and formed an alliance with his former enemy, Louis XIV, in exchange for a subsidy (1701). But with the defeat of the Sun King and his allies at Blenheim, the elector was compelled to flee Bavaria. Thus began a decade of parsimonious exile (1704–15), first in the Netherlands, then in France. From Boffrand the elector commissioned the Hunting Pavilion of Bouchefort in the forest of Soignes in 1705, but his forced departure from Brussels precluded its completion. In 1713 he purchased a house at Saint-Cloud and had Boffrand redesign the interior.[41] During this crucial period Max Emanuel's eyes were opened to the glories of French Baroque architecture:

> I must have *maisons de campagne*, gardens, forests, the hunt, ground plans, furniture, and the like. . . . I could not exist without sketching designs. I form an idea of the sites and then draw and make plans, . . . being content to scribble on paper without worrying about execution. These drawings may be useful later on. When I look at my drawings and papers, just the thought of a prospective building gives me pleasure.[42]

Upon the Peace of Rastatt in March 1714, the elector prepared for the return to Bavaria and resumption of work on his country estates. Hopeful of obtaining French ideas for Schleissheim and Nymphenburg, in June 1714 he requested that plans and memoranda on their status be sent to Paris.[43] There is no evidence that de Cotte responded to the matter of Nymphenburg, but he did formulate two projects for Schleissheim, either as alternatives or as successive schemes (we cannot be certain).[44] This must have taken place some time between August 1714, when plans were mailed from Munich, and March 1715, when the elector left France—hence the lack of written correspondence between architect and client. De Cotte did mention Schleissheim in the letter of 12 February 1715 addressed to the Spanish minister Jean Orry, in which he compared his palatial projects for the Buen Retiro, Schleissheim, and Bonn.[45]

De Cotte's first proposal for Schleissheim appears on a large plan showing the relationship between the palace, stables, and gardens (fig. 34). Aside from using the foundations of Zuccalli's new *corps-de-logis*, the project disregards Lustheim and calls for sweeping away the Altes Schloss. So extreme a proposal may have been prompted by a lack of information concerning the site, or by the state of disrepair of the buildings, left unattended while Bavaria was occupied by imperial troops. As in the instance of de Cotte's first proposal for the Buen Retiro, Versailles is the source for the U-shaped structure and the placement of the outbuildings, as well as the three-part formal garden and the canal, all located on a single longitudinal axis (compare fig. 26).

In the Schleissheim plan the visitor's path into the palace precinct is marked by three increasingly narrow spaces along the main axis—*place*, *avant-cour*, and *cour d'honneur*—that are separated in turn by a stirrup-shaped moat and a screen entry wall. Unlike the curved hemicycle of the Buen Retiro, the screen wall enclosing the court at Schleissheim is straight (visible in the large site plan and lightly indicated in ruled graphite lines on the plan of the *premier étage*, figs. 34–35; some plans omit this feature). Entrance walls of this type were usually one-storied and served to connect the lateral wings of a palace to an entrance pavilion on the longitudinal axis. Such pavilions were frequently domed; although it is clear that the one for Schleissheim was to be built over a central plan, no elevation drawing for it exists.[46] Mansart's Louvre projects provided inspiration for the complicated articulation of the ends of the lateral wings in de Cotte's plan, with their multiple pavilions and diagonally canted corners.

The desire to enclose the courtyard reflects a functional aspect of protocol that differed between French and German courts. Unlike the situation at Versailles, where access to the palace was virtually unlimited, in Bavaria entry into the precinct was carefully controlled, and the right to drive into the *cour d'honneur* was regulated by strict rules reflecting rank. As Friedrich Carl von Moser phrased it in a book on German court etiquette (1754–55):

Outer courtyards serve 1) for magnificence and to enhance the visibility of the building; and 2) for the security of the owner, as by custom the right of entry may be refused to commoners, foreigners, or otherwise suspicious persons. Inner courtyards serve 3) for the maintenance of peace and quiet and for the convenience of the owner, in so far as permission to drive into these in carriages is very limited. For this reason 4) the division into separate courtyards has an influence on rank and ceremonial.[47]

Turning to the building proper, we find that an early sketch of Schleissheim, which includes various trial solutions and is thus asymmetrical, follows the prototype of Versailles in several details (figs. 25, 36) The ceremonial stair on the right-hand side of the courtyard is patterned after the double-branch design and location of Louis XIV's Escalier des Ambassadeurs; in the wing at the

34. Plan, first proposal, Neues Schloss and gardens, Schleissheim, c. 1714–15 (Vd 29, t. 1, 106).

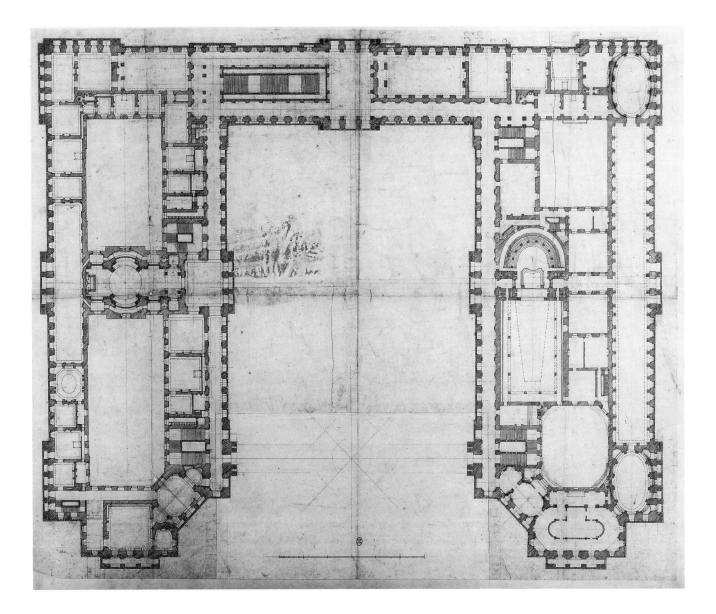

35. Plan, *premier étage*, first proposal, Schleissheim, with penciled lines showing location of the courtyard screen wall and entrance pavilion (Vd 29, t. 1, 100).

back of the court a gallery bracketed by a pair of *salons* mimics the layout of the Galerie des Glaces, and in like manner separates the apartments of the ruling couple. Two trial locations in the left wing for a palatine chapel exhibit a single-nave design with side aisles and vestibule familiar from the Versailles chapel.[48]

The three-wing plan of the first proposal is comparable to the Palace of Versailles in its vast dimensions, but a comparison of the two layouts shows that, as in the instance of the Buen Retiro projects, the new plan is more logical and advanced (fig. 35). Around three sides of the forecourt a covered gallery on the ground floor protects visitors from the rain; directly overhead on the main floor (reproduced here) corridors provide easy circulation between the wings. Formal entryways appear midway down these wings, as at Versailles, and more logically on the central axis, where de Cotte inserted the key introductory areas—entrance vestibule and ceremonial staircase. Placed in the thin western wing, where it would be flooded with light from windows on both sides, the straight flight of steps, broken by two landings, would be surrounded by a seemingly floating gallery and set within a columnar cage reminiscent of a Louvre project by Claude Perrault (c. 1667–69).[49] Such elements were explored further and brilliantly realized in German palace architecture later in the century.

Having ascended the great stair to the main floor, the visitor would turn back to reach the *appartement de parade* of the elector. It contains the following sequence of rooms *en enfilade*, commanding prestigious views of the gardens: guard room, first antechamber, second antechamber, bedchamber (the bed is placed behind a balustrade in an alcove), and *cabinet*. The presence of three rooms preceding the *chambre* matches the layout of the electoral apartment in some of Zuccalli's early projects for Schleissheim (1690s); in his 1700 project, there are four anterooms, the same number as in the final building, and comparable to the suite of public and semipublic rooms in the Alexanderzimmer at the Residenz.[50] The Munich court based its etiquette on the Burgundian-Spanish model brought by Charles

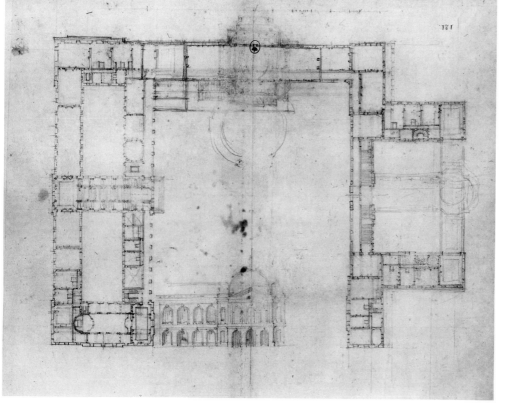

36. Preliminary plan and court elevation, first proposal, Schleissheim (Ha 19, 121).

V to Vienna, which required numerous anterooms for reception, and reserved the *chambre* and *cabinet* for the private use of the elector and immediate family.[51] Since state functions were only occasionally performed in country residences, the full number of prescribed anterooms was not of the strictest necessity, and rooms often served multiple functions.

In de Cotte's plan the elector's apartment communicates with an *appartement de commodité* composed of three small rooms immediately adjacent (the bedroom faces an inner court), a loo, and service stairs.[52] The order of the rooms in the electress's apartment, to the left of the stair, is similar to that in the elector's, while allowing for an additional antechamber.

Emphasis in the *corps-de-logis* is given the stair rather than the Grande Galerie, here shifted from its central position at Versailles to the right-hand wing. In the center of this wing the *opéra*,

which features a Palladian screen of columns in the elliptical audience hall and a deep stage accommodating flats, balances its ecclesiastical counterpart in the left wing, the chapel, a modified Latin cross whose curved transepts echo the shape of the domed crossing.[53]

No exterior elevations for the first proposal survive. Nevertheless, we may infer from the plans that the elevations were based on the Garden Front of Versailles (fig. 35; see fig. 7). The central axis of the *corps-de-logis* would probably have been crowned by a dome that was visible from both the courtyard and the garden, as in the elevations of the first proposal for the Buen Retiro (figs. 29–30). This is suggested by the early sheet of sketches, which includes a court elevation in the lower center (fig. 36). Here a square dome, not oval like that for Madrid, rises above a second-story order and triangular pediment.

De Cotte's second proposal for Schleissheim is

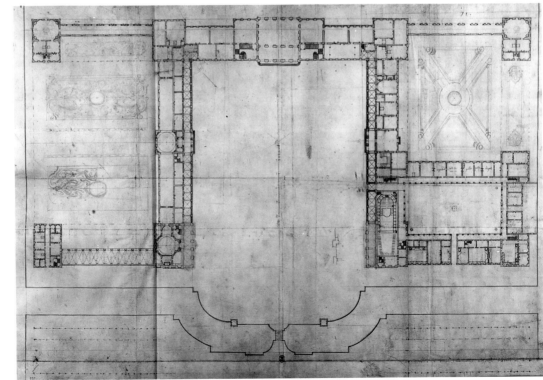

37. Plan, ground floor, second proposal, Schleissheim (Vd 29, t. 1, 120).

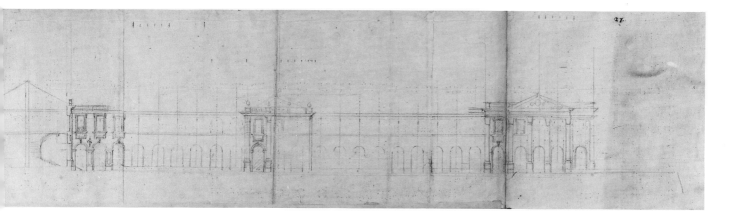

38. Preliminary sketch, south court elevation with section of *corps-de-logis*, second proposal, Schleissheim (Ha 19, 130v).

not so much for a garden palace as a *maison de plaisance*, Trianon-like in its meandering extensions (fig. 37). This project also calls for demolishing the Altes Schloss to allow for a great oval *place* and an *avant-cour* flanked by stables. The plan is based on a three-wing project by Zuccalli from c. 1700–1702 and largely incorporates the already constructed *corps-de-logis* with its wide central projection and corner pavilions facing the garden.[54] A pair of corridors lead outward from both ends of the *corps-de-logis* to independent blocks repeating the lateral pavilions of Lustheim. De Cotte's plan alters Zuccalli's room layout in the central wing and surprisingly disregards the established height of two main stories and a mezzanine. The second proposal comprises only a ground floor for the main rooms and an attic overhead for minor apartments and service quarters. The visitor would enter the vestibule on axis, proceed to the *salon à l'italienne*, and move left or right into the electoral suites. The gallery is now in the left wing, where it leads to a domed central-plan chapel; the latter is again balanced by the *opéra* in the corresponding right-hand wing.

A single surviving elevation, a tentative sketch showing the right-hand (south) court fa-

çade, employs a giant order of pilasters articulating the pavilions only, a motif associated with Le Vau (figs. 38, 3). The arcade of the ground-story corridor is vertically linked to the rectangular attic windows above by means of small tablets, a visual device earlier employed by de Cotte for the garden façade of the Abbey of Saint-Denis (figs. 180, 182). This reduced presence of the order is consonant with the scaled-down size and less formal layout of the second proposal.

De Cotte's schemes were too impractical to have an impact on later work at Schleissheim, particularly since the elector decided to retain the Altes Schloss as a cost-saving measure. The dream of a palatial residence faded, and the task of installing interiors (1719–26) went to a new court architect, Joseph Effner, who replaced Zuccalli as chief designer, having trained in Paris probably under Boffrand. Dominique Girard, a Frenchman imported from Paris in 1717, completed the gardens.[55]

Electoral Residenz, Bonn

Like his elder brother, Max Emanuel, whom he revered, the Archbishop-Elector Joseph Clemens of Cologne (1673–1723) lived in exile from 1704 to 1714, residing at Naumur, Lille, and Valenciennes, and spending time with his brother-in-law, the grand dauphin, at Meudon.[56] He was disheartened by the thought of returning to his unfinished palace at Bonn, Zuccalli's closed rectangle of wings with heavy towerlike pavilions at the angles (1697–1704; fig. 39, shaded area). The palace incorporated a cramped Grand Appartement "with which," the elector wrote, "I am utterly disgusted, having viewed the spacious and superb buildings recently erected in Paris and its environs."[57]

Fifty-six extant letters concerning plans for the Bonn Palace and country residences at Poppelsdorf, Brühl, and Godesburg, sent by Joseph Clemens to de Cotte between 1712 and 1720, make clear the elector's passionate involvement in the designs and his familiarity with monumental French architecture.[58] The elector's tone is consistently one of flattery: "No one is capable of giving me better ideas on these matters than you, and I always yield with pleasure to your sage advice concerning all of the projects that I find it appropriate to undertake."[59] Yet, he continually pleaded that his financial limitations be taken seriously: "I beg you, Monsieur, to give more consideration in all this to good taste and *commodité* than to magnificence, which underlies all of the beautiful things that you have conceived for [Louis XIV]: he must justifiably have palaces that correspond to his grandeur and power, but my

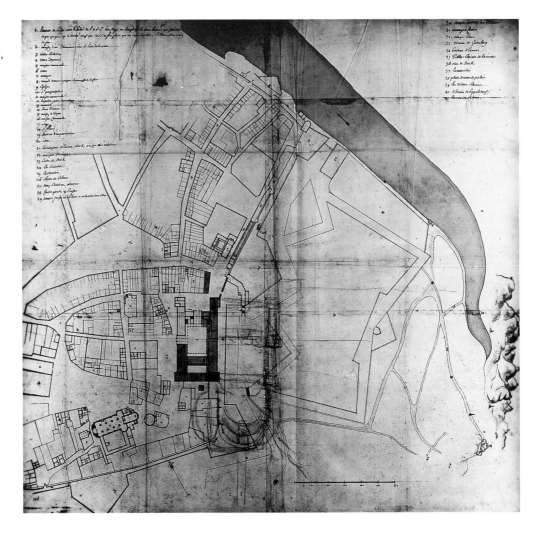

39. Site plan, Electoral Residenz and environs, Bonn, with de Cotte's first proposal, 1714 (Ha 19, 115).

buildings must be equal to my means, which are nothing compared to his."[60]

The elector continued to seek de Cotte's advice on every detail after the arrival in Bonn of two assistants, Benoît de Fortier and Guillaume Hauberat, sent in 1715 and 1716 respectively to oversee work.[61] A large number of drawings were transported from capital to capital between 1713 and 1721. On the basis of relatively few sheets surviving in Paris we can infer de Cotte's intentions.[62]

In a crucial letter of 25 June 1713 the elector described three alternative ideas that he had in mind for the Bonn Palace. He admitted that the proposal calling for an entirely new structure on the banks of the Rhine was impractical. The other two concepts utilized the southern *corps-de-logis* of Zuccalli's palace, with its outmoded electoral suite, as the left-hand wing of a new open three-wing palace based on the Versailles model. The court would be closed by an iron grill; the longitudinal axis of the second design was supposed to link with that of the suburban villa, Schloss Poppelsdorf, located outside the city one-half mile to the west. The elector listed the chambers that he required in his new Grand Appartement: "It is absolutely necessary that the apartment I am obliged to occupy be composed of the following rooms": a great staircase, a vestibule, a *salon*, a guard chamber, an *anti-salle*, first and second *antichambres*, an audience or throne room, a *grand cabinet* serving as council chamber, and a state bedchamber.[63] These were to be followed by twelve more rooms for personal use, including a gallery, a chapel, and a billiard room. The large number of spaces resulted from the rules of court etiquette, which, as Joseph Clemens acknowledged, had been borrowed from the imperial court and that of his brother at Munich.[64] Ordinances divided the courtiers into four categories—court officials and servants, clerics, military personnel, and foreign visitors—

each further divided and assigned a separate place for waiting.

De Cotte replied by sending two projects on 25 March 1714. The surviving evidence for the first proposal is sketched on the site plan of Bonn showing the palace and its environs. To the main wing de Cotte added a new rectangular structure enclosing two large courtyards (fig. 39, southern or right-hand side). The complex was to be entered from the west, where a curved hemicycle—presumably a one-story colonnaded or arcuated corridor like that proposed for the Buen Retiro in Madrid—enclosed the forecourt (fig. 39, bottom center; fig. 27). The covered hemicycle would serve a functional purpose: in the elector's words, "to provide shelter from the rainstorms that come quite often in the heat of summer."[65]

In the second proposal, shown in a pair of plans that include Zuccalli's main wing, de Cotte shifted the hemicycle to the northern side, the original point of entry from the town (fig. 40, left).[66] Concentric outlines on the entry pavilion suggest that the central axis of the hemicycle would be distinguished by some manner of domed structure, following French royal tradition and possibly resembling that for Schleissheim (figs. 34–35). On the southern side of Zuccalli's *enfilade* de Cotte spread three new wings surrounding a courtyard and containing a magnificent suite of generously proportioned rooms to be entered from the vestibule on the west (fig. 41). The visitor would ascend to the main floor by means of a spectacular pavilion lit from windows on three sides, in which the staircase is of the imperial type, as in the Buen Retiro designs; this pavilion, a modern revival of the late medieval and Early Renaissance stair tower, was probably suggested by the courtyard location of imperial stairs in François Mansart's fifth and sixth plans for the Louvre.[67]

Most of the rooms stipulated by the elector are provided in the plan of the new wings, although in a different sequence. From the stair, the visitor would proceed through the upper vestibule and two guard chambers, then turn left into the oval *salon* with its gallery for musicians. One would then continue through two *antichambres* to the *chambre* or state bedroom; beyond in the eastern wing lie a *salon*, the elector's private chapel, a gallery, and a dining room. As in the drawings for Schleissheim, ceremonial rooms face the garden while smaller dressing rooms, service stairs, corridors, and a loo give onto the court. The *salon* on the axis of the south wing—an element used similarly for the Buen Retiro designs—ranks among the earliest appearances in German palace design of the oval *salon à l'italienne*. The elector rejected de Cotte's projects as "trop vaste," choosing instead to maintain Zuccalli's grand apartment (fig. 42).

40. Plan, *premier étage*, second proposal, northern half, Electoral Residenz, Bonn, 25 March 1714 (Ha 19, 118).

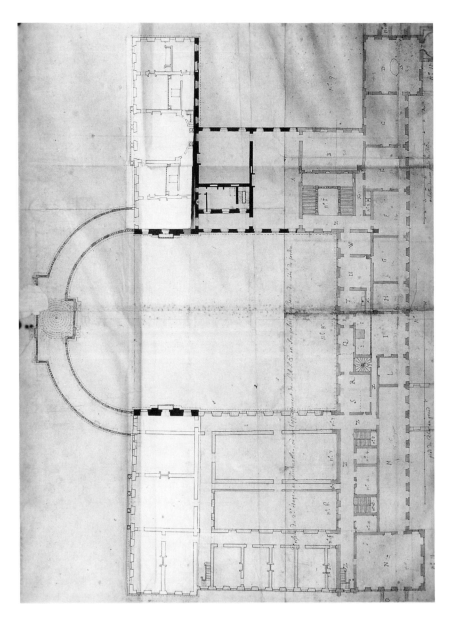

41. (*Opposite*) Plan, *premier étage*, second proposal, southern half, Electoral Residenz, Bonn (Ha 19, 1014).

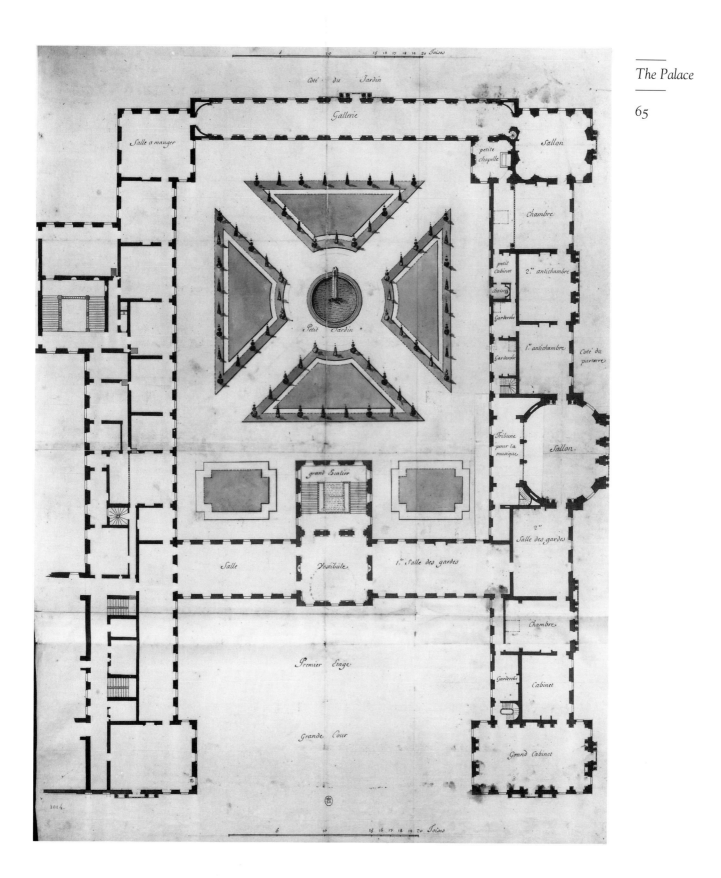

Coté du Jardin

Gallerie

Salle a manger

Sallon

petite chapelle

Chambre

petit Cabinet

2.e antichambre

chaise

Garderobe

Garderobe

1.re antichambre

Coté du parterre

Petit Jardin

Tribune pour la musique

Sallon

grand Escalier

2.e Salle des gardes

Salle

Vestibule

1.re Salle des gardes

Chambre

Premier Etage

Garderobe

Cabinet

Grande Cour

Grand Cabinet

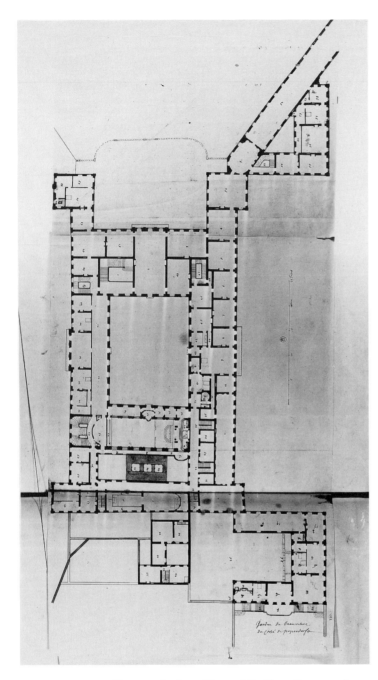

42. Plan, *premier étage*, Electoral Residenz, Bonn, 23 August 1715 (Ha 19, 110).

43. (*Opposite*) Elevation, south (garden) front, Electoral Residenz, Bonn, November 1714 (Ha 19, 149).

The ecclesiastical sovereign also desired a small menagerie and a private garden sealed by a gate: "One of my greatest pleasures [is] to cultivate plants and fresh greens with my own hands; it is a form of amusement that pleases me above all things: but in order to do this, it is necessary that I engage in this pursuit without being seen by anyone; also I enjoy, as does His Majesty at Marly, keeping fine chickens, rare ducks, and curious carp."[68]

Furthermore, he requested a pavilion on the Rhine to use as a summer retreat and waiting station for German princes arriving by boat. They would be escorted back to the palace through a *grande galerie* "like the one that goes from the Tuileries to the old Louvre" (fig. 42, upper right).[69] A courtier pointed out a planning error in de Cotte's scheme that routed visitors, retinue, and honor guard through the elector's bedroom and *cabinet*. The patron wrote to his architect, "There is a difference in our customs, so that while in France everybody enters and passes through the apartments of the king and princes, here very few people enjoy this honor and have this advantage. Being in Germany, I must therefore conform to the manners of the country, so as not to offend the nobles."[70]

In February 1715, Joseph Clemens discarded the idea of the hemicycle, since it projected too far into the town, and he shifted the principal entrance to the east wing (fig. 42, top center). In August of that year he and de Fortier conceived the Buen Retiro wing (fig. 42, lower right), an *appartement de commodité* decorated in the French style and facing Schloss Poppelsdorf; it would be balanced by an apartment for guests on the south side of the *grande galerie* (upper right).[71] In the end, the elector gave up his wish for a grandiose palace in the French manner and contented himself with furthering construction on the north and east wings and decorating his public and private apartments with designs and fur-

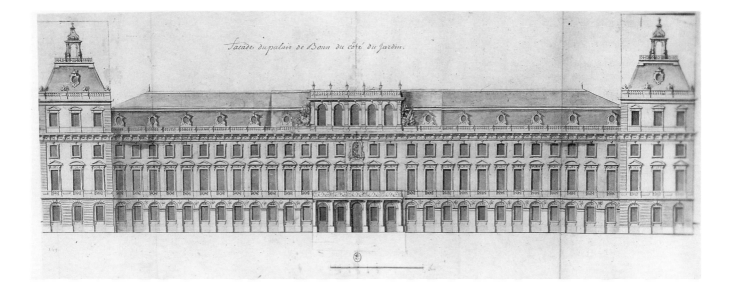

Facade du palais de Bonn du côté du Jardin.

nishings supplied by de Cotte from Paris (principally late 1716–18).[72] An imperial staircase was constructed near the east entrance (1717–21).[73] In addition to the minor wings projecting from the main block, the elector adopted some of de Cotte's suggestions for enlivening the south garden elevation, which called for channeled rustication, a blind arcade along the ground floor, more elegant roofs on the corner towers, and a classical frontispiece and an ornamental iron balustrade on the central axis (fig. 43).[74]

Episcopal Residenz, Würzburg

In January 1723 Johann Philipp Franz von Schönborn, prince-bishop of Würzburg (1673–1724), sent Balthasar Neumann to Paris to seek de Cotte's opinion of plans for the new Residenz.[75] Neumann spent three months in France informing himself of the newest trends, hiring craftsmen to work at Würzburg, and purchasing furnishings to be sent to Germany. All the while he continually revised the plans and sent drawings to the prince-bishop. Neumann was just beginning his career as an architect at this date, and the project was largely the collaborative ef-

fort of the patron and a team of designers in Würzburg, Mainz, and Vienna. Why was Neumann sent to Paris and not to Italy, given the Italian orientation of the Schönborn? Johann Philipp Franz had in fact familiarized himself with Italian architecture while traveling extensively in the south. The idea of tapping French sources, which arose as early as 1719, was in part instigated by a collaborating architect, Philipp Christof von Erthal, who had connections in Paris.[76] In Frankfurt in 1721, Neumann viewed the vast collection of architectural publications and engravings belonging to Johann Friedrich von Uffenbach, who had undertaken exhaustive research of French architecture during a seven-month sojourn in Paris (1715–16).[77]

The foundation stone of the new Residenz had been laid on 22 May 1720, and work on the north wing was tentatively begun, as indicated on the earliest plan to receive de Cotte's attention: "coste comme cela est commencé" (fig. 44, left-hand side). De Cotte communicated his ideas orally and in sketches rather than in letters or memoranda. We may infer his criticisms from two sources: Neumann's abundant and highly descriptive correspondence with his patron, and a handful of drawings—five sheets surviving in the Fonds de Cotte and one in Germany.[78]

Despite de Cotte's preoccupation with the affairs of his studio, he met with and greatly impressed Neumann on several occasions: "I am unaware of whether de Cotte is known at all in Germany, [but] I find him and his son to be very intelligent."[79] Neumann also sought the expertise of Boffrand, "with whom," he said, "I deal less formally."[80] The tenor of the relationship between the two French masters is evident from Neumann's acknowledged wish to visit privately with Boffrand: "I didn't show either one the plans of the other, nor did I make positive comments, in order to prevent jealousy."[81]

In addition, Cardinal Armand-Gaston de Rohan-Soubise received Neumann warmly, showing great interest in the Würzburg project: "I

44. Plan, *rez-de-chaussée*, project, Residenz, Würzburg, 1723 (Vd 29, 1195).

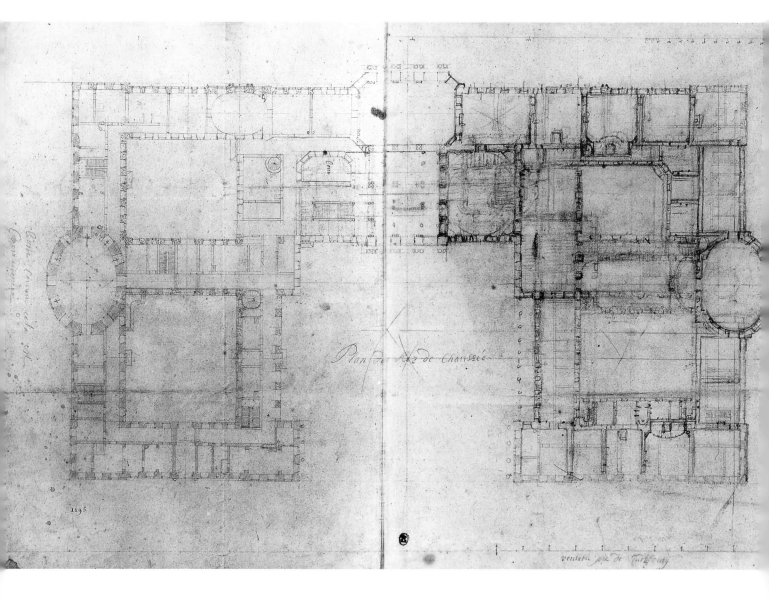

myself am amazed that His Holy Eminence, the cardinal de Rohan, has invested so much effort" in the plans.[82] By 15 February Neumann met with the cardinal, who measured the drawings with a compass. In response to the architect's request, the cardinal provided drawings of his Château de Saverne in Alsace, where Neumann, on his way to Paris, had admired the seventeenth-century imperial staircase lit from two sides and surrounded by a platform.[83] Most important, the cardinal served as liaison with de Cotte.

The Premier Architecte's response to the project was recorded by Neumann: "After Monsieur de Cotte and his son, who is equally qualified, had inspected the plans, the father commented that the design showed many features in the Italian manner, and a few German ones." By Italianate features he probably meant the oval rooms and the exterior elevations. He doubtless took the pinched size of the rooms and their sequence to be German. He was satisfied with the size of the *corps-de-logis* but found the stairs too narrow and small, and had the same criticism for the two apartments following the *salon*, which he said should be combined into one. He approved of the audience chamber but advised that the bedroom, *cabinet*, and entire adjoining pavilion be combined into a *grand cabinet*. "He said that if he had a plan drawn in graphite [instead of ink], he could work on it," and so Neumann, unable to find an assistant, spent the night at the drafting table.[84]

Of the four plans that remain, two are reproduced here as a means of demonstrating de Cotte's reactions. In the first of these, Neumann's drawing survives intact on the northern half, where an oval chapel is visible in the center of the left-hand wing (fig. 44). In spontaneous strokes on the right or southern half, de Cotte enlarged all of the rooms and created several *enfilades* by placing doors on a single axis near the windows. In a manner comparable to his earlier

palace plans, behind the apartments he placed smaller service rooms, a corridor, and an *appartement de commodité* facing the inner courtyards, thus substantially reducing their size. He altered the shape of the oval salon in the center of the south front to conform to current French practice by attaching to the exterior wall a rectangular pavilion with columns, such as he had proposed for the new wing at Bonn (fig. 41).

From de Cotte's point of view, the most problematic aspect of the plan was the pair of twin imperial stairs on either side of the vestibule. Although he was certainly familiar with François Mansart's use of double imperial staircases in the Louvre projects, their inclusion here seemed redundant.[85] Nonetheless the patron fervently supported this feature as an element providing visual grandeur. Initially de Cotte enlarged the right-hand stair and changed it to the newel type (fig. 44); then he replaced the left-hand stair with a large chapel and redesigned the stair as an imperial type, five bays wide, set within a voluminous space (fig. 45). The resulting central emphasis on the combination of the staircase, vestibule, and chapel is a restatement of a theme used twenty years earlier by de Cotte and his collaborators for the cross axis of the Castello di Rivoli (fig. 50). He extended the stair area a full bay southward along its length to allow illumination from an interior courtyard in the right-hand wing as well as from the *cour d'honneur*. The columnar staircage and the seemingly suspended gallery that surrounds the stair on the *premier étage* resemble a similar arrangement proposed for the stair at Schleissheim (fig. 35), as well as that constructed at the Château de Saverne; Perrault's projected staircase for the Louvre likewise featured a columnar gallery.

In light of the patron's connections with the Viennese court, the number of rooms preceding the bedroom in each of the two *grands appartements* lining the east front appears inevitable, re-

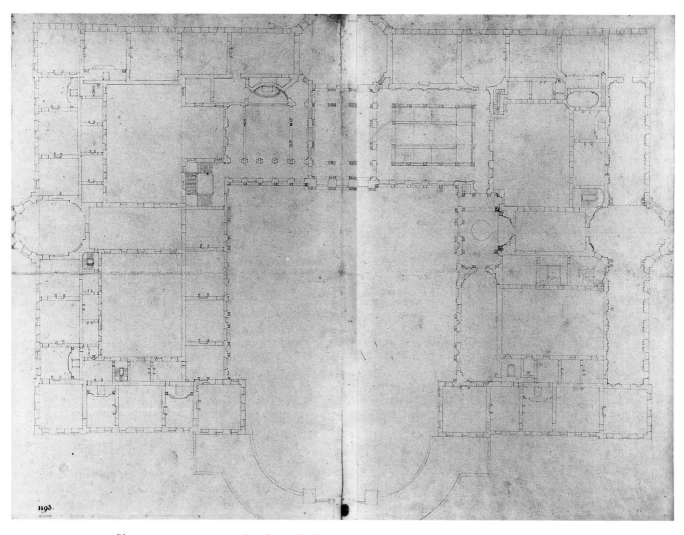

45. Plan, *premier étage*, project, Residenz, Würzburg
(Vd 29, 1193).

calling the formal suites in de Cotte's Schleissheim and Bonn designs.[86] Upon arriving in the
cour d'honneur, the visitor would pass through
the following: the ground floor vestibule, the
staircase, an upper vestibule, and the *salon*; then
continue left or right into one apartment or the
other by means of a guard chamber, anteroom,
and audience chamber. The more private space
of the bedroom follows, where the bed is indicated behind a balustrade in an alcove. (There is
no key that clarifies the specific use of all of the

rooms.) De Cotte transformed the south wing
into a gallery (as in the right-hand wing of the
first Schleissheim proposal, fig. 35), with a great
oval space in the center, its axis turned ninety
degrees, and matching *salons* at either end—the
whole concept reminiscent of the galleries at
Versailles and Clagny. Although the north wing
was already under construction, de Cotte also ro-
tated the axis of the north oval (the former
chapel), thus providing a strong cross axis for the
building, while turning the ovals into roughly octagonal shapes. In the north wing the apartments
intended for lesser inhabitants also have their

smaller service rooms adjacent to them, facing the courts. Another characteristic feature of de Cotte's palace plans, the stirrup-shaped moat, increases the depth of the *cour d'honneur*, which is supervised by twin sentry boxes to left and right of an iron grill. Hence, compared to the original German plan, the French drawings are more grandiose and up to date.

Only two elevations are extant, these being consecutive proposals for the garden façade. As Neumann reported to the prince-bishop in typically rambling prose, de Cotte had his own ideas about the court and garden elevations:

Monsieur de Cotte has also changed the [elevations] for the garden wing; instead of an attic story over the *salon*, he proposed an octagonal dome; he removed the attic level from the principal courtyard, and put the frontispiece on freestanding columns, not for structural reasons but according to local [French] usage; on the garden façade facing the bastion, all of the ground floor windows are arched, the ones above have curved lintels, and the mezzanine windows are on top.[87]

These points deserve clarification, beginning with the courtyard façade. In de Cotte's correction to the right-hand side of the first plan he proposed a covered colonnaded passage joining the pavilions on the side of the court (to be duplicated on the left-hand side; fig. 44), similar to the lateral corridors bordering the courtyards projected for Schleissheim and Buen Retiro. He eventually dropped this feature, along with the pair of pavilions at the back of the court (figs. 44–45). Nevertheless, as the plans show, he used the orders extensively on the courtyard walls, with engaged columns and pilasters separating the bays, and freestanding columns comprising the frontispiece—all in a manner comparable to the courtyard elevations for Schleissheim and Madrid.

With respect to the garden façade, it is clear that the earlier of de Cotte's two elevations (not

reproduced here) matches Neumann's description of three levels of varying window shapes. The narrow three-bay end pavilions in this drawing, derived from the first plan (fig. 44), were broadened to five bays in the subsequent elevation to give the pavilions greater visual weight (fig. 46). The two-story pedimented frontispiece on axis, topped by a dome supporting a royal crown (see Buen Retiro, fig. 30), derives from the tradition that includes Vaux-le-Vicomte and Clagny (figs. 3, 5). The second Würzburg elevation consists of two stories of arcades across the entire length of the façade, whose planar sweep is broken slightly by columnar projections on the upper floor of the wings connecting the pavilions. De Cotte eliminated from the German project the mezzanine level between the two main floors, much to the patron's chagrin; following Italian and Viennese practice the prince-bishop wished to house his domestics there, and its inclusion rendered the main stair higher and more impressive. Unlike the garden elevation for Buen Retiro, this for Würzburg emphasizes the wings and pavilions as independent entities by virtue of separate roofs and sharply contrasting articulation.

Neumann expressed disappointment with de Cotte's inflexibility regarding the prince-bishop's wishes: "He did not adhere to Your Highness's stipulations, which I had indicated to him in the presence of His Eminence, the cardinal. I could not therefore make changes; the plans will serve to demonstrate [French] taste."[88] The cardinal de Rohan offered to intervene on the prince-bishop's behalf to persuade de Cotte to work further. But Neumann felt it useless to press "Monsieur de Cotte, who likes his own drawings best":[89]

I cannot ask Monsieur de Cotte for further drawings, and convince him that Your Highness cannot make the courtyards so small, and the windows so large, since the winter and the seasons [in Germany] are

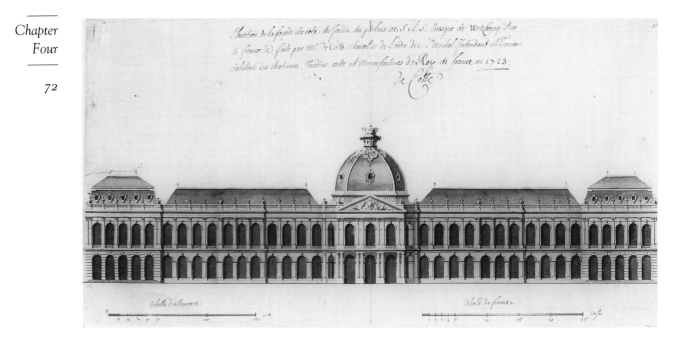

46. Elevation, garden façade, project, Residenz, Würzburg
(Staatliche Museen zu Berlin, Kunstbibliothek, Hdz 4682).

longer and more unpredictable . . . ; Monsieur
de Cotte did not want to move the chapel from the
location [that he preferred in the *corps-de-logis*], failing to consider [the necessity of] direct access from
the street, whereas [in his plan] people would have to
walk through the *cour d'honneur*.[90]

In other words, the courtyard, as at Schleissheim,
was to be a restricted area. Moreover, Johann
Philipp Franz was unwilling to relinquish the
twin stairs. Neumann spoke of using de Cotte's
design for the imperial stair, even though he felt
it was too large.[91] In the last analysis, the Ger-
mans judged the dome on the garden front to be
redundant, since domes had already been projected for the two side elevations.[92] It is evident
that de Cotte saw his role as that of advisor, not
designer. On the other hand, Boffrand was more
amenable in this respect and was thus invited to
Würzburg, where he resided June to September
1724.[93]

The untimely death of Johann Philipp Franz

in 1724 brought to a close the French phase in
the planning of the Residenz before the resolution of fundamental problems in the design.
While certain of de Cotte's proposals did make
their way into the final stages of the conception—notably, the single stair, its surrounding
platform and abundant lighting, the *enfilade*, the
addition of commodious secondary spaces, and
the reduction of the Italianate oval—he was not
the only architect to recommend these features.
His precise contribution therefore remains difficult to assess. There is no question, however,
that he was an active participant during part
of the lengthy design process. Neumann ultimately built the celebrated imperial staircase for
Friedrich Karl von Schönborn on the left-hand
side of the vestibule.

Château de Fontainebleau

Late in his career de Cotte received a commission from his own sovereign for extensive remodeling of one of the great *maisons royales*. The appeal of Fontainebleau lay in the informality of
court life there and the superb hunting and pic-

turesque beauty to be found in the rock-strewn Forêt de Bière. Since the entire court made the Voyage de Fontainebleau every autumn, the need for extensive and comfortable accommodations was increasingly felt. Louis XIV had not initiated any major additions to the palace during his reign, but Louis XV, the only monarch to marry at Fontainebleau, took an interest in refurbishing the complex from the time of his coronation, beginning with the erection of the Salle des Comédies in the Aisle de la Belle Cheminée and the

restoration of the Galerie François I (1724–25). Later he undertook remodeling of the Appartement des Reines Mères, the Galerie des Cerfs (1727), and the Grand Cabinet du Roi (1729).[94]

The year 1729 marked the first time in well over a century that an important building program was considered for the château. Although the extant plans—which were not realized—are by de Cotte, the commission would also have involved his brother Louis, who had been *contrôleur* there from 1699. The project calls for a new south wing (fig. 47, bottom center) connecting the Aisle de la Belle Cheminée (right) with the Aisle des Reines Mères (left), thus sealing off

47. Plan, *premier étage*, Château de Fontainebleau, with proposed additions in red ink, 1729 (Va 77, t. 6, 1481).

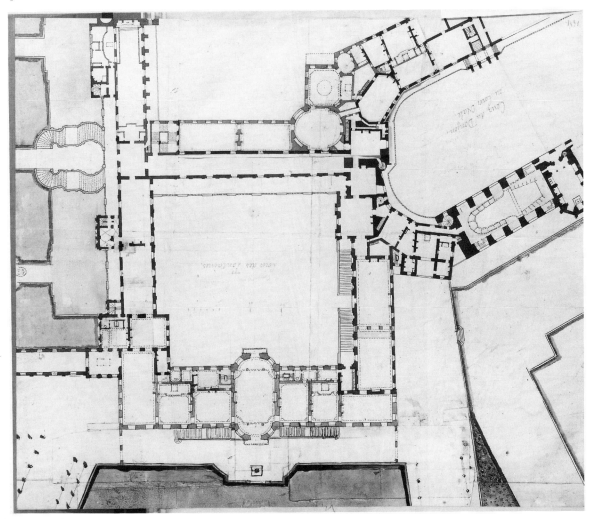

the Cour de la Fontaine from the carp pond to the south.[95] Construction of the wing and its waterfront terrace would have required filling in the northern end of the pond. The chief disadvantage of the proposal was that it marred the symmetry of the finest façade at Fontainebleau, Primaticcio's Aisle de la Belle Cheminée (1568). In addition, the plan calls for doubling the width of the north wing containing the Galerie François I (Louis XVI commissioned this change in 1785). The old royal suite on the northwest side of the Cour de l'Ovale was to be transformed into two new apartments connected to the gallery by an oval *antichambre*.

The dominant feature of the new royal wing on the south is the great oval *salon* separating two Grands Appartements on the *premier étage*. The motif of an elongated oval *salon* bisecting a wing longitudinally, so that its curved short ends project toward both the court and the garden, was introduced by Le Vau in the Château du Raincy (early 1640s; destroyed early 1800s). In the Fontainebleau design the *salon* is not a true oval, and its interior shape is complicated by a pair of tribunes supported by columns on the curved ends. Each royal suite consists of the basic French sequence of rooms—*antichambre* for waiting, *chambre* wherein the bed is placed in an alcove behind a balustrade, and *grand cabinet*—the very trio of chambers that François I had provided for himself on the Cour de l'Ovale as part of the remodeling of the castle that commenced in 1528.[96] Despite the expanded need over two centuries for additional *petits appartements* and service rooms (here they face the court, as usual), the French system continued to differ from German and Spanish court systems by virtue of the relatively small number of rooms required by the king and the more public nature of his existence.

The new wing would have provided a splendid modern façade for Fontainebleau, particularly impressive when viewed across the carp pond and reflected in its waters. The billowing projection of the central *salon* was to be repeated in the shape of the terrace jutting into the water, and as indicated on the plan, the central axis would be further marked by monumental sculpture on a pedestal. Two elevations remain, each with several flaps proposing alternative details (figs. 48–49). Compared with the projects for Buen Retiro and Schleissheim, these elevations feature minimal use of the orders; the relative austerity of the blind arcade and simple window shapes is in harmony with the Renaissance parts of the building. Moreover, this degree of restraint is appropriate from the standpoint of *convenance*, since the building was not the king's major residence but a royal country house. Against the picturesque roofs of the old château de Cotte sought to juxtapose a serenely contained and emphatically horizontal mansard roof, or alternatively, a skyline *à l'italienne*, the latter solution eliminating much needed attic lodgings. In one variation a double flight of steps, rising in triangular formation against the plane of the façade, augments the apparent Italianism of the design while facilitating direct access to the oval *salon*. An unprecedented motif in de Cotte's oeuvre, this exterior stair is the most important link with the past: two similar monumental exterior stairs had been built at Fontainebleau, the Escalier de la Reine in the Cour de l'Ovale (1531, removed c. 1579), and Primaticcio's staircase on the Aisle de la Belle Cheminée.

Of the five palatial projects considered in this chapter, the Bonn Residenz was the only building carried out in part according to de Cotte's directives. But as we have seen, he was a major player on the international team of designers for the Würzburg Residenz, and his unexecuted proposals for the Buen Retiro, Madrid, provided the

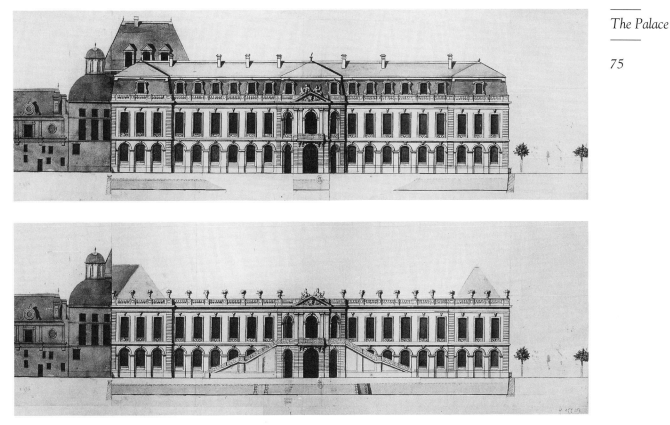

48. (*Top*) Elevation, garden façade, proposed south wing, Fontainebleau (Va 77, t. 6, 1478, without flaps).

49. (*Above*) Elevation, garden façade, proposed south wing, Fontainebleau (Va 77, t. 6, 1478, with flaps).

basis for the layout and elevations of the most important Italian palace constructed in the eighteenth century, Vanvitelli's Caserta. The influence of the projects was perhaps greatest in France, however, where de Cotte's palace drawings were available for study by successive generations of architects in the Bâtiments. A dramatic example of their impact may be found in the series of Grands Projets executed by Ange-Jacques Gabriel for the remodeling of Versailles and the construction of the Château de Compiègne in the 1740s and 1750s.[97] Thus it was as official disseminator of the formal rules of French palace design that de Cotte left a substantial legacy.

The Country House

*Houses situated in the city offer great advantages: the owner is well located for
attending to business; one has the freedom to enjoy the company of one's choosing;
one may cultivate the sciences and the arts, indulge in one's inclinations, and vary one's
pleasures. But houses in the country possess charms that may well be preferable. Every year
we see the nobility and the well-to-do get away from it all for a while in order to
benefit from the peacefulness of life in the country. People at the top go there
to leave behind important occupations that bind them to the welfare of the state;
others go to gather the fruits of their domain. . . . In this manner each
according to his rank, office, and means joins friends and family
in savoring the simple pleasures that reign in the country.*[1]

WITH THESE WORDS Jacques-François Blondel characterized the recreational goals of urban and court society in the ancien régime. Being normally bound to rules of hierarchy and ceremony, the French sought refuge in a less structured existence in the suburbs and the countryside.

From the standpoint of theory, a *maison de plaisance* was a building designed for pastoral enjoyment by a prince, a noble, or an exceptionally wealthy *bourgeois*. In contrast, the country residence of a member of the middle class, which might have components for farming and husbandry, was categorized as a *maison de campagne*.[2] The proper names of these buildings usually incorporated the word "château," despite the origins of the term in a type of fortified building. As explained in Daviler's *Cours d'architecture*: "A château is a royal house or manor house built in the form of a fortress, with moats and a draw-bridge. A château without a real system of defense is also called a *maison de plaisance*, in which the moats are merely ornamental. . . . It is so called because it is destined more for the pleasure than the profit of the owner."[3] A smaller building of two or three rooms, located within the park of a *maison de plaisance*, would be named a *pavillon*, *trianon*, or *hermitage*; these little structures provided places for specific activities, such as hunting, bathing, or dining.

The extreme popularity of country house architecture in France during the eighteenth century is apparent from two important handbooks that feature designs suited to a variety of economic levels: Blondel's *De la distribution des maisons de plaisance* (1737–38) and Charles-Etienne Briseux's *L'art de bâtir des maisons de campagne* (1743, 1761). They summarize the developments in layout and decoration that appeared during the first third of the century. To the great Baroque exemplars of Le Vau and Hardouin-

Mansart, such as Vaux-le-Vicomte and Marly, the architects of the period brought the latest innovations in *distribution* and *commodité*. These practical concerns were also foremost when a commission called for remodeling an ancestral château or erecting a new villa on old foundations.[4]

It is clear from the variety of floor plans reproduced by Blondel and Briseux that there was no single layout, method of massing, or scale employed for *maisons de plaisance*. The rule of *convenance* required that the design correspond to the status and financial means of the occupant.[5] Even so, by the beginning of the eighteenth century the principal longitudinal axis of the plan inevitably incorporated two public rooms: an entry vestibule and a tall, spacious *salon* intended for concerts, balls, important dinners, and gatherings after the hunt.[6] The large windows of the *salon* provided an unimpeded view of the "spectacle du jardin."

Since a country house principally served relaxation rather than business or ceremony, private quarters were located away from public areas and usually consisted of the four basic rooms in the French *appartement:* the *antichambre* or waiting room for visitors, domestics, and valets; the *chambre* or bedroom for both sleeping and reception; the more private *cabinet* for reading and intimate conversation; and the *garde-robe* for washing, dressing, and storage.[7] In a large country house the master might have both a formal *chambre de parade* that served principally for receiving, and a smaller bedroom, more easily heated during the winter, located either in an *appartement de commodité* or on the mezzanine level.

In his Italian travel diary de Cotte confirmed that it was the purpose of the *maison de plaisance* and its attendant garden to render life in the countryside "extremely agreeable."[8] This was the function uppermost in his mind when designing domestic structures away from an urban context.

Six country-house projects involving his talents form the substance of this chapter. Schloss Poppelsdorf, near Bonn, was the only one built, but all are of great interest insofar as they provide clear evidence of contemporary requirements for princely retreats.

Castello di Rivoli

The geographic location of the Duchy of Savoy, adjacent to the southeast border of France, brought Victor Amadeus II (1666–1732) into an alternating series of conflicts and alliances with Louis XIV, who wished to dominate the Savoyard state.[9] Following the Sun King's example, the prince of Piedmont created institutions that focused power on the central government, and he indulged a passion for architecture by erecting monuments to his *gloire*. In 1684 the duke married the niece of Louis XIV, Anne d'Orléans, and in 1702 he gave the hand of his daughter, Maria Luisa, in marriage to Louis's great-grandson, Philip V (see Buen Retiro, chap. 4). However, during the war against France in the Piedmont (1690–96) and the War of the Spanish Succession (hostilities in Piedmont-Savoy, 1704–6), French armies under Maréchal Catinat ravaged the duchy. Two of the duke's country retreats to the west of Turin sustained heavy damage: the Venaria Reale and the Castello di Rivoli (neither is mentioned in de Cotte's travel diary, despite two visits to Turin).

The Castello di Rivoli, a medieval structure that had been enlarged by Ascanio Vittozzi and the Castellamonte family through much of the seventeenth century, was burned by French troops in 1693. Four drawings in the Fonds de Cotte, comprising two different schemes, are all that remain to confirm the involvement of the Bâtiments in its reconstruction.[10] Although they are unsigned and undated, the presence of de Cotte's hand in the pencil sketches suggests that he played a significant role in their conception. The drawings were most likely produced in 1699, the year of closest rapprochement between the two powers, simultaneous with a request to Hardouin-Mansart for assistance with the Venaria Reale,[11] or at least before the eruption of new hostilities in 1704. They may thus represent Hardouin-Mansart's thoughts as visualized on paper by de Cotte, or a collaboration between the two men and Michelangelo Garove, the duke's architect in Turin. Equally, they could be the product of responsibility delegated by Mansart to his subordinate upon reorganization of the Bâtiments in 1699, the year that de Cotte was assigned the job of giving shape to the new Abbey of Saint-Denis. What is certain is that only much later, as Piedmont-Savoy emerged victorious from the wars with France, did work on Rivoli actually commence, following the plan by Garove for reconstructing the east wing (documented 1711–14).[12] The death of Garove in March 1713—the year of the Treaty of Utrecht and of Victor Amadeus's resolve to revive his architectural program—left the duke without a designer until he enlisted the services of Filippo Juvarra the following year.

While the first of the two proposals (not illustrated here) is likely a correction of Garove's plan, the second appears to be an alternative conceived independently (fig. 50). The building is situated in such a way as to reuse some of the foundations of the old structure. Compared to the much larger seventeenth-century building being replaced, as well as the gigantic palace later envisioned by Juvarra, the Paris drawings show a modest albeit princely *maison de plaisance*. The building is essentially a freestanding block with projecting corner pavilions; public rooms are concentrated toward the main axis and more private, symmetrically disposed apartments are located at the sides. This layout derives from the tradition of Renaissance country houses: the Italian archetype, the Medici villa at Poggio ai Cai-

ano (Giuliano da Sangallo, begun c. 1487), influenced the plan of the first French example, François I's Château de Madrid (1527–40).[13] The principal Baroque manifestation of the type in France is Vaux-le-Vicomte (fig. 3).

The apartments of the duke and duchess comprise a sequence of rooms originating to right and left respectively of the entry vestibule. Each apartment contains a guard room, two antechambers, a *chambre* in the middle of the lateral façade (the bed is shown behind a balustrade), and two *cabinets*. Piedmontese emulation of French court life accounts for the similarities between French and Savoyard systems of the *appartement*.[14] Rivoli was not intended exclusively for recreation: the duke's second *cabinet* is designated a "cabinet de conseille" on the plan. A pair of *petits appartements* have been loosely sketched in graphite in the end pavilions on the court side.[15]

The plan also features a gallery bordering the façade opposite the entrance. On the cross axis the architect placed the staircase, an oval chapel, small light wells providing illumination (visible in the section, fig. 51, upper right), and, behind the *chambres*, minor rooms for domestics and *lieux d'aisance*. The stair is of the imperial type, which de Cotte later used in his palace projects for Bonn and the Buen Retiro, Madrid; however, it is discreet in size and location, since the principal rooms are on the ground floor.

The designs for Rivoli give considerable prominence to the transverse axis and lateral fronts, particularly because the main garden was to be located on the cross axis, extending from the left-

50. (*Opposite, top*) Plan, *rez-de-chaussée*, with de Cotte's handwriting, second project, Castello di Rivoli, near Turin, c. 1699–1704 (Vb 5, 12).

51. (*Opposite, bottom*) West garden elevation; section showing *salle des gardes*, inner court, and gallery; south court elevation; with de Cotte's handwriting, second project, Castello di Rivoli (Vb 5, 1515).

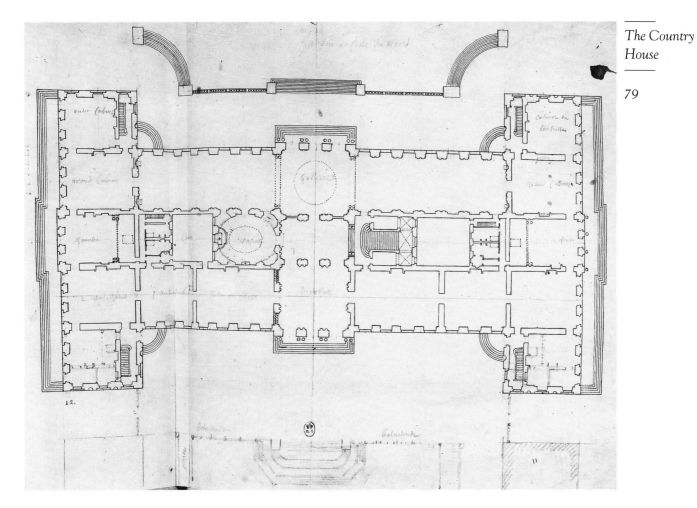

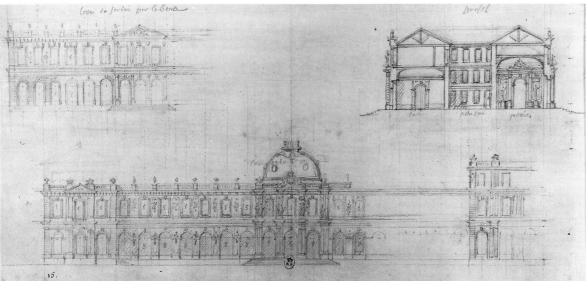

hand façade along the ridge of a hill. The siting of Rivoli corresponded to the dictates of Italian and French theory. Blondel, like many writers, favored placing a country house on a natural eminence: "At elevated sites the air is most pure, and one enjoys the most perfect health."[16] In addition, such a location provided optimum views of the formal garden and the surrounding landscape.

A sheet of three studies conveys some idea of the elevations (fig. 51). Bertrand Jestaz recognized the drawing style of de Cotte in the rapid, freehand sketches with diagonal hatching, and his handwriting in the captions.[17] The long, low-lying court façade below, featuring a square dome on the central pavilion and a tripartite composition for the end pavilions, is based on the work of Hardouin-Mansart, whose garden façade of Clagny is the chief source (fig. 5). The elevation differs from Clagny in the use of a blind arcade all around the ground floor and the absence of a visible roof. Lightly sketched attic stories on the end pavilions of this façade are a tentative concession to traditional *castello* design, reflecting the original towered corners of the old Rivoli.

In accordance with contemporary theory, the classical orders are used sparingly on the exterior, appearing only on the pavilions. Concerning exterior elevations, Briseux wrote, "There are two sorts of decoration for buildings: the first consists of the architectural orders, suitable only for palaces, large châteaux, churches, and other public monuments. . . . The second is no more than the harmonious arrangement of simple parts and the judicious relationship they bear to each other, the whole based on the principles of *convenance*, [an understanding of] which requires more than a little genius and study."[18] Indeed, most theorists felt that while the orders could be employed all across the exterior of a palace, they should be restricted to the main entrance of a *maison de plaisance*. Windows were thus one of the salient fea-

tures of country house exteriors. As Briseux declared, "The beauty apparent from a glance at a façade depends also on the forms given the window openings. Those terminated in an arch, curved lintel, or flat molding are the most approved; one may also employ a flattened arch or basket-handle arch in order to procure more variety in the façades; but these forms must be used judiciously."[19]

In sum, the project for Rivoli was conceivably de Cotte's earliest for a *maison de plaisance*, or equally, it may have been an example of collaboration among several hands in the Bâtiments. Although not executed, it reveals an attempt to combine both stately and comfortable quarters within the genre of the freestanding block with corner pavilions.[20]

Schloss Brühl and Schloss Godesberg

In late March 1715 Joseph Clemens, the elector of Cologne, for whom de Cotte prepared designs for the Palace of Bonn (see chap. 4), wrote to the Premier Architecte in order to initiate planning on his country houses: "Now that the time has come, Monsieur, to work on my *maisons de campagne* of Poppelsdorf, Brühl, and Godesberg, you would do me a great favor by sending to me as soon as possible a sketch of your ideas concerning these."[21] One month later he acknowledged de Cotte's response: "I am grateful . . . for the beautiful design that you sent to me for the hill of Godesberg. The layout is very fine, and I am extremely pleased; but to tell the truth, Monsieur, the projects for Poppelsdorf and Brühl are the most pressing, since I have no house to which to retire during the summer. . . . It would please me if you would send these projects as soon as you can."[22]

The old moated castle of Brühl, situated on the road from Bonn to Cologne in an area famous for falconry, had been damaged by the French during the War of the League of Augsburg

(1688–97). Financially pressed, the elector determined to make the most of the existing structure. On 4 May 1715 he sent a plan of the building to Paris along with a sketch in his own hand showing the new outbuildings he envisioned around the old house (fig. 52). A long memorandum keyed to the plan explains his ideas in detail.[23] He wished to conceal the square keep ("vieux château," bottom of plan), originally entered from the south, behind a new entrance façade on the east (K), matching that of the Bonn Residenz, in which direction it faced. Two new

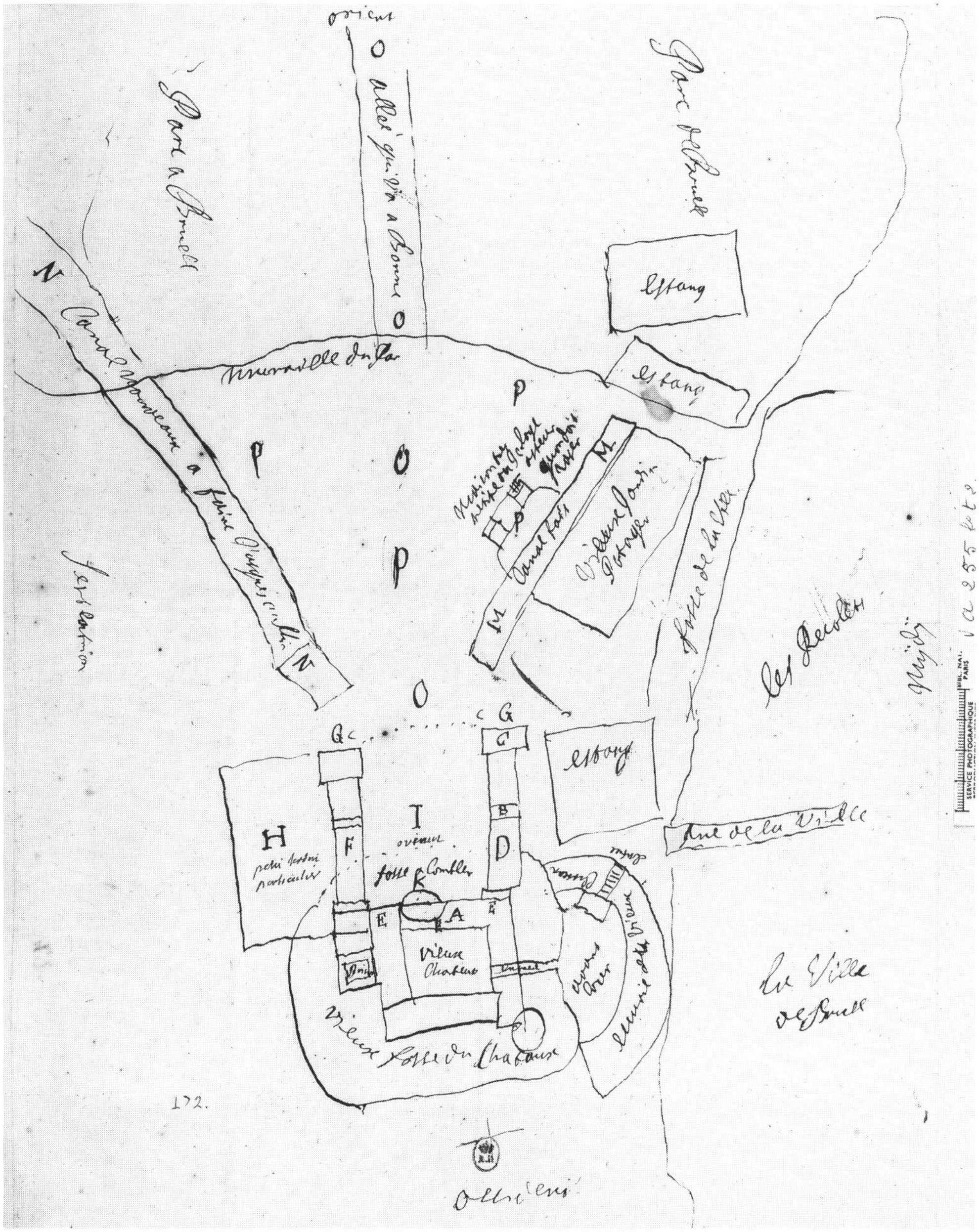

52. Joseph Clemens, elector of Cologne, sketch of the old Schloss Brühl with suggestions for a new *maison de plaisance*, 4 May 1715 (Vc 255, t. 2, 172).

wings containing the elector's apartments (F, D) would project eastward from the old building, producing a forecourt closed by an iron gate. He desired that the longitudinal axis (O) be continued by an avenue leading toward Bonn, while two canals (M, N) would radiate diagonally northward and southward from the pair of wings. Versailles was the model for the *patte d'oie* configuration of three axes converging on a grill-enclosed courtyard bordered by subsidiary buildings (fig. 4). As at the Palace of Bonn, the elector desired a small private garden (H) where he could indulge his passion for horticulture.

53. Plan, project, Schloss Godesberg, April 1715 (Vc 254, 138).

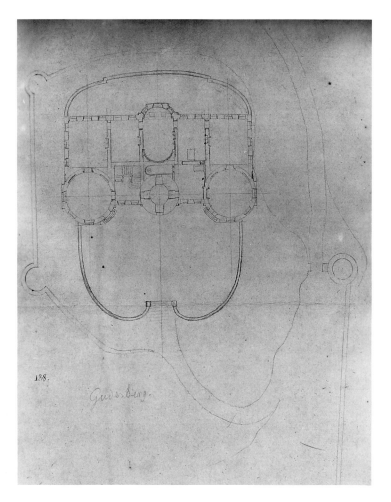

In spite of the exchange of letters, no plans by de Cotte for Brühl are extant, if indeed any were drawn up. A decade later Joseph Clemens's successor, Clemens August, reconsidered the problem of Brühl with the aid of Guillaume Hauberat, de Cotte's assistant (1724), and Johann Conrad Schlaun, the architect of the new building (1725).[24]

In the letter of April 1715 the elector announced receipt of the presentation drawings for Schloss Godesberg, three miles southeast of Bonn, but these sheets have not survived. A graphite drawing of the plan, a reduced variant of Jean-Baptiste Bullet de Chamblain's Château de Champs (1701–7),[25] the most influential reduced-scale variant of Vaux-le-Vicomte, did remain in the Paris studio (fig. 53).[26] De Cotte kept only the tower of the medieval ruin (which still stands) as the center of a new court façade, repeating its circular shape in projecting entrance pavilions on either side. An elongated oval *salon* on the opposite façade likewise projects from the plane of the wall. In any event, the château was never rebuilt.

Schloss Poppelsdorf

As early as 1704 the elector of Cologne solicited ideas from Hardouin-Mansart for a *maison de plaisance* to replace the old ruined castle of Poppelsdorf on the southwest outskirts of Bonn, but there is no evidence that Mansart responded.[27] In 1715 Joseph Clemens renewed his program with de Cotte, envisioning a broader scheme that would link visually a new *villa suburbana* with the *enfilade* of the remodeled Bonn Palace one-half mile to the north. The idea of a canal connecting the two structures is based on the example of Versailles and its subsidiary, the Trianon de Marbre (fig. 4). On 24 May 1715 the elector wrote to de Cotte, "I received your project for my Maison de Poppelsdorf, which pleased me infinitely, and I know of nothing more beautiful or

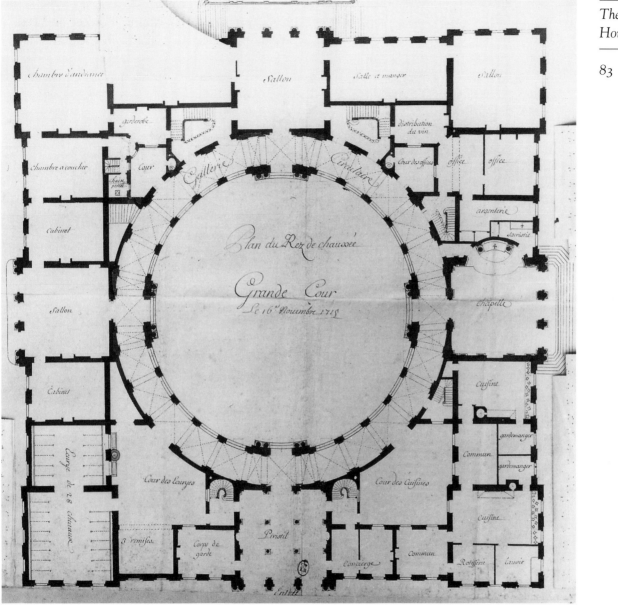

---

better conceived, but we are now obliged to consider the site on which it must be built."[28] The commission thus illustrates problems that de Cotte frequently faced when designing for a site he had not personally inspected.

The first project (May 1715), for which no ground plan remains, may be deduced from extant letters and later plans.[29] Biaxially symmetri-

54. Plan, *rez-de-chaussée*, second project, Schloss Poppelsdorf, Bonn, 16 November 1716 (Vc 254, 132).

cal for the most part, it consisted of four two-story wings surrounding a circular court that was bordered by an arcaded gallery. The circle-in-square plan was similar to the contemporary cross-in-square second proposal for the Buen Retiro, Madrid (fig. 31). The elector deemed this too elaborate, requesting de Cotte's assistant at Bonn, Benoît de Fortier, to reduce three of the wings to a single story, allowing the garden wing to dominate (second project, 16 November 1716; fig. 54):

> I am sending . . . , Monsieur, the [revised] plan of the house that I wish to build at Poppelsdorf. You will find that we have essentially followed your concept in accordance with the grand and magnificent design that you had made: however, I realized that it would be quite useless to erect so large a building on that site, which is but a cannon shot from town, and to and from which one can go in very little time. Thus, for the most part my retinue returns to the city at night, and I keep near me only those who are absolutely necessary to serve me.[30]

In this plan a vestibule with twelve columns, freestanding or engaged, leads to a covered ambulatory circumscribing the courtyard, and thence to a *salon à l'italienne* on the opposite side of the main axis, from which the elector's apartment is accessible by turning to the left. The sequence of rooms in the apartment is an abbreviated version of the more extensive *enfilade* in the Bonn Palace: *grande salle, chambre d'audience, chambre à coucher,* and *cabinet.* Stables, kitchens, offices, a chapel, and a dining room occupy the other wings. Minor rooms, stairs, a loo, and small inner courts face the arcaded gallery.

To a considerable extent de Cotte's choice of a central plan with a circular court was the result of his familiarity with Italian Renaissance architecture and sixteenth-century theoretical literature, interests that were stimulated by his Italian sojourn. He would have known two important precedents for a country retreat with a circular interior court, the Villa Madama, Rome (Raphael, begun c. 1516, not completed), and the Palazzo Farnese at Caprarola (Vignola, begun 1559), although there is no record in his travel

diary of visits to these sites. As we saw in the discussion of the central-plan second proposal for the Buen Retiro, de Cotte presumably had knowledge of Serlio's manuscript and proofs for the Sixth Book, *Delle habitationi di tutti li gradi degli uomini* (composed 1540s); this may account for the parallel between the Poppelsdorf plan and Serlio's ideal project for a villa for a prince (fig. 55).[31] Based on the fortress type, Serlio's plan consists of four large towers anchoring the corners of a square plan that encloses a circular courtyard. Serlio's plans for bilaterally-axial châteaux were the source for elaborate and fanciful villa designs (many analogous to Poppelsdorf) published by Jacques Androuet du Cerceau in the *Premier livre d'architecture* (1559; projects XLIV, XLVIII) and the *Troisième livre d'architecture* (1582; projects XX, XXX, XXXII, XXXV, XXXVIII).[32] Just as these sixteenth-century projects owed their origins to the four-wing *château-fort* with an enclosed inner court, so too de Cotte's Poppelsdorf design stemmed in part from the elector's wish to reuse the ruined foundations of an earlier fortified residence on the site.[33] A connoisseur of French architecture, the elector surely appreciated the fact that the Poppelsdorf plan also resembled the central-plan design of Marly, the Sun King's retreat, even though the latter differed insofar as an enclosed circular *salon* occupied the center (begun 1679; fig. 9). It should be recalled that Marly was Hardouin-Mansart's homage to Palladio's Villa Rotonda, whose origins have been traced to the central-plan designs in Serlio's Sixth Book.[34] Whatever the chain of influence, de Cotte was clearly operating under the spell of sixteenth-century Italian architecture.

Proof of this interest appears in an anecdote regarding Nicodemus Tessin the Younger's first project for the rebuilding of the Louvre (1704), which incorporates a large circular courtyard within the old Square Court of Lescot, Lemercier, and Le Vau.[35] The architect's agent in Paris, Daniel Cronström, wrote to Tessin in Stockholm that de Cotte had reacted to the project more favorably than the other academicians as a result of his sympathy toward Italian architecture: "I took Monsieur de Cotte aside with several courtiers and read your report to him. He is sharp, and before I could name them, he guessed the places in Italy that you have cited to justify the arcades and the circular court [e.g., Caprarola]. He approved of your reasoning, eagerly requested your memorandum in order to copy it, and returned it to me three hours later."[36]

The most impressive drawing among the series of exterior elevations produced by de Cotte and de Fortier is that for the first project, which, like the court elevation for the Castello di Rivoli, derives from the garden façade of Clagny (figs. 5,

55. Plan, Villa for a Prince, pl. XXVIII, Sebastiano Serlio on Domestic Architecture, the Sixteenth-Century Manuscript of Book VI in the Avery Library of Columbia University, New York.

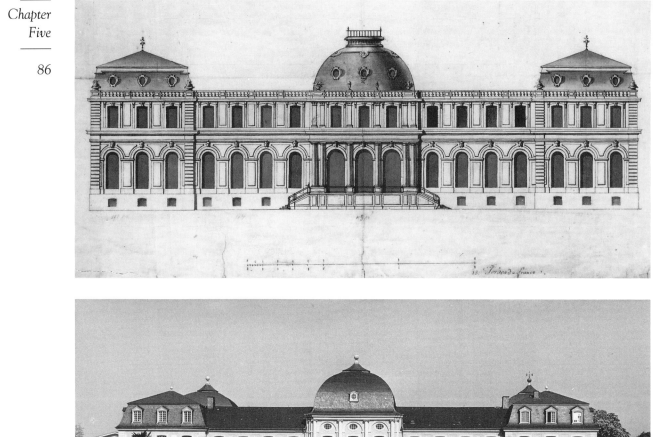

56). A continuous arcade on the main floor unifies the strongly horizontal, chiefly planar front that rises over a short plinth. A balustrade tops off the attic story, whose windows alternate with raised panels. In concert with contemporary theoretical writings, the order is limited to the central pavilion—engaged columns below, dwarf pilasters above.[37] The roof is not continuous. Rather, the end pavilions have short mansard roofs, and the central pavilion bears a circular rather than square dome, fully in keeping with the smooth, elegant feeling of the whole. The blind arcade and dwarf pilasters repeat motifs from the early works of Hardouin-Mansart (respectively, the Château du Val, 1674, and Hôtel de Noailles, Saint-Germain-en-Laye, 1679), while the contrast between mansard roofs and curved dome harks back to Le Vau (Vaux-le-Vicomte, fig. 3). Through the combination of sculptured keystones, rusticated strips, and delicate low-relief surfaces, de Cotte successfully achieved "un heureux mélange d'ornemens"— Briseux's phrase describing the effect desired of the exterior elevations of a typical maison de plaisance.[38] At the same time, the architect sought to avoid the congested appearance of the sculptural decoration of the Italian villa exteriors that he had criticized on his study trip.

The character of the Poppelsdorf elevations changed once the elector and Fortier assumed control of the design (November 1716) and at subsequent times during construction. De Cotte had no power to influence what was built. Work came to a halt upon the death of the patron; beginning in 1745 his successor Clemens August

initiated the final building campaign. We are fortunate nonetheless to have a structure that reflects de Cotte's basic conception of a noble maison de plaisance, despite the intrusion of such Germanic elements as the polychrome exterior and bulbous roofs (now part of the University of Bonn; fig. 57).

Schloss Tilburg

During the same period, c. 1715–17, the Premier Architecte undertook a similar commission for Prince William VIII of Hesse-Kassel (1682–1760), governor of Breda, who wished to fashion a maison de plaisance out of the nearby medieval estate of Tilburg in North Brabant (Holland; not executed).[39] In a manner comparable to the circumstances prevailing at Poppelsdorf, the rectangular shape of the old castle suggested a cross-in-square plan anchored in a moat (figs. 58–59; compare the contemporary second proposal for the Palace of Buen Retiro, fig. 31). Unlike the Poppelsdorf plan, there is no central court. The longitudinal axis bisects a vestibule and a salon, both two-storied; U-shaped dining and billiard rooms lie on the cross axis.[40] Billiard rooms were popular in country houses, although Briseux advised placing them away from the bedrooms on account of the noise, and the frequency of accidents led Blondel to recommend simple wooden paneling rather than paintings and mirrors for decoration.[41] In each of the four corners of the square the architect inserted comfortable apartments with cabinets in towerlike pavilions, similar to those on the courtyard side of Godesberg (fig. 53).

As at Poppelsdorf, the decision to superimpose a basically central plan on medieval foundations yielded a design analogous to several French Renaissance châteaux that developed out of the tradition of the medieval donjon. For example, both the Château de Chambord (1517–32) and Pierre Chambiges's Château de Challuau (c. 1540) fea-

56. (Opposite, top) Elevation (without later flaps), first project, Schloss Poppelsdorf, May 1715 (Landeskonservator Rheinland).

57. (Opposite, bottom) Garden wing, Schloss Poppelsdorf (Schloss Clemensruhe).

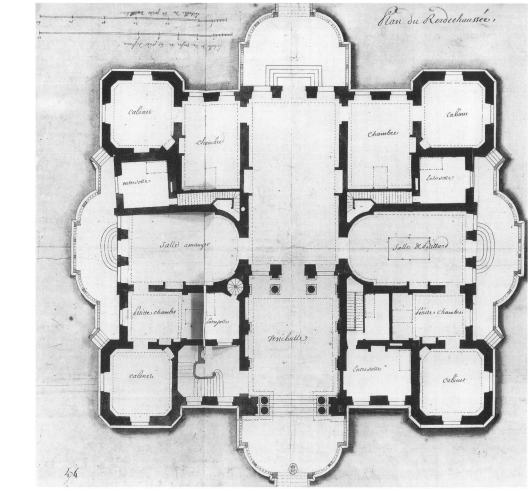

58. Plan, *rez-de-chaussée*, project, Schloss Tilburg, c. 1715–17 (Vc 75, 476).

ture public rooms on the axes and secluded apartments in the pavilions.[42] In consideration of the strong interest in Italian planning stimulated by de Cotte's southward travels, and the admiration and familiarity he had developed for Palladio's work, one feature of the Tilburg plan requires special comment, the axial pairing of an open vestibule and a longitudinal hall, flanked by symmetrically disposed rooms. This was also a feature of Palladio's villa plans (compare loggia-*salone* combinations at the Villa Valmarana-Scagnaroli, c. 1563–66, and Villa Foscari, Malcontenta, c. 1558–60; *I quattro libri dell'architettura*, book 2, pls. XXXIII, LXII). Whether or not these ele-

ments are of specifically Palladian inspiration in the Tilburg layout, the plan belongs to a group of early eighteenth-century French designs that demonstrate a return to Renaissance ideals.

In a detailed *mémoire* de Cotte emphasized the degree to which every consideration was given to comfort, privacy, and the clever use of space both horizontally and vertically. *Entresols* and doubled up *garde-robes* are tucked away throughout. A stair on the left side of the vestibule leads to seven small apartments in the attic story. Domestics' rooms and *garde-meubles* are situated below the roofs.

As was customary for country dwellings, the

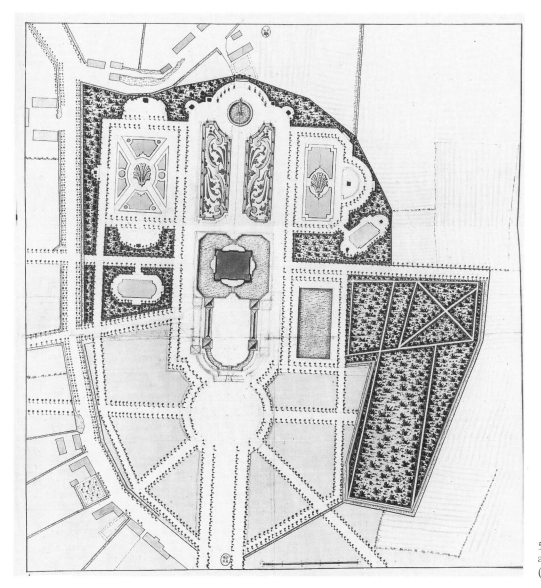

59. Plan, project, château and garden, Schloss Tilburg (Vc 75, 472).

order appears sparingly in the elevations, columns being paired in depth along the entry alone (figs. 58, 60). The entrance pavilion is a sophisticated composition that corresponds in its horizontal division to the two stories of the elevation, but appears visually as a single vertical unit, capped by a mansard roof. The open vestibule is of a type favored for large houses; de Cordemoy wrote in 1714, "The entire bay of the vestibule adjacent to the façade must be completely open to the height of the *premier étage* only, so that the beauty of the interior strikes the eye at first sight even before one enters."[43] The pavilions with their crested roofs, an elaboration of the square dome, retain the medieval character of the original structure.

The plan of the domain was altered to fit the type preferred by de Cotte (fig. 59). A large circular *place*, from which many paths radiate, stands before the court of the château. The fore-

60. Elevation, court façade, project, Schloss Tilburg (Vc 75, 478).

court is enclosed by a stirrup-shaped moat and parallel wings for offices, kitchens, and stables. The main axis is continued on the garden side of the building, with *parterres de broderie* leading to a basin. Blondel summarized the importance of ornamental grounds as follows:

Gardens comprise the most pleasurable part of a country house. . . . The art of gardening was taken to the highest perfection in the last century, especially in France, which evidently serves as a school for all other nations. . . . The elements of a formal garden are lawns, fountains, basins, thickets, *salons, salles de verdure,* cloisters, bowling greens, woods, trellis arbors, little retreats, etc. But it is the *distribution* of all these parts that lends charm to a park; their arrangement and variety cause surprise and amuse agreeably. One must take care that all of a garden's beauties are not visible at a single glance, and it is good to arouse curiosity by concealing some of the ornaments that will satisfy it.[44]

Wary of changes that might be introduced by non-French builders, de Cotte concluded his memorandum by saying, "If these drawings are suitable and [the patrons] wish to execute them, it will be necessary for me to be in touch with the men charged with the work, in order to conserve the style and spirit [of my design]."[45]

Château de Compiègne

The Château de Compiègne, located north of Paris in the Ile-de-France, was virtually the only royal building that did not undergo major transformation under Louis XIV. He contented himself with remodeling some apartments within the complex that enveloped the original *château-fort* of Charles V. Louis XV, attracted by opportunities for hunting offered by the site, was disappointed on his first visit in 1728 to find inadequate housing.[46] The earliest attempt to provide a more modern retreat was de Cotte's proposal for a *pavillon de chasse* (hunting lodge) situated away from the town in the center of a vast ensemble adjacent to the forest (fig. 61).[47] The proposal, which went unrealized, probably dates from 1729, the year that the young king put de Cotte to work on remodeling the Maison Royal de Fontainebleau (see chap. 4). In 1751 Louis XV charged Ange-Jacques Gabriel with construction of the palatial château that dominates the site today.

De Cotte's scheme is a reduced replica of Versailles (fig. 4): the visitor would enter the complex via the main axis leading between two U-shaped stables, comparable to Hardouin-Mansart's Grandes Ecuries. On the other side of the moat, to left and right of the *cour d'honneur*, lie two buildings incorporating service wings. The design of the symmetrically composed garden echoes the multiple axes of the château.

Like the plans for Poppelsdorf and Tilburg, the X-shaped ground floor of the pavilion offers the geometric precision of an aesthetic ideal combined with the practicality of withdrawn, private suites giving directly onto the garden (fig. 62). Four entrance vestibules, rectangular with semicircular lateral spaces, join a central circular *salon à l'italienne* rising three stories. Each of the wings contains an apartment. Those for the royal couple are located on the garden side, where the inscriptions clearly designate the *antichambre*, *chambre*, *grand cabinet*, *petit cabinet*, and *garde-robe et chaise*. Suites of rooms on the second floor, reached by a pair of stairs beside the court vestibule, are smaller and more numerous in order to accommodate lesser members of the family and the king's guard.

During the previous two centuries the X-shaped plan had become closely identified with the *pavillon de chasse* as an architectural type. One of its earliest appearances was Pierre Chambiges's plan for the Château de la Muette of François I in the forest of Saint-Germain (1542).[48] The radiating plan also appeared in the

realm of theoretical architecture in the publications of Serlio (Seventh Book, chap. 13) and Du Cerceau (*Premier livre d'architecture,* 1559; projects XVI, XXVIII, XLIII, XLIV, XLIX). Moreover, during his trip on the Brenta Canal in 1698, de Cotte had seen the Palazzo Contarini, X-shaped in plan and domed over the central core (attributed to Baldassare Longhena; c. 1630s). In addition, while in Rome he visited a similar central-plan structure on the grounds of the Villa

61. Plan, project, stables, outbuildings, château, and gardens, Compiègne, c. 1729 (Va 434, 1652).

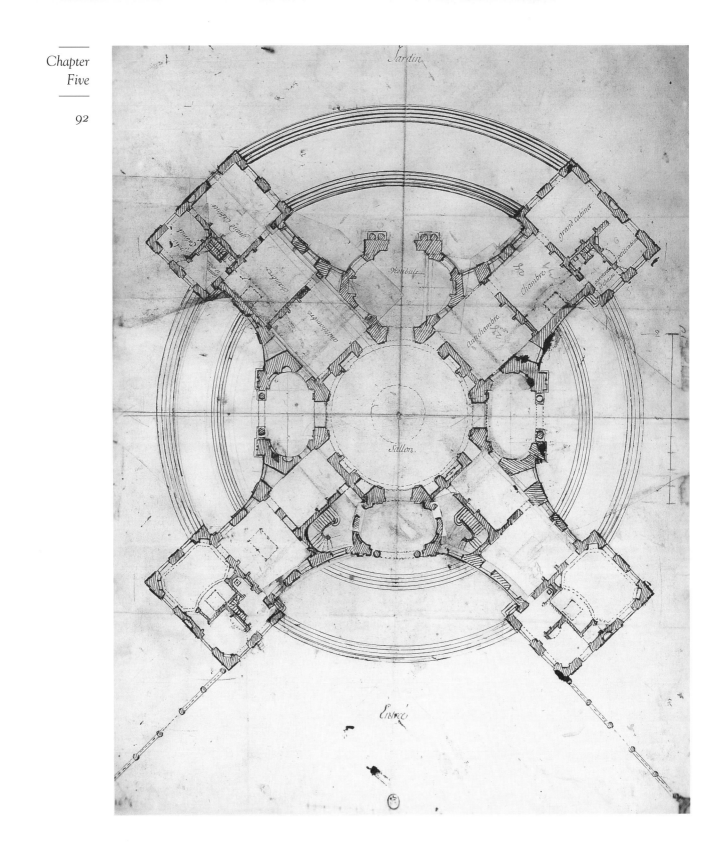

62. (*Opposite*) Plan, early sketch, *rez-de-chaussée*, Château de Compiègne (Va 60, t. 14, 1654).

63. (*Below*) Boffrand, plan, Malgrange II, 1711 (*Livre d'architecture*, 1745, Ha 22).

Ludovisi, the Casino dell'Aurora; its plan is a Greek cross, whose central section rises to form a belvedere (before 1577). However, the most influential building of this type to be constructed was J. B. Fischer von Erlach's Gartenpalais Althann in the Rossau, Vienna (c. 1693).[49] It was the source for Boffrand's unexecuted second scheme for the Château de Malgrange, commissioned by Léopold, duc de Lorraine (1711; fig. 63).[50] De Cotte's Compiègne project resembles the latter pair of examples in its incorporation of an apartment in each of four wings projecting from a central rotunda; it differs in that the arms of the cross are equidistant from each other and are fully revealed on the exterior. During the same years that de Cotte was at work on this plan, Filippo Juvarra devised the X-shaped com-

position of the Royal Hunting Lodge of Stupinigi outside Turin (1729–31), based on the designs of both Fischer and Boffrand.

The greater degree of biaxial symmetry in the Compiègne plan and its geometrical coordination with the domain suggest a second line of sources. The centralized plan of the Pavillon du Roi at Marly has the same disposition of four vestibules separating four apartments on equidistant axes, although in this instance a square plan encloses an octagonal central room (fig. 9). Another influential work, Boffrand's Pavillon de Chasse de Bouchefort, was based on a similar Greek cross; the difference here lay in the use of an octagonal block enclosing an octagonal *salon*, and four porticos projecting from the exterior walls in emulation of the Villa Rotonda. One further example is the partly centralized plan of Jacques de la Guêpière's Pavillon de la Ménagerie at Sceaux (undated; perhaps second decade of the century).[51] Ange-Jacques Gabriel, who took over the work at Compiègne at mid-

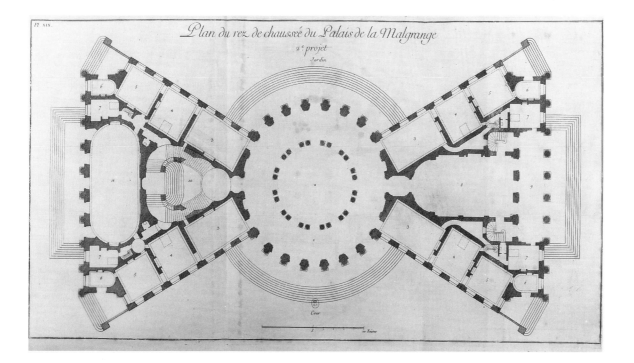

century, later employed a small version of the X-shaped plan for the Pavillon Français in the garden of the Petit Trianon, Versailles (1749).

In his project de Cotte not only utilized the theme of the central plan that had preoccupied him in the mid teens, but in the elevations he also employed features from his earlier designs for *maisons de plaisance* (fig. 64, differing from extant plans in some details; compare Poppelsdorf, fig. 56). A blind arcade pierced by windows runs the length of the ground story, simple windows of *bombé* profile illuminate the attic level, and the order appears only on the entrance bays and the drum. There is no roof over the wings, which are crowned by a stone balustrade. An ornamental ironwork railing perches atop the dome. Four concave balconies directly above the vestibules would have provided elevated views of the landscape and a means of taking the air, while three circular stairs within the drum would have led to the terrace atop the dome, with its grand pan-

orama. Such lookout points, even when relatively inaccessible, had been used frequently in French royal country houses—for example, the rooftop platform of Chambord, the pseudo-*loggie* of the Château de Blois (1520–24), and the recessed terrace of the Enveloppe, Versailles (1668)—all of which suggested in architectural terms the king's surveillance over his domain.[52]

Pavillon des Bains, Saverne

One of the major figures of the period was Cardinal Armand-Gaston de Rohan, whose career as bishop of Strasbourg spanned the years 1704–49. A member of the Académie des inscriptions et belles-lettres and the Académie française, a great bibliophile, and a distinguished patron of the arts, the bishop was widely celebrated for his intelligence and taste. Because of the princely status of his family, he was able to obtain the services of prominent designers in the Bâtiments. His first important undertaking was

64. Elevation, court façade, château, Compiègne (Va 60, t. 14, 1656).

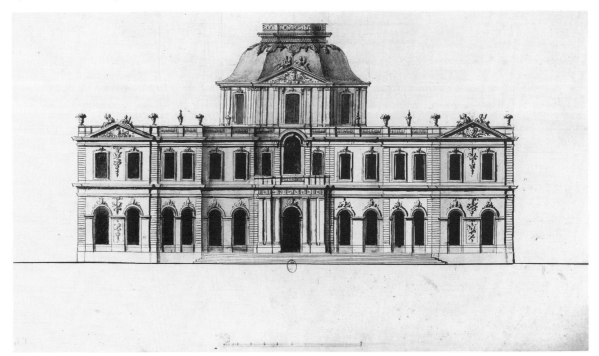

the Hôtel de Rohan, Paris (1705–12), built on a site neighboring the *hôtel* of his father, François de Rohan, prince de Soubise. During the course of construction de Cotte and Boffrand replaced the initial architect, Delamaire (see chap. 1). The cardinal's second big scheme comprised a series of additions to his main seat, the Château de Saverne, overseen by de Cotte (1712–30).[53] A third large-scale project was the erection of a new Palais Episcopal in Strasbourg, for which de Cotte provided designs (1727–28) and his deputy, Joseph Massol, oversaw construction (1731–42; chap. 10).

The Pavillon des Bains (Pavillon de la Grille) was one of the cardinal's last projects for Saverne. It was intended for a site on the eastern border of the grounds where a double *allée* of trees met the gate. The extant suite of drawings, which is incomplete, calls for a small garden building devoted to submersion bathing, a new type of luxurious and healthful recreation that employed advances in plumbing as a means of stimulating the senses.[54] On the basis of a letter from the cardinal to de Cotte (1 October 1730), it appears that planning evolved through three stages.[55]

The first project, whose layout is comparable in some respects to the centralized plans for Poppelsdorf, Tilburg, and Compiègne, consists of a one-story block (fig. 65). This faces the narrower of two *allées* forming a perspective view from the cardinal's *cabinet* in the château. The plan resembles a Latin cross circumscribed by a rectangle. A square vestibule and an oval *salle des bains* occupy the longitudinal axis of the plan; each of three alcoves surrounding the *salle* contains an oval bathtub. So that the languorous activity of bathing might be followed by relaxation in bed, a pair of symmetrically disposed *appartements*, each with a *chambre de repos* and a *cabinet*, lie on either side of the central rooms. The plan follows seventeenth-century developments in the type of small blocklike *maison de plaisance* exemplified by

Pierre Bullet's Château d'Issy (1681), which is also only three rooms wide.[56]

The *appartement des bains* was not a feature of de Cotte's *hôtel* or château designs during the teens. Its appearance here reflects the greater incidence of this type of accommodation by 1730. Blondel states, "The function of such an *appartement* requires cool air, and this is why it is most often placed on the ground floor of a building in the shade of some woods and near a fountain. Thus, upon emerging from this kind of building, one may breathe fresh air in the shade of some pleasant greenery."[57] De Cotte's plan calls for three bathtubs, presumably to be made of tin-lined copper; his subsequent plans show two tubs

65. Plan, first project, Pavillon des Bains, Saverne, 1730 (Va 67, t. 3, 1251).

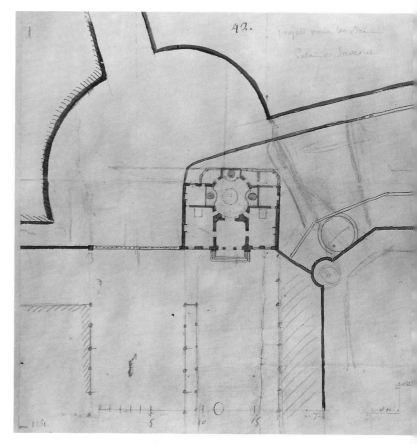

arranged symmetrically (second project; fig. 66). Two was the usual number according to Blondel, "either so that two persons may keep each other company and amuse themselves in privacy; or so that the layout of this type of room possesses more symmetry; or so that one of the basins may be used for tepid water, and the other warm, depending on the season."[58]

In the second project, the building was shifted to the broader site facing the main *allée* (fig. 66). In a curious reversal of the previous plan, the architect altered the *salle des bains* to rectangular

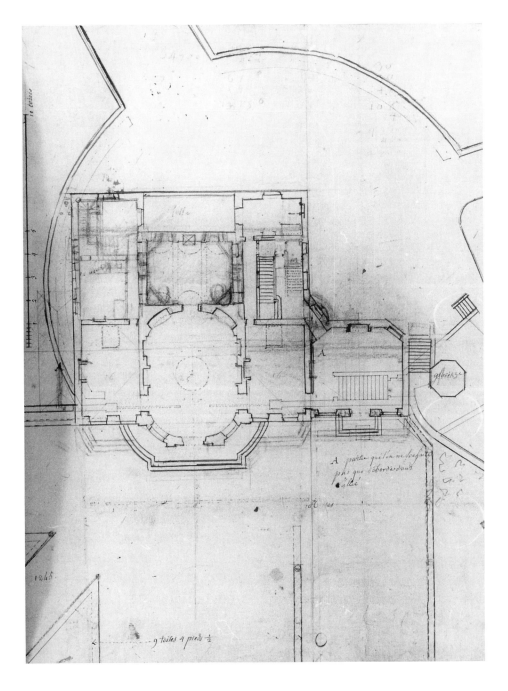

66. Plan, *rez-de-chaussée*, preparatory ink drawing with graphite corrections, second project, Pavillon des Bains, Saverne (Va 67, t. 3, 1245).

shape, while he changed the entrance vestibule to an oval, so that it projects from the wall in a manner mimicking many a château garden front. The second project includes a pair of water closets on the main floor (not shown in fig. 66), an amenity specifically associated with an *appartement des bains* because of the plumbing system.[59] In this project the building grew to two stories; a one-story pavilion attached to the right-hand side provides a focal point for the smaller *allée*. This, however, did not please the cardinal, who wrote to de Cotte, "When I resolved to examine, my dear Sir, the plan that you had the kindness to prepare for the Pavillon des Bains in the square by the iron gate near the ice house, it appeared to me that the projecting block containing the stairwell, which gives onto the *allée* opposite my *cabinet*, produces a disagreeable effect." He had de Cotte's newest assistant on the site, Le Chevalier, rework the plan, reducing the width of the pavilion. He then sent the corrected design to Paris: "I beg you to examine the new [plan] to see if the proportions are the same, the exterior steps are all right, etc."[60] The third project for the most part repeats the *distribution* of the second.

The definitive elevation (fig. 67) derives from the *maison de plaisance* tradition established by the Bullet family. The Château d'Issy popularized the narrow, tripartite elevation lacking lateral pavilions; the Château de Champs set the standard for the suave integration of the customary elements—the flat, planar projection of the *salon* wall, the prominent forged-iron balcony, and the pediment supported by rusticated strips in lieu of a classical order.[61] In the drawing, tall floor-to-ceiling windows and doors articulate the exterior shell. A flap attached to the drawing offers an alternative for the high mansard roof enclosing an attic—a simple balustrade with no visible roof, hence *à l'italienne*. In an alternative elevation, the central bay is capped by a semicircular arch, a château-motif whose lineage descended through the Du Cerceau, Salomon de Brosse, and François Mansart.

Sections of the interior show rococo paneling and mirror-topped mantles intended to complete the image of an *architecture élégante* according to the standards of the day.[62] There is insufficient evidence to confirm construction of the building. Late eighteenth-century references to a "maisonette . . . dite les bains" on another site in the park may describe a comparable structure of subsequent date.[63]

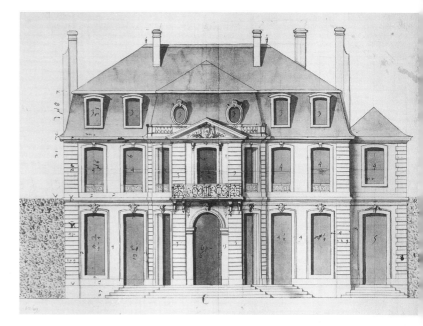

67. Elevation, principal façade (facing château), third project, Pavillon des Bains, Saverne (Va 67, t. 3, 1249).

Chapter Six

The City: Paris

*Paris, the model for other cities, surpasses them completely in grandeur, beauty,
and magnificence, although it has arrived at this state of perfection only gradually;
it is the work of many centuries. The taste and splendor of our kings, the wealth of the
citizens, and the concerns of civil government have contributed to make this capital
the most accommodating and most flourishing city in the world.*[1]

IN THIS MANNER Le Cler du Brillet proudly described France's greatest urban center in 1738 (fig. 68). He further remarked that Paris, according to current theory, possessed the three essential requirements for a thriving metropolis: industrious, peace-loving citizens, good government, and a propitious geographical location furnishing necessities for the construction of buildings and streets.[2]

Historians of Parisian urbanism traditionally view the period 1700 to 1735 as a hiatus between two eras of brilliance—the late seventeenth century, which witnessed the great building campaigns of Louis XIV, and the mid-eighteenth century, when competitions for the Place Louis XV heralded that monarch's interest in large-scale public architecture. This view fails, however, to take into account the dramatic upswing in private construction in the intervening years, its impact on urban planning, and the efforts to accommodate commercial and social activities by providing new public buildings and squares.

Robert de Cotte belonged to a team of city and royal officials who oversaw the expansion of Paris in these years. The general goal was the completion of the Ludovican program instituted by Colbert in the 1670s. The great minister had sought to transform the *ville royale* into a new Rome—a well-organized, prosperous city, whose monuments would withstand the vicissitudes of time as concrete evidence of the monarch's *gloire*. Colbert's master plan, embodied in the *Plan de Paris* published by François Blondel and Pierre Bullet in 1676, called for projects dedicated "à la commodité des Habitans, & à la décoration des Edifices publics."[3] Its main objectives were still in force in the early eighteenth century, but on a larger scale: improvement of circulation by the opening of new thoroughfares and the broadening of streets; development of quays along the river; expansion of the utility matrix comprising water and sewage systems; and completion of the new tree-lined ramparts that girded the city's perimeter.

At the same time, the ever-increasing recreational needs of Parisians received consideration from urban planners. In particular, a large network of social arenas within the city provided a backdrop for the most prominent leisure activity during the ancien régime, the *promenade à la mode.* "There are no People," observed Martin Lister in 1699, "more fond [than Parisians] of coming together to see and to be seen."[4] Strollers viewed the city as a sequence of pictures or stage sets—gardens, shops, theaters, and squares—to and from which they whirled, performing their individual roles in the spectacle of public life. This outdoor activity served to stimulate business transactions, dangerous liaisons, gossip, and such parental obligations as finding a suitor for an eligible daughter. Paris was aptly dubbed the theater of the universe.

The early decades of the eighteenth century also saw the publication of a concise theory of urbanism, the *Traité de la police*, begun by Nicolas Delamare (vols. 1–3, 1705–19) and continued according to established guidelines by his assistant, Anne-Louis Le Cler du Brillet (vol. 4, 1738). An antiquarian who had traveled to Rome, Delamare (1639–1723) worked as commissioner at the Châtelet and as chief advisor to Nicolas de la Reynie, the man installed by Colbert in 1667 as first Lieutenant Général de la Police.[5] Delamare's treatise was the earliest comprehensive French history of urban public governance, or *police*. In it he explicitly defined the relationship of civil law to urban planning.[6] His thesis was that good government is reflected in the "image" of a town, and that civil law ensures harmony, which in turn brings beauty to the city. That he adopted Colbert's theme of the new Rome is clear from constant references to Roman prototypes in his discussions of different aspects of Parisian life and building types. The insistence on three major goals of urban architecture—*commodité*, *utilité*, and *décoration*—in addition to *bienséance*, harks back to Vitruvian as well as Albertian ideals. The *Traité* culminates in a discussion of urban projects carried out in Paris during the years central to de Cotte's career in the Bâtiments—1699 to 1734.[7] For this reason, and for the purpose of understanding the theoretical aims of the period, we will often consult Delamare and Le Cler du Brillet as guides to the Parisian scene.

It is more difficult to trace de Cotte's role in the formation of urban projects than in the development of domestic and ecclesiastical schemes because of the elaborate official hierarchy that oversaw changes in the fabric of Paris. An outline of this hierarchy will serve to clarify the structure of the collaborative process. Delamare asserted the common belief that the chief planner of Paris was the king, whose laws and edicts governed urban life. Large-scale civic buildings were a royal obligation: "The prince is the only person who may permit the erection of public monuments."[8] Indeed, the opinion held by Saint-Simon and others, that Louis XIV gradually lost interest in Paris after his decision in 1682 to rule from Versailles, is not wholly justifiable. Although he made but four visits to the city between 1700 and 1715, the Sun King remained its first citizen and chief defender. As Christian prince he was duty-bound to ease the suffering of less fortunate citizens by maintaining sanitary conditions, opening new water resources, and providing hospitals and other public institutions for the afflicted. Lacking its own charter of liberties, the city was subject to the direct civil and military control of the Crown. The king and his ministers, rather than the submissive municipal governors and conservative *parlement*, were the instigators of urban change. In those inevitable circumstances where private property infringed on royal construction, the Crown possessed the right to compulsory acquisition of land without compensation. However, the king resisted use of this prerogative for the sake of good relations, with the result that obstinate property owners often delayed or blocked work on royal projects.

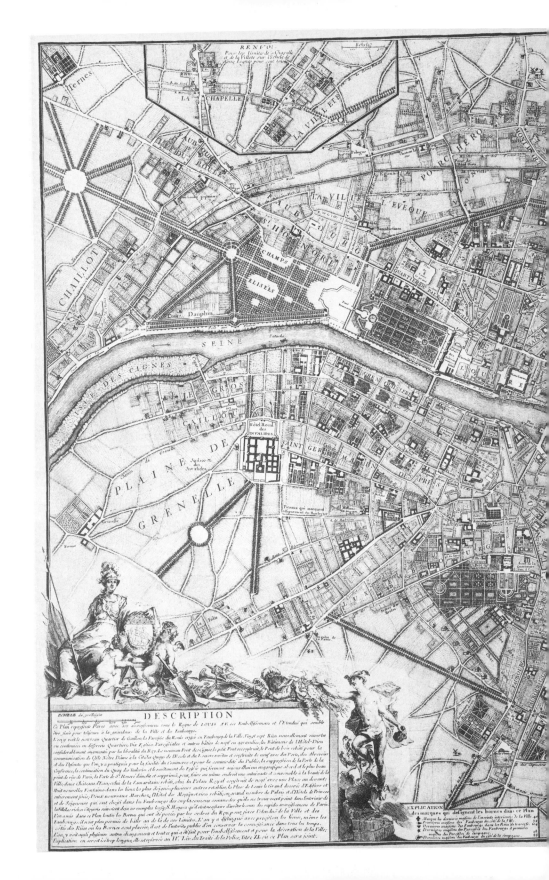

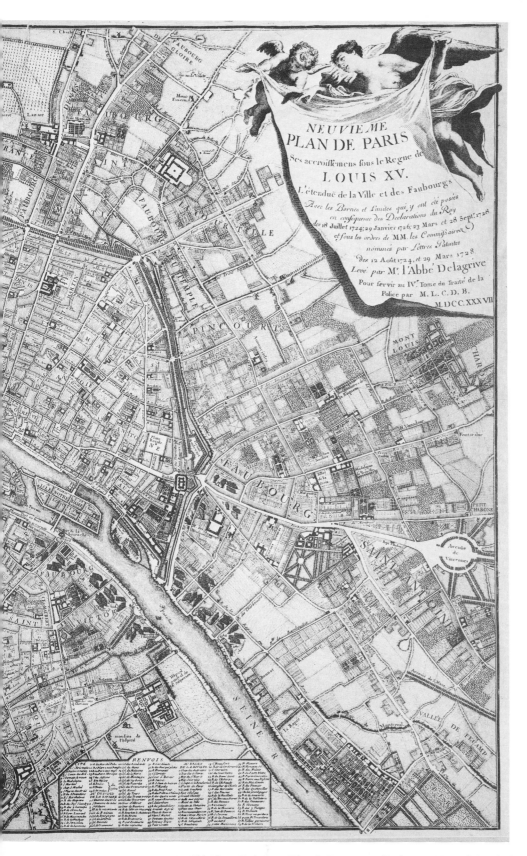

68. Abbé Jean Delagrive, *Plan de Paris*, 1737 (Delamare, *Traité de la police*).

The principal representative of the king in Paris was the Lieutenant Général de la Police, one of the most powerful figures in France from the institution of the office in 1667 until the Revolution. In the early eighteenth century two men holding the post, Marc René de Voyer d'Argenson (served 1697–1718) and René Hérault (served 1725–40), exerted considerable influence on the growth of the city. A pair of further royal agents responsible for construction in Paris were the Surintendant des Bâtiments— Hardouin-Mansart until 1708, followed by the duc d'Antin, in part as Directeur Général, until 1736—and the Premier Architecte. Thus de Cotte's role in the development of Paris cannot be overestimated, given his successive positions, initially as assistant to Hardouin-Mansart (c. 1676–99), then as head of the Département de Paris (1699–1708), and finally as Premier Architecte (1708–34). This sequence guaranteed that his advice and participation were sought for all major urban projects.

Although royal funds paid for a good deal of construction in the capital during the seventeenth century, the transfer of the court to Versailles in the 1680s required the raising of city taxes to cover further embellishments in Paris. Le Cler du Brillet considered the construction and maintenance of certain public works, such as walls, bridges, ports, streets, and warehouses, to be the responsibility of the city fathers.[9] The city was represented in the decision-making process by the Prévôt des Marchands (provost of the Parisian merchants), a relatively powerless honorary official who coordinated the interests of the échevins (elected representatives of the urban bourgeoisie). Charles Trudaine (served 1716–20) and Michel-Etienne Turgot (served 1729–40) were the most active administrators in this position. Jean Beausire, head of a large architectural dynasty, held the position of city architect from 1680 to 1743.[10] His legacy consists principally of numerous fountains, sober and utilitarian in style. Decisions on new projects were always made by committee, and the work was inevitably collaborative, involving representatives of both the Crown and the city.[11]

While in other chapters of this book I focus on de Cotte, in the present chapter I emphasize the commissions themselves, mostly from the period 1699–1735. Artistic and political personalities receive less consideration, but de Cotte's role is stressed whenever possible. In sum, this chapter has three principal aims: to demonstrate the highly collaborative nature of much of de Cotte's work in a field where his precise contribution cannot always be ascertained; to broaden current notions about the history of Parisian urbanism by considering a variety of projects from the late years of Louis XIV's reign and the transitional period of the Régence; and to provide a context for a discussion of de Cotte's town houses, the subject of the next chapter.

City Ramparts

The approach to Paris was designed to heighten the expectations of the traveler. Edward Wright, entering by the northern route in 1720, commented, "For about ten leagues before we arriv'd at Paris, the roads were very pleasant, with rows of trees planted on each side [of] the way."[12] As may be seen in the Abbé Jean Delagrive's *Plan de Paris* of 1737, which accompanies Le Cler du Brillet's text in volume 4 of the *Traité de la police*, several long avenues leading to the city had been cut through the surrounding natural landscape: the avenue des Tuileries (Grand Cours) from Saint-Germain and Neuilly on the northwest; the avenues leading from Meudon to the Place du Dôme des Invalides on the southwest; and the Cours de Vincennes and Cours Saint-Antoine from the Château de Vincennes on the east (fig. 68).

One of the first urban elements visible from

outside the city was the ring of ramparts that surrounded much of Paris. Having gradually replaced the old fortified walls, the ramparts (*boulevarts*) took on a new form—a sort of elevated terrace, about twelve feet in height and bearing a broad avenue. The main purpose of the ramparts was to restrict the growth of the city and separate it from the suburbs, long considered dangerous parasites.[13] Cognizant of the problems precipitating the decline of ancient cities, Louis XIV and Colbert reasoned that the very process of growing too large would contribute to the ruin of Paris. Edict after edict prevented further expansion, but each new set of prescribed boundaries was disregarded in turn. A series of royal decrees in 1704, 1715, and 1724 called for the continuation of the ramparts in the newly developing faubourgs Saint-Honoré and Saint-Germain on the western side of the city, where construction exceeded imposed limits.[14] However, as Delagrive's plan shows, in 1737 the southern rampart was still far from complete. In areas lacking *boulevarts*, stakes and street plaques signaled the new boundaries.

Although the ramparts failed to inhibit growth, they did serve symbolic and recreational purposes. As Delamare pointed out, "Instead of walls, ramparts, and bastions, which in the past reflected the fear of the citizens," a new boundary was undertaken, "a promenade planted with trees for their enjoyment, which at the same time exhibits the magnificence of the city and its present safety."[15] Oak trees planted in four rows demarcated a broad central drive for carriages, bordered by pedestrian sidewalks on either side. These provided elegant strolling grounds for well-to-do Parisians. The new avenues perched on the *boulevart* were the ancestors of the tree-lined Parisian boulevard.

Western Periphery: Right Bank

During much of the seventeenth century, the eastern side of Paris had provided the most fashionable places for strolling—the Place Royale, the Marais, and the Ile Saint-Louis. By 1700 the focus had shifted to the west, partly as a result of the construction of the Place Vendôme and the magnetic pull of Versailles (fig. 68). A large colored plan in the Fonds de Cotte by the royal surveyor, Jacques Dubois, shows the western periphery of the Right Bank as it appeared around 1720 (fig. 69).[16] The region was described by contemporary chroniclers as one of the chief *endroits délicieux* of the city, with its carriageways, trees, and superb views of the river (fig. 70). Defining pleasure grounds of this type, Le Cler du Brillet wrote, "Public walks, avenues, and other places planted with trees, near and on the outskirts of cities, contribute no less to their beauty than to the pleasure of the citizenry; these plantings and lanes constitute an outward embellishment, and at the same time create magnificent promenades, which the public enjoys free of charge."[17]

Along the right bank of the Seine, above the chemin de Versailles, ran one of the lengthiest perspectives in Paris, the carriage drive called the Cours la Reine, laid out in 1616 by Marie de' Medici in imitation of the *corso* of the Cascine gardens bordering the Arno in Florence. "Every evening, from Easter to the end of autumn, society people come here by coach to take the air," wrote Henri Sauval. "Before setting out, the ladies do all they can to heighten their beauty in order to please."[18] Since the original iron gate on the eastern end could accommodate only one carriage at a time, in 1700 Hardouin-Mansart designed flanking gates leading to the pedestrian walks on either side of the main drive, in order to relieve congestion around the entrance.[19] By 1723 the roots of the old elms lining the Cours had gradually encroached upon the retaining

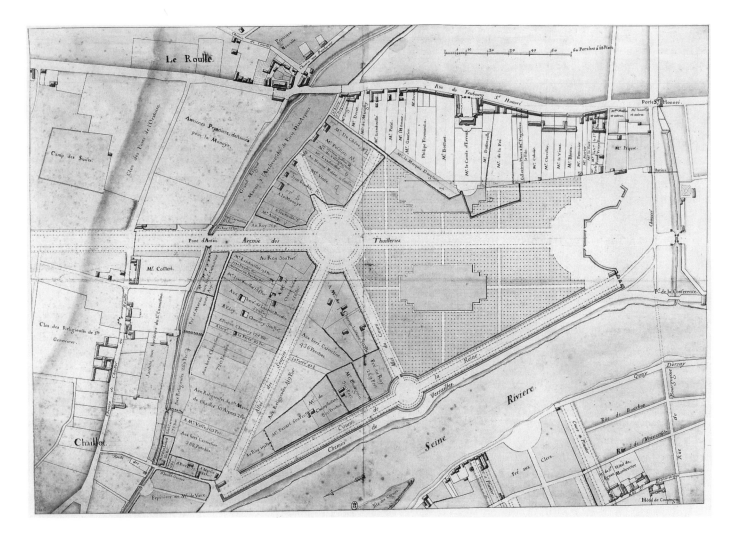

69. Jacques Dubois, plan, Right Bank, Paris, showing the faubourg Saint-Honoré, Champs Elysées, esplanade of the Tuileries (Place du Pont Tournant), and Cours la Reine, c. 1720 (Va 444, 1615).

walls of the quay, and so city officials replanted the trees along the avenue. The duc d'Antin ceremoniously positioned the first tree.[20]

To the north of the Cours la Reine, the Champs Elysées consisted of parallel rows of trees divided by the avenue des Tuileries (fig. 69, center). The extension of the Champs westward toward Chaillot was contingent upon the appropriation of numerous small, privately owned plots, mostly gardens with modest houses. The

difficult task of buying these for the Crown occupied many years; documents mention dates principally from 1716 through 1719. The involvement of de Cotte, the duc d'Antin, and others is confirmed by a *procès-verbal* reporting the surveying and appraisal of the various estates.[21] Just west of these properties along the avenue des Tuileries, the Pont d'Antin, named for the surintendant, was constructed in 1710 over the Grand Egout de Chaillot (fig. 69, left center).[22] Its purpose was to facilitate circulation between the *rond-point* and the Grille de Chaillot, the great iron gate that terminated the Grand Cours (fig. 69, far left center).

Early eighteenth-century plans show that the esplanade between the Champs Elysées and the Jardin des Tuileries, occupied today by the Place de la Concorde, consisted of little more than an open field crossed by a few irregular paths (fig. 69, right center). The site, connected to the Tuileries by means of a swing-bridge, the Pont Tournant, was not fully developed until 1753, when Ange-Jacques Gabriel's project for the Place Louis XV was accepted. Attempts to define the

area as a coherent entity were drawn up as early as 1664, however, when Le Nostre began the work of transforming the neighboring gardens.[23] Bullet's plans of Paris (1675–76) show the stirrup-shaped moat projecting toward the Champs Elysées. The seventeenth-century projects propose a *patte d'oie* arrangement of avenues converging at the entrance to the garden: the avenue des Tuileries, the Cours la Reine, and a truncated *allée* to the north connecting with the faubourg Saint-Honoré (see fig. 71, oriented with west at the top).

A notice in the *Gazette d'Amsterdam* of 1700 records numerous suggestions for the site: "They are talking about building another bridge at the end of the Grande Allée des Tuileries facing the Cours [la Reine] and erecting new gates at either end of the Cours, modeled after the Porte Saint-

70. View of the Seine with the Pont Royal des Tuileries, 1684; on the Left Bank, the quais Malaquais, d'Orsay, and de la Grenouillère, and the faubourg Saint-Germain; on the Right Bank, the quai des Tuileries with the old Porte de la Conférence, the palace and garden of the Tuileries, the Cours la Reine bordering the river, and beyond, the Champs Elysées, late seventeenth century (print by Perelle, Va 228).

Antoine [the eastern entry into Paris], with a *place* between the Cours and the Tuileries to contain a statue of the king."[24] A large colored plan of this area served as the foundation for a series of proposals in the Bâtiments from about 1700 to 1720 (fig. 71).[25] Swatches and *pentimenti* accrued

as new ideas developed. Hardouin-Mansart and de Cotte—presumably the key designers working on the *place*—conserved the stirrup-shaped moat but reworked its borders into arabesques and added iron gates framed by guard houses at points of entry into the square. The plan also

71. Plan, project for gates, moats, and pavilions, esplanade of the Tuileries (Place du Pont Tournant; present Place de la Concorde), Paris, c. 1700–1720 (Va 444, 2353, oriented with west at the top).

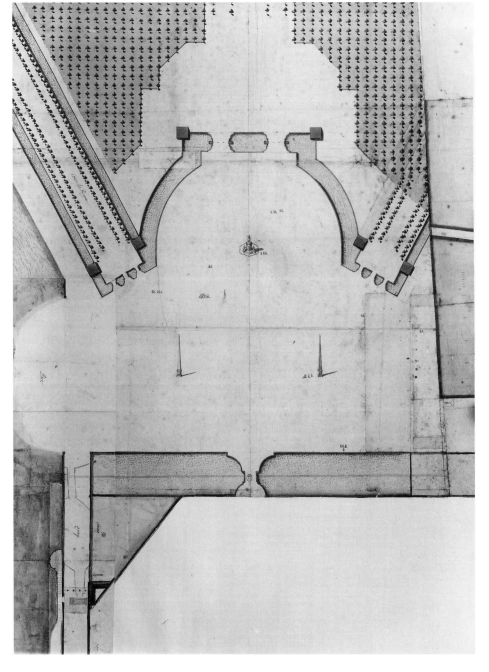

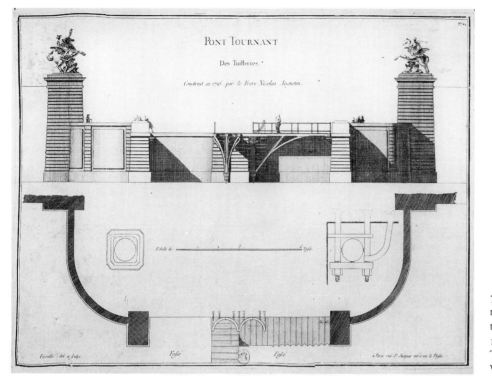

72. Nicolas Augustin, Pont Tournant des Tuileries, 1716, and Antoine Coysevox, *Mercury* and *Fame*, 1702, moved to the Jardin des Tuileries in 1719 (print by Fierville, Va 220).

proposes enlarging the moat adjacent to the Tuileries. An equestrian statue of the monarch appears at the center of an imaginary circle formed by the western moat, while minor foci are introduced by two obelisks located on the axes of the two diagonally-radiating avenues.[26] A landing area for boats was to be devised along the Seine on the axis formed by the obelisks. The *place* differs from seventeenth-century Parisian squares, such as the Place Vendôme, in its less constricted boundaries, greater number of axes, and natural as opposed to architectural vistas—specifically, the Seine, the Tuileries garden, and the Champs Elysées.

Relatively little work was actually accomplished on the esplanade during these years (in fact, some elements of the large project, such as the moat, the equestrian statue, and an obelisk, were incorporated into the *place* at various times later in the eighteenth and nineteenth centuries). A sudden burst of planning was precipi-

tated by the death of Louis XIV and the return of the court from Versailles. In 1716 several houses were destroyed in order to clear the site, and Nicolas Augustin built the new Pont Tournant, which gave its name to the esplanade—the Place du Pont Tournant (fig. 72).[27] Masonry from the recently demolished triumphal arch at the Barrière du Trône on the eastern side of the city (Cours de Vincennes) was used for the reconstructed moat. In 1717 the duc d'Antin approved a project for forged-iron gates leading from the square into the Champs Elysées, but they were not executed (fig. 73).[28] The elevation drawings of the gates and pavilions make extensive use of rustication, an Italianate formal device associated with garden gates, because of its "natural" character. The classical orders are present on the piers only, where the columns are ringed with vermiculated bands.

One of the latest additions to the large project concerns changes to the Porte de la Conférence,

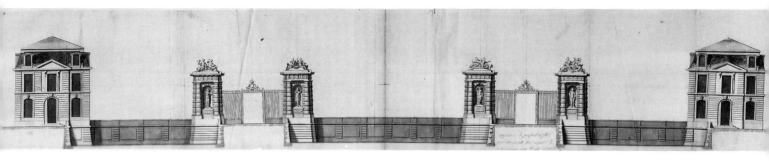

73. Elevation, project, pavilions and gates at the moat separating the esplanade of the Tuileries from the Champs Elysées, Paris, 7 January 1717, signed by the duc d'Antin (Va 444, 2354–2356).

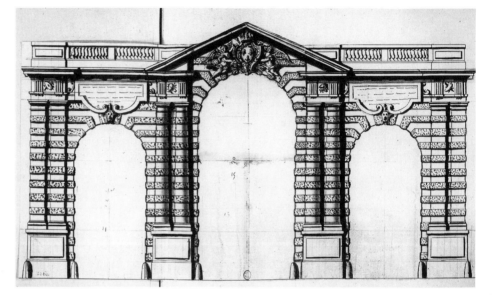

74. Elevation, third project, Porte de la Conférence, Paris, c. 1717–19 (Va 220, 2360a).

located on the quai des Tuileries outside the southwest corner of the garden (fig. 69, center right, fig. 71, lower left). The plan calls for destruction of the old city gate (late sixteenth century, reconstructed early seventeenth century, razed 1730),[29] widening the quay, and erection of a new portal and attendant tollhouse. According to Le Cler du Brillet, the old gate, which allowed only a single coach to pass, was too narrow to accommodate heavy traffic from Versailles. Furthermore, it obscured the view of the Tuileries and gave a poor first impression of the city (the *porte* is visible in fig. 70).[30] An initial proposal for an iron fence (c. 1700; not reproduced here) provided an economical solution, since decoration was limited to sculpted trophies, obelisks, and foliage on four stone piers supporting the

grills.[31] Four later extant proposals for a masonry portal featuring the classical orders, vigorous rustication, and decorative sculpture are in harmony with the 1717 design of the gates to the Champs Elysées (fig. 74). These unexecuted projects show an entry that would have been the visual counterpart of the rusticated Porte Saint-Antoine, located at the eastern entrance to the city (François Blondel, 1671–72, incorporating earlier elements).[32] A date of about 1717–19 and an attribution to de Cotte seem reasonable: several features in the third drawing of this series, such as the central aedicule of paired rusticated Doric columns, the broken pediment framing the royal coat of arms, and the alternation of channeled and vermiculated rustication, are comparable to de Cotte's design of 1719 for the Château d'Eau du Palais Royal, Paris; in addition, the drawings for both are by the same hand (see fig. 75). We should recall that on his southern travels de Cotte had studied many Italian city portals.

According to Brice, it was the opinion of experienced travelers that the Jardin des Tuileries was one of the most beautiful promenades in Europe, offering every sort of diversion.[33] Its charm consisted of sweeping vistas, elevated terraces, and private, small-scale amusements to be enjoyed in the *bosquets*, where fashionable society, in the words of Sauval, "often [took] refuge in the shade in order to abate the intense heat of the sun—and of passion."[34] In 1700 the *Gazette d'Amsterdam* reported the possibility of changes in the layout of the garden, and early in the cen-

tury new garden ornaments were proposed for the sheltered areas to either side of the central *allée*.[35] Draftsmen in the Bâtiments employed line, wash, and discreet touches of color in a series of undated projects for architectural additions to the garden, such as aviaries and pavilions (fig. 76).[36] Antoine Coysevox's equestrian statues of *Mercury* and *Fame*, originally located at the horse pond of Marly (1702), were transferred in 1719 to the western terrace of the Tuileries, where they were mounted on piers high above the Pont Tournant (fig. 72).[37]

Western Periphery: Left Bank

The Place du Dôme des Invalides was intended to be the major set piece among the city's

76. Elevation, project, aviary, Jardin des Tuileries, n.d. (Va 220, t. 1, 2377).

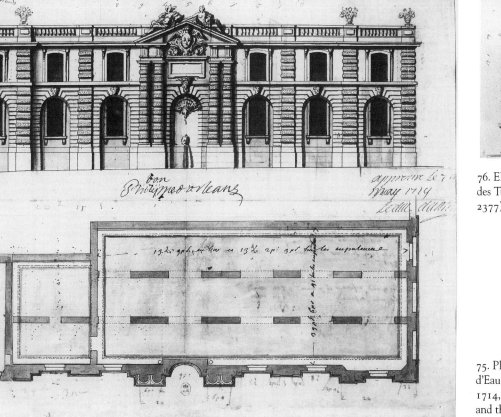

75. Plan and elevation, Château d'Eau du Palais Royal, Paris, 7 May 1714, signed by Philippe d'Orléans and the duc d'Antin (Va 232b, 1748).

peripheral squares (fig. 68). When Louis XIV founded the Hôtel Royal des Invalides on the plaine de Grenelle in 1670, he established not only a public hospital for soldiers employed in the wars but also an architectural monument that proclaimed the military prowess of the Bourbon dynasty. The relationship of the complex to its site was of vital interest to city planners, including de Cotte, who was involved in the design, construction, and decoration of the Invalides.[38]

In his description, "De la situation et des dehors de cet Hôtel," Sauval declared that all four sides of the complex presented admirable views, and that a tour around the building revealed different aspects of its manifold purpose.[39] Moreover, he felt that the surrounding greenery, being composed of the natural countryside as well as man-made *allées*, was visually pleasing and offered salutary benefits. There were two chief areas for development: the Place de l'Eglise du Dôme on the south, and the Esplanade des Invalides stretching to the Seine on the north (fig. 77, oriented with south at the top).[40] In addition, the eastern flank of the *hôtel* acted as a backdrop to new construction in the faubourg Saint-Germain, while the western flank formed a commanding prospect when seen from Meudon and Saint-Cloud.

Initially, it was intended that three radiating avenues comprising a *patte d'oie* would focus on the Eglise du Dôme. Two of these avenues already existed, one on the main axis from the south and a second from the Château de Meudon to the west (fig. 77 includes various proposals for the square). The third radiating avenue, on the eastern side, was supposed to link with the southern ramparts (fig. 68). Hardouin-Mansart incorporated the *patte d'oie* concept into a scheme for a large *place* (fig. 78) bordered by two wings radiating from the Dôme in a manner reminiscent of

Bernini's colonnaded Piazza di S. Pietro, Rome (from 1656; de Cotte had seen and critiqued this piazza on his Italian trip).[41] A similar composition had been employed by Le Vau for the Collège des Quatre Nations, Paris (1662–72); in general, the concept is Palladian (see *I quattro libri dell'architettura*, book 2, pl. XLIII). The arms, conceived in the tradition of ancient porticoes bordering public spaces, were to consist of vaulted corridors fronted by a Roman arch order of engaged columns and framed by four domed pavilions. The Invalides square was not planned as a *place royale*, since a statue of the king was to be erected within the Cour Royal of the Hôtel. Nor did the *place* provide direct entry into the city; the avenues flanking the building would serve this function. Most likely the Place du Dôme was intended as a military parade ground and ceremonial auditorium, with accommodation for spectators behind the balustrade of the semicircular arms.[42]

Documentation from the earliest phase of planning consists only of Louvois's letters to Mansart on 8 April 1676 and 12 September 1678, when in requesting drawings he mentions "the oval wall that would enclose the square."[43] It was only later, in July 1698, that Daniel Cronström reported to Nicodemus Tessin the Younger in Stockholm that work on a monumental square for the Dôme was finally under way.[44] The highly finished style of the extant projects and the presentation drawing in curving perspective suggests a date of 1699 or later, when de Cotte was head of the Département de Paris and Contrôleur of the Invalides (1699–1707); the details were probably worked out at this time.[45] The aerial view was reproduced as the frontispiece to the publications of Bellocq (1702) and Félibien (1706), where formations of drilling soldiers occupy the *place*.[46] The concept remained on plans of the area into the 1720s.[47] Only later did the

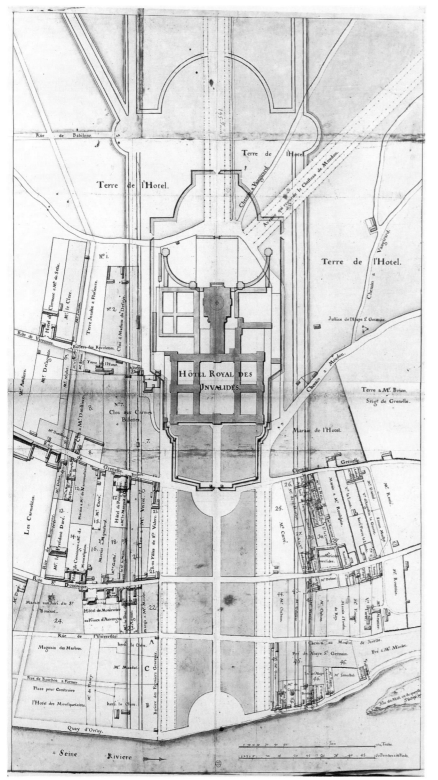

77. Jacques Dubois, site plan (oriented with south at the top), faubourg Saint-Germain and southwest periphery of Paris, with the Place du Dôme (top center), Hôtel des Invalides, and Esplanade des Invalides (bottom center), c. 1717–20 (Hc 14, t. 1, 1716).

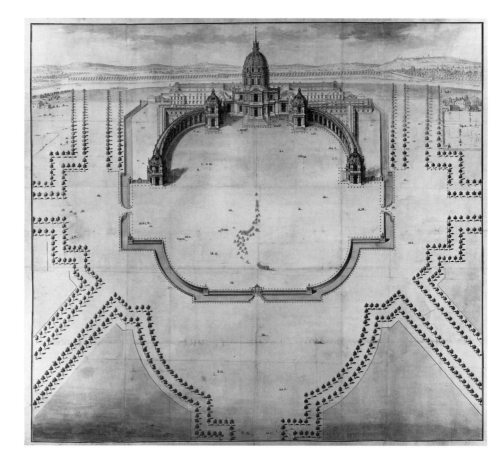

78. Project, Place du Dôme des Invalides (Va Grand Rouleau, 1672).

idea of a simple *patte d'oie* reemerge. Yet nothing more than a plain moated rectangular court was ever fashioned.

Plans were also made in about 1698 to cut avenues along both sides of the Invalides from the Place du Dôme to the river. Despite efforts to purchase from private owners the necessary land along the flanks of the *hôtel*, particularly in 1720 and 1726, this proved to be an impossible task (fig. 77 bears the names of proprietors).[48]

The design of the Esplanade des Invalides between the northern entrance to the building and the Seine was also a matter of consideration (fig. 77). The idea was to create a public promenade by incorporating *allées* of trees into a geometrical composition of arbors and *parterres* intersected by

several paths. Jules-Robert de Cotte was responsible for the completion of this "endroit délicieux" (Pérau) in 1750.[49]

Places royales

In the *Traité de la police* Le Cler du Brillet defined three types of public squares: those dedicated to commercial activity, such as market-places, quays, and bridges; those accommodating public and religious meetings, such as squares in front of town halls, churches, law courts, and other civic buildings; and *places royales*, which serve the purpose of glorifying the reigning monarch. He further defined the latter type as a public square with uniform façades along its boundary and a statue of the king in the center. Such *places*, he wrote, were not born of necessity, as were the other types, but were "the fruits of peace and tranquility among nations."[50]

The earliest documented work by de Cotte in connection with a *place royale* was for the Place des Victoires. The duc de La Feuillade initially conceived this square in 1684–85 as a tribute to the military glory of Louis XIV.[51] Hardouin-Mansart designed a circular space at the intersection of five streets in the rapidly developing financial district east of the Palais Royal. In the center stood Martin Desjardins's sculpture of the king dominating four captives, while on the circumference four lanterns supporting relief medallions of the king's martial exploits burned in perpetual homage. By 1692 two arcs of the circle had been built. The completion of two more on the south, temporarily hampered by the existence of houses on the site, was supervised by de Cotte, who signed the final plans (fig. 79).[52] The elevation of these blocks continued Mansart's use of a giant Ionic order of pilasters supported by a rusticated blind arcade, with an alternating rhythm of dormers projecting from the roof (fig. 80).

Hardouin-Mansart's original conception of the Place Louis-le-Grand (Place Vendôme), a three-sided arcaded square framing François Girardon's *Equestrian Louis XIV* and housing several royal foundations, such as the academies, the mint, and the library, also dates from 1685 (first scheme; fig. 81).[53] The façades were erected rapidly, but by 1698 it was clear that the Crown could not afford so ambitious an undertaking. The king presented the land to the city so that it could finance construction of a new system of uniform façades on the plan of an irregular octagon (second scheme; fig. 81). It was left to well-to-do citizens and entrepreneurs to erect private houses behind these walls.

Most eighteenth-century sources credit Man-

sart with the plan of the second scheme, but contemporary evidence confirms the collaborative handling of this project in the Bâtiments.[54] For example, after the rejection of the first scheme, Pierre Bullet complied with a request on 11 April 1699 for drawings proposing new elevations (these were not employed).[55] Furthermore, on 12 May 1699 de Cotte was charged with overseeing construction of the definitive plans.[56] On a drawing of the quarter, in which the second solution was superimposed in red ink on the first design, an inscription apparently in de Cotte's hand attributes the octagonal plan to him: "Place de Louis le grand areste par le roy suivant lide [l'idée] de M. de Cotte" (undated; fig. 81).[57] No

79. Plan, Place des Victoires, Paris, 1692, with de Cotte's handwriting and signature (Va 441, 1569).

80. Elevation, Place des Victoires (Va 230e, 930).

other evidence exists to corroborate this asser-
tion, but it should be recalled that in February
1699 he had taken charge of the bureau of the
Département de Paris, and shortly thereafter he
was designated Architecte Ordinaire. It is entirely possible that Mansart accepted a proposal
by de Cotte for the second layout. As usual,
Mansart retained the privilege of putting his own
signature on all designs issuing from the Bâtiments (as did de Cotte upon succeeding to the
post of Premier Architecte), such as the definitive elevations for the Place Vendôme (dated 6
June 1699).[58] These elevations derive from those
of the Place des Victoires, although the bays are
more slender and possess richer detailing, such as
the Corinthian order and curved lintels over the
attic windows (fig. 10).

Quays and Bridges

In the Baroque age the lifeblood of Paris was
the Seine, providing both drinking water and a
transport route for comestibles and other natural

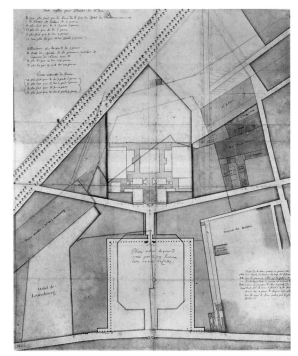

81. Site plan, faubourg Saint-Honoré, incorporating first
and second schemes for the Place Louis-le-Grand (Place
Vendôme), Paris, with de Cotte's handwriting and signature, 1699 (Va 234, 1804).

resources brought by boat from the furthest corners of France to docks along the quays (fig. 68). The Seine was also among the earliest urban rivers to be exploited for its visual effect.[59] Buildings and monuments faced onto it, fireworks, illuminations, and popular fêtes employed the river as backdrop, and social life gravitated toward the bridges (fig. 70). In accordance with the wishes of Henri IV, the Pont Neuf was the first bridge to lack houses so as not to obscure the splendid views in all directions. The magnificent ensemble of quays and bridges was praised by contemporaries, Le Cler du Brillet among them:

The Seine river flows between two quays that serve as embankments from one end of the city to the other: in several places one sees these superb walls support buildings and delightful houses right up to the water's edge; . . . in other parts along the same stretch they bear the enormous weight of broad and spacious avenues, whose beauty, combined with the elegance and symmetry of the royal, public, and private edifices bordering them, deservedly captures the admiration of inhabitants and foreigners alike. In fact, if one considers that fine ports, quays, and beautiful views are priceless things, Paris, which contains so many marvels, will always exceed expectations.[60]

Contemporary theorists considered the quay to be a building type comparable to the palace and triumphal arch in monumentality and beauty, and equally capable of immortalizing the sovereign through its solidity and permanence.[61] The incorporation of docking places and lengthy promenades along the ridge satisfied both utilitarian and aesthetic concerns.[62] Many of the quays bordering the Seine had been built by the 1660s, but the task of hauling the brilliant white stone into place continued in the eighteenth century.

One of the primary urbanistic goals of the period was the construction of the quai de la Grenouillère along the south bank of the river, from the Pont Royal westward to the Hôtel des Invalides (figs. 70, 82–83). According to a royal decree of 18 October 1704, which outlined a comprehensive scheme for the faubourg Saint-Germain, this quay presented in its natural state "a most disagreeable prospect when seen from the Louvre and the Tuileries."[63] The decree also required the king's approval for any houses built on the quay. Numerous plans of the quarter show the intended alignment of the new shoreline with the grid of streets crisscrossing the faubourg.[64] As a result of a similar decree in 1707, a short strip at the eastern end was built, called the quai d'Orsay; it was the wish of all concerned that the industrial dockyards occupying several blocks parallel to the quay would be relocated outside the city, thus opening up sites for large *hôtels*.[65] De Cotte was involved in several projects in this exclusive area, most prominently the Hôtels du Maine (1716–19) and de Torcy (c. 1711–15), part of a cluster of large private houses located midway down the length of the quay. On a site near the Pont Royal and bordering the rue de Bac, de Cotte built the Maisons de Robert de Cotte (facing the quay; 1723) and Maisons de Jules-Robert de Cotte (facing the rue de Bourbon; 1728), a complex of two pairs of imposing *maisons*, which the Premier Architecte briefly considered inhabiting (figs. 84–85; the site is visible in fig. 82, far left; see the designs for his interiors, fig. 22).[66] The houses were let to prestigious tenants throughout the century (destroyed 1870–71, 1900–1901). With Beausire he prepared projects for barracks for the Mousquetaires Gris: first, for a new *caserne* on the Pré aux Clercs, bordered by the quay and the rue de Bourgogne (19 January 1718; fig. 86); second, for a narrower building bordered by the rue de Bourbon (16 July 1719); and finally, for the remodeling of the old structure, the former Halles Barbier, one block south of the Pont Royal (1720–21; fig. 83).[67]

Other schemes in these years included remod-

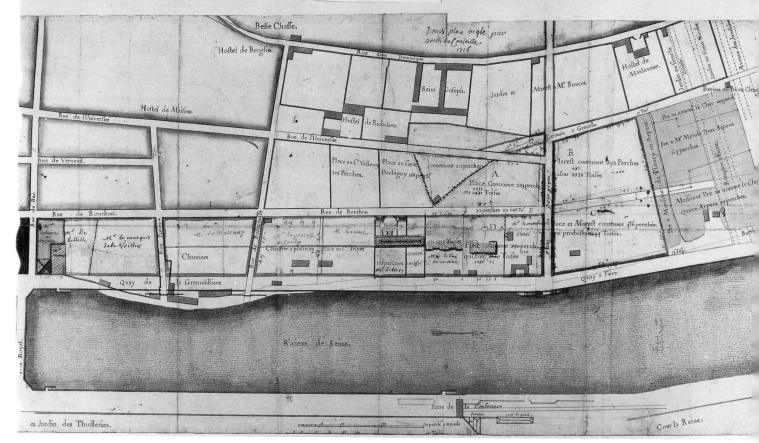
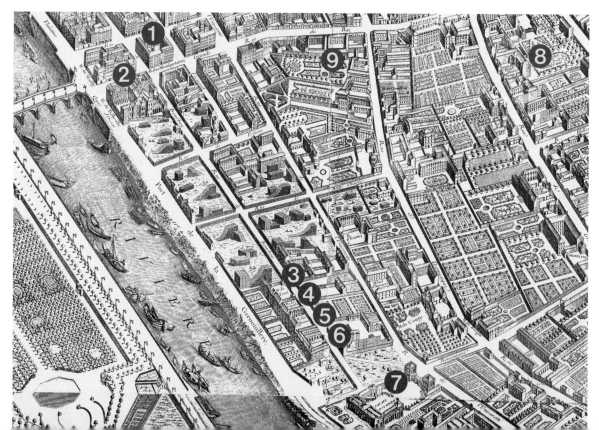

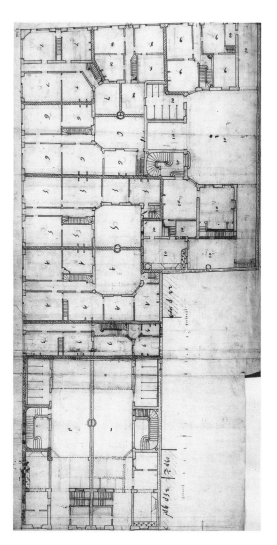

85. Elevation facing quai d'Orsay and partial elevation, rue de Bac, with boutiques at left, Maisons de Robert de Cotte (Va 270a, 2754).

82. (*Opposite, top*) Jacques Dubois, plan, faubourg Saint-Germain (oriented with south at the top), with project for the quai de la Grenouillère, site of the Maisons de Robert de Cotte and Maisons de Jules-Robert de Cotte (left center, by the rue de Bac), sites of the Hôtels de Torcy, de Seignelay, du Maine, and d'Humières (clustered in center), late seventeenth-century(?) map with subsequent additions, dated 1716 (de Cotte's hand? Va 444, 2648).

83. (*Opposite, bottom*) Detail, Louis Bretez, *Plan de Turgot,* 1739, showing (left) the quai des Tuileries, and (right) the quai de la Grenouillère and the faubourg Saint-Germain; (1) Hôtel des Mousquetaires Gris; (2) Maisons de Robert de Cotte and de Jules-Robert de Cotte; Hôtels (3) de Torcy, (4) de Seignelay, (5) du Maine, and (6) d'Humières; (7) Palais Bourbon; (8) Hôtel d'Estrées; (9) Hôtel du Lude.

eling of the quai du Louvre and nearby quai de l'Ecole (1719); widening of the quai des Orfèvres (1716) and quai du Marché Neuf (1734), both on the south side of the Ile de la Cité; and enlargement of the quai des Tuileries (1730).[68] These quays already consisted of docks and stairways extensive enough to handle heavy commercial traffic; it was for the purpose of widening the road along the river and creating more impressive public areas that new projects were developed.

With the expansion of the western side of Paris, circulation between the area around the

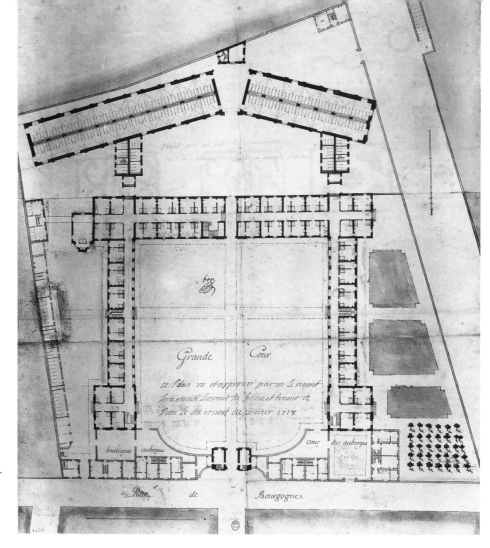

86. Robert de Cotte and Jean Beausire, plan, project, Hôtel des Mousquetaires Gris, Paris, approved by
the regent 19 January 1718
(Va 444, 1036).

Tuileries and the faubourg Saint-Germain increased, and the burden of heavy traffic crossing
the river was thrust upon the Pont Royal, the
single bridge west of the Pont Neuf (adjacent to
the Palais des Tuileries; fig. 70). Sorely needed
was a bridge further down the river near the esplanade by the Tuileries, and indeed such a
bridge appears in projected form on the Dubois
plan, linking the Porte de la Conférence with the
rue de Bourgogne (fig. 69).[69] In 1725 the king allowed the city to borrow money for financing
construction of a wooden bridge supporting a hydraulic machine that would furnish water to the
western faubourgs.[70] Nothing was actually built

until 1787, when the Pont de la Concorde was
erected slightly to the west of the previous site
on the axis of the Place Louis XV.

During the severe winter of 1709, thawing
ice and high waters inflicted heavy damage on
the Pont de Bois, the early seventeenth-century
wooden bridge connecting the Ile de la Cité with
the Ile Saint-Louis. According to Le Cler du Brillet, "This accident greatly inconvenienced the
inhabitants of the two islands and the quarters
nearby."[71] The bridge was dismantled soon after-
ward and replaced only in 1717, when a private
contractor offered the city a scheme for financing
new construction (fig. 68, where the bridge is

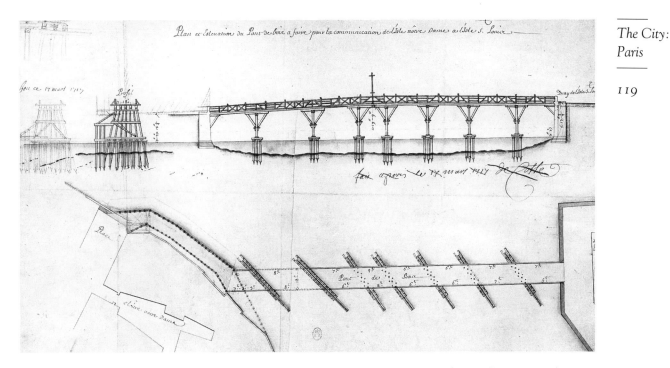

87. Plan and elevation, Pont de Bois (Pont Rouge), Paris, with de Cotte's signature, 17 March 1717 (Va 255m, 731).

called by its new name, the Pont Rouge). Although Beausire was certainly involved, the documents credit de Cotte with the new design, and it was he who, as Premier Architecte, approved and dated the drawings including one on which his signature is canceled and alternative solutions appear for the elevation of the wooden piles and the rebuilt profile of the quai d'Anjou (fig. 87).[72] In the following year fire weakened the structure of the Petit Pont, one of several masonry bridges contructed since the twelfth century on a site along the south side of the Ile de la Cité; it was restored in 1718 after lengthy deliberation.[73]

Pompe de la Samaritaine

The provision of water was one of the chief preoccupations of the king and city magistrates. Water was necessary not only for consumption and public health, but for the preservation of a city susceptible to frequent fires.[74] The complexi-

ties of transport and the size of the local population made this a difficult task.[75] Delagrive's *Plan des fontaines de la ville et des faubourgs de Paris*, published in the fourth volume of the *Traité de la police* (1738), gives a comprehensive view of the utility matrix formed by conduits, reservoirs, and sewers. Water for the city originated in three places: *eaux de Seine* was either pumped by hydraulic machines on the bridges or carried directly from the quays by street vendors;[76] *eaux de sources* traveled through a system of aqueducts and pipes from the countryside to various fountains in the city; and well water was drawn in private courtyards. Distribution obeyed rules of social hierarchy rather than serving the needs of the general public.

The installation of hydraulic machines on the Pont Neuf, the Pont des Tuileries, and the Pont Notre-Dame facilitated the transport of water to various neighborhoods in Paris (the three pumps were erected in 1602, 1632, and 1671, respectively). The Louvre, the Jardin des Tuileries, and the Palais Royal received water from the Pompe de la Samaritaine, located adjacent to the second bay of the Pont Neuf near the Right Bank. Much restored and in poor condition, the pump was the object of repairs in 1712; work was suspended until late 1714, when a new building was erected according to plans by de Cotte, being complete by August 1715 (destroyed 1813; figs. 88–90).[77]

This curious edifice consisted of two parts. The upper half, a three-story pump house, contained the quarters of the Gouverneur de la Samaritaine, who was also responsible for maintenance of the *Equestrian Henri IV*.[78] The lower half comprised the machine proper and wooden piles driven into the river bed. The exterior of the pavilion was composed of timber covered with a coat of plaster cleverly designed to look like ma-

88. Jean-Baptiste Nicolas Raguenet, *La chaussée du Pont Neuf,* viewed toward the south, showing the *Equestrian Henri IV* and the Pompe de la Samaritaine, 1777; detail (Musée Carnavalet, Paris).

sonry. Blondel, ever mindful of *bienséance*, approved of the detailing: "Its decoration is very elegant and is in a genre analogous to its use."[79] Thus while an early sketch of the west façade employed pilasters (fig. 90), in the final solution the order gave way to strips of channeled rustication (fig. 89, left). The utilitarian link with the element of water required the use of such rustic motifs as vermiculated *bossages* framing the central bay of the east front.

The sculptural group by Etienne Blanchard of *Christ and the Samaritan Woman at the Well*, after which the old building was named, was replaced by a new pair of larger-than-life figures in lead that comprised a metaphor for the quenching of the Parisians' thirst through benefits provided by the king and city fathers. Philippe Bertrand fashioned the *Christ Seated by the Well of Jacob* and René Frémin the standing *Samaritan Woman,* installed together on the upper level of the east front, facing traffic on the Pont Neuf.[80] The carillon was the joy of Parisians, playing on the strike

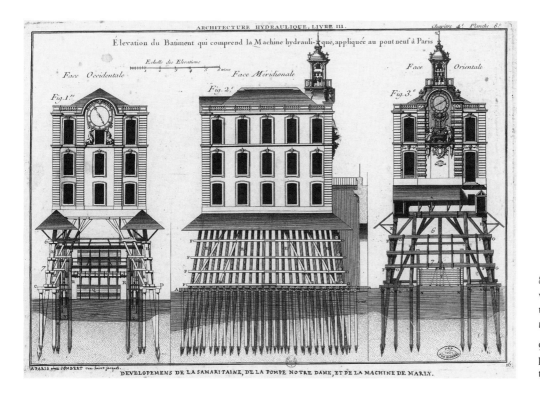

89. West, south, and east elevations, Pompe de la Samaritaine, Paris (Belidor, *Architecture hydraulique*, Va 244b).

90. Elevation, west façade, project, Pompe de la Samaritaine, 1715 (Va 224b, 2562).

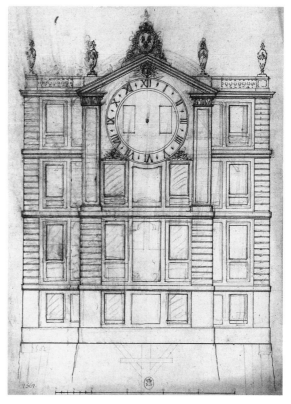

of the hour and during occasions of public celebration. Reporting the success of the monument, Blondel wrote, "Although the water that it distributes is hardly considerable, [the building] nevertheless produces a good impression, presents a splendid sight, amuses the people, and pleases foreigners—motives that must always be deemed worthy in the construction of an edifice as important as that considered here."[81]

Château d'Eau du Palais Royal

In 1719, de Cotte designed a water reservoir that was constructed along the south side of the Place du Palais Royal on the former site of the barracks of the Corps de garde. This was a rare commission instigated by the regent, who signed the drawings himself—"bon Philippe d'Orleans" (fig. 75).[82] The *raison d'être* for the building is clear when we recall that the duc d'Orléans occupied the Palais Royal during the Regency (1715–23) and installed the young Louis XV at the Palais des Tuileries nearby. The Château d'Eau du Palais Royal provided water for the Palais Royal, the Tuileries, and the Louvre, and additionally improved the irregular and unattractive space in front of the regent's palace. Le Cler du Brillet praised the Château d'Eau with these words: "The beauty of the edifice, its advantageous location, the fountain constructed there, and the expansion of the square have further embellished the city: this building encloses reservoirs that contain about four thousand *muids* of water, which assure the surrounding royal houses of the best and most prompt aid in case of fire."[83]

Several sheets of drawings remain in the Fonds de Cotte, showing two reservoirs on the upper floor that received water from the Pompe de la Samaritaine and the Aqueduc d'Arcueil.[84] The lower floor provided space for the system of pumps and storage; a concierge inhabited the left pavilion.

The location of the portal of the Palais Royal slightly to the west of the north-south axis of the square and the mélange of private structures along the periphery precluded overall symmetry and regularity in the *place* itself. In the elevation of the Château d'Eau, however, de Cotte repeated motifs from the palace façade, such as horizontal channeled rustication and paired columns flanking the central bay, so that there would be visual correspondences between the two. Although the building was destroyed during the Commune of 1848, early views give an idea of its appearance within the context of the square.[85]

Writing in the 1750s, Blondel criticized de Cotte's placement of the attic story directly on the heavily rusticated *rez-de-chaussée*. Blondel failed to recognize that, in accordance with the concept of *bienséance*, the low proportions and roughly dressed masonry proclaimed the utilitarian function of the building, while the central aedicule enclosing the royal coat of arms reflected the official character of the commission. The exterior elevation follows an important precedent, the Réservoir du Cloître de Saint-Germain-l'Auxerrois, located not far to the east.[86] In both examples, channeled rustication enhances the arched bays on the ground floor, and a pediment interrupts a balustrade crowning the attic story.

For the cornice of the pediment Guillaume Coustou sculpted a reclining river god and nymph representing the Seine river and the Arcueil spring.[87] Elaborate shell and *rocaille* incrustations decorated the niche in the lower central bay, and the water spigot took the form of a bronze dragon. However, from Blondel's point of view, the building failed to exercise its representational function, due to the lack of a full-scale fountain: "With respect to this trickle of water, we feel that an edifice of such importance should present itself outwardly in a more striking manner, either by means of a pool, a waterspout, or a torrent of water. In this way the spectator would have recognized the magnificence of the prince who erected this monument, the city would have been embellished, and a sense of the magnitude of the river and the spring that provide the water would be apparent."[88] In fact Blondel was insensitive to the reality of the situation: Paris traditionally suffered a shortage of water too severe to allow lavish fountains. The inscription on the building—"QUANTOS EFFUNDIT IN USUS" [How greatly it flows in use!]—was hyperbolic at best.[89]

The standard Parisian fountain, rather than being freestanding, was normally incorporated into the frontage of neighboring buildings lining a narrow street. The design usually depended on architectural features and minimal use of sculpture—never on the play of water; in other words, the very features that made Italian fountains so attractive to de Cotte on his southward journey were in short supply in Paris, where water was conserved through the use of faucets.[90]

* * *

The Château d'Eau typifies the urbanistic goals undertaken in the capital during the first third of the century, insofar as its design responded equally to utilitarian, emblematic, and aesthetic demands and it stood primarily as an independent monument, not as an element of a cohesive environment. There were no plans for renovating the narrow, crowded spaces of the older districts of Paris during de Cotte's tenure as Architecte Ordinaire and Premier Architect, although efforts were undertaken in the new faubourgs to introduce a more orderly gridlike network of avenues. In one way or another, many projects involved the Seine, through enlargement or straightening of the quays or attempts to increase the water supply. As a result of the westward march of new construction, the royal architects drew up plans for embellishing the Left and Right Banks on the western periphery. Significantly, several schemes responded to the recreational needs of Parisians, while at the same time affirming the power and prestige of the Crown.

Chapter Seven

The Town House

PRIVATE CONSTRUCTION in Paris, which had languished during the height of Louis XIV's reign at Versailles, experienced an upswing in the opening decades of the eighteenth century—even before the death of the monarch in September 1715 and the subsequent abandonment of Versailles by the regent and the court.[1] To the ranks of the nobility and established upper bourgeoisie requiring mansions in the capital came a new economic elite comprised of financiers and speculators; having realized sudden and immense wealth during the wars of the Sun King, they were now bent on copying the lifestyle of the aristocracy. Closely related to this phenomenon was the acceleration of several trends that had been underway since the mid-seventeenth century: the blurring of class lines through marriage, the purchase of offices and noble titles, and extravagant expenditure on such status symbols as magnificent houses.[2] To accommodate the need for construction sites in the crowded city, as well as to meet the demand for luxurious houses on spacious grounds, residential quarters sprang up along the western boundary of Paris. As recounted in the previous chapter, on the Right Bank the faubourg Saint-Honoré replaced the Marais as a fashionable neighborhood, while on the Left Bank the faubourg Saint-Germain developed into a network of impressive streets lined with mansions giving onto long, airy gardens (figs. 68, 70, 82–83). It was in this rapidly expanding environment that the intensification of private patronage secured the triumph of the French urban dwelling in its most representative form—the *hôtel particulier*.

The Parisian town house was one of the most remarkable inventions of the French Renaissance. Despite the numerous and varying conditions contributing to its layout, a few basic types emerged during the sixteenth century, the most important being the *hôtel-entre-cour-et-jardin*, so called because the principal block, or *corps-de-logis*, was placed halfway down the site between the courtyard and garden.[3] Narrow wings framing the courtyard usually extended forward to the street, where the court was closed by a wall with a classical portico in the center. If the site allowed, service courts were placed to either side of the main court and out of the visitor's view. The appeal of so simple a formula lay in its flexibility: by the judicious placement of the parts, a building erected on an irregular urban site could be designed to appear ordered and symmetrical.

The interior layout of the *corps-de-logis* comprised a few common rooms, such as the *salle* or *salon* for large gatherings and concerts, and a series of independent suites called *appartements* for the habitation of individual members of the household. Husband and wife had separate, spacious apartments, while the rest of the family received less splendid accommodations. The secretaries, tutors, priests, domestics, and other dependents were given lodgings on the upper floors or over the stables, usually near the place where they worked.[4] Over the years the *appartement* rarely deviated from the basic combination of rooms, employed in a comparable manner, as we have seen, in the French palace and *maison de plaisance*: the *antichambre* or waiting room; the *chambre* or bed-sitting room, used for both sleeping and reception; and the *cabinet*, the least public place, to which only the most important visitors were admitted. An adjoining *garde-robe* served as dressing room and closet.[5] The sequence in which the rooms were to be viewed, and their actual number (which could be expanded, for example, to include a first, second, and third *cabinet*) were dependent on many factors, particularly the status and wealth of the patron.[6]

De Cotte and his contemporaries embraced many of the formulas and devices developed during two earlier phases in the evolution of town-house design. The first phase was one of trial and error, beginning just before the mid-sixteenth century and lasting about eighty years. It was Serlio who initially combined classical principles of regularity with the French interest in practicality in his plan for the Grand Ferrare in Fontainebleau (1544–46). Serlio's innovation was adopted soon after in Paris for the Hôtel Carnavalet (1548–50) and other structures.[7] The *corps-de-logis* in the first phase was only one room deep (designated an *appartement simple*), and elevations were often austere in the extreme, with only stringcourses and quoins articulating the flat walls. The second phase, commencing in the 1620s and terminating toward the end of the century, saw an emphasis on *distribution*, the judicious placement of rooms as a means of easing circulation. The *appartement double*, a double suite of rooms, was used in Paris at the Hôtel de Châlons-Luxembourg (Jean Thiriot? 1623–28) and reappeared in two influential houses, the Hôtel Tambonneau (Le Vau, 1644) and the Hô-

tel de Jars (François Mansart, 1648).[8] This made possible two apartments on a single floor and/or space for chambers of more specialized function, such as the *salle à manger*, which came into use around 1640.[9] The marquise de Rambouillet and others put into practice the concept of separating public from private rooms in the house around 1620—an idea that in its most significant form involved the differentiation of the *appartement de parade* for show or display from the more intimate *appartement de commodité*.[10] Elevations in this period fluctuated between severity and richness, tending in the later seventeenth century toward complicated effects through lavish use of the orders.[11]

The transition to the third phase of *hôtel* design was chiefly the work of Hardouin-Mansart.[12] The extensive use of corridors and many other new features introduced by Mansart for the provision of *commodité* in the minor floors and wings of those buildings housing the court—for example, the Château de Clagny (1676) and the Château Neuf at Meudon (1706–9)—were absorbed into the vocabulary of *hôtel* architecture. In addition, Mansart's method of laying out an urban mansion became something of a commonplace during the early eighteenth century. His Hôtel de Noailles in Saint-Germain-en-Laye (1679) employed an unobstructed longitudinal axis running from the courtyard through a paired vestibule-*salon* configuration into the garden, with symmetrically placed apartments on either side of the axis.[13] For the elevations of his *hôtels* and several structures for the royal family, Mansart tended to restrict the placement of the orders to the central pavilion alone, as at the Château Neuf (fig. 11). Many of these features were absorbed by Lassurance, a draftsmen for Mansart from 1684 to 1700 who became the first major figure in *hôtel* design during the third phase of activity, 1700–1730.[14] His Hôtel Desmarets,[15] an important monument of this phase, was erected in the faubourg Saint-Honoré in 1704, that is, about the same time de Cotte was beginning his career as a remodeler of older *hôtels*.[16] In this chapter we will consider six of de Cotte's built designs and several related unexecuted plans. Like other members of the Bâtiments, he worked for wealthy members of the upper middle class and the great noble families attached to the court, including several prominent widows.

Hôtel du Lude

De Cotte constructed his first private house, the Hôtel du Lude, on the rue Saint-Dominique in the faubourg Saint-Germain for the speculative builder François Duret, Président de la Chambre des Comptes (fig. 83).[17] Duret leased the *hôtel* for life to the wealthy and well-connected Marguerite-Louise de Béthune, dowager of the duc du Lude, Grand Maître et Capitaine Général de l'Artillerie. Work was carried out in the years 1708–10, just after de Cotte was named Premier Architecte. The building, situated in front of an immense private garden, was destroyed in 1861. None of the original plans survives, but a record of the architect's intent appears in the engravings of Mariette and later drawings.[18] The design in part incorporated an early seventeenth-century house already standing on the site.

The visitor entered the house by means of a vestibule on the right-hand side of the courtyard, which led directly into the most public room, the *grande salle*, intended for receptions and entertainments, and from there into the *appartement de parade*—a suite of three chambers along the garden façade (fig. 91). The depth of the suite was visible at a glance through the *portes en enfilade*. The apartment was essentially *simple*, thus having the advantage of receiving natural light on two sides, and was composed of an *antichambre, chambre du dais*, and *grand cabinet*. The location of the chimneypieces on the walls con-

fronting the viewer leaves no doubt about the direction in which the rooms were to be experienced; a fireplace was usually located opposite the door leading into a room so that heat would not escape from the hearth and a sudden draft of cold air would not chill anyone warming by the fire.[19]

A vestibule on the left side of the court led to the more private *appartement de commodité*, consisting of an *antichambre, chambre à coucher*, and *cabinet*. This last room was the most private in the house, where the owner might read, compose letters, or enjoy the company of intimates surrounded by a collection of paintings, books, or curiosities. Its counterpart in the *appartement de parade*, the *grand cabinet*, was still subject to the rigors of contemporary etiquette, although it was not nearly as formal as the *chambre du dais*. In the seventeenth century, the main reception rooms had often been on the upper floor; de Cotte, following the lead of Lassurance and others, here situated a major apartment on the ground level, eliminated the usual grandiose stairwell, and made the garden immediately accessible through a series of doors.

Several felicitous details may be seen in the plan, such as the insertion of the porter's lodge to the left of the main entry from the street, rendering the courtyard symmetrical. The broad site allowed the placement of a service court to the left, leaving to the main court the public ceremony of the arrival and departure of guests. At first glance the kitchen, with its companion rooms, the *salle du commun* (servants' dining hall) and *garde-manger* (pantry) (fig. 91, lower right), seems far removed from the *salle à manger*, but according to contemporary writers it was considered infinitely preferable to have meals carried a distance across the courtyard to the dining room in *plats couverts* and reheated if necessary than to suffer the noise, fumes, and odors of a kitchen located within the *corps-de-logis*.[20] Nevertheless, in his description

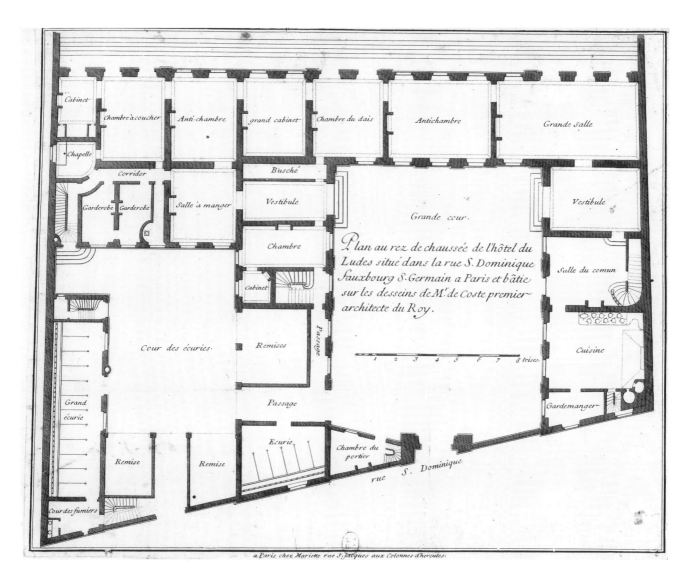

Labels within the plan:

Cabinet · Chambre à coucher · Anti-chambre · grand cabinet · Chambre du dais · Antichambre · Grande Salle
Chapelle · Corridor · Busché · Vestibule
Garderobe · Garderobe · Salle à manger · Vestibule
Grande cour.
Chambre · Salle du comun
Cabinet · *Plan au rez de chaussée de l'hôtel du Ludes situé dans la rue S. Dominique fauxbourg S. Germain a Paris et bâtie sur les desseins de Mr. de Coste premier architecte du Roy.*
1 2 3 4 5 6 7 8 toises.
Cour des écuries. · Remises · Passage · Cuisine
Grand écurie · Passage · Gardemanger
Remise · Remise · Ecurie · Chambre du portier
Cour des fumiers · rue S. Dominique

a Paris chez Mariette rue S. Jacques aux Colonnes d'hercules.

91. Plan, *rez-de-chaussée*, Hôtel du Lude, Paris, 1708–10
(Blondel, *Architecture françoise*, Va 273h).

of the Hôtel du Lude Jacques-François Blondel did point out that the positioning of the dining hall off the stable court can hardly have produced an appetizing view.[21]

Both representational stateliness and personal comfort were the goals of the plan.[22] It must be remembered that the occupant of an *hôtel* used it as a place to conduct business and to socialize, in addition to a residence: through the overt display of wealth, an individual could widen his or her orbit of power. The owner wished to impress not only callers of lesser and equal status, but also those of higher rank.

The elevations of the Hôtel du Lude, completely devoid of columns and pilasters, are characterized by plainness and reserve (fig. 92). The compact unity of the design, with the roofs pulled together to form a single volume, contrasts with the lavishly bedecked *hôtel* façades of the late seventeenth century. Only a few bands of lightly incised quoins and some keystones re-

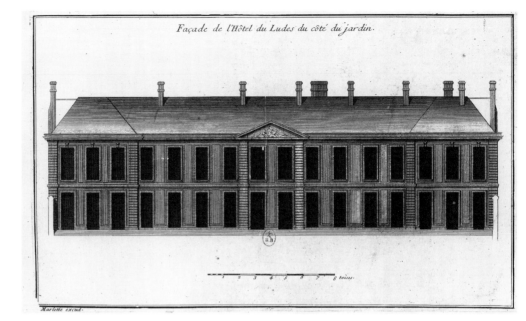

Façade de l'Hôtel du Ludes du côté du jardin.

Mariette excud.

92. Elevation, garden façade, Hôtel du Lude (Blondel, *Architecture françoise*, Va 273h).

lieve the general impression of severity. The primary motif is the tall, narrow rectangle of the French window, repeated to form a rhythm of dark accents across the white stone wall; these windows provided abundant illumination for the interior. To be sure, this degree of sobriety had been seen in the previous period of *hôtel* design, as well as in the first phase, but the detailing was rarely so delicate or so low in relief. The moldings around the windows and the flat, raised panels between them imply several planes within the surface of the wall. By abandoning the orders, de Cotte endeavored to create an example of *la belle architecture*, an architecture whose natural and simple beauty was the result of symmetrical composition and the clear, harmonious relationship of the parts.

Hôtel d'Estrées

De Cotte's next major commission was the *hôtel* erected on the rue de Grenelle in the faubourg Saint-Germain between 1711 and 1713 for Madeleine-Diane de Bautru de Vauban, duchesse d'Estrées and widow of François Anni-

bal, third duc d'Estrées (fig. 83).[23] It is the only Parisian *hôtel-entre-cour-et-jardin* by the Premier Architecte to have survived in a state comparable to its original condition, although the building was disfigured in the nineteenth century by the addition of a full third story (fig. 93). At the street entrance de Cotte made use of the classical orders (fig. 94). Unlike the *porte-cochère* of the Hôtel du Lude, where a segmental arch framing the coat of arms was poised on two rusticated piers, that of the Hôtel d'Estrées consists of a pair of Doric columns supporting an abbreviated entablature on which the d'Estrées coat of arms originally rested. The concave wall served several functions: it discreetly hid the awkward relationship of the axis of the *hôtel* to that of the street, aided in the maneuvering of carriages, and sheltered the columns from possible damage by passing vehicles (fig. 95).[24] On the court side the concavity is reproduced in reverse to form porters' lodges on either side of the gate.

The plan does not repeat the scheme of the Hôtel du Lude. The doubling of rooms in the *corps-de-logis* and the presence of a longitudi-

93. Garden façade, Hôtel d'Estrées, Paris, 1711–13.

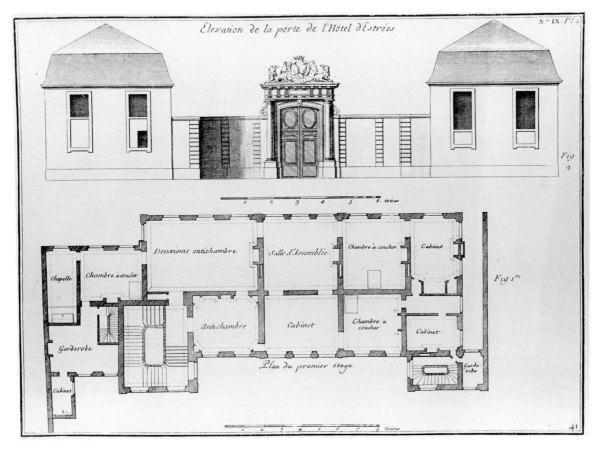

94. Elevation, street façade, and plan, *premier étage*, Hôtel d'Estrées (Blondel, *Architecture françoise*, Va 270d).

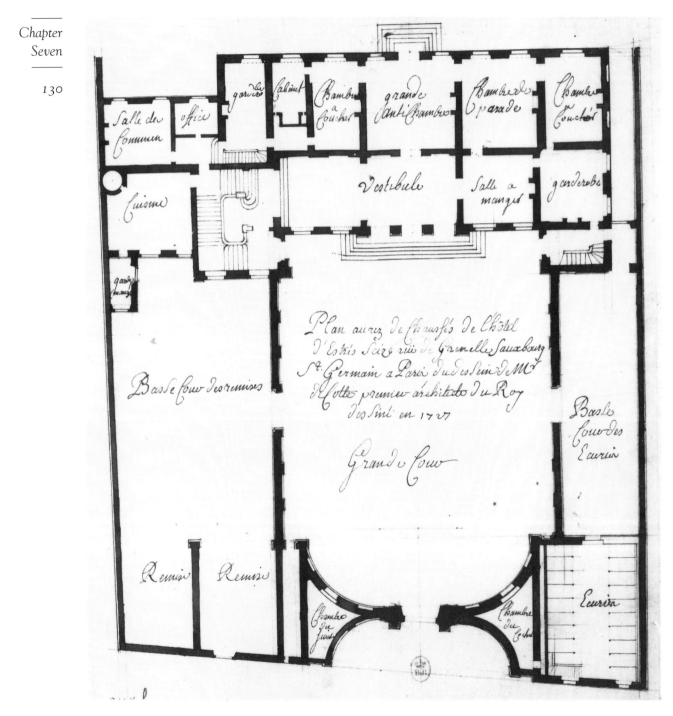

95. Plan, *rez-de-chaussée*, Hôtel d'Estrées (Va 270d, 2115a).

nal axis through the vestibule and *grande anti-chambre*, linking the court and the garden, bring the layout closer to contemporary developments. The major difference is that the garden façade is not allowed to run the entire width of the building site; the *corps-de-logis* proper, when viewed from the garden, gives the impression of a free-standing block. The elegant stair situated in the left-hand pavilion resulted from the importance given the upper story (fig. 94). Here, in a magnificent *enfilade* on the garden side—an arrangement not unlike the *appartement de parade* of the Hôtel du Lude—de Cotte provided splendid living quarters.

The dining room is located on the lower floor on a direct line from the kitchen across the stair and vestible and independently of the suites, so that the table could be laid or cleared out of sight. The apartments on the ground floor had the advantage of the immediacy of the garden, while those on the upper floor could claim the prospect of the ornamental *parterres*. It cannot be assumed automatically that each of the apartments was intended for a separate member of the household. The various rooms and apartments did not always serve the same purpose: the time of day, the season, or the presence of important guests could determine, for example, whether the duchesse would dine upstairs or down, and whether she would sleep in a *chambre* exposed to the north or south. The chapel was a standard feature in a large house, and here it was appropriately located on the second floor to the far left of all mundane activities.

At the head of the courtyard de Cotte erected one of his simplest and most agreeable façades (fig. 96). The upper floor features a Roman arch

96. Elevation, court façade, Hôtel d'Estrées, Paris (Va 270d, 2115f).

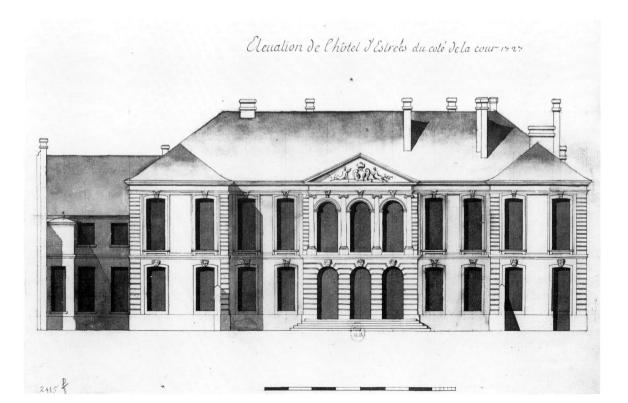

Eleuation de l'hôtel d'Estrées du coté de la cour 1727

order whose three bays of Ionic pilasters stood on a rusticated triplet of arched bays and supported a pediment. The richly articulated central pavilion contrasts with the simple walled masses to either side, a compositional feature that both Hardouin-Mansart and Lassurance had in turn inherited from the previous age (see Le Vau's courtyard elevation of the Hôtel Tambonneau).[25] These elements, when combined with the suggestion of a freestanding block, took on a pronounced Palladian flavor. It will be recalled that de Cotte had recorded in his Italian notebooks a fondness for Palladio's works, particularly the villas along the Brenta, such as Palladio's Villa Foscari at Malcontenta, which features a similar emphasis on the block and a restricted use of the order (fig. 16). At the same time, de Cotte was transferring from the country to the city several features of the *maison de plaisance*. In view of the popularity of Italianate design and the increasing interest in Palladianism, it was inevitable that changes would take place in the sphere of the *hôtel*: as early as 1700 Boffrand had already produced an imposing house with Palladian overtones, the Hôtel Le Brun, Paris.[26] The originality of de Cotte's adaptation of these sources lay in the flatness and delicacy of the forms, and in the unification of the elements by means of the large, simple shape of the roof, from which he eliminated the standard motif of the dormer. Furthermore, it was the consistent interest in the isolated block that set de Cotte's plans apart from those of his contemporaries.

Hôtel de Torcy and Related Projects

Nowhere in de Cotte's work is this ideal better expressed than in the drawings for the Hôtel de Torcy, one of five unexecuted proposals for Parisian town houses forming a single group.[27] Although there is no firm evidence for dating, they were almost certainly produced in the second decade of the century, when de Cotte was actively engaged in *hôtel* design.

The project for the Hôtel de Torcy was intended for Jean-Baptiste Colbert, marquis de Torcy (1665–1746), nephew of Le Grand Colbert and his successor as secretary of state, who moved with his family from the Richelieu quarter to the faubourg Saint-Germain. The Premier Architect's design was not adopted. On 14 November 1715 the marquis purchased the celebrated *hôtel* erected between the rue de Bourbon (de Lille) and the quai de la Grenouillère by de Cotte's colleague in the Bâtiments and his major rival in the *hôtel* field, Germain Boffrand (figs. 82–83).[28] Boffrand had purchased the site in 1713; he also built on a speculative basis the neighboring *hôtel* to the west, inhabited by Torcy's nephew, Charles-Eléonor Colbert, comte de Seignelay. The evidence suggests that Torcy solicited projects independently from both architects; it is also possible that, as was so often the case, de Cotte was invited as Premier Architecte to critique a set of drawings and in response produced his own variant.[29] The street frontages of both plans measure approximately twenty-three *toises* and all of the other dimensions are similar. Thus the designs offer an unrivaled opportunity to compare, detail for detail, the stylistic features peculiar to the two major figures in French architecture during the first half of the century.

De Cotte's plan for the Hôtel de Torcy amplifies certain tendencies already noted at the Hôtel d'Estrées (fig. 97). The curvilinear walls on the courtyard side of the *porte-cochère* usher the visitor into the *grande cour*, and to an even greater degree the *corps-de-logis*, virtually a freestanding block, sits isolated within the site. The chief rooms are on the ground floor, and the stair is placed in the right-hand pavilion beyond the large *salle*. By blocking the axis and carefully sealing off the apartments, greater privacy is gained.

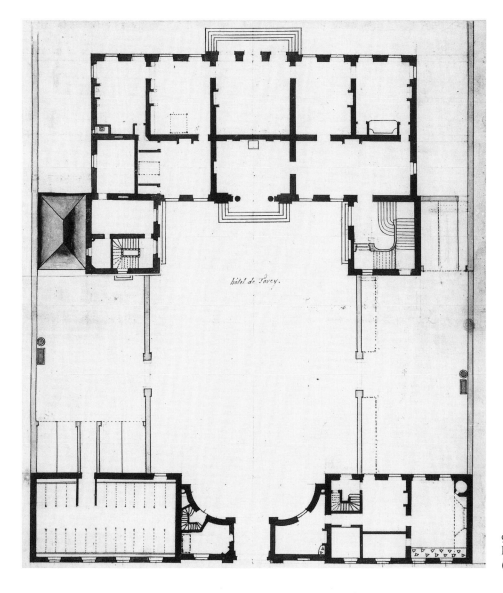

97. Plan, *rez-de-chaussée*, project,
Hôtel de Torcy, Paris, c. 1711–15
(Va 273e, 305).

Indeed, the organization of the plan is now annular, so that the visitor would proceed through the rooms in counterclockwise movement. In contrast, Boffrand's Hôtel de Torcy fills the width of the site, and he maintains the vestibule-*salon* combination on axis while spreading an imposing suite of rooms across the garden façade (fig. 98). His upper floor, like de Cotte's, consists of three *appartements*, but the larger floor space allows for a gallery on axis.

In the elevations, the differences between the two architects appear even greater. Boffrand's courtyard elevation (fig. 99) is typical of his robust style, eschewing utterly the graciousness of de Cotte's façades. The wall is composed of three planes advancing toward the center, with stark windows at the ends giving way to superimposed arcades in the midsection. Not only the orders but even rusticated strips are lacking, leaving only blank expanses of wall. If such a style looks

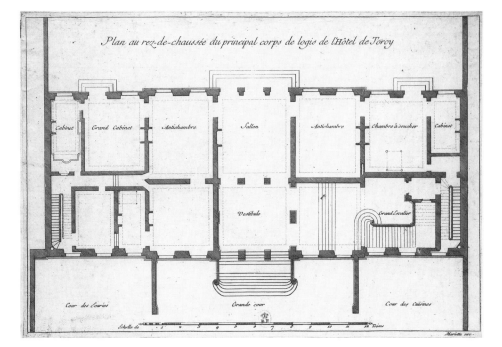

98. Germain Boffrand, plan, *rez-de-chaussée*, Hôtel de Torcy, Paris, 1713–15 (Blondel, *Architecture françoise*, Va 273e).

99. Germain Boffrand, elevation, court façade, Hôtel de Torcy (Blondel, *Architecture françoise*, Va 273e).

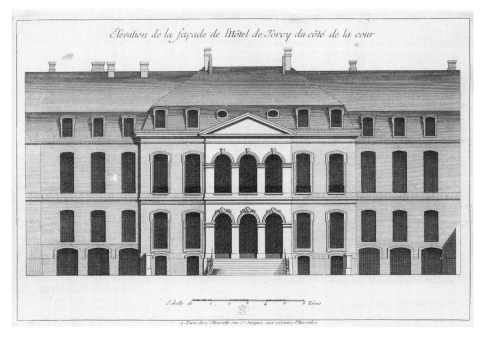

forward to the boldly expressive designs of late eighteenth-century architects, de Cotte's courtyard façade (fig. 100) looks back toward a composition stated eloquently earlier in the century: the courtyard front of Bullet de Chamblain's Château de Champs (1703–7).[30] The traditional pavilions, the simple outline of the roof, and the superb frontispiece, open below and closed above, were reworked by de Cotte into a harmonious whole. The central pavilion provides a

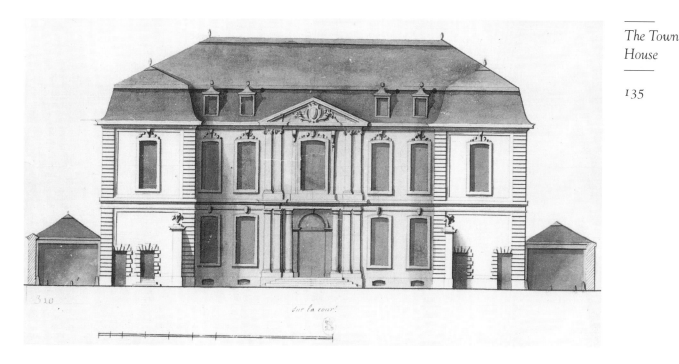

100. Elevation, court façade, project, Hôtel de Torcy
(Va 273e, 310).

strong axial focus. In addition, the unglazed vestibule would have had the double advantage of
revealing from a distance the beauty of the interior while allowing visitors easy access upon
descending from a carriage during inclement
weather. The open vestibule is another instance
of underlying Palladianism (see the recessed
portico-loggia on the garden front of Palladio's
Villa Pisani, Montagnana [1552/3–59], as well as
the court façade of Schloss Tilburg [1714–17;
fig. 60]).

Boffrand's street front resembles that of the
Hôtel d'Estrées in emphasizing the autonomy of
the components; *porte-cochère*, screen walls, and
pavilions are each articulated differently. De
Cotte in his masterful Torcy design pulled the
various parts together into a single horizontal
shape capped with low hipped roofs and punctu-
ated all across by vertical windows and pilaster
strips (fig. 101). Blondel would have approved of

this homogeneous composition, wherein the end
pavilions are as suavely articulated as the central
portico, so that the entire ensemble might form
a worthy accompaniment to a *grande rue* in the
capital city.[31] De Cotte's cross section of the
building shows the screen walls enclosing
the court, as well as the height and depth of the
rooms (fig. 102).

Of the group of five unexecuted projects, the
Hôtel de Torcy comes closest to de Cotte's ideal.
Despite the lack of a precise chronological relationship, the others may be seen as variations on
the same general concept, with references to the
Hôtel d'Estrées as well. The project identified
in de Cotte's hand as "un maison pour la rue
de grenelle pour la place de Mr le marechal
de montesquiou" is very similar to the Hôtel de
Torcy in its dimensions, but here the *corps-de-
logis* occupies the full width of the lot, allowing
for a more intricate pattern of rooms and a stair
that spills into the space of the vestibule (fig.
103).[32] The elevations are also expanded ver-
sions of those in the Torcy series (garden front,

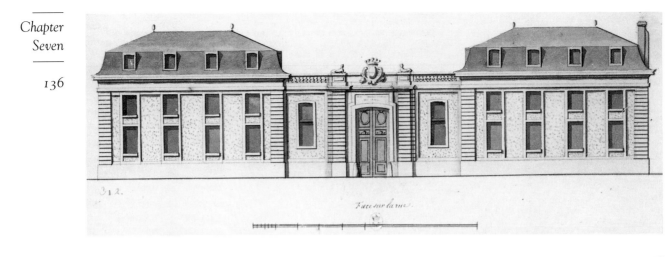

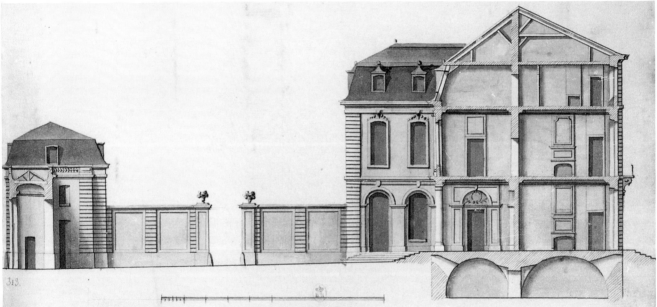

fig. 104). In the project for Alexis-Marie-Rosalie, comte de Châtillon, probably for a site on the rue Saint-Dominique, the layout of the court and service wings follows the pattern of the d'Estrées house, while the plan of the *corps-de-logis* is similar to that of the Hôtel de Torcy, but with two major changes: the sequence of rooms in the annular plan is followed in clockwise progression, culminating in the *chambre de parade* on axis; there are no side pavilions on either the court or garden façades, which recede on the ends to form

101. (*Top*) Elevation, street façade, project, Hôtel de Torcy (Va 273e, 312).

102. (*Above*) Cross section, *corps-de-logis*, and view of left-hand court wall, project, Hôtel de Torcy (Va 273e, 313).

shallow planes in depth (fig. 105).[33] The type of frontispiece employed on the Torcy court façade is used on the corresponding fronts of both the Hôtel de Châtillon (fig. 106) and the project for an unidentified *hôtel*, whereas variations of the d'Estrées frontispiece are the focal points of the

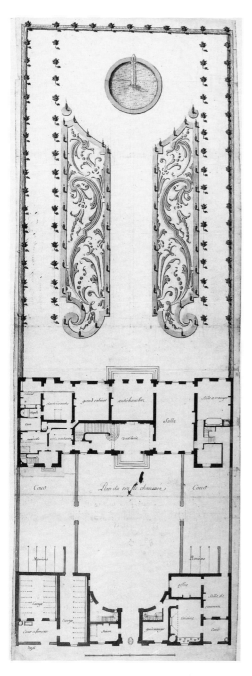

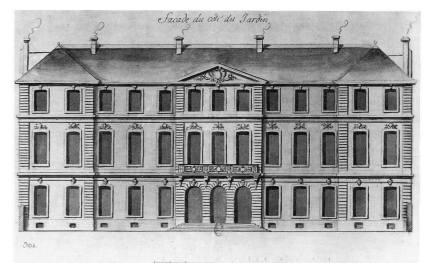

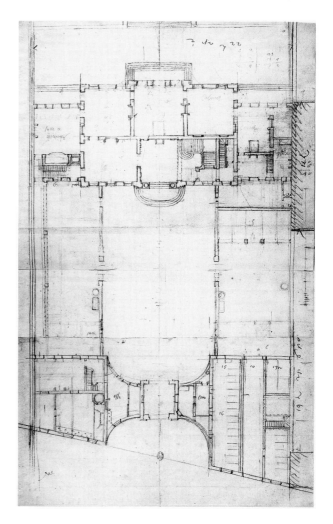

103. (*Above*) Plan, *rez-de-chaussée*, project, Maison pour le maréchal de Montesquiou, n.d. (Va 444, 296).

104. (*Above, right*) Elevation, garden façade, project, Maison pour le maréchal de Montesquiou (Ha 18, t. 1, 302).

105. (*Right*) Plan, *rez-de-chaussée*, project, Hôtel de Châtillon, Paris, n.d. (Va 270a, 705).

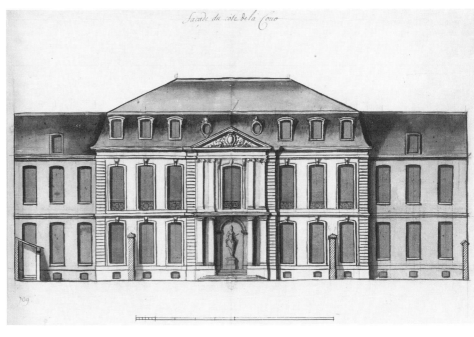

106. Elevation, court façade, project, Hôtel de Châtillon (Va 270a, 709).

107. Elevation, garden façade, project, unidentified *hôtel*, n.d. (Ha 18, t. 1, 435).

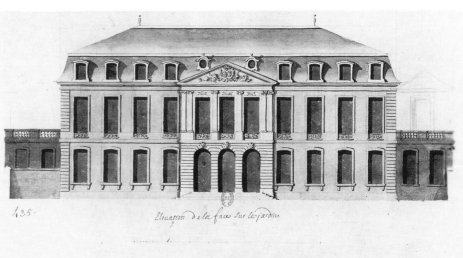

garden façades of these same buildings (unidentified *hôtel*, fig. 107). All of the elevations, including the deceptively simple sketches for the "hôtel, rue de Richelieu," demonstrate that the architect, by eliminating overly elaborate devices from his vocabulary of decorative forms, was free to concentrate on the harmonious coordination of large masses (fig. 108; both handwriting and sketchy style suggest an autograph work by

de Cotte). In addition to the simple motifs of rectilinear window frames and rusticated quoins, the designer used forged-iron balconies and railings to animate the wall surfaces.[34]

Certain general observations may be made concerning the group as a whole. De Cotte followed the normal practice of making the courtyard more deep than broad, so that the viewer standing at the *porte-cochère* would perceive it as

108. Garden and court elevations, project, *hôtel*, rue de Richelieu, Paris (Ha 18, t. 3, 2524).

square. Despite variations in the ground plans, their layout is always the result of the posing of two questions—how to route the visitor through the public rooms, and how to ensure seclusion in the private chambers. The annular plan is favored over the axial plan. Unlike Boffrand, who followed the tradition of Le Vau in devising room sequences of contrasting geometrical shapes, de Cotte designed primarily square or rectangular rooms, commonly thought to provide more usable space and to be less expensive to construct.[35] He preferred not to employ an oval *salon* projecting from the center of the garden façade, despite its popularity among his colleagues (e.g., Boffrand's Hôtel Amelot de Gournay, 1712; Courtonne's Hôtel de Matignon, 1722–24), probably for reasons related to *bienséance:* as we have seen (chaps. 4–5), the motif had palatial

connotations. The major stairs are of the *à la française,* or open-well, type, placed to the side of the vestibule so as not to disturb the grand suite of chambers. Smaller service stairs free the grand stair of the presence of servants. The kitchen (identified on the plans by the hood over the fire) is usually located opposite the stables in an area adjacent to the street; food would be carried across a service court on the same side of the house to a dining room (identified by the built-in buffet) situated on the garden side of the *corps-de-logis* (figs. 97, 103, 105). *Lieux d'aisance* are located conveniently by a bedroom or *garde-robe.*[36]

The glimpses of interior walls visible in the sections (fig. 102) enhanced the presentation drawings but were not usually intended as literal guidelines. As discussed in chapter 3, when supervising an interior scheme de Cotte provided at most the underlying pattern of the wall surfaces; the invention of the interior decor was the province of a *dessinateur* or a sculptor. Ironically, as rococo interiors became increasingly intricate, *hôtel* exteriors became simpler, the result of the strict observance of *convenance,* according to which the orders and sculpture were to be reserved for the exteriors of buildings of consequence—not *hôtels,* but palaces, churches, princely châteaux, and public monuments.[37]

One of the most pleasurable areas of an *hôtel* was the garden. In 1713, Antoine-Joseph Dezallier d'Argenville observed, "There is nothing more agreeable and delicious than a beautiful garden, nicely laid out and well kept, whose appearance contents the eyes and gives satisfaction to men of good taste."[38] Although an occasional *jardin fruitier* or *jardin potager* might appear, the *jardin de propreté* remained the standard type, so that for his *hôtels* de Cotte usually provided a detailed scheme incorporating *parterres, compartiments de broderie,* fountains, basins, terraces, and stairs in the tradition of the seventeenth-century formal garden (fig. 103).[39]

Hôtel Legendre d'Arminy

That the freestanding block became a possibility within the conservative tradition of the *hôtel* was certainly related to the development of generous and regular-shaped sites on the western side of Paris. But ingenious planning was still frequently required, as in the instance of an exceptionally narrow lot, nearly six times as long as wide, north of the Place Vendôme and west of the neighboring Couvent des Capucines, between the rue des Capucines and the northern city ramparts. Here in 1713 de Cotte laid out an *hôtel* for François Legendre d'Armini, director of the Compagnie de Saint-Domingue and brother-in-law of Pierre Crozat.[40] The house no longer exists, but drawings in the Fonds de Cotte demonstrate that the Premier Architecte experi-

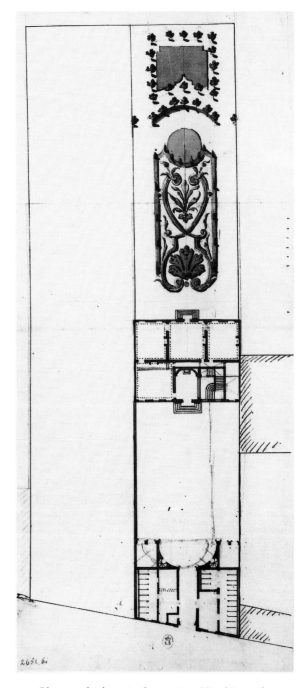

109. Plan, *rez-de-chaussée,* first project, Hôtel Legendre d'Armini, Paris, 1713 (Va 235, 2562*bis*).

mented with different solutions to the problem. The first plan called for a rectangular block located midway down the corridor of space (fig.

110. (*Right*) Plan, *rez-de-chaussée*, Hôtel de Réauville, Aix-en-Provence, 1714–17 (Va 13, t. 2, 878).

111. (*Right, bottom*) Cross section, Hôtel de Réauville (Va 13, t. 2, 884).

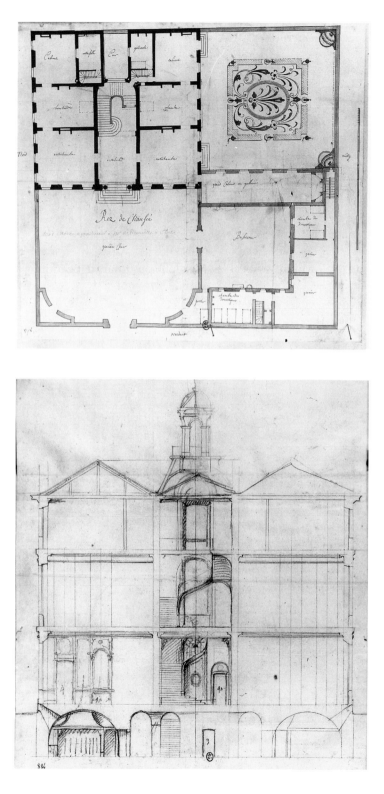

109). The *corps-de-logis* was to be entered on axis and experienced in clockwise movement; the main apartment occupied the garden side of the ground floor. The simplicity of this plan yielded in the second solution to a more practical arrangement in which the architect extended a service wing down the right-hand side of the courtyard and moved the entrance to the stair pavilion on the right, while introducing a counterclockwise progression of rooms. In the definitive project, illustrated by Blondel, few changes were made in the plan (the oval vestibule became an octagon), but the classical order was eliminated from the exterior in favor of a simple sequence of window openings more befitting a modest house.

Hôtel de Réauville

A site of equally unusual shape—a square—received a remarkable treatment by de Cotte in 1714–17. The *hôtel* in question, later called the Hôtel de Caumont, was commissioned by François de Tertulle, seigneur de Réauville, président à la Cour des Comptes de Provence. It still stands at the intersection of the rues Goyrand, Joseph-Cabassol, and Mazarine in the old aristocratic district of Aix-en-Provence, thus offering an opportunity to experience firsthand the grandiose spaces, abundant natural light, and high ceilings common to de Cotte's town houses.[41] The building is also a good example of the means by which Parisian ideals were introduced to the provincial capitals.

In this instance, de Cotte subdivided the terrain into four sections, one each for the courtyard, main block, service wings, and garden (fig. 110). The plan of the *corps-de-logis* is not comparable to any of the *hôtels* discussed above. Indeed, the *hôtel-entre-cour-et-jardin* never became popular in Aix, and de Cotte's freestanding block matches the cubist character of Provençal houses. The building is entered on axis through a vestibule that merges with a stair chamber rising three floors at the hub of the design. The showpiece of the place, the stair is breathtaking in its curvilinear outlines, superbly wrought iron railing, and overhead lighting; to crown the vertical axis, de Cotte designed a lantern that no longer exists, if it was ever built (fig. 111; compare figs. 32, 147). Two complete apartments are situated parallel to the central axis, while the kitchens of necessity inhabit the basement (fig. 111). A single-story gallery is situated at right angles to the garden façade.

Although de Cotte's plan was followed during construction (1714–17), the court elevation was modified by the local builders (fig. 112). De Cotte's subtle play of four varying window designs on the courtyard elevation was reduced to a single arched shape. Whereas his triangular pediment appropriately marked the *étage noble*,

the frontispiece was erected with two pediments, triangular over segmental. Moreover, the intended freestanding columns flanking an open vestibule were changed to pilasters. Thus, although the play of volumes in golden Aixois stone, which may be still admired today, is that established by de Cotte, the loss of his detailing only points up the subtlety of the Premier Architecte's vision.

Hôtel du Maine

Few of the *hôtels* discussed above had so complicated a history as that of the Hôtel du Maine, formerly located on the rue de Bourbon, two houses to the west of Boffrand's Hôtel de Torcy, and like the latter, having the garden façade command a view of the Seine (figs. 82–83).[42] The land was purchased from Boffrand on 30 May 1716 by Marie-Thérèse de Bourbon-Condé, princesse de Conti, but it was de Cotte who drew up the plans a month later. The following year, before the building was habitable, the princess

112. Court façade, Hôtel de Réauville.

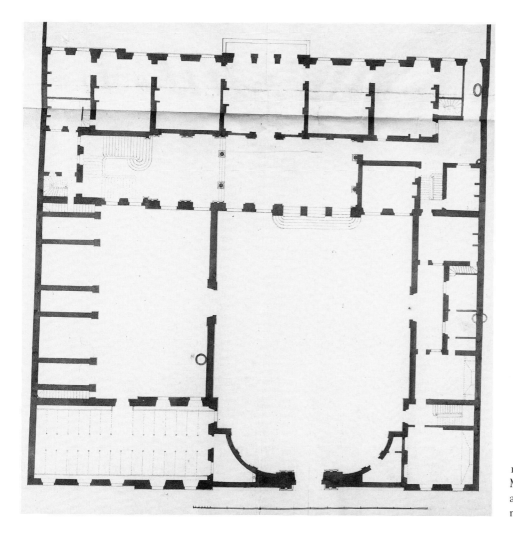

113. Plan, *rez-de-chaussée*, Hôtel du Maine, Paris, 1716, before alterations by Claude Mollet (MS 1037, no. 31).

sold the partially constructed *hôtel* to her brother-in-law and sister, the duc and duchesse du Maine (27 December 1718). Armand-Claude Mollet, who was then achieving prominence in domestic architecture (Hôtel d'Humières, located on adjacent terrain to the west, 1716–17, fig. 83; Hôtel d'Evreux, 1720), succeeded de Cotte and altered the original plans. As the legitimized son of Louis XIV and Madame de Montespan, the duc (Louis-Auguste de Bourbon; 1670–1736) was showered with honors and favors, including the right of succession to the throne; naturally he became the enemy of the regent. Their rivalry culminated in the imprisonment of Maine and his wife; during their exile from Paris the duc's *intendant* oversaw completion of the *hôtel*.[43]

De Cotte's original design for the Hôtel du Maine is revealed by a pair of drawings in the collection of the Bibliothèque de l'Institut, Paris (figs. 113–14).[44] They may be compared with drawings by Jean-Michel Chevotet for plates published by Blondel, which show the house as built. De Cotte's *corps-de-logis* was kept intact, while Mollet's principal change consisted of eliminating the stable court, so that the resulting courtyard was now wider than deep, in violation of the rules for town-house design. This also upset the proportions of the courtyard façade,

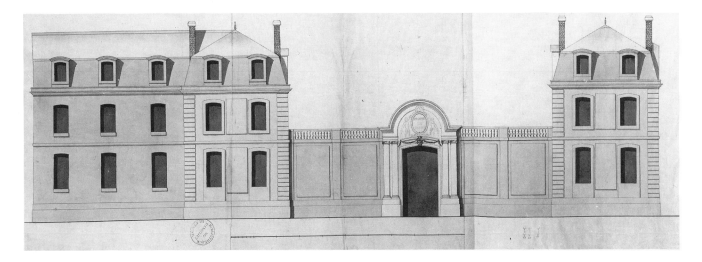

114. Elevation, street façade, project, Hôtel du Maine (MS 1037, no. 22).

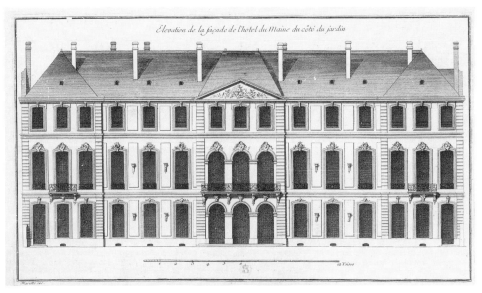

Élevation de la façade de l'hôtel du Maine du côté du jardin

115. Elevation, garden façade, Hôtel du Maine, 1716–19 (Blondel, *Architecture françoise*, Va 270e).

whose three-bay entry was expanded to seven bays. Mollet kept de Cotte's design of the individual features of the street elevation (fig. 114), but adjusted the location of the imposing side pavilions and the entry portal to create a symmetrical composition across the entire frontage.

The general layout of the *corps-de-logis* as conceived by de Cotte is an expanded version of the Hôtel d'Estrées, here extending laterally to fill the width of the site (figs. 113, 95). One enters the vestibule on the axis of the courtyard; the axis then shifts discreetly to the left to incorpo-rate on the garden side a *salon* separating two *appartements* opposite each other. Once again the *grand escalier* is on the left, preceded by a double vestibule. The arrangement of the upper floor of the Hôtel du Maine bears many features of the d'Estrées house, including the location of the *appartement de parade* overlooking the garden on the right side of the plan.

The hand of de Cotte is evident in the elevation of the garden façade, which was not altered by Mollet. The large volume consisting of two stories and an attic, broken vertically by three pavilions and capped by a simple continuous roof, is almost identical to the design for the garden façade of the Montesquiou house (figs. 115, 104). In both elevations the emphasis is on the central pavilion with its arcade, forged-iron balcony, and pediment, while the flourish of sculptural detail over the windows brings a note of richness to an otherwise restrained performance.[45] The ultimate source for this composition is Hardouin-Mansart's garden elevation of the Château Neuf, Meudon, where the pavilions and the wings between them each consist of three bays (fig. 11). This is a good example in the private sphere of the influence of the mentor on his protégé.

Palais Bourbon

The principles formulated by de Cotte during the teens were subsequently absorbed into domestic projects varying in intent from the standard Parisian house. For example, the *hôtel* type took on palatial qualities in de Cotte's series of projects for the Parisian dwelling of Louise-Françoise, duchesse de Bourbon-Condé (1673–1743), the legitimized daughter of Louis XIV and Madame de Montespan and sister of the duc du Maine. By 1719 the duchesse owned a considerable part of the old Pré aux Clercs on the quai d'Orsay, the proposed site of the Hôtel des Mousquetaires Gris in the faubourg Saint-Germain (fig. 116, northern portion at top; figs. 82–83).[46] Since funds for the new barracks were lacking in the end, the duchesse acquired most of the Crown property for herself in 1720. The generous riverfront site, which afforded splendid views toward the Tuileries, was bounded by the rue de Bourgogne, the rue de l'Université, and the Esplanade des Invalides. The western sector was reserved for the *hôtel* of her intimate, the marquis de Lassay. It was inevitable that de Cotte should draw up plans for the duchesse c. 1720: not only were he and Jean Beausire involved in the Mous-

quetaire project, but de Cotte had also worked a few years earlier on the *hôtels* of her brothers, the duc du Maine and comte de Toulouse.

The starting point for de Cotte's design of the Palais Bourbon was the typical layout of an urban *hôtel particulier* (figs. 116–17).[47] The street façade consists of a concave wall between two pavilions, with a *porte-cochère* on axis. Service courts are situated to the left and right of the *avant-cour*. However, the deep plot provides for a *cour d'honneur* beyond the first courtyard, a small-scale variation on de Cotte's double-court palace schemes for the Buen Retiro and Schleissheim (figs. 26, 34). The second courtyard is enclosed by covered colonnaded passages, a commonplace in de Cotte's palace plans but an extravagance in the realm of the Parisian town house—the U-shaped court on the site plan (fig. 116) is modeled after the magnificent courtyard of that great anomaly among Parisian houses, the Hôtel de Soubise (Delamaire; 1704–9).[48] Thus, although

116. Site plan, project, Palais Bourbon, Paris, c. 1720 (Va 272, 1021).

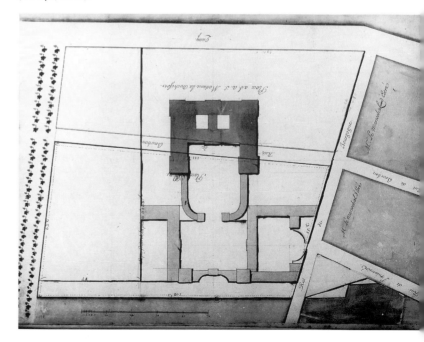

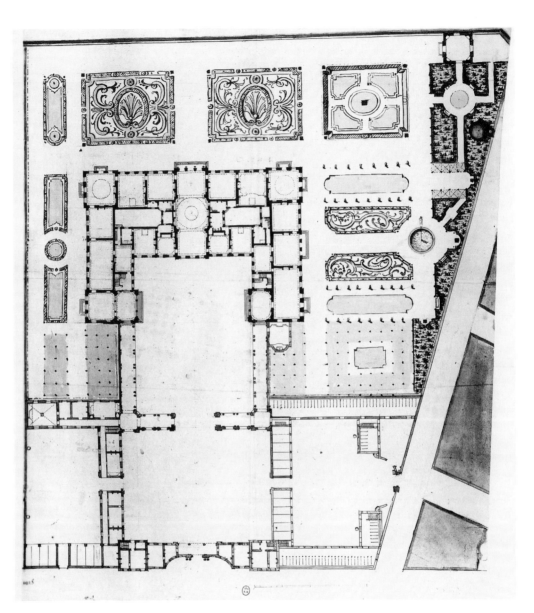

117. Plan, *rez-de-chaussée*, project, Palais Bourbon (Va 444, 1028).

the building was not intended to function as a palace in the literal sense of a seat of power, both architect and patron visualized the Palais Bourbon as more than either a town house or a *maison de plaisance* on the city's edge. Such distinct borrowings from de Cotte's earlier palace projects suggest that the building was intended to have certain palatial connotations appropriate to the daughter of the Sun King.

For the *distribution* of the interior the duchesse required doubled *appartements de parade* and *appartements de commodité*, allowing flexibility for living arrangements according to season. Three of the proposals are based on the three-wing palatial plan. In one of these, related to the first proposal for the Buen Retiro, the colonnaded walkways lead to two suites of state rooms along the west and east walls, while four apartments are clustered on either side of a domed *salon* on the main axis (fig. 117; compare fig. 27). Stairs and small rooms for private use are clustered around the inner light wells. The lack of a large staircase suggests that the main rooms are on the ground floor. The emphasis on the *rez-de-chaussée* in the three-wing plan and the use of a great number of doorways to bring nature within easy reach are elements reminiscent of the Château de Clagny, the suburban mansion of the duchesse's mother,

Madame de Montespan, located on the outskirts of Versailles (at this time in the possession of the comte de Toulouse; fig. 5), and of de Cotte's earlier design for the Castello di Rivoli (c. 1699–1704; fig. 50).

In a remarkable alternative to this proposal, de Cotte drew on his experience of centrally planned structures and devised a four-wing building with a small square courtyard in the center (fig. 118). The placement of the major rooms

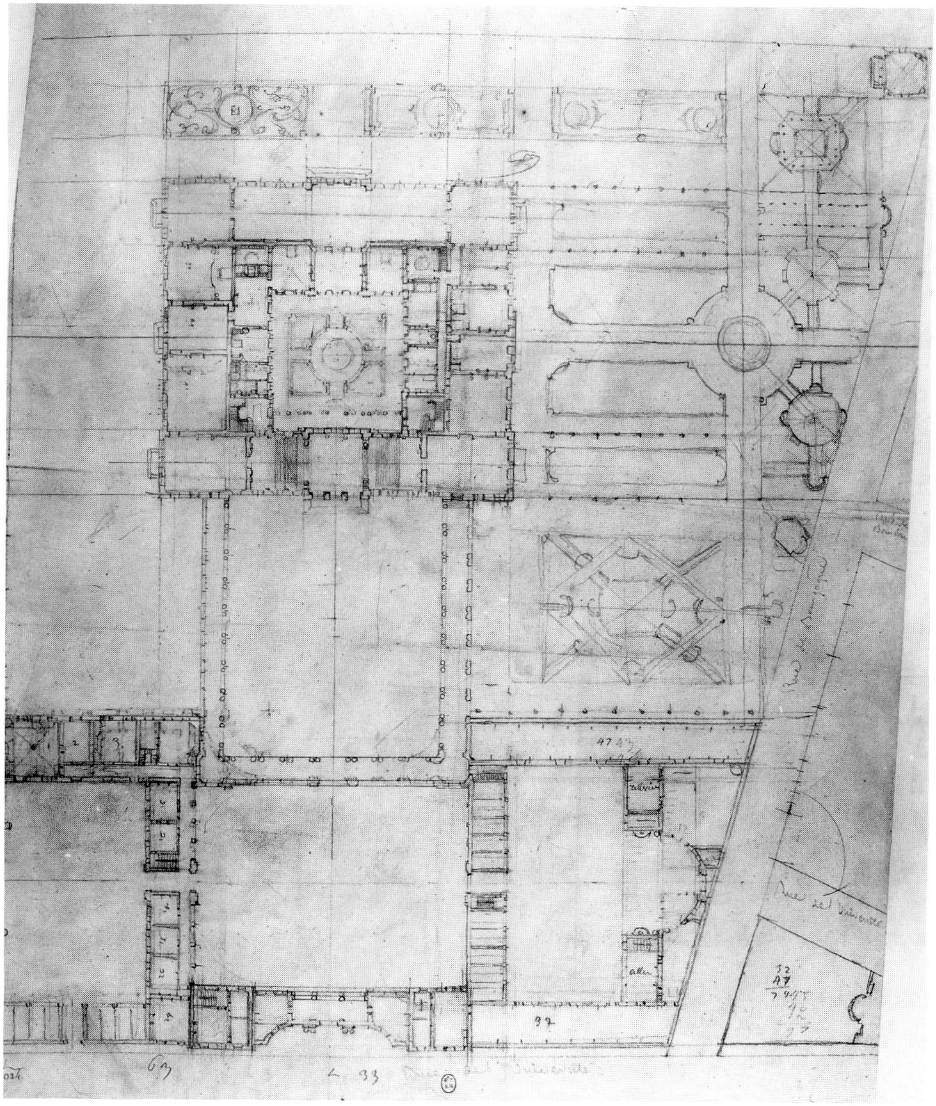

118. Plan, *rez-de-chaussée*, project, Palais Bourbon (Va 444, 1024).

toward the gardens and the ring of smaller rooms toward the inner court brings to mind de Cotte's layout of the second proposal for Buen Retiro and that of Schloss Poppelsdorf (figs. 31, 54). As required, the formal apartments are two in number, located in the east and west wings. This leaves space on the south for a grandiose vestibule and on the north for a gallery situated between two square *salons*, in the manner of Versailles (fig. 25).

The three surviving elevations do not match the extant plans. A longitudinal section shows a three-wing building consisting of a single court with a hemicycle at the street entrance (fig. 119). The *corps-de-logis* is two rooms deep and consists of a vestibule and *salon oval* on axis. An elevation for the garden façade with paired pilasters all across the *premier étage* repeats on an abbreviated scale certain features of the garden front of the first Buen Retiro proposal (figs. 120, 30).

De Cotte was but one of many architects to work for the duchesse on this project: Giardini, Lassurance, Aubert, and Gabriel followed. The final building, even more palatial in its details than originally imagined, was celebrated for the contrast on the interior between grandiose state rooms and intimate, comfortable chambers.[49]

119. Section showing *salons*, vestibule, and colonnaded courtyard, project, Palais Bourbon (Va 272, 2497).

120. Elevation, garden façade, project, Palais Bourbon (Va 272f, 2498).

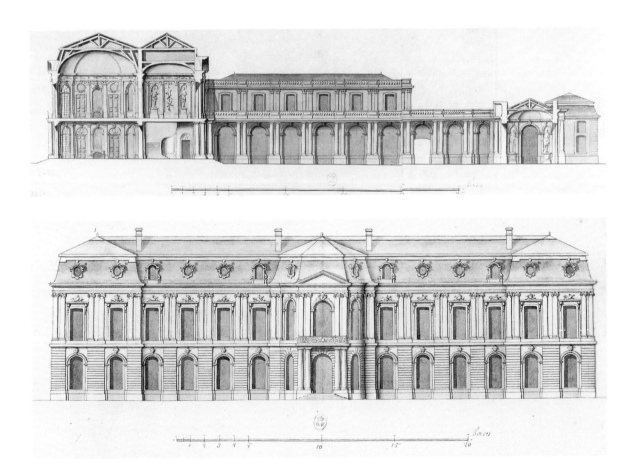

121. Wooden model, Palais Thurn und Taxis, Frankfurt am Main, c. 1730 (Fürst Thurn und Taxis Zentralarchiv, Museale Gegenstände, Regensburg).

Palais Thurn und Taxis

Chief among de Cotte's later designs for large urban dwellings is the residence of Prince Anselm Franz von Thurn und Taxis, postmaster general of the Holy Roman Empire and the Netherlands (1681–1739).[50] Although the family resided in Brussels, Charles VI persuaded this Catholic prince to relocate in Protestant Frankfurt am Main, one of four cities in the Empire possessing a free constitution. De Cotte wisely utilized the *hôtel* form so that the street façade would project a dignified if sober appearance to the passerby, while princely richness was relegated to the garden front and the interiors, elements hidden from public view.

The prince sent the initial plans prepared by a local architect to the Bâtiments for evaluation. Typically, de Cotte rethought the problem and submitted his own design. The Palais Thurn und Taxis was planned in 1727 and carried out between 1731 and 1740 on Grossen Eschenheimer Strasse, the avenue leading north from the medi-

eval sector. Guillaume Hauberat, de Cotte's superintendent at Poppelsdorf, oversaw construction, for which a wooden model was prepared (fig. 121).[51] Although splendidly decorated, the building was inhabited little more than a decade; in 1748 the Thurn und Taxis moved their seat to Regensburg, the site of the Imperial Diet of Princes. Only the street front of the Frankfurt *hôtel* survived bombing in 1943–44, to be incorporated into the modern complex of the city post office (fig. 122).

De Cotte's justification of his design comprises a *mémoire* mailed to the prince with the plans;[52] it bears quoting at length, since it encompasses many of his thoughts on the subject of domestic architecture (8 September 1727; see fig. 123):[53]

I have examined the plans sent to me for the construction of a large *hôtel* in the city of Frankfurt for His Highness Monseigneur the Prince von Thurn. I found the layout and *distribution* well disposed: the architect who made the plans, and who appears to me to be skillful and capable of their execution, has evidently followed the specifications given to him.

122. Street façade, Palais Thurn
und Taxis, designed 1727, constructed 1731–40.

Since my opinion has been requested, I believe upon reflection that, this being the house of a *grand seigneur*, it would be more appropriate to put but one *grand appartement* on the *rez-de-chaussée*—this is where the *seigneurs* and nobility assemble—and to put two *appartements* facing the garden on the *premier étage*, and others in the wings. . . .

Since the street on which this house must be built is not wide, I thought that in order to render access easier and to make the entry more elegant, one would have to create two curved walls, which would have a fine effect.

Inside, I designed a peristyle on the courtyard side of the portal, where normally people assemble in a certain order throughout the day; this adds considerable charm and is appropriate for the house of a nobleman. In addition, this peristyle leads to arcaded galleries to right and left of the courtyard, providing sheltered passage from the peristyle to all parts of the house while aggrandizing the court.

Thus de Cotte altered the design of the portal according to the preferred concave type, and in-

corporated covered passageways comparable to those in his earlier *hôtel* and palace designs. He then considered the *distribution* of the interior, emphasizing the separation of public and private spaces and giving his reasons for introducing an annular rather than axial arrangement of rooms:

At the back and in the center of the courtyard is the vestibule. Instead of allowing immediate access into the *salon* (which faces the axis of the garden), the room where men of high status would assemble, I closed the passageway on the axis, thus depriving entry to those of inferior rank and to servants. This is why one enters towards the right into a great *salle* illuminated by the courtyard; here servants are normally in waiting. From there one passes through three arches into an *antichambre* on the garden side, where the officers and valets of the house stay; next one enters a *salon* of oval shape where there are two fireplaces or wood stoves, and an alcove to accommodate a sofa on the main axis facing the garden: as I said, this is the room in which *seigneurs* and nobility convene. One moves from the *salon* into the *chambre de parade*, and from there into the *grand cabinet*, and beyond this to a bedroom which has its *commodités*—*petits cabinets* and a *garde-robe*; an advantageously located *antichambre* has its own separate entrance from the gallery on the left side of the court, so that the prince and princess may frequently withdraw from the company to give orders without their officers and domestics passing into the *grand appartement*. In the plans communicated to me I found that the *chambres* and *cabinets* were too small.

Next de Cotte proceeded to a consideration of three principal spaces requiring easy access:

To the left of the vestibule I placed the great stair, which rises on the axis of the vestibule to the *premier*

123. Working plan, *rez-de-chaussée*, Palais Thurn und Taxis, with de Cotte's handwriting (Vc 325, 1199).

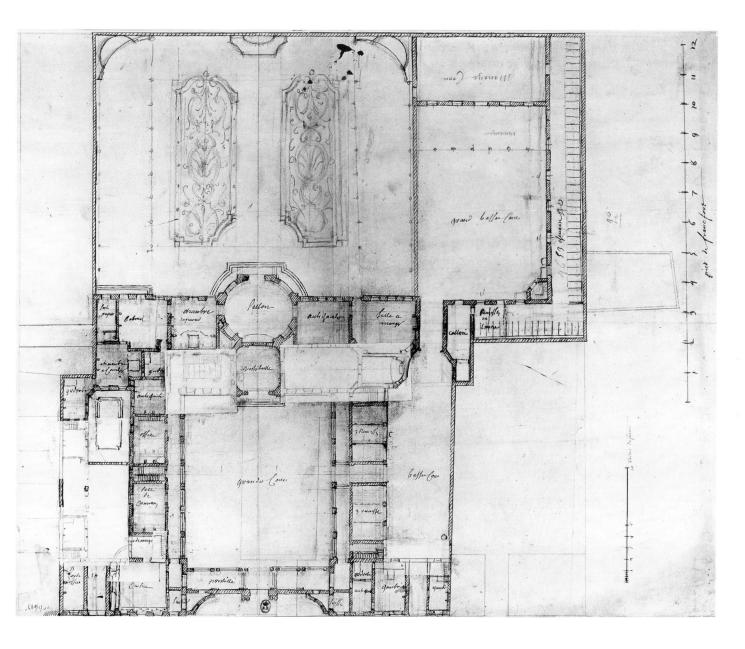

étage only, leading to two *grands appartements* facing the garden on either side of the oval *salon,* and to other apartments in the wings. Additional stairs placed in various locations will lead to all the stories as well as descend to the *caves.*

I felt obliged to place the chapel on the ground floor, with its entrance at the back of the first *salle;* there is a tribune accessible from the *premier étage;* the entire staff of the house may easily hear Mass on the *rez-de-chaussée,* even from the *salle.*

Concerning the dining hall, since it is an important room where people frequently assemble, I thought that I must take care to situate it well, and that it must be sufficiently large. That is why I put it on the garden side to the right of the *antichambre* in the *enfilade* of the *grand appartement,* also being accessible to the servants from the first *salle:* thus the table may be set and cleared easily from the service rooms and kitchen, which are situated much as in the plans mailed to me, except that I brought the room used during the day for refreshments closer [to the kitchen].

The Premier Architecte went on to describe the layout of the second floor, the stables, and the carriage garages. His final summary included the following points:

These are my thoughts on this *hôtel.* If this layout is agreeable, you may give it to the architect who furnished the first designs, so that he may have occasion to rethink them. I prepared this project solely to please a prince whose acquaintance I have not had the honor of making. If your architect is ill-disposed and the project pleases His Highness, he need only let me know his intentions, to which I will conform. But at the same time, in order to work with assurance, it is necessary to have an instructive memorandum of indispensable *commodités* and the number of lodgings needed for officers and domestics.

Despite de Cotte's preference for the annular plan, in the final layout for the house a door leading from the vestibule directly into the *salon oval* provided passage along the main axis, while two *appartements* of roughly equal size flanked the *salon,* each containing an *antichambre, chambre,* and *cabinet.* In addition, a narrow gallery for din-

ing was appended to the left-hand *enfilade,* and the chapel was moved to the upper floor.[54]

The simple articulation of the Frankfurt street elevation is typical of de Cotte's town houses, but the height and prominence of the side pavilions is unusual (the original hipped roofs have been replaced by flat roofs and a balustrade; figs. 121–22). In most Parisian *hôtels* the lateral walls of the courtyard are little more than screens hiding the service courts. At Frankfurt, however, the court was bordered by lateral wings whose elevations consisted of arcades on both stories, the upper ones being blind (the model shows open arcades on both floors; figs. 121, 124). For the design of the elevation at the head of the court, de Cotte borrowed from his own earlier unexecuted composition for the Hôtel de Torcy (fig. 100).

On the garden front the energetically curving walls of the oval projection were checked by the planar frontispiece with its flat pilasters (fig. 125). De Cotte considered the domed *salon* to be a princely motif and employed it prominently in palace and country-house designs for patrons of the highest rank. Its use for the Thurn und Taxis, therefore, was appropriate, although the oval *salon,* comprising two separate stories, was not a true *salon à l'italienne.* An early sketch in the Fonds de Cotte for the central pavilion shows a curved forged-iron railing crowning the dome, thus repeating a motif found in de Cotte's drawings for the domed fronts of Poppelsdorf and Compiègne (figs. 56, 64). The rail was changed in the definitive drawings to an urn-shaped finial.

The designs for the Palais Bourbon and the Palais Thurn und Taxis demonstrate the means by which the *hôtel* as a building type could be altered and aggrandized to suit the requirements of a particular patron. Similarly, the *hôtel* form provided the basis for three city mansions created by de Cotte for bishops of the Catholic church; these *palais épiscopaux* are the subject of chapter 10.

124. Courtyard façade, Palais Thurn und Taxis (before destruction).

125. Garden façade, Palais Thurn und Taxis.

Chapter Eight

The City: Provincial Capitals

THE PROVINCIAL CAPITALS of France followed the lead of Paris in showing a keen interest in urban planning.[1] The most ambitious form of city square in the provinces was the *place royale*, which paid homage to the king, embellished the urban scene, and provided a promenade ground for the citizenry. The *places royales* honoring Louis XIV in Paris—the Place des Victoires and the Place Vendôme—set the standard for the type, which required an imposing sculptural representation of the monarch, usually on the principal axis, and magnificent uniform façades surrounding the symmetrically composed space. Robert de Cotte, ever the willing consultant, brought his experience as Hardouin-Mansart's assistant at the Parisian sites to projects for two major *places royales* discussed in this chapter, those for Lyon and Bordeaux.

In addition, the provincial capitals needed new buildings and squares to accommodate mercantile activities. Such complexes added to a city's economic fortunes by providing places for business transactions, while at the same time celebrating the town's prosperity through the presence of inscriptions and emblematic sculpture. Unlike the *place royale*, whose elevations normally incorporated a giant order, commercial buildings received less noble articulation on the exterior; the chief formal element was often bold rustication, sometimes with vermiculated bosses.

This was the case with the designs from de Cotte's *atelier* for commercial schemes in Lyon and Rouen.

Although some city projects were the direct result of royal patronage, most were promoted by provincial governing bodies or local *intendants*, who acted as financial liaison between the municipal government and the Crown. The goal was to transform an old, usually medieval city into an attractive and efficient center of government and commerce. This required the collaborative efforts of numerous individuals, such as the Premier Architecte, his deputy on the site, the *intendant*, one or more provincial committees, and a local architect. It follows that the gestation process was lengthy. It was common for the provincial authorities to alter and even reject designs produced in the Bâtiments.

Place Bellecour, Lyon

In 1686 the Consulat of Lyon (board of city magistrats) decided to commission a bronze equestrian statue of Louis XIV to be erected on a prominent site in the city. Martin Desjardins's sculpture was finally ready for delivery in July 1701, when it was shipped from Paris. The previous year, from mid-September until 2 October, de Cotte visited Lyon in his capacity as Architecte Ordinaire for the purpose of presenting Mansart's design of the pedestal for the monument.[2] He was accompanied by a draftsman, since it was also his charge to draw up plans of various squares and bridges that might serve as possible locations for the work.

The statue was erected in 1713 in the center of the chosen site, the projected Place Louis-le-Grand (Place Bellecour). However, the immense size and irregular shape of this area proved to be an obstacle to the fashioning of a coherent *place royale*. As early as 1677 Hardouin-Mansart had proposed for this region an ideal, centrally planned complex of administrative and recreational buildings set in a garden, but his design failed to take into account the limitations imposed by the space.[3] As Premier Architecte, de Cotte wrestled with the problem from about 1711 to 1714. Extant plans of the quarter in its undeveloped state probably date from his visit in 1700,[4] but the chronology of the various projects, of which there are at least a dozen (counting alternatives suggested on the flaps), is difficult to reconstruct because of the lack of dates on most of the plans and the disappearance of several drawings. Even so, the variety of solutions is re-markable, although the continual rearrangement of elements suggests that the architect, the Consulat, and the provincial governor, the maréchal de Villeroy, had differing opinions concerning use of the space.

In what is presumably de Cotte's earliest proposal (c. 1711) he filled the trapezoidal site with buildings on three sides in an effort to give the square the more regular shape of a rectangle and to reduce the overall area of the *place* proper, thus making it more intelligible to the eye.[5] On an informally inked site plan de Cotte sketched this proposal rapidly and summarily, using his characteristic hatchings (fig. 126). He also redrew the streets leading from the square to the rivers on the east and west, the Rhône and Saône, respectively, and in addition he altered the Pont de l'Archevêche on the Saône, so that all of these thoroughfares would be consistent with the geometric shape of the *place* and not at an angle to it. Although the statue remained the primary focus at the center of the *place royale*, de Cotte provided a secondary focus to the west on the side

126. Plan, project, Place Bellecour, Lyon, c. 1711 (Va 436, 590).

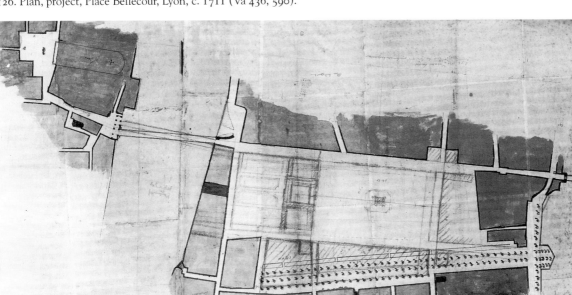

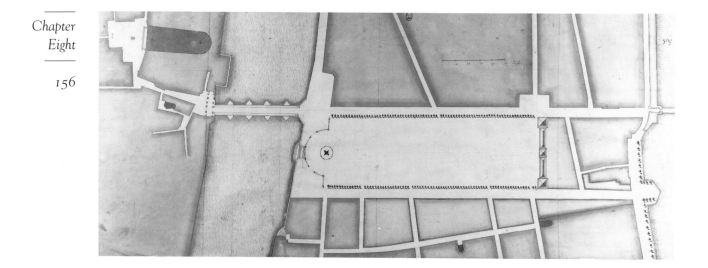

127. Plan, project, Place Bellecour, c. 1711–13 (Va 69, t. 6, 598).

of the Saône in the form of a great civic building comprised of wings surrounding three large courts. However, the Consulat did not approve the reduced size of the original square.[6]

The space remains largely intact in a comparable plan wherein the building is placed on the eastern, Rhône side facing a long, open rectangular *place* bordered by trees (c. 1711–13; fig. 127).[7] Here de Cotte proposed erecting the statue on a balustraded hemicycle permitting views westward onto the Saône, to which the spectator could descend by means of a monumental stair.

On 31 May 1713 Louis XIV and the maréchal de Villeroy approved an entirely different plan calling for no new construction of any significance; the emphasis would be completely on the sculpture in the center and on surrounding *parterres* and trees articulating the space.[8] A few preexisting structures were to be demolished to make way for an *allée* of trees along the south side of the square and a large formal garden on the side of the Rhône. Although this was the least costly of the solutions, it must have been apparent to everyone involved in the project that a square lacking monumental architecture would

not only constitute a feeble gesture toward the king but would represent the loss of an opportunity to enhance the city.

Further possibilities were proposed in the final group of plans (1713–14). One of these involved erecting on the long, southern side of the *place* a major façade of fifty-three bays, with smaller blocks of thirteen bays to the left and right of it.[9] On the shorter extremities of the square to the east and west, there would be medium-size buildings of thirty-one bays. The cross axis thus achieved prominence, particularly in an alternative project drawn on a superimposed flap: here the chief façade is hollowed out and the statue is placed before a great concavity (fig. 128). As an iconic image of power and glory, the conjunction of sculpture and architecture might have comprised one of the great *places royales* of France, but economic and physical restraints prevented its adoption.

In fact, the king approved a new proposal on 1 May 1714. It shows an *allée* of trees on the south to give the *place* rectangular shape, and two identical façades on the shorter ends facing the sculpture in the center (fig. 129).[10] The buildings were intended to be private dwellings, each composed of rental flats independently financed and constructed, similar to the final, more economical solution of the Place Vendôme in Paris. Yet even in this definitive plan, the underlying problem of the square remains unsolved: the distance spanning the buildings is so vast—some 158 *toises*—that the pair of façades fails to control the space, and the statue is left adrift in the middle.

As might be expected, de Cotte's earliest proposals for elevations (1711–12) are based on the precedents of the Place Vendôme and the Place des Victoires (figs. 10, 80). However, when the Consulat exhibited the projects, they were criticized for being insufficiently Italianate.[11] Hence the elevations of 1714 for blocks of various widths on three sides of the *place* are a hybrid of French and Italian elements.[12] For example, in

128. Plan, project, Place Bellecour, c. 1713–14 (Va 69, t. 6, 597, with flap).

129. Plan, project, Place Bellecour, 1714 (Va 436, 592).

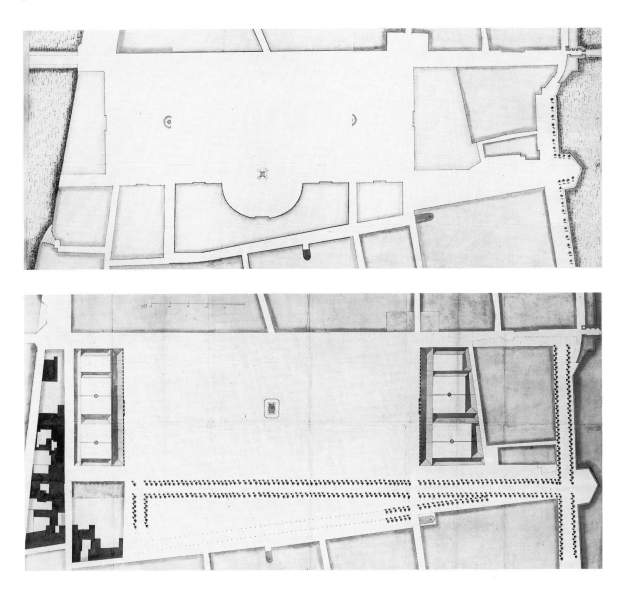

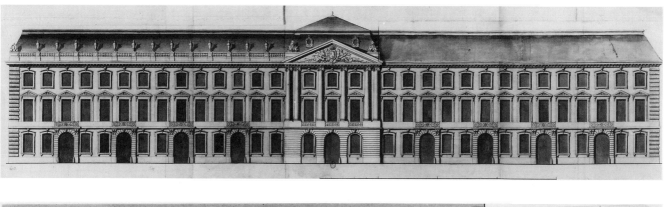

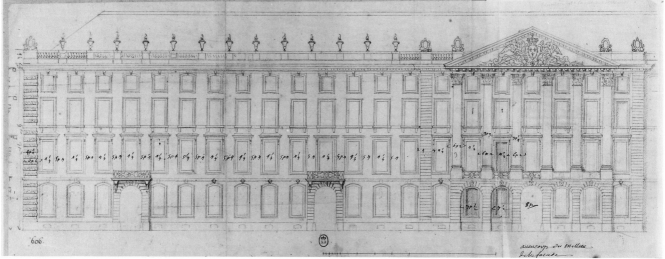

130. (*Top*) Elevation facing the square, east and west blocks, project, Place Bellecour, 1714 (Va 69, t. 6, 605).

131. (*Above*) Elevation facing the square, east and west blocks, final scheme, Place Bellecour, 1714 (Va 69, t. 6, 606).

the elevation of the east and west façades, the central pavilion consists of a colossal order standing on a rusticated base and embracing two stories in a manner similar to the temple-front motifs on the pavilions of the Place Vendôme (fig. 130; compare the corresponding plan, fig. 128). But the elimination of the order from the side wings and the abandonment of the standard French end pavilions in favor of vermiculated quoins at the edges, which is even more striking, derive from Roman palazzo design. The pedi-

mented window moldings set into the bare wall of the *premier étage*, and the rusticated portals on the *rez-de-chaussée* marking the entrances to the houses, bring to mind the most famous of secular façades in Rome, the Palazzo Farnese, which de Cotte had admired in 1689, exclaiming, "This palace is the most beautiful and the most perfect and correct in Rome."[13] It is significant, therefore, that in this commission de Cotte departed from the prototypical elevations of Hardouin-Mansart's *places royales* in response to demands from his patrons.

The definitive elevation for the matching pair of blocks erected on the shorter sides of the square appears in two graphite sketches (fig. 131).[14] It differs from preceding solutions in the following ways: the addition of a fourth story; the appearance at the center of evenly spaced pilasters, not columns, bracketed by rusticated strips; the removal of the domed roof of the central axis; and the elimination of the pediments over the second-story windows. The result is a flatter and more monotonous façade. Minor changes were made during construction (1715–26).

The final scheme was not the most coherent of de Cotte's proposals, and indeed, the Place Bellecour does not rank among the most aesthetically successful *places royales* created in the eighteenth century. Nevertheless, it constituted a royal presence in Lyon of such power that the buildings were pulled down during the Revolution, along with the statue (1792–93).

Place du Change, Lyon

The relatively small dimensions of the Place du Change, the center of commercial activities in Lyon, allowed for a more cohesive design than that of the Place Bellecour. The original seventeenth-century exchange building bordering the *place*, the Loge au Change, was a response to a demand by the local community of Italian merchants for a place of business. Serlio's unexecuted proposal for a structure with a merchant's loggia on the ground floor and two stories of apartments overhead (c. 1542; published in his Seventh Book) provided the basis for the building constructed by Simon Gourdets as part of a city block facing a small square adjacent to the right bank of the Saône (1634–53; letter A on the plan, fig. 132).[15] Almost immediately the loggia was deemed too small to accommodate the merchants, and late in the century plans were solicited from another Italian, Francesco Fontana, for a larger, freestanding loggia of classical design to be erected in the middle of the square (elevation D; fig. 133).[16] His work was not executed, but Fontana's four proposals, along with an undated descriptive memorandum in Italian and

French, were presumably given to de Cotte in 1700 while he was considering various locales in Lyon as appropriate sites for the statue of Louis XIV.

Three undated projects by de Cotte are extant.[17] The first two were evidently composed around 1700, since the *Equestrian Louis XIV* figures prominently in a plan, and an accompanying *mémoire* argues for placement of the royal image in this square (fig. 134). While Fontana concerned himself exclusively with the design of the new loggia, de Cotte considered enlarging the irregular-shaped *place* by demolishing structures on all four sides, including the old Loge, and erecting a new pavilion within the space toward the side of the square opposite the river. He reshaped the square along symmetrical lines so that a controlling longitudinal axis intersects the Loge, the statue, and the street descending to the bridge crossing the Saône. For the elevations, de Cotte appropriated various motifs from Fontana's designs. The somber massiveness of the latter's trabeated loggia reappears in de Cotte's design for a screen of Doric columns supporting an entablature and superimposed balustrade (fig. 135). From Fontana's drawing de Cotte also borrowed the crowning motifs of the clock and the bell tower, motifs commonly employed on the exterior of civic buildings, such as town halls (see the Pompe de la Samaritaine, Paris, 1715, figs. 88–90).

The third project, for which the elevations are in a more tonal drawing style comparable to de Cotte's designs of the teens, was a later rethinking of the problem, probably about 1711–14, when he drew up proposals for the Place Bellecour.[18] The presentation drawings for this project, which were sent to Lyon, have been lost, but three sheets are preserved in Paris. On the site plan of the square de Cotte lightly sketched four possible ground plans for the Loge, either rectangular or T-shaped, as well as four possibili-

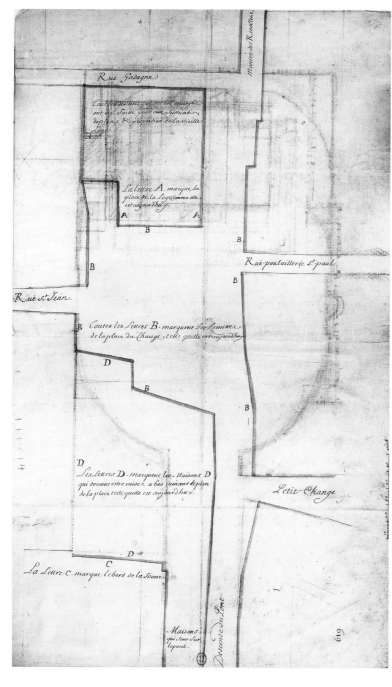

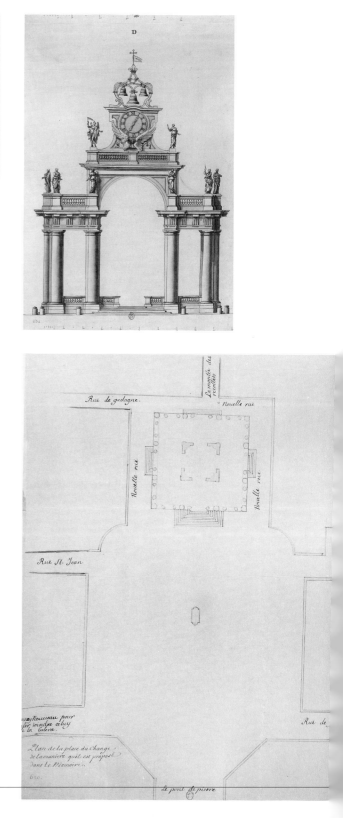

132. Site plan, Place du Change, Lyon; third project sketched in charcoal, c. 1711–14 (Va 69, t. 11, 619).

133. (*Top, right*) Francesco Fontana, elevation D (narrower front), Loge au Change, Lyon, 1690s(?) (Va 69, t. 11, 631).

134. (*Right*) Plan, first project, Place du Change, c. 1700 (Va 69, t. 11, 620).

135. Elevation, first project, Loge au Change, c. 1700 (Va 69, t. 11, 625).

136. Elevation, third project, Loge au Change and Place du Change, c. 1711–14 (Va 69, t. 11, 632).

ties for the perimeter of the new *place*, being either rectangular or having concave walls smoothing the angles at the corners (fig. 132). The projected elevations of the façades on the perimeter of the *place* are simple: arcaded shop fronts appear on the ground floor and apartment windows on the second; relief sculpture, a fountain, and an inscription provide decoration for the large pavilion located on the long wall (fig. 136). On the side elevation of the richly textured Loge, the architect placed paired pilasters on a rusticated arcade, and surmounted the structure with a clock tower and a balustrade topped by gesticulating sculpted figures. The result is comparable to several pieces of Parisian urban decor conceived by de Cotte in the teens, such as the Château d'Eau du Palais Royal (1714; fig. 75) and the Porte de la Conférence (c. 1717–19; fig. 74). As it turned out, the Consulat did not approve such an extensive scheme of reconstruction. Only later did Jacques-Germain Soufflot commence substantial remodeling of the old Loge au Change (1747).

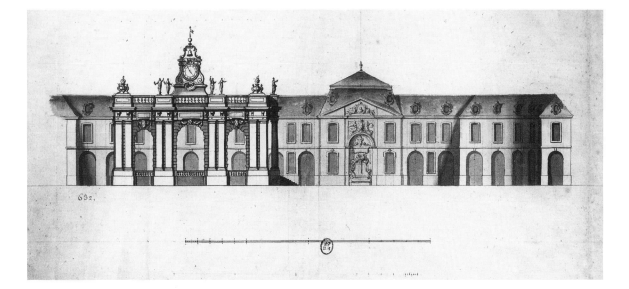

Place Louis XV, Bordeaux

The Place Louis XV, Bordeaux, as it appears today (Place de la Bourse), was the creation of Jacques V Gabriel, who was appointed as architect for the site in 1729, and of his son Ange-Jacques, who took charge on his father's death in 1742. It was the first *place royale* of the open-square type, in which an architectural backdrop faces onto a promenade along a quay, with pleasant views toward a river; as such, it was the principal model for the Place Louis XV (Place de la Concorde), Paris. Ideas for a Bordelaise square germinated as early as 1688, when the local *jurats* (members of the city council) decided to commission a bronze image of the sovereign.[19] Despite several decades of delays, the Intendant

137. Héricé, plan, project, Place Royale, Bordeaux, April 1728 (bottom); de Cotte, plan, project, July 1728 (flap, top) (Va 431, 1317).

Claude Boucher pressed ahead early in 1728 by commissioning from a local architect, Héricé, a design for a series of uniform façades bordering the Garonne River between the Porte des Paus and the Cour des Aides (fig. 137, bottom).[20] Until this time Bordeaux had remained medieval in character, having turned its back on the river, from which it was separated by a wall. Plans for the new site call for a structure located beyond the wall and facing the water, thus initiating an outward direction in the city's development. There was also a built-in mercantile element: the long open quay, much admired for the beauty of its vistas, was the principal port of the maritime city.[21]

Héricé's proposal requires a vast edifice of fifty-seven bays, whose central concavity balances a convex projection of the new, enlarged quay. The center of the intervening oval space provides the location for a statue of Louis XV. As indicated

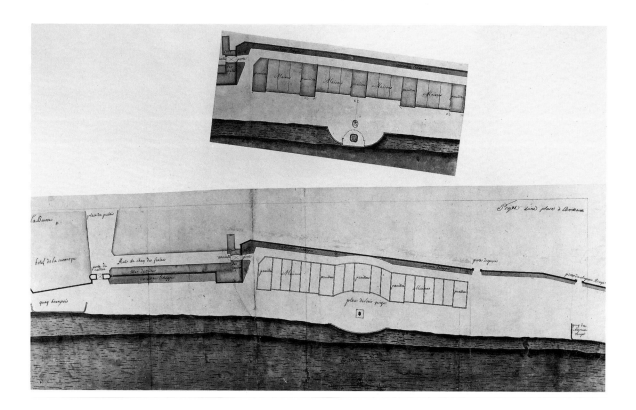

on the plan, the building would shelter nineteen separate houses to be purchased by independent buyers. In Hérice's two-story elevation a blind arcade runs along the entire lower floor, and the orders appear on the pavilions only—Corinthian over Ionic.[22] The imposing central pavilion supports a tall mansard roof crowned by a belvedere to be used as an observatory by members of the recently formed Académie des sciences.

In April 1728, Boucher submitted the project to the duc d'Antin, a personal friend and native of Gascony, for approval and correction. The latter found the composition unworthy of so admirable a site and requested improvements from de Cotte: "Since charcoal costs you nothing, please oblige me with a sample of your expertise, . . . for in truth I confess that I shudder to see public buildings constructed by the first comer lacking genius and experience."[23] "The Bordelais," he further claimed, "much prefer to sell their wine than to erect beautiful buildings."[24] The drawings sent to Bordeaux by de Cotte have been lost, but the following remain in the Paris files: a plan, preliminary drawings for the elevation, a cross section, and a draft of a *mémoire* with marginal notes in his hand dated 14 July 1728.

The Premier Architecte was frank in his criticism of Hérice's design:

I examined the proposed plan and elevation that were sent to me, and found that the *place* in the shallow curved space was too narrow, being but eighteen to nineteen *toises* in diameter; moreover, the curved part was too shallow to allow buildings of appropriate design, and the promenade was too constricted [as a result of] the pedestal in the center and the steps and stone posts required to surround it [see de Cotte's use of a giant exedra for Lyon; fig. 128]. This gave me another idea, which I drew on the paper overlapping the plan that was sent to me, that of extending the curved wall on the bank of the Garonne further, without altering the river bed or its current [fig. 137, top]. The result, I believe, would be a better placement of the equestrian figure; by this means the quay

would be open and the space larger, and nothing would spoil the buildings or the space, of which we hope to make the most.[25]

Thus de Cotte moved the proposed location of the statue to a more prominent position on a terrace projecting toward the river. (The following year he used a similar arrangement in the design for a new wing and waterfront terrace incorporating sculpture at the Château de Fontainebleau; fig. 47). By means of a new system of pavilions he reduced Hérice's nineteen houses of varying widths to seventeen of roughly equal breadth.

De Cotte further stated, "Although I did nothing to alter the building's length, I found the façade sent to me too low for its considerable breadth";[26] therefore, he introduced an attic story in the revised elevation, which is loosely based on the *ordonnance* of the Place Vendôme—a giant order over a rusticated arcaded base (figs. 138, 10). As a means of enlivening the length, he subdivided it into nine parts, five of which constitute pavilions. In the center section the plane of the front is pushed back by one bay, so that twenty-one bays recede in depth, while all of the pavilions project forward slightly. Realizing that cost was a major factor, de Cotte eliminated the expensive mansard roof, made the belvedere an optional feature, and drew up an alternative elevation (not extant) that dropped the use of columns altogether and employed pilasters on the pavilions only. Typical of designs from the Bâtiments, the finished drawing had several flaps "pour satisfaire les curieux," in this case showing alternative roof designs for the pavilions.

Although excavation of the site commenced in September 1728, the Parlement caused further delays. The arrival in May 1729 of the Architecte Ordinaire, Jacques V Gabriel, initiated his long association with Bordeaux and a series of new proposals. Gabriel divided de Cotte's mono-

138. Elevation, project, Place Royale, Bordeaux, July 1728 (Va 431, 1318).

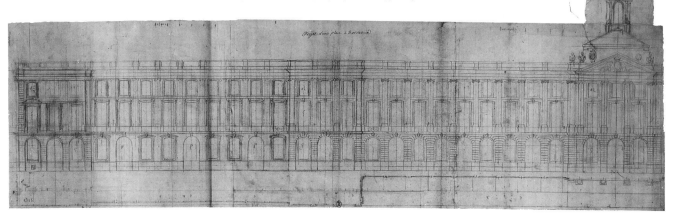

lith into several smaller buildings, increased the area of the *place* by making it half-octagonal, integrated the *place* with the town by means of connecting avenues, and based his elevations more closely on those of the Place Vendôme.

The Douane, the Bourse, and the Grenier à Sel, Rouen

Like Bordeaux, Rouen owed its prosperity to maritime commerce and its propitious location on the banks of a river—in this case the Seine in northern Normandy. Not until the mid-eighteenth century did the city fathers take an interest in erecting a *place royale* or improving the network of streets.[27] Instead, the urbanistic goals of the first third of the century focused on the large, impressive quays with their numerous ports, and on three buildings that would stand isolated along the Seine—the Douane, the Bourse, and the Grenier à Sel. A suite of projects for these exists in the Fonds de Cotte, dating from the period of his tenure as Premier Architecte. There is no extant correspondence, but the plans were probably conceived according to the standard method of collaboration as described above,

whereby de Cotte worked variously with the Intendant Goujon de Gasville, the Conseil des échevins, and the Chambre de commerce.

In 1699 the Conseil des échevins convened to discuss building a new customshouse to replace the old one. There were no tangible results at first, but in 1714 the issue was raised again; the earliest plans may date from this time. Finally, on 13 October 1722, Louis XV authorized funds for the Douane, which was erected in 1723–26 on the basis of designs produced in the Bâtiments.[28] In the Fonds de Cotte there is a memo for a dedicatory inscription to Louis XV within a cartouche on the façade (9 December 1725).[29]

The Douane, also called La Romaine after the Roman balance used within for weighing goods, straddled the city walls on the quai du Havre (figs. 139, bottom left, and 140). On either side of the building stood a pair of city gates, the Porte de la Vicomté and the Porte de la Haranguerie, which were constructed anew with the Douane. The simple elevation of the ensemble, incorporating discreet use of the orders, triangular pediments enclosing sculpture, and bands of vermiculated rustication, is consistent with de Cotte's

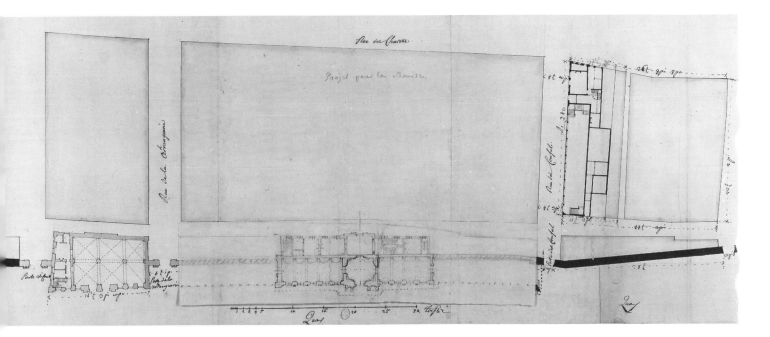

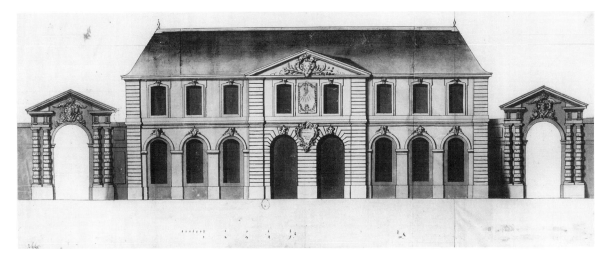

139. Plan, quai du Havre, with (left to right) Porte de la Vicomté, Douane, Porte de la Haranguerie, Bourse Découverte with flap showing project for the Bourse, and old Palais des Consuls, Rouen (Va 449, 2429).

140. Elevation, Douane, Porte de la Vicomté and Porte de la Haranguerie, 1723–26 (Va 76, t. 15, 2440).

Parisian urban projects of the teens (e.g., gates and pavilions for the esplanade of the Tuileries, fig. 71). Nicolas Coustou sculpted the large bas-relief in the central pediment representing *Mercury with the Attributes of Commerce*.[30] A large vaulted room on the ground floor accommodated the reception of goods, while smaller rooms on the upper story provided lodgings for officers.[31]

Just east of the Douane lay the Bourse Découverte, an open-air promenade along the quay where traders and manufacturers assembled to do business. A low wall lined by a file of trees marked the limits of the area along the quay between the Porte de la Haranguerie and the Porte

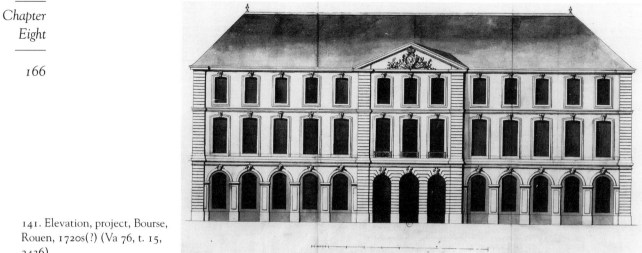

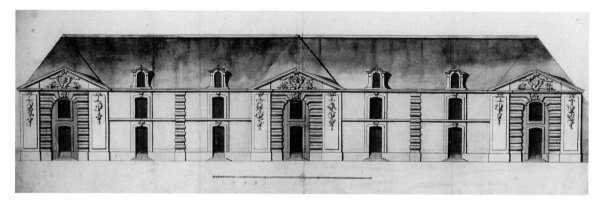

142. River elevation, project, Grenier à Sel, Rouen, c. 1713 (Va 76, t. 21, 2456).

des Consuls. A pair of projects in the Fonds de Cotte call for erecting on this site a Bourse, two rooms deep and alternatively two or three stories in height, to provide indoor space for the merchants (figs. 139, bottom center, and 141).[32] The drawings are in the same style as those for the Douane and probably date from the same years. The plans were not carried out, although a comparable building, the Palais des Consuls, was constructed on a site within the city walls on the rue des Consuls (Jean-François Blondel, 1734–39).[33] In 1753 the Bourse Découverte was restored and decorated with an obelisk, sculpted trophies, and a relief portrait of Louis XV.

Transport of salt down the Seine was a major source of revenue for the Rouennais. Traditionally salt was brought to a port on the quai au Sel (later, quai Saint-Sever) on the south side of the river, opposite the Douane and the Bourse Découverte. Twenty-two sheets in the Fonds de Cotte comprise several projects for a new Grenier à Sel on this site.[34] The building, construction of which began in 1713, consisted of two parts: a row of seven warehouses, whose entrances faced northward along the quay (fig. 142); and lodgings and offices for officials, facing eastward toward the Petit Château in the Seine.[35] The strong, simple style of the elevation drawings is consonant with that of the drawings for the Douane and the Bourse. The boldly overscaled vermiculated rustication, suggestive of the forces of nature, is appropriate for a building devoted to the storage of salt.

De Cotte's projects for the provinces reflect the same diversity of urban needs that he attempted to satisfy in his Parisian designs. However, one concluding point deserves emphasis here. In the *Traité de la police* Le Cler du Brillet strongly differentiated the *place royale*, a concept exemplified by the great prototypes, the Place des Victoires and the Place Vendôme, from the public square devoted to commerce. Nevertheless, among de Cotte's designs for provincial capitals only the Place Bellecour corresponds to this narrow definition—an architectural setting whose *raison d'être* is the royal image. As we have seen, two of de Cotte's designs, the Place du Change (first and second schemes) and the Place Louis XV at Bordeaux, merged royal and mercantile elements, producing a somewhat different iconography: here the city's prosperity appeared as one of the benefits of royal government.[36] At the same time, the extreme importance attached in the eighteenth century to the business fortunes of the rising middle class is illustrated in de Cotte's work by the predominantly commercial character of his buildings for Rouen.

Chapter Nine

The Church

THE WAVE of new construction that engulfed Paris and the provincial capitals in the early eighteenth century provided numerous opportunities for the planning and remodeling of religious buildings: new city quarters required local parish churches; many older basilicas still lacked appropriate façades; and several religious orders had yet to construct a monumental chapel within their monastic complexes.[1] De Cotte's strong interest in ecclesiastical architecture was in part a result of his firsthand experience of Italian church design during his southern journey in 1689–90. It is significant that the majority of his drawings and notes from the trip concern religious rather than secular buildings. The judgments expressed in his notebooks reflect critical points of view instilled during his formative years through familiarity with a considerable number of French seventeenth-century basilicas and central-plan churches. In reviewing his most important projects for the clergy, we shall see that although his designs primarily follow French precedents, there are echoes of buildings he had seen on Italian soil.

De Cotte's earliest opportunities in the ecclesiastical field permitted only a limited exploration of the major building types. As Hardouin-Mansart's assistant, he worked in 1687–88 on drawings for the parish church of Marly, a small rectangular space encompassing a nave and aisles, with a pedimented but otherwise un-

adorned façade.[2] After 1697 he probably assisted Mansart in the completion of Montauban Cathedral, taking full charge of operations there when he became Premier Architecte in 1708.[3] Later, in 1722, he altered the Montauban portal by adding bell towers to the lateral bays in a manner resembling the composition of Hardouin-Mansart's Notre-Dame de Versailles (1684–86; fig. 8). Similarly, in 1708–9, de Cotte stepped into Mansart's position as royal advisor for the completion of the Gothic cathedral of Sainte-Croix d'Orléans.[4] Extant designs for a two-towered portal and a belfry over the crossing represent the efforts of the Premier Architecte in collaboration with an undistinguished local architect, Guillaume Hénault. The projects owe their surprisingly original character to the neo-Gothic detailing—a condition imposed by Louis XIV as a means of maintaining stylistic homogeneity throughout the building. Although the design was largely the work of Hénault, the harmonious proportions and monumental grandeur of the new portal elevation most likely reflect de Cotte's influence.[5] However, nothing was built at this time. Upon resumption of the project in 1723, Jacques V Gabriel reworked the Hénault–de Cotte solution to achieve his own façade project.

Couvent de la Visitation, Paris

De Cotte's first independent ecclesiastical commission was for the rebuilding of the church and forecourt of the Couvent de la Visitation in the rue Saint-Jacques, Paris. Established in 1626, the convent was located just north of the Val-de-Grâce in an area favored for nunneries.[6] Following a pattern typical for such foundations, the nuns initially installed themselves in several old houses, using one as a chapel; when funds became available, they commissioned a church and cloister from François Mansart. However, of his project for a new Latin-cross church and conventual building, only a few cloistral wings were erected (1632–34).

A suite of plans, sketches, and presentation drawings dating principally from 1710 testifies to three stages in the design process under de Cotte's guidance.[7] His solution was not carried out, and indeed, no major changes to the convent were made until 1767, when Marie-Joseph Peyre initiated rebuilding of the church and parts

143. Plan, first project, Couvent de la Visitation, Paris, 1710 (N III Seine 124, detail).

of the convent (demolished after 1908). Be that as it may, the projects by de Cotte are of great importance as examples of his approach to chapel and portal design.

The Premier Architecte's plans call for completion of the northwest angle of Mansart's cloister and erection of minor wings on the street (the church faces west; fig. 143). Furthermore, they propose construction of quadrant-shaped wings extending from the portal to form a semicircular courtyard in front of a domed church. A masonry wall or an iron grill with a central gate would separate the court from the street. On the opposite side of the church de Cotte provided the layout of a formal garden about eighty *toises* in length and featuring geometrically aligned paths, *parterres*, fountains, and basins.

The dual purpose of the church is expressed in the first project: to provide a modestly scaled nave for the laity and a choir for the nuns, both areas sharing a common domed crossing (fig. 143). Three differentiated spaces occupy the lon-

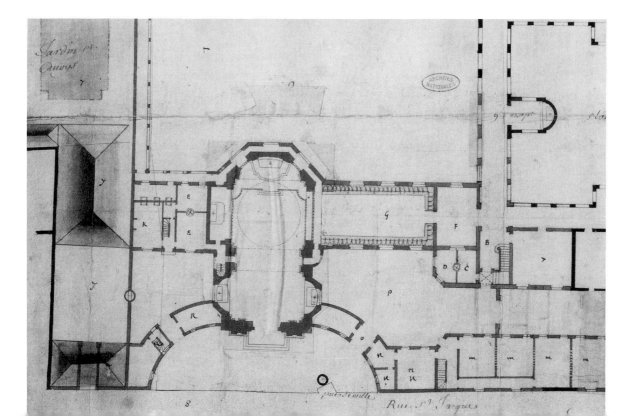

gitudinal axis in succession—the single nave bay, the crossing, and the concave apse. The transverse axis is reserved for the women of the order, who could approach the nuns' choir from the convent by means of a vestibule (marked G, F, respectively). A forged iron grill separates the choir from the crossing. In the plan reproduced here, a corridor running behind the sanctuary allows the nuns access to a communion rail close by the high altar.

Street elevations for the first and second projects are missing, but their appearance may be in-

144. Façade, project, church of the Couvent des Capucines, Paris, 1721–22 (Ha 18, 2612).

ferred from the corresponding plans. Those for the first project show closely paired pilasters framing a central door, a configuration that brings to mind François Mansart's single-bay portal of the church of the Couvent de la Visitation in the rue Saint-Antoine in the Marais (1632–34).[8] The path of influence is a logical one, since Mansart's building, belonging to the same order of Filles de Sainte-Marie de la Visitation, had become an approved model of Visitandine design. De Cotte's elevation probably resembled his similar, later elevation for the portal of the Couvent des Capucines, Paris, in which paired pilasters support a semicircular break in the entablature (1721–22; fig. 144). The concept of curved walls framing a central portal recalls such French Baroque prototypes as Le Vau's Collège des Quatre Nations, Paris (begun 1662), and the projected colonnade for the Place du Dôme des Invalides, Paris (1690s; fig. 78).

For the second and third projects de Cotte expunged the truncated nave to allow a deeper semicircular forecourt (fig. 145). He based the church on the central-plan theme of an octagon supporting a circular dome about six and one-half *toises* in diameter. The combination of rotunda and semicircular walls abutting the portal is a standard theme in religious architecture known to de Cotte from three monuments that he had studied in Rome: the sixth-century church of SS. Cosma e Damiano in the Forum Romanum; Borromini's S. Agnese in Piazza Navona; and Bernini's S. Andrea al Quirinale (see chap. 2). However, the primary source for de Cotte's centralized Visitation plan is François Mansart's central-plan church of the Visitation in the rue Saint-Antoine.[9] There are important differences, nonetheless: whereas in Mansart's building the chapels are in satellite areas, in de Cotte's design the spaces inhabited by the principal altars, as well as those containing the secondary altars in the four beveled piers, are

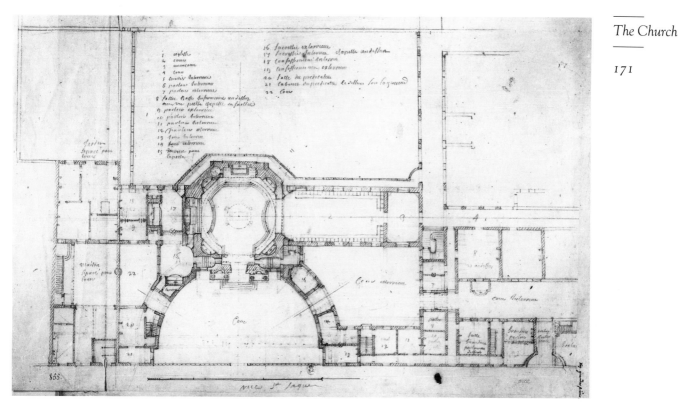

145. Plan, second project, Couvent de la Visitation, 1710, with legend in de Cotte's hand (Va 258d, 855).

continuous with the space of the rotunda (see de Cotte's domed centralizing schemes for palace chapels in his projects for the Buen Retiro, Madrid, 1715, and Schloss Schleissheim, c. 1714–15; figs. 27, 31, 35, 37).

Turning to a consideration of exterior elevations, we find that in the plan for the second Visitation project paired freestanding columns, spaced at an interval, are located in front of the wall (fig. 145). Such an arrangement implies an elevation incorporating two stories of superimposed columns that support a crowning pediment—similar to the portal of Notre-Dame de Versailles (fig. 8).

The church front of the definitive third project is loosely based on the façade of the most conspicuous central-plan church in Paris, the Dôme des Invalides (figs. 146, 6). The elevation now comprises two full stories, with paired en-

gaged columns rising through a broken entablature to make up the central aedicule and single pilasters framing the outer boundary of the adjacent bays.[10] The terminal bays of the lower story lack the order altogether, in a manner similar to the Invalides church. The third project may also reflect the influence of Boffrand's exterior elevation of the Eglise de la Merci, Paris, itself a flattened and narrowed version of the Dôme façade, which features a similar gradation from planar lateral bays to high-relief elements in the center (1709).[11]

Like the front of the Dôme des Invalides and certain Roman portals, such as Carlo Maderno's S. Susanna (1593–1603), de Cotte's Visitation façade was intended to be the focal point of a larger scheme.[12] The lateral conventual walls curving to left and right bear a system of quoins and stringcourses that corresponds to the articu-

146. Elevation, church portal and conventual wings, third project, Couvent de la Visitation, 1715 (Va 258d, 856).

lation of the lower level of the church and is linked to the upper story through elegantly scrolled volutes and the tapering outline of the roofs (fig. 146). The strong vertical lines of the order achieve climactic resolution not in an exposed dome, as at the Invalides, but in a large lantern.

One of a pair of extant cross sections reveals that this lantern was to be the major source of light for the interior (fig. 147). The section also shows the typically French timberwork of the mansard roof, and the spare use of ornamental detailing within—barely a few cherubs' heads. A sketch for a cross section of the nuns' choir indicates that this equally austere space would be brightly illuminated by great roundheaded windows. It is evident that on the interior wall sur-

faces the architect wished to maintain the proportional relationships established for the façade, such as the relative height of the order and moldings (compare in this regard de Cotte's section of Palladio's Redentore, Venice; fig. 19). Continuity between major and minor parts and between exterior and interior is thus the chief principle governing the overall conception.

Saint-Etienne, Dijon, and Notre-Dame de Bonne-Nouvelle, Orléans

The Premier Architecte turned to the more purely Italianate format of the two-story basilican façade in unexecuted projects for Saint-Etienne, Dijon, where only the portal was lacking (c. 1718; fig. 148),[13] and Notre-Dame de Bonne-Nouvelle, Orléans, where a new church

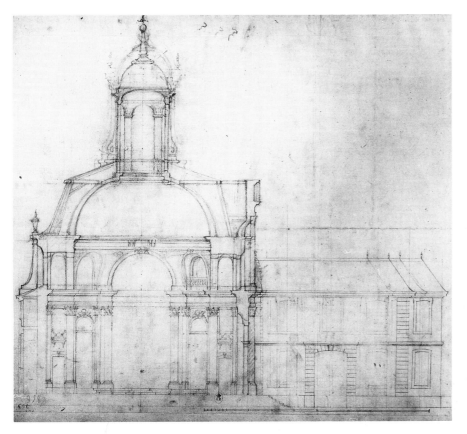

147. Longitudinal section of the church and elevation of the conventual wing, third project, Couvent de la Visitation (Va 258d, 858).

148. (*Left, below*) Façade, project, Saint-Etienne, Dijon, 1718 (Va 21, t. 4, 267).

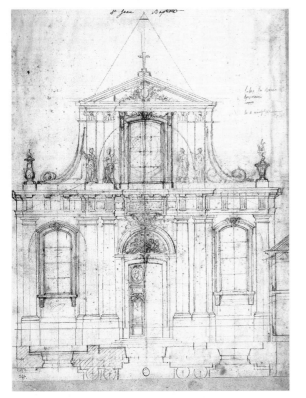

was to be built (1724–25; figs. 149–50).[14] In both cases the task of designing a small-scale façade with a single entrance resulted in a solution consisting of flat, neutral planes divided into regular bays by an aedicule of superimposed orders applied to the surface and bearing a pediment. In each, the languidly unfurled volutes are of a character very different from the tautly coiled volutes for the Visitation (fig. 146). In this way the elevations resemble certain sixteenth-century Italian façades, such as that of the Basilica of Loreto (Giovanni Boccalini, Giovanni Battista Ghioldi, and Lattanzio Ventura, 1571–87), which de Cotte drew while in Italy,[15] as well as seventeenth-century French portals of a restrained, academic cast—for example, Jacques Lemercier's west entrance to the church of the Sorbonne, Paris (begun 1626). Unlike the Italian examples, de Cotte's compositions incorporate a

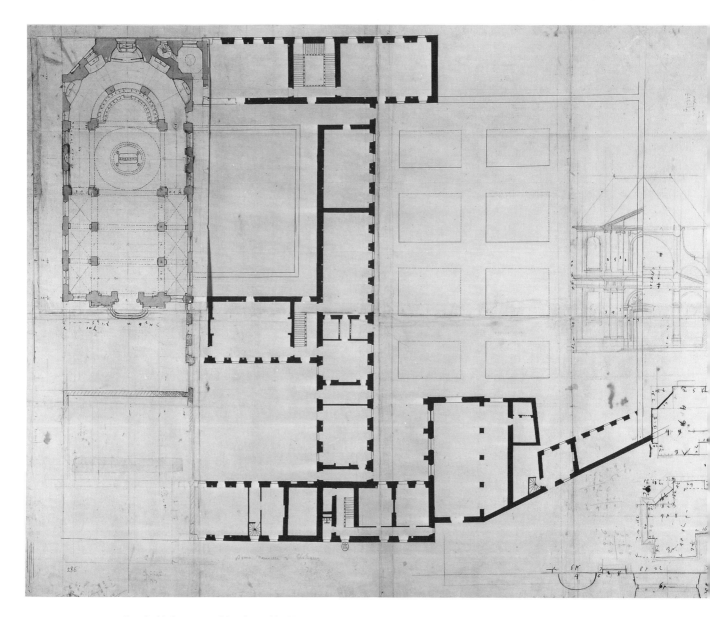

149. Plan, half elevation of façade and half interior section, project, with existing house for the order, Notre-Dame de Bonne-Nouvelle, Orléans, 1724 (Va 432, 286).

gabled roofline, following French tradition.

In the design for Saint-Etienne, the reduced height of the upper floor, where dwarf pilasters support an abbreviated entablature, produces an unorthodox if not ungainly effect, which he hoped to mitigate by placing four freestanding figures of saints in front of the second-story order (fig. 148). In the accompanying memorandum, in which he approved two of the designs sent from Dijon for his opinion, de Cotte attempted a point-by-point justification of his own composition on the basis of the restrictions at hand. These included the shape of the wall to be covered, the presence of the church *trésorerie* bordering the portal on the right, and budgetary limitations. Even so, his project was rejected, and the

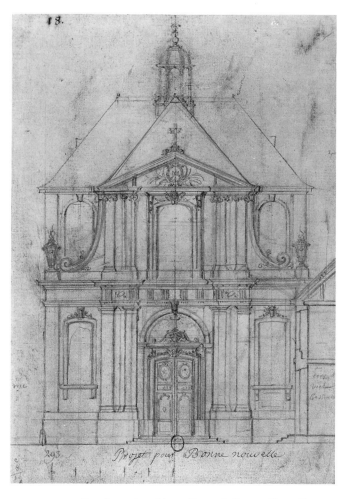

150. Façade, project, Notre-Dame de Bonne-Nouvelle
(Va 408, t. 1, 293).

commission went to Martin de Noinville, whose central bay rises a full second story, with engaged columns on both levels.

The commission for the Benedictine church of Notre-Dame de Bonne-Nouvelle was originally in the hands of Hénault, the architect with whom de Cotte had worked in 1708–9 on the proposals for the façade of Sainte-Croix d'Orléans. On 19 May 1718, Hénault wrote to the Premier Architecte to request an appraisal of a project for a new church of Notre-Dame de Bonne-Nouvelle to replace a former chapel on the restricted site bordered by the rue de Bour-

gogne; the plans awkwardly combine Gothic and classical styles. Subsequent documents date to 1724, by which time de Cotte had full responsibility for the work. Three phases in the design process are implied by the correspondence, but extant drawings show a single solution with minor variations in the configuration of apsidal chapels. De Cotte retained for the most part the old conventual buildings and garden, while proposing a modern church entirely classical in style (fig. 149). The plan shows a nave and side aisles extending three bays toward a domical crossing, in which a double-faced high altar accommodates both the lay community in the nave and monks in the choir stalls (compare the smaller three-bay nave with apse proposed by de Cotte for the palace chapel of the Würzburg Residenz, 1723, and a similar chapel for Schloss Poppelsdorf, 1715; figs. 45, 54).

Both the small sketch of the portal on the right-hand side of the plan and a more detailed elevation show a façade three bays wide (figs. 149–50). The major limitation was the width of the site, bounded on the right-hand side by the house of the order. De Cotte superimposed a variation of the Dijon composition on this format, reusing many of the same idiosyncratic elements. The central bay acquires prominence through the presence of fully articulated pilasters and a Doric frieze, while the lateral bays feature simple vertical strips and less decorated entablatures. Thus de Cotte's approach to façade design for Dijon and Orléans was similar in a significant way to that for the Visitation: whereas Roman Baroque architects had regularly treated church façades as autonomous units, his portals are more closely related, in dimensions and design, to the body of the church behind them.

Saint-Louis de Versailles

De Cotte's most challenging ecclesiastical project came in the early 1720s with the design

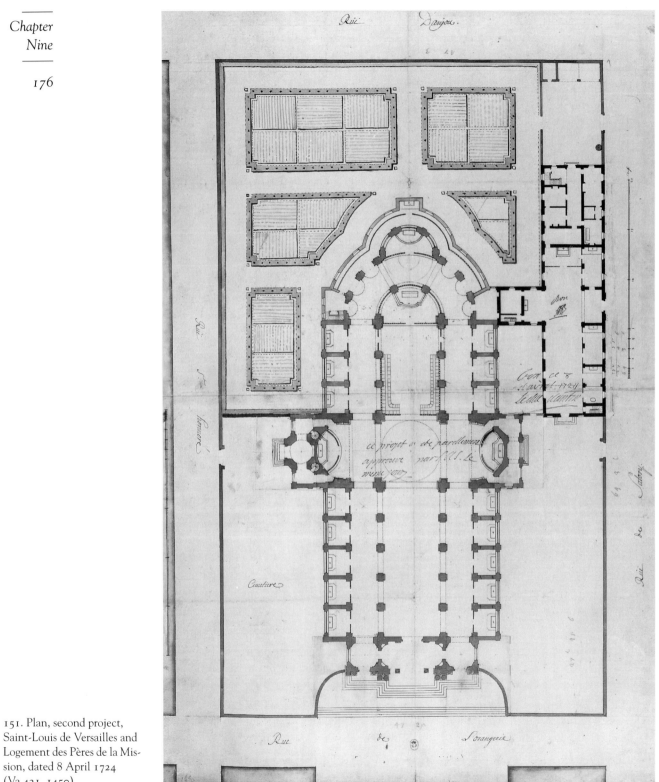

151. Plan, second project,
Saint-Louis de Versailles and
Logement des Pères de la Mis-
sion, dated 8 April 1724
(Va 421, 1450).

of Saint-Louis de Versailles, the single instance in his oeuvre of a commission for a longitudinal basilica. The rapid growth in the early eighteenth century of the Parc-aux-Cerfs, a new district in the southern quarter of the town of Versailles, produced an urgent need for a parish church to serve the local populace (fig. 4, bottom left).[16] When Louis XV attained his majority in 1722 and the court returned to Versailles, the Crown determined to sponsor a foundation dedicated to Saint-Louis, the French royal saint and ancestor of the Bourbon dynasty.

The design and construction of Saint-Louis developed in two phases. During the first phase, from 1724 to about 1730, de Cotte drew up plans for a pair of structures lying adjacent to each other: a house for the Lazarist priests, called the Logement des Pères de la Mission, which was built immediately (1724–27); and a large Latin-cross basilica to be erected when funding was available (fig. 151, right and center, respectively).[17] As a temporary measure until the basilica was constructed, religious services for parishioners took place in the Chapelle Provisoire de Saint-Louis located in the Logement des Pères (the high altar is visible in the plan, fig. 151). At first Saint-Louis was a succursal of Notre-Dame de Versailles, the parish church of the northern Ville Neuve; independent parish status was granted in 1730.[18]

During the second phase in the development of Saint-Louis, 1742–54, construction was carried out on the basilica itself.[19] The definitive plans were the work of Jacques Hardouin-Mansart de Sagonne, who used de Cotte's projects as a point of departure. Our concern is with the first phase of activity, evidence for which consists of a series of drawings from the de Cotte studio.[20] We begin with the Logement des Pères. Extant drawings of this building are of particular importance, since the house was razed in 1760 to provide space for the present bishop's palace.[21]

The Logement may be studied in the plan approved and dated 8 April 1724 by Louis-Henri de Bourbon, premier ministre, and the duc d'Antin (fig. 151).[22] The Logement stands on the southwest corner of the site near the ambulatory of the basilica, to which it was eventually attached (the church portal faces north). Modest living quarters for the religious community are situated in the south part of the Logement and on the upper stories. The plan of the Chapelle Provisoire de Saint-Louis derives from the figure of a Latin cross, with the main altar at the end of the longitudinal axis.

The single remaining exterior elevation of the Logement des Pères is in the drafting style associated with de Cotte's *atelier*—drawn almost entirely freehand with a brush, boldly shaded to give a striking impression of depth, and sparingly colored with tinted washes; it does not match the existing ground plans in all details (fig. 152).[23] The façade on the rue de Satory is conceived as a symmetrical composition of extreme sobriety. The arched shape of the central doorway, which gives onto the right transept of the chapel, reappears in the arched gateways leading alternately to the enclosed churchyard on the left and the service court on the right.

A plan and an elevation of the sanctuary of the Chapelle Provisoire bear notations of dimensions in de Cotte's handwriting (fig. 153). The altarpiece is bordered by paneled pilasters and crowned by a segmental arch echoing the motif employed in the street elevation. The frame for the painting features a broad semicircular arch at the top and joined volutes below, elements frequently employed in designs for interior paneling produced under de Cotte's supervision.[24]

Turning to extant plans and elevations for the basilica of Saint-Louis, we find that de Cotte's goal was to create a magnificent church whose design would mirror Hardouin-Mansart's Notre-Dame de Versailles, the chief architectural mon-

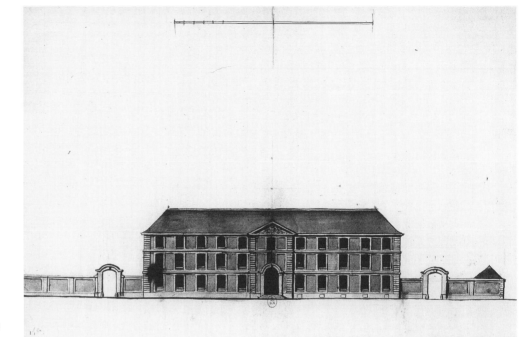

152. Street elevation, Logement des Pères de la Mission,
Versailles, 1724 (Va 78h, t. 3,
1457 recto).

ument in the Ville Neuve (1684–86; fig. 4, bottom right; figs. 8, 154).[25] Although not simultaneously visible, both churches face toward the
major east-west axis of the town, the avenue de
Paris. Ever mindful of *bienséance*, de Cotte respected the dual function of Saint-Louis: as a
royal commission it required a degree of grandeur
worthy of the king; as a parish church it needed
various spaces for the rituals performed daily by
the clergy and local inhabitants. Close inspection of the surviving plans, and particularly of
transitional drawings and pasted-on corrections,
reveals a series of three alternative solutions conceived sequentially, of which the second received
official approval in April 1724.

In laying out the first project (fig. 155),
de Cotte rejected the Italianate basilican plan
exemplified above all by the church of Il Gesù,
Rome (Vignola and Giacomo della Porta, 1568–
73), with its broad nave and attendant side chap-

153. Plan and elevation, Chapelle Provisoire de Saint-
Louis, 1724 (Va 78h, t. 2, 1456).

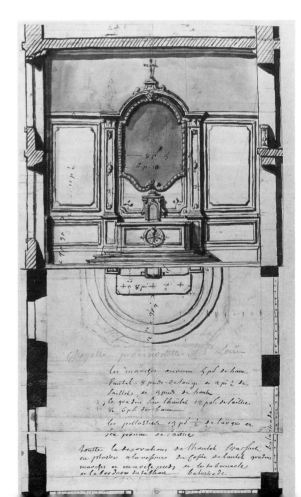

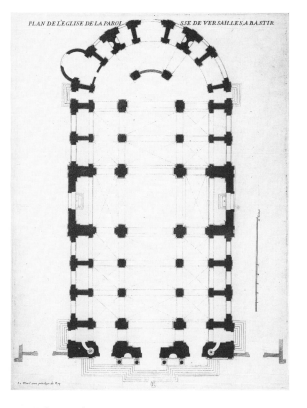

PLAN DE L'EGLISE DE LA PAROI.....SSE DE VERSAILLES A BASTIR

154. Jules Hardouin-Mansart, plan, Notre-Dame de Versailles, 1684–86 (print by Le Blond, Va 421).

155. (*Right*) Plan, first project, Saint-Louis de Versailles, 1724 (Va 421, 1453).

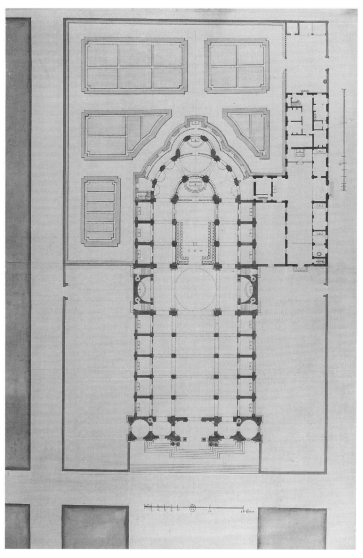

els, which had been adopted in France by François Mansart and others during the seventeenth century.[26] Instead, like Hardouin-Mansart (fig. 154), de Cotte chose a more traditional, essentially medieval floor plan, similar to that of the great French Gothic churches, such as Notre-Dame de Paris (begun 1163). In both de Cotte's first project for Saint-Louis and Hardouin-Mansart's plan of Notre-Dame de Versailles, aisles line the nave and an ambulatory encircles the sanctuary, thus allowing ease of movement through and around the interior. The profusion of chapels bordering the considerable length of each plan provides a large number of altars to facilitate the offering of Mass and other devotions. The location of the crossing midway down both plans ensures a large choir area for communal prayer and chanting the Divine Office. Finally, the arrangement of the choir stalls (not shown in fig. 154)[27] just beyond the crossing and the disposition of the transepts, aligned with the side chapels, are comparable in both plans.

In his first project de Cotte also borrowed from another design by Hardouin-Mansart. The interpenetration of spaces around the oval Chapelle de la Vierge, which overlaps the ambulatory at the end of the main axis, is based on Hardouin-

Mansart's composition of intersecting circular and oval spaces in the domed Chapelle de la Vierge at the sanctuary end of Saint-Roch, Paris (1706–10; fig. 156).[28] Like the plan of Saint-Roch, the Saint-Louis proposal requires the placement of three altars in sequence down the main axis: the high altar in the choir, followed by altars in the Chapelle de la Vierge and the Chapelle de la Communion at the far end.

De Cotte conceived the façade of Saint-Louis as a focal point within the urban complex, dominating an open square. No elevation is extant for the first project, but the plan suggests that the Premier Architecte initially devised a portal similar to Hardouin-Mansart's façade for Notre-Dame de Versailles (figs. 155, 8). The paired col-

156. Plan, Saint-Roch, Paris, portion in black showing Jules Hardouin-Mansart's plan to complete the structure, 1706–10, and façade and bell tower in red by de Cotte, c. 1728 (Va 441, 2567 with flap).

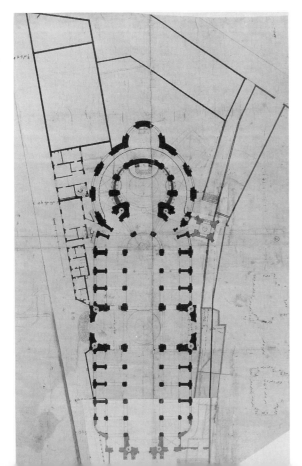

umns visible in de Cotte's plan on either side of the entrance were probably intended to support superimposed columns that in turn carried a pediment, the whole arrangement thus forming an aedicule. In the same plan, pilasters bracket the end bays of the façade, which presumably were intended to support towers. De Cotte altered Mansart's conception in one respect. Instead of closing the portal by means of a door on the central axis, he opened the vestibule to the street. Although rarely used in French churches, the open vestibule was a device commonly employed in French domestic architecture, since it allowed a visitor to alight directly from a carriage into a sheltered space during inclement weather (see the Hôtel de Torcy, Paris, and Palais Rohan, Strasbourg, figs. 97, 100, 171, 174).

On a duplicate plan of the first project, de Cotte made important revisions to the façade and transept areas by pasting over them newly drawn swatches of paper, thus producing the second of his three projects for Saint-Louis (fig. 151).[29] The chief modification of the interior space consists of the extension of rectilinear transepts from the body of the church. The larger transepts allow prominent entrance vestibules, while retaining the concave disposition of the altar walls. The significant change incorporated in the façade of the second project is the elimination of the end bays.

The third project for Saint-Louis developed out of the second scheme.[30] In the definitive solution, the exterior contour of the ambulatory wall is simpler in outline, both transept walls are curvilinear in plan, and the chapels lining the nave are more shallow (fig. 157). From a liturgical point of view, the most important new feature is the exchange of elements in the choir. The choir stalls are now situated along the inner periphery of the ambulatory, while the high altar has moved to the crossing, where it is freestanding and double-faced, like the one proposed for

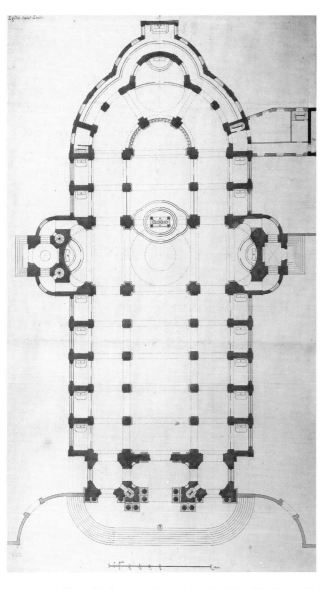

157. Plan, third project, Saint-Louis de Versailles (Va 448f, 1454).

Notre-Dame de Bonne-Nouvelle, Orléans—one altar toward the nave and the other toward the sanctuary. One final change incorporated in the plan is the repositioning of the altars in the side chapels so that they would be visible simultaneously to the spectator upon entering the church.

An elevation of the façade and sections of the interior and the vestibule in the fluid style associated with de Cotte have survived (fig. 158). On the lower story of the portal, engaged columns bracket the side doors, while in the center the paired columns of the aedicule are repeated in paired columns located perpendicular to the wall on either side of the entrance (visible in the section and on the plan, fig. 157). The result is a total of twelve columns ranged across the lower story, eight of which are echoed by columns and pilasters on the upper level, where four sculpted figures front the pilasters in a manner earlier used for Saint-Etienne, Dijon (fig. 148). The side doors are placed in concave niches that enhance the curvilinear theme of the design, and the façade is terminated by pilasters intended to have the effect of solid piers when viewed diagonally. Low concave walls, present only in the plans, mark the transition from the façade to the street. Unlike de Cotte's previous façade designs, the wall is no longer a neutral surface to which the order is applied, but a mass whose depth is revealed by layered ranks of rounded columns, cubic sections of entablature, and scooped-out niches—all carved as if by the hand of a sculptor.

The flourish of columnar accents on the exterior recalls the façade of Hardouin-Mansart's Dôme des Invalides (fig. 6). In addition, the façade for the third project clearly shows the influence of Roman Baroque portals, particularly the façade of SS. Vincenzo ed Anastasio, which is comparable in its massing of freestanding columns (Martino Longhi the Younger, 1646–50; fig. 21).[31] De Cotte drew the plan of this church during his Italian sojourn, noting that Cardinal Mazarin had commissioned the work. Even so, in the design for Saint-Louis he avoided typically Italian Baroque details, such as encased pediments or the crowded overlapping of elements.

Since the third project is the most fully developed design in the series, we may ask why it was not the one that received official approval. The answer appears to be that it was produced some

158. Cross section of the nave, façade elevation, and longitudinal section of the narthex, third project, Saint-Louis de Versailles (photographic montage of Va 448f, 1447 verso).

time after the initial period of activity in April 1724. Since the plan of the Logement des Pères is included in only two of the five plans for the third project, and the layout is that as built, it is reasonable to assume that the Logement was either under construction or already completed by then. Even so, we cannot be certain of when the third project was conceived—whether in 1724, soon after the granting of official approval for construction; in 1727, when the Logement was in use; or as late as 1730, when the problem of accommodating lay worshippers was more pressing, and efforts were undertaken to elevate the succursal chapel to independent parish sta-

tus. It was not unusual for architects in the Bâtiments to revise an approved design at a later date. In any case, the third project represents de Cotte's final solution, prompted as much by liturgical as by aesthetic needs.

Several years ago Pierre Moisy intuited that the similarities shared by Mansart de Sagonne's final design for Saint-Louis de Versailles (constructed in 1742–54) and Jacques V Gabriel's plan for the Cathedral of La Rochelle (1741; also dedicated to Saint-Louis) were due to the use of a common model.[32] We are now in a position to see that this model was de Cotte's series of designs for Saint-Louis de Versailles. Mansart de Sagonne drew heavily from de Cotte's first and second projects in producing the definitive ground plan of the Versailles basilica,[33] while Gabriel, as Architecte Ordinaire, would have been familiar with these projects in the 1720s. Thus, although de Cotte's proposals were themselves never realized, they had a measurable impact on designs for later basilican churches.

Eglise des Capucines and Chapelle de la Charité, Paris

De Cotte also participated in the remodeling of two smaller Parisian façades, that of the church of the Couvent des Capucines (1721–22), formerly on the present rue de la Paix facing the north entrance to the Place Vendôme, and the façade of the chapel of the Hôpital de la Charité on the rue des Saints-Pères (1732; much altered in 1798). The design of the Capucine portal was limited by the necessity of following the basic arched motif and overall dimensions of the original front erected by François d'Orbay in 1688, which had fallen into disrepair.[34] The new

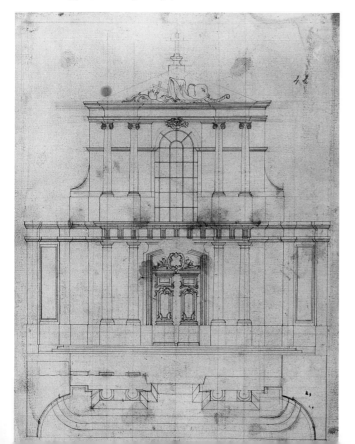

159. Façade, chapel of the Hôpital de la Charité, Paris, 1732 (MS 1604, no. 42).

façade made greater use of both the classical orders and decorative sculpture. The principal designer may have been the sculptor Sébastien-Antoine Slodtz, who probably submitted his designs to the Premier Architecte for criticism. The latter evidently responded with a corrected version of his own—a fine graphite and wash drawing of a single-bay façade of the arched type presumably employed for his first Visitation project (fig. 144).[35] Both designs ultimately owe a debt to François Mansart's portal for the Visitandine Convent on the rue Saint-Antoine. De Cotte's drawing possesses a more even balance between architecture and sculpture and more satisfactory proportions than the façade that was actually built.

The portal of the Charité is generally attributed to de Cotte, although the eighteenth-century sources also mention Nicolas Pineau and an obscure figure, Cholot, again implying a collaboration.[36] The possibility of the Premier Architecte's involvement is confirmed by a drawing in the de Cotte albums at the Bibliothèque de l'Institut, Paris (fig. 159).[37] Many of the details are related to motifs found in de Cotte's earlier portal designs: the standard two-story aedicule applied to a composition that broadens in the lower level; the Doric frieze restricted to the central bay; vestigial volutes; and pilasterlike strips located on the concave extremities (compare figs. 146, 148, 150). However, the elements have not been welded into a cohesive whole.[38]

Saint-Roch, Paris

With the façade of Saint-Roch in Paris, erected 1736–38, de Cotte created an arresting visual image that heralds the church to the passerby and enriches the rue Saint-Honoré with its magnificence (fig. 160). The commission called for completion of one of the city's major basilicas, which had been under construction for over three-quarters of a century.[39] As early as 1706,

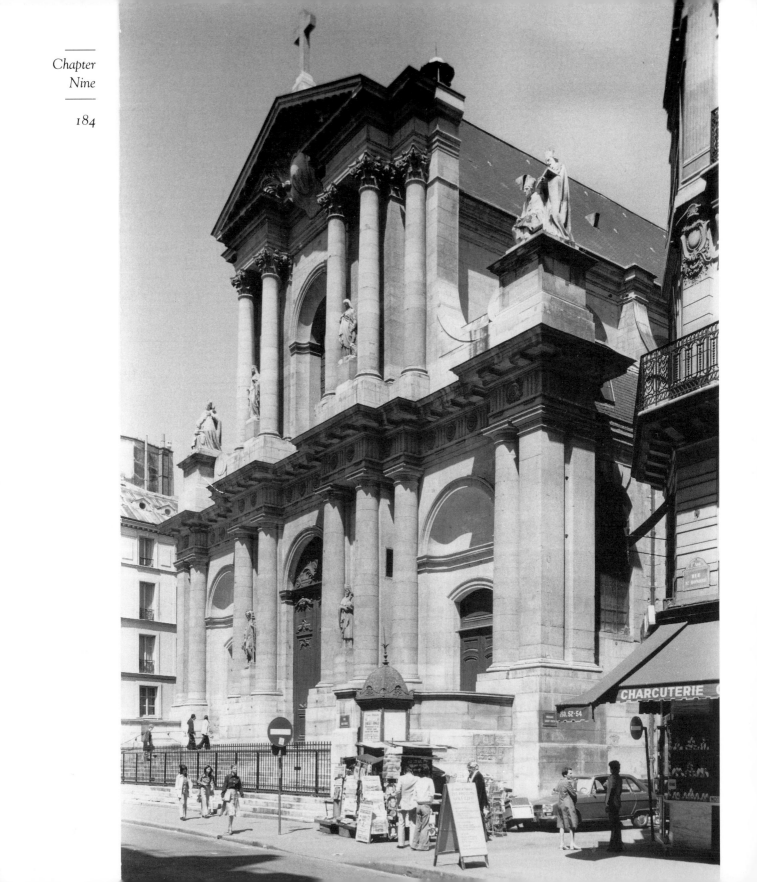

during a period of rapid expansion in the quartier Saint-Honoré, Hardouin-Mansart had pressed ahead with new plans for the church (fig. 156). His projected two-towered façade, based on his own front for Notre-Dame de Versailles, was not carried out.[40] Later, between 1722 and 1726, Bullet de Chamblain submitted a pair of proposals for a façade of the two-story rectangular type, related compositionally to Hardouin-Mansart's Primatiale, Nancy (1706).[41] De Cotte's involvement at Saint-Roch dates at least from 1723, when he was active in the decoration of the nave interior.[42] Most likely around 1728 he attached

to Hardouin-Mansart's plan of 1706 his first proposal for the façade and a plan for a bell tower (the tower was built in 1728–36 on the right-hand flank of the church along the sanctuary; figs. 156, 161).[43] The Premier Architecte did not live to see the façade erected (d. 1735). His son Jules-Robert commenced construction in 1736.[44]

The development of the façade project may be inferred from two plans and three elevations, including a pair of superb tonal wash drawings highlighted with flashes of color, and incorporating *pentimenti* in the form of bits of paper pasted down and redrawn (figs. 162–63).[45] While retaining Bullet de Chamblain's concept of reduced breadth—the wider bulk of the nave chapels and transepts is visible in the elevations—de Cotte developed the first elevation along the lines of the Roman basilican type. The close similarity between the Saint-Roch elevations and that for the third project of Saint-Louis de Versailles (fig. 158) suggests the possibility of influences between the two commissions. As we have seen, the third project may postdate 1724, while the Saint-Roch drawings could predate 1728, but without more precise information we cannot be certain of their relationship.

In the central bay of the first elevation for Saint-Roch the large apertures of entryway and window, together with the relief sculpture covering the remaining surfaces, have the effect of nullifying the architectonic value of the recessed plane, giving dominance to the projecting aedicule of paired freestanding columns (fig. 162). The muscular quality of the latter contrasts effectively with the flatness of the pilasters bordering the aedicule on both stories. In the lower side bays shadowed pilasters alternate with full pilasters pulled inward from the edges of the façade. As in the Saint-Louis drawings, shallow niches in the side bays enhance the play of expanding and receding surfaces.

In the second elevation for Saint-Roch, de

160. (*Opposite*) Façade, Saint-Roch, Paris, constructed 1736–38.

161. Cross section of the nave and project for the bell tower, Saint-Roch, with notes on other Parisian church towers, 1728 (Va 233, 2568).

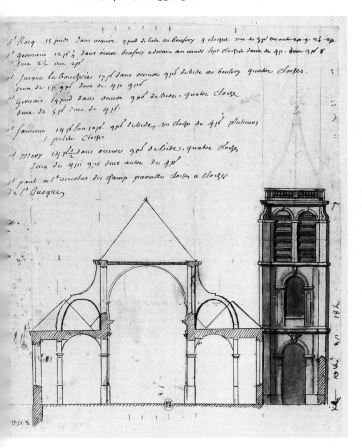

162. Façade, first elevation,
Saint-Roch (Va 441, 2569).

163. Façade, second elevation, Saint-Roch (Va 441,
2570).

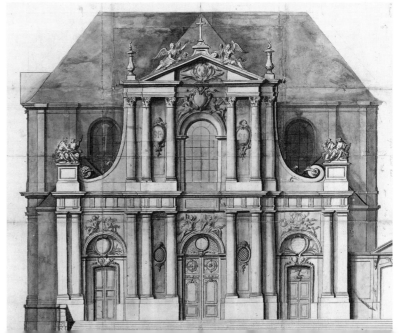

164. Façade, Jacques Hardouin-Mansart de Sagonne, Saint-Louis de Versailles, 1742–54.

tect's goal: the Doric order is an extension of that lining the nave walls; the lateral doors open directly onto the axes of the side aisles.

In a lengthy analysis Jacques-François Blondel objected to many details of the finished portal, blaming Jules-Robert for spoiling the original conception during construction (fig. 160).[46] However, the criticisms reflect a more conservative approach to classical architecture at midcentury. In fact, the son was largely faithful to his father's design, the only change being a reduction in the quantity of relief sculpture, resulting in a loss of the pictorial vitality characterizing the drawn elevations.

It may be said in sum that even though the two-story composition with columns massed at the center is ultimately related to the Roman Baroque tradition (compare SS. Vincenzo ed Anastasio; fig. 21), Renaissance classical models are recalled by the conscious equality of the bays along the lower story, as well as the general style of the sloping volutes and the depressed central bay (e.g., the façade of the Basilica of Loreto). Even so, the portal belongs principally to the French tradition: Hardouin-Mansart's influence is unmistakable, and the combination of robustness and restraint is a characteristic that distinguishes many early portals, such as the archetypal church façade, Salomon de Brosse's Saint-Gervais, Paris (1616).

Although Saint-Roch provided the model for a few subsequent portals, these generally fail to exhibit the boldness of the original. Frère Claude's façade of Saint-Thomas d'Aquin, Paris, for example, consists of frail columns pressed evenly against the neutral plane of the wall (1765–69).[47] The single dramatic restatement is Mansart de Sagonne's façade of Saint-Louis de Versailles, which follows the example of Saint-Roch rather than de Cotte's Saint-Louis projects (fig. 164). The disposition of the order and the breaking of the entablature imitate de Cotte's

Cotte increased the overall plasticity by substituting columns for most of the pilasters, and he widened the spacing between the paired columns of the aedicule to create minor bays enclosing relief sculpture (fig. 163). A motif shared with the Saint-Louis elevation is the pairing of column and pilaster at the extremities of the lower story, so that the transition from curved to flat shapes signals a strong visual termination at the ends of the façade, especially when viewed from an angle. Indeed, de Cotte had the pedestrian in mind, since the narrow street, lacking an open square, imposes a diagonal view of the portal, in which its depth is revealed fully. A flight of steps bridges the difference in height between the street and the butte Saint-Roch. The use of a rich Corinthian order over Roman Doric follows the organization of the orders at the Dôme des Invalides (fig. 6), but the stepping back of the upper entablature below the pediment negates the subtle association with the classical temple front favored by Hardouin-Mansart, and stresses instead the powerful verticals of the aedicule. Continuity with the interior is once again the archi-

system closely. Some differences are evident in the Versailles front—for example, the closer pairing of the columns of the aedicule and the substitution of columns for corner pilasters. The effect is one of splendid redundancy, with the verticals creating a dominant upward force. In a deliberate reference to Notre-Dame de Versailles (fig. 8), the composition was broadened to incorporate two towers set back from the inner-most plane of the façade. The exposed outer surfaces of the basilica undulate gently in fluid curves—all, that is, except the planar surface of the aedicular front, which Mansart de Sagonne failed to bring into rapport with the rest of the exterior. The comparison serves to demonstrate de Cotte's greater artistic powers as a result of his long experience in designing ecclesiastical façades.

Chapter Ten

The Bishop's Palace

ROBERT DE COTTE produced designs for three bishop's palaces in eastern France, the *palais épiscopaux* of Châlons-sur-Marne, Verdun, and Strasbourg.[1] All were intended to replace old-fashioned, dilapidated structures; two were built. The high status of the patrons is evident from the fact that the Premier Architecte, prior to drawing up plans, inspected the sites personally.

French bishops inevitably came from aristocratic families and enjoyed privileged associations with the royal house. As *grands seigneurs*, they ruled vast territories, had large personal retinues, and were often the chief representatives of both Church and Crown in the provincial towns. Because a bishop's lifestyle was so similar to that of the high nobility, the building type of the *palais épiscopal* (or *évêché*) generally took the form of a large *hôtel particulier* located close by a cathedral and incorporating large ceremonial rooms and administrative offices for the diocese. According to Jacques-François Blondel, a typical bishop's palace required "grand *appartements de parade*, several private apartments, a chapel, a library, an ecclesiastical courtroom, secretaries' offices, an archive, and, lastly, lodgings for vicar-generals, chaplains, secretaries, and other officers in the personal service of the bishop."[2] Furthermore, an *évêché* included accommodations for important guests, above all the king. Blondel stated, "The decoration of *palais épiscopaux* must be akin to that of the dwellings of crowned heads;... the extent of their sumptuousness must accord with the rank of the prelates building them."[3] These circumstances explain why de Cotte, in designing such structures, enhanced the plan and elevations of the standard *hôtel* through the addition of rooms and architectural motifs specifically palatial in character.

Theoretically, it was expected that bishops would shun the display of luxury. However, the revenues attached to ecclesiastical offices supported a way of life that allowed an urban *évêché* adjacent to the cathedral, a château in the country, and a house in Paris. Outraged by the worldly ambitions of bishops in the late seventeenth century, Fénelon, archbishop of Cambrai, was prompted to remark:

> The passion for architecture is as addictive as gambling; a house becomes a sort of mistress. In truth, the clergy charged with the care of so many souls should not have time to embellish their houses. Who will check this building craze, so extravagant in this century, if the good bishops themselves approve of this scandalous behavior?[4]

A final measure of the princely status of this particular building type during the ancien régime may be gauged from a newspaper report of 1792 that concerns de Cotte's *évêché* at Verdun. During the upheaval of the French Revolution, when the ransacking of châteaux and churches served to obliterate the authority of the monarchy and the Church, a law decreed the destruction of coats of arms on bishop's palaces. The report stated, "The people clamor for the elimination of the heraldic devices decorating the house at Verdun occupied by the bishop of the province, and of its pompous name of *palais épiscopal*."[5]

Palais Episcopal, Châlons-sur-Marne

As the agent of the Crown in the province of Champagne, the bishop of Châlons-sur-Marne traditionally enjoyed special privileges in the *pays châlonnais*: civic, ecclesiastical, and military authority were united in his person. Since Châlons was on the main route between Paris and eastern France, the French kings often lodged in the *chambre du roi* of the fifteenth-century Palais Episcopal.[6] Louis XIV made a number of trips to the city as guest of the bishop, and important royal marriages took place there—notably those of Philippe d'Orléans (1671) and the Grand Dauphin (1680).

The severe winter of 1709 caused considerable damage to the old *évêché*, which had already shown such signs of age that the bishops preferred to reside nearby in the Château de Sarry. By April 1719, Bishop Jean-Baptiste-Louis-Gaston de Noailles (1669–1720) secured financial assistance from the regent of France for rebuilding the house; he therefore requested de Cotte's expertise in devising plans.[7] Hailing from a distinguished French family, the patron was the brother of Louis-Antoine de Noailles, archbishop of Paris, for whom de Cotte worked in the same years on the interior remodeling of Notre-Dame de Paris (altar of the Virgin in the south transept, 1718–19).[8]

De Cotte recounted his efforts on behalf of the bishop in this way: "In order to work efficiently, it was necessary for me to go to Châlons several times and to send and oversee the draftsmen who prepared site plans of the old palace, the surrounding areas and houses, the great church of Saint-Etienne, parts of the monks' cloister, por-

tions of the ramparts, the [Porte du] Jaar, the river, and the pitch of the sloping site—everything necessary for the execution of the project": in other words, "two or three portfolios filled with my drawings, reports, specifications, estimates, contracts, plans, sections, and elevations for each project."[9] Only one trip by de Cotte to Châlons is documented (May 1719), but in any case the bishop told him, "You may oversee the progress of the work from your office."[10] The Premier Architecte did provide the customary on-site services of three representatives: Meusnier, Collin, and the better-known René Carlier, who had performed a comparable task with respect to the Alcázar and the Buen Retiro in Madrid.

Demolition of the former chapel and part of the *corps-de-logis* was underway by June 1719, and excavation for the new foundations commenced the following September. However, the bishop's untimely death in September 1720 put an end to the work. What remained of the old *évêché* continued to serve the bishopric for the duration of the ancien régime.[11]

In his projects for a new *palais épiscopal*, de Cotte chose not to utilize the foundations of the old building. He applied the format of the *hôtel-entre-cour-et-jardin* to the irregular-shaped site, which was hemmed in between the western portal of the cathedral and the Main River on the southwest (fig. 165, oriented with north at the bottom). The plan, which evolved through two projects, is comparable to de Cotte's plan for the Hôtel du Lude, Paris (1708–10; fig. 91), in the use of the *appartement simple* (a single file of rooms) in the *corps-de-logis* rather than a double range, on account of the shallow site.[12] Service courts are located to the right of the entry court.

From the main portal on the cathedral square the visitor would step into a concave space bor-

165. (*Opposite*) Plan, *rez-de-chaussée*, second project, second variant, Palais Episcopal, Châlons-sur-Marne, inscribed "dernier plan de 15 janvier 1720" (Va 443, 646).

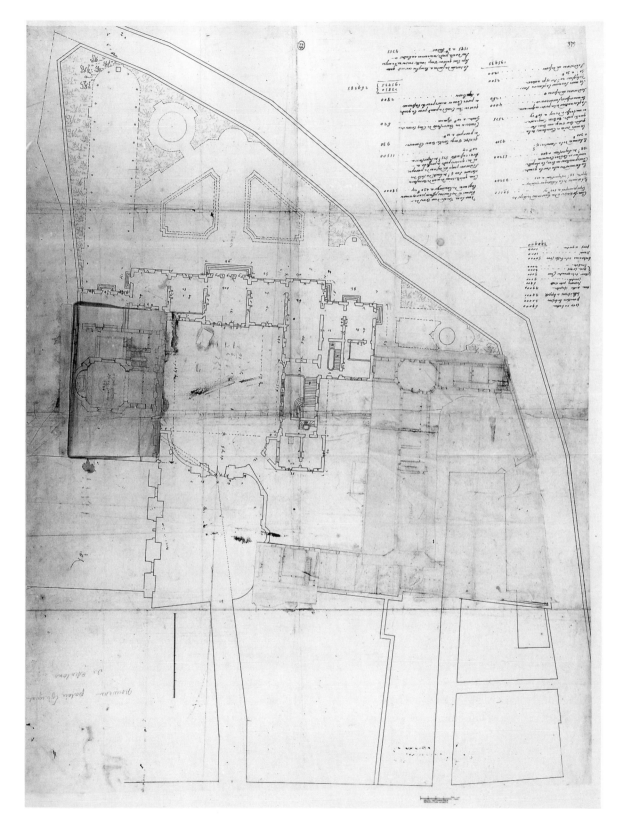

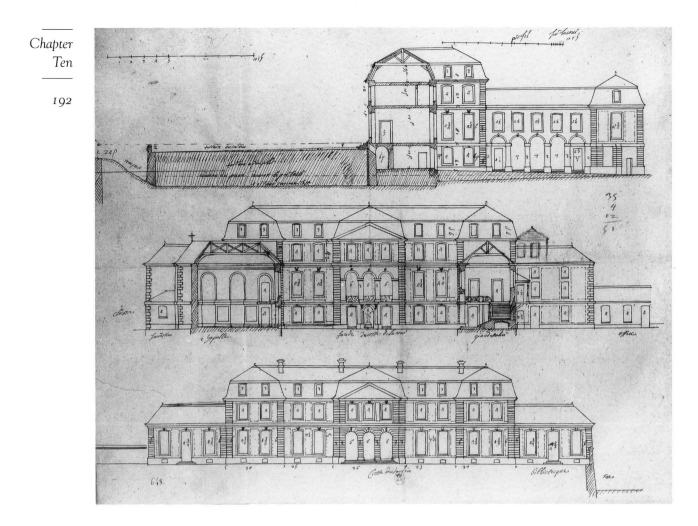

166. Longitudinal section, court elevation, and garden elevation, second project, first variant, Palais Episcopal, Châlons-sur-Marne (Va 51, t. 3, 648).

dering the *cour d'honneur* and proceed to the entrance in the right-hand wing. Here the *grand escalier* would lead to the principal rooms on the *premier étage*, whose layout repeats that of the ground floor. Although the *appartement de parade* occupying the *corps-de-logis* functioned primarily as the bishop's reception area, it would also have housed royal guests, just as the *chambre du roi* in the old *évêché* had done. The order of rooms marked on the plan beyond the stair is as follows: *grande salle*, two *antichambres*, the *chambre*, and a

grand cabinet. The library and chapel are located in the wing on the left side of the courtyard, where a short corridor provides direct access to the cathedral. The bishop's private *appartement de commodité* faces a small garden on the right-hand side of the main block. The remaining rooms constitute offices and lodgings for the bishop's staff and servants.

The court elevation is three stories in height, while that of the garden is two stories, as a result of a garden terrace raised to the level of the retaining wall (fig. 166).[13] The elevations are comparable in their simplicity to those of contemporary *hôtels*: de Cotte's garden elevation of the Hôtel du Maine, Paris, offers many points of similarity (1716; fig. 115). The classical orders do not appear in the Châlons elevations; instead, simple rusticated strips mark the vertical edges of the pavilions. Tall windows headed with curved lintels and bordered by flat linear frames are the chief elements in the composition of the walls.

Palais Episcopal, Verdun

In 1722 de Cotte's assistance was solicited for the planning of a new *palais épiscopal* to be built at Verdun, some forty miles northeast of Châlons-sur-Marne on the western border of Lorraine (fig. 167).[14] On 14 May 1724 he left Paris to visit the site and report on the condition of the late sixteenth-century *évêché*. He summarized his findings as follows:

The extant buildings, being irregular and unsightly, although not entirely in ruins, are worth little on account of their age and poor condition; likewise, almost all of the roofs, scarcely covered with worn tiles, are swept bare with the arrival of strong winds. Instead of making . . . repairs, which

167. Palais Episcopal, Verdun, court façade, design completed May–June 1724, constructed 1724–80.

will never yield a house fit for a bishop, I advise that we keep only the chapel and the principal entry portal, carrying out the restorations indicated in the above report, and that we pull down the remaining structures in order to proceed with construction of a new episcopal residence according to the plans, specifications, and estimates that we have drawn up.[15]

The patron, Charles-François d'Hallencourt (bishop of Verdun, 1723–54), played a major role in the development of the plan during the period of May 1724 to February 1726, requiring continual modifications and dickering over the least detail. For example, on 17 July 1725 he wrote to the Premier Architecte, "Summon your patience to hear a good many disagreeable arguments from me. However, they concern only the arrangement of the interior, for despite the bizarreness of my ideas, I could never imagine it possible to change the drawing that you have made for the overall layout of the house."[16] Although the bishop lived at the Abbaye de la Charité, near Besançon, he had a residence in Paris, allowing frequent consultation with the architect: "There are many little things in this new plan concerning the *distribution* of the interior and even the

design of the exterior, my observations of which I would like to have the honor of conveying to you; but this is a subject for conversation rather than for letters, and it will be easier for me to persuade you when we speak for a quarter of an hour, than by means of a voluminous correspondence."[17]

The documents name three assistants directing work on the site: Delespée (a member of the Delespine family?), an unknown, Guillain, and the most important, Denis Jossenay, who drafted some of the plans. The bishop was irritated by the need to translate for the builders the official language of the specifications: "The workers in this region are so ignorant that they would just as easily understand Hebrew."[18]

Work began late in 1724 on a terrace supporting the structure along the crest of a small bluff. By October 1731 low wings bordering the court were substantially complete, and by September 1732, Jules-Robert de Cotte succeeded his father as director of the project. But as late as 1744, when Louis XV passed through Verdun following his recovery at Metz, the bishop had difficulty providing suitable accommodations in the unfinished building. The *palais* was not completed until after his death, with some alterations made to the original design.[19] The structure suffered bombardment in 1916–17, and the interiors are only partially restored; nevertheless, the building's scale and commanding position form an impressive sight.

As seen in the plan of the second of three projects, the bishop's palace is located by the western front of the Cathedral of Notre-Dame (May–June 1724; fig. 168).[20] The plan, like that for Châlons-sur-Marne, is based on the building type of the *hôtel* (compare de Cotte's Hôtel d'Estrées, 1711–13, fig. 95). In this case, a small public square precedes the entrance to the *cour d'honneur*, while the *corps-de-logis* overlooks a terraced garden at the back, facing the citadel of Verdun. In the plan a sequence of curved walls greets the arriving visitor: the rounded street front, an unvaulted oval "vestibule," and the concave façade of the *corps-de-logis*. The latter is an element normally not present in *hôtel* architecture, but concave fronts figure prominently in projects for princely residences in France, such as Le Pautre's fourth design in the *Desseins de plusiers palais* (1652), Bernini's first and second schemes for the Louvre (1664), and Boffrand's Palais Ducal, Nancy (1715–22).[21] Thus de Cotte may have introduced it into the Verdun plan in an effort to lend palatial overtones. It is worth noting that on his Italian sojourn de Cotte had admired the similar-shaped forecourt of the Palazzo della Sapienza, Rome (Giacomo della Porta, begun c. 1575), which he described in his Italian notebook: "One enters a very beautiful courtyard, longer than wide, with a concavity circular in plan."[22]

The entrance vestibule and *salon* defining the main axis subdivide the *corps-de-logis*. To the right within the main block the bishop's *appartement de commodité* faces the garden. To the left the central *salon* is joined by means of two transverse arcades to a pair of further public rooms, a *salle* for dining and an *antichambre*. That the use of these public rooms was subject to contemporary rules of etiquette is clear from the bishop's letters: "Liveried retainers would remain in the *salon* [and] *valets de chambre* in the *grande salle* measuring four bays."[23] On the far left of the *corps-de-logis*, the *appartement de parade*, or *appartement d'honneur*, as named by the bishop, consists of the following rooms en enfilade (starting with the left-hand garden pavilion): *cabinet d'audience*, *antichambre*, *chambre*, and *cabinet*. The patron appreciated the visual benefits offered by

168. (*Opposite*) Plan, *rez-de-chaussée*, second project, second variant, Palais Episcopal, Verdun, May–June 1724 (Va 55, t. 5, 1534).

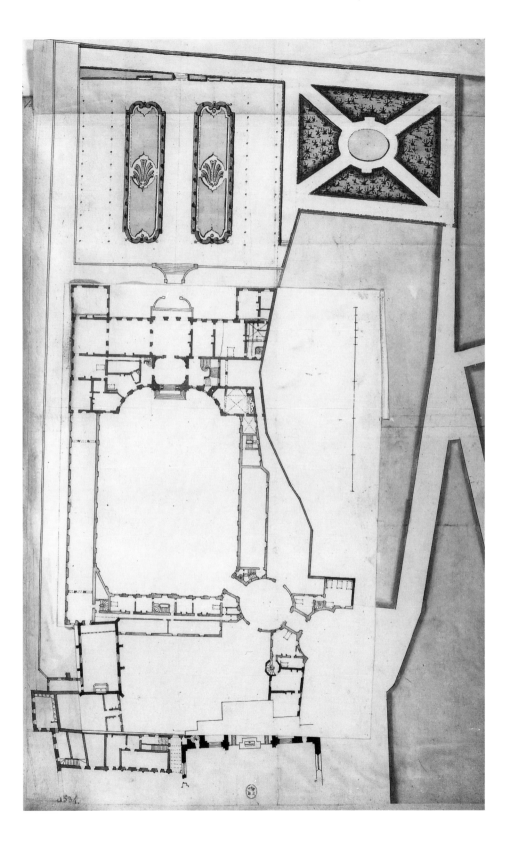

a gallery positioned in the left-hand wing border-ing the court, for he requested large windows to provide optimum illumination and a broad pan-oramic view.[24] His desire for two square rooms framing the gallery probably had its origins in the archetypal arrangement at Versailles of the Gal-erie des Glaces. Yet he also realized that problems of etiquette arose by the necessity of having visi-tors proceed through his *chambre* and *cabinet* in order to reach the gallery; at one point he even proposed reversing the order of the rooms of the *appartement de parade* since, as he said, the public "must not pass through my *chambre* in order to enter these rooms," that is, the gallery, and so forth.[25]

One of two process drawings for elevations shows an early scheme for the garden façade (fig. 169). The sheet discloses three steps in the

method of visualization at the Bâtiments: a *dessi-nateur*'s precise, finely ruled rendering; a flap pro-posing a tall pedimented central pavilion capped by a dome; and de Cotte's(?) robust redrawing of the right-hand pavilion. The axially positioned dome, most likely a traditional French square dome, is a motif, like the concave court façade, that is rare in *hôtel* architecture but is closely as-sociated with the building type of the palace. Recognizing this, de Cotte normally reserved it for buildings of princely status, according to the principle of *convenance* (see the discussion of domes in chaps. 4, 5). Therefore, like the con-cave court façade, the proposed dome for the gar-den front of the Verdun *évêché* was certainly in-tended to add a princely air to the bishop's domain.

Although the garden elevation never received a dome, the courtyard was further aggrandized through addition of an extensive sculptural pro-gram (fig. 167). In accordance with the patron's

169. Garden elevation, project, Palais Episcopal, Verdun, n.d. (Va 55, t. 5, 1544).

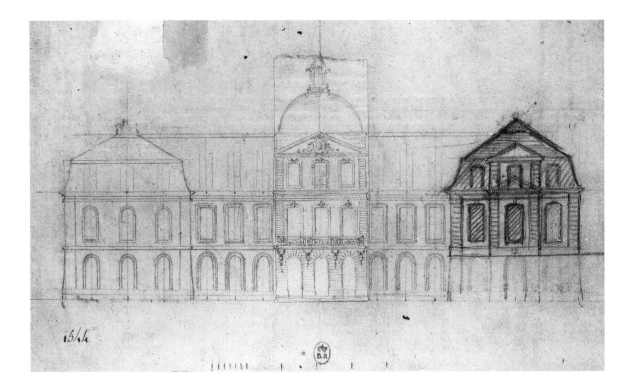

wishes, coats of arms of the bishops of Verdun, their names, and the dates of their bishoprics, circled by garlands, were placed in the spandrels of the blind arcade girding the space: "I was struck by an idea that would very much enhance the courtyard façade of my building. . . . This frieze would relate in chronological order the history of the diocese of Verdun."[26] In a similar vein, escutcheons of the bishop's allies appeared over the entrance to the *corps-de-logis* on either side of his coat of arms. All were obliterated, as noted above, in the Revolution.

Palais Rohan, Strasbourg

With the surprise capture of Strasbourg by French troops in September 1681, the local citizenry exchanged a loose alliance with the Hapsburgs for the strict domination of the Bourbons. The triumphal entry of the Sun King into Strasbourg was paralleled by the return of the bishop to the cathedral, defiled by Lutheran rites ever since the Mass was abolished during the Reformation. Catholic rule soon became the source of power in the municipality. The ideal representative of church and state appeared in the figure of Cardinal Armand-Gaston de Rohan-Soubise (1674–1749), the first of four princes who held in succession the office of bishop of Strasbourg and title of Landgrave de Basse-Alsace from 1704 until the Revolution. With the aid of Louis XIV, Armand-Gaston achieved nomination to the Grand Chapitre in 1690 and was named bishop in 1704. He became a cardinal in 1712.

Despite efforts at modernization undertaken by his predecessor, Cardinal Guillaume-Egon de Fürstenburg, Armand-Gaston considered uninhabitable the medieval *palais épiscopal* located on a site bordered by the south transept of the Cathedral of Notre-Dame and the Ill River.[27] Louis XV sanctioned financing of new construction by special revenues levied on the bishopric. De Cotte was the natural choice as the architect,

having worked on additions to the family compound in Paris, which comprised the Hôtels de Rohan and de Soubise (c. 1710–15), and the remodeling of the cardinal's principal residence, the Château de Saverne (1712–30; see chap. 5).[28] A keen interest in architecture had prompted the cardinal to discuss de Cotte's designs for the Würzburg Residenz with Balthasar Neumann during the latter's mission to France (1723; chap. 4). In mid-1727 de Cotte journeyed to Strasbourg to draw up a *procès-verbal* reviewing the condition of the old *évêché* and to acquaint himself with the site.

Although plans and a wooden model were ready by 1728, construction was delayed until 1731 so that work at Saverne could be completed first. Le Chevalier, resident at Saverne, was considered in 1730 as on-site assistant at Strasbourg, but it was Joseph Massol (1706–71) who supervised building operations from 1731 to 1742, at the same time overseeing design and erection of the nearby Hôtel de Hanau in Strasbourg, for which de Cotte made an early proposal (1727).[29] The *évêché* underwent few changes during the century, since it was not the major domicile of the Rohan cardinals, being used only when they were resident in the city. Damaged by bombardment in 1944, the building has been magnificently restored (fig. 170).

The layout of the main floor was established by de Cotte from the first (1727), being altered only in details through a sequence of five schemes (fig. 171).[30] As expected, the plan owes its origins to the Parisian *hôtel-entre-cour-et-jardin*. For example, the entrance portal stands at the center of a semicircular wall, flanked by two pavilions (compare the Hôtel d'Estrées, fig. 95). On either side of the *cour d'honneur*, lateral walls mask service courts, stables, and coach houses. However, the shallow site, which slopes toward the Ill, imposed two departures from the norm: there is no garden, and a basement story, not vis-

170. Palais Rohan, Stras-
bourg, aerial view from cathedral tower, designed
1727–28, constructed
1731–42.

ible from the court, elevates the river front to three stories (fig. 172).

At the rear of the court the architect employed a pair of entrances facing each other in the large pavilions to left and right of the *corps-de-logis*, recalling the arrangement of the Hôtel du Lude (fig. 91). The smaller vestibule on the right is intended for members of the household and staff, while the octagonal *vestibule d'honneur* on the left leads to the main rooms (fig. 171). A pair of public chambers consisting of a *salle* and *salle à manger* (in early plans, the chapel) are joined visually yet separated by an arcade, similar to the ensemble of *salon*, *salle*, and *antichambre* at Verdun (fig. 168). The *grand appartement*, intended for ceremonies and the lodging of official guests, faces the river: to the right of the *salle* lie an *antichambre*, *chambre*—with the bed behind a balustrade in an alcove framed by columns—and *cabinet*. The prince-bishop's *petit appartement*, also accessible from the *vestibule d'honneur*, faces the court. The location of his bedroom on the central axis invites comparison with the similarly sited Sun King's *chambre* at Versailles (fig. 25).

The acquisition of land along the right-hand side of the plan allowed the addition of a chapel adjacent to the right-hand vestibule and a library toward the river (not shown in the plan, fig. 171, but visible on the left side of the river front, fig. 172).

The design of the elevations, for which two projects remain, underwent considerable change. Again the starting point was the Parisian *hôtel*, evident in the contained horizontality of the roofs, the plain design of the windows, and the unadorned simplicity of the wall surfaces. However, important elements were introduced into the composition of the façades, particularly a thin overlay of horizontally drafted strips and certain palatial devices that proclaim the status of the building to be superior to that of an *hôtel particulier*.

The effect of the street façade is one of exulta-tion, with its agitated skyline and dynamic plan (figs. 170, 173). The entrance is developed spa-tially by means of blocky pavilions, a hemicycle, and a freestanding Doric order, so that the view from the diagonal has tremendous visual impact.

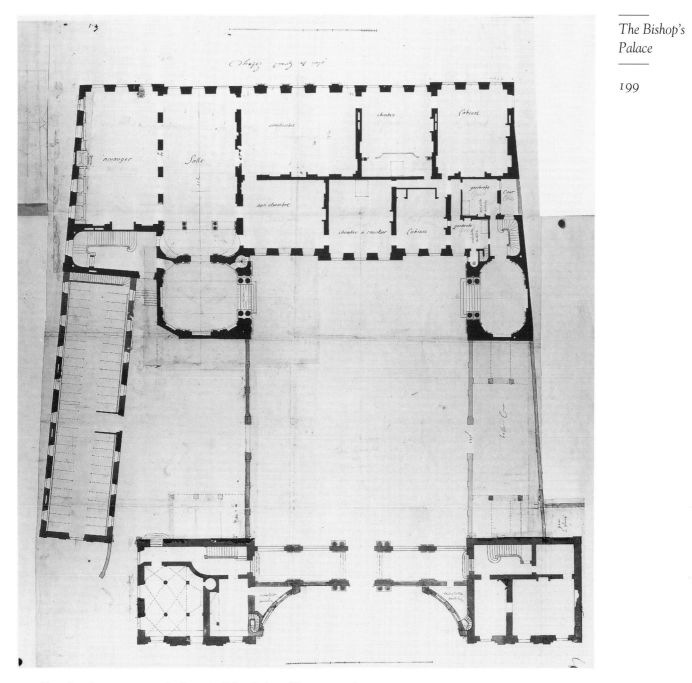

171. Plan, fourth variation, *rez-de-chaussée*, Palais Rohan (Va 435, 1215).

172. River façade, Palais Rohan.

The elevation reaches an exuberant climax at the center with the robust, paired Doric columns ringed with vermiculated bands. The pavilions, containing kitchens (left) and episcopal tribunal (right), are more richly articulated than those of a Parisian *hôtel* (compare the Hôtel d'Estrées; fig. 94).

Passing through the gateway, the visitor reaches the bounded space of the court (fig. 170).

By means of a few devices de Cotte solved the problem of how to link formally the surrounding walls, normally a group of dissonant elements in the urban house: the pavilions at the four corners of the court are roughly the same size; the roof lines are of equal height; and the wall articulation is unified on all four sides through lavish use of the Ionic order. The basic composition of the entrance pavilions, open on the ground floor and

173. Street façade, Palais Rohan.

closed overhead (fig. 174), appears frequently in de Cotte's *hôtel* designs (e.g., Hôtel de Torcy, Hôtel de Chatillon, Paris; Palais Thurn und Taxis, Frankfurt; figs. 100, 106, 124). De Cotte also employed the configuration of paired columns perpendicular to the plane of the wall on either side of an open entrance in the project for Schloss Tilburg (c. 1715–17; figs. 58, 60) and the third project for Saint-Louis de Versailles (1724 or later; figs. 157–58).

Whereas the invitingly open, walkable space of the horizontal street façade draws the viewer in, the river front is not a point of entry but a boundary without access whose function is emblematic and ceremonial (fig. 172). The façade achieves its grandeur through the presence of the giant order—considered by de Cotte appropriate for buildings of princely rank—in the form of a pedimented temple front rising from a podium. Appropriately, the richest of the orders, Corinthian, appears on the last of the succession of façades. In a late phase of planning, not present in extant drawings, the design was further en-

174. Left-hand vestibule, *cour d'honneur*, Palais Rohan.

hanced by the incorporation of a square dome, which, as in the case of the project for Verdun, lends palatial associations to the building.

This princely use of the giant order capped by a pediment and a dome, contrasting strongly with the astylar walls to left and right, is related to Boffrand's similar use of classical elements for the frontispiece of the ducal château at Lunéville, in nearby Lorraine (1719).[31] On a smaller scale, the temple-front motif had likewise appeared on a rusticated base but without a dome in de Cotte's *hôtel* designs (Hôtel d'Estrées, unidentified *hôtel* project; figs. 96, 107). The inspiration for these elevations is ultimately to be found in the villas of Andrea Palladio. In the case of the river front of the Palais Rohan, the blocklike silhouette, the chaste linear incising of the rustication, and above all, the towering portico reflected in the water are all distant echoes of Palladian prototypes. One thinks particularly of the Villa Foscari at Malcontenta, which de Cotte had seen on his Italian sojourn some four decades earlier, when he expressed his admiration for this Renaissance master in his notebooks and drawings (c. 1558–60; fig. 16).

In the Strasbourg river façade, the order has sunk halfway into the surface, and the pavilions barely interrupt the prevailing flatness. The façade pulsates with a gentle rhythm of repeated linear accents. Horizontal moldings running behind the order link with the vertical quoins and thus bind together the composition. The window shapes with their bouyant lintels are repeated the length of each story and thus likewise serve to unify the whole. The Rohan river front is one of de Cotte's chief artistic triumphs—elegant and rich, but not excessively so.

The resemblance of the Palais Rohan to the Palais Thurn und Taxis on the opposite side of the Rhine in Frankfurt (designed and built in the same years, 1727, 1731–40; figs. 121–25) is striking. The Strasbourg elevations, however, are much more harmoniously integrated, except for the library façade, constructed on the left side of the river front as an independent composition. The great segmental arch supported by paired pilasters repeats the composition of de Cotte's earlier proposal for the church façade of the Couvent des Capucines (1721–22; fig. 144).

Robert Le Lorrain, who worked for the cardinal at the Hôtel de Rohan and the Château de Saverne, oversaw the extensive sculptural program, which exceeds that at Verdun.[32] Heraldic coats of arms dominated the chief elevations, symbolically uniting the Rohans with the monarch and the diocese of Strasbourg. Allegorical statues on the entrance portal alluded to the cardinal's roles as prince, judge, and ecclesiastic, while figural masks on the keystones, following Cesare Ripa's *Iconologia*, represented the harmony of the Baroque world.

With the Palais Rohan, Bourbon taste and politics invaded an essentially German medieval environment. Significantly, the cardinal, fifth son of François de Rohan, was rumored to be the illegitimate offspring of Anne de Rohan-Chabot and Louis XIV.[33] This may explain certain details of the interior decor, the general outlines of which were the work of de Cotte. In the *petit appartement* the cardinal hung copies of paintings, both religious and secular, that decorated the private rooms of the old king at Versailles. In the *grande antichambre* the visitor awaiting admittance to the *grande chambre* could study the portraits of the prince and his seven predecessors, a dynastic allusion comparable to the sculpted reliefs of the Verdun courtyard. In the library, portraits of the Evangelists rubbed elbows with the images of Louis XIV and Louis XV, proclaiming the doctrines of Divine Authority and Divine Right. The alcove behind the railing in the *grande chambre* was hung with tapestries depicting Rubens's *Life of Constantine*, first protector of Christianity and overlord of vast territor-

175. Chambre du roi of the *grand appartement*, Palais Rohan.

ies, an antecedent and model for the king of France (fig. 175).

Louis XV's six-day sojourn in Strasbourg during October 1744, following his recovery at Metz, entailed a series of sumptuous celebrations in and around the building. The bedroom of the *grand appartement* was henceforth called the Chambre du Roi. This event, and many more like it, such as the arrival in France from the empire of the Dauphine Marie-Josèphe de Saxe (1747) and later that of Marie-Antoinette (1770), witnessed the use of the Palais Rohan in the manner intended, not only as the bishop's house in Strasbourg, but as a temporary residence for members of the royal family, as a public stage for courtly ritual, and as a viewing box for fireworks and other emblematic fêtes—in short, as an instrument in diplomatic relations.[34] The Palais Rohan at Strasbourg is not only de Cotte's finest extant work but also bears the distinction of being one of the most complete ensembles in France of architecture and decorative arts to have come down to us from the eighteenth century, thanks to a meticulous program of restoration.

Chapter Eleven

The Monastery

THE RECONSTRUCTION of the Abbey of Saint-Denis was the first large-scale commission undertaken by Robert de Cotte as an independent designer rather than as Hardouin-Mansart's assistant and collaborator. The plans date from 1699, the year de Cotte was promoted to the position of Architecte Ordinaire (fig. 176). Consequently, they represent his newly won status as a creative force in the Bâtiments. The design reveals the importance attached by de Cotte to the principal of *convenance*: he employed the standard layout and wall articulation commonly found in monastic complexes. Although the abbey was erected over a long period of time, with changes made in the plan after his death, the building nonetheless reflects his ideal with respect to the architectural type of the monastery.

A Benedictine foundation, Saint-Denis enjoyed considerable prestige among the religious houses of France through its close association with the French monarchy, particularly as the royal necropolis.[1] The funeral ceremonies of the French kings, queens, and members of their family occurred there, before interment in the basilica. Furthermore, the queens of France were crowned at Saint-Denis, and the ensuing banquets took place in the monastery, where Their Majesties would spend the night prior to returning to Paris the next day. Thus, periodically the abbey lacked the customary silence of a sanctuary and took on the bustle of a royal dwelling.

The Hundred Years War and the Wars of Religion, together with the ravages of time, left many French monasteries in poor condition by the end of the seventeenth century, including the old Abbey of Saint-Denis, a conglomerate of twelfth- through seventeenth-century buildings. In 1666, Colbert decreed that as an economic measure no further monastic houses were to be founded without royal permission, but he encouraged rebuilding.[2] The Congrégation de Saint-Maur, to which the Benedictines belonged, had its own architect-brethren working at various sites. Many abbey churches were reconstructed, but the Gothic basilica of Saint-Denis was not altered for reasons of economy and its cultural position; the Congrégation, which placed strong emphasis on historical scholarship, supported the preservation of Gothic structures.

However, it was Dom Arnoult de Loo, grand prieur de Saint-Denis in the years 1696–1702 and 1708–11, who determined to construct a new monastic complex at Saint-Denis. While no funds were forthcoming from the king, as a royal institution the abbey had access to architects in the Bâtiments. Hardouin-Mansart had just assumed the mantle of Surintendant with its extensive obligations, and so the task of designing for the Benedictines went to de Cotte, who a decade earlier had visited several Italian monasteries on his southern study trip and had marvelled at the grandeur and spaciousness of their interiors. He too was burdened with responsibilities at

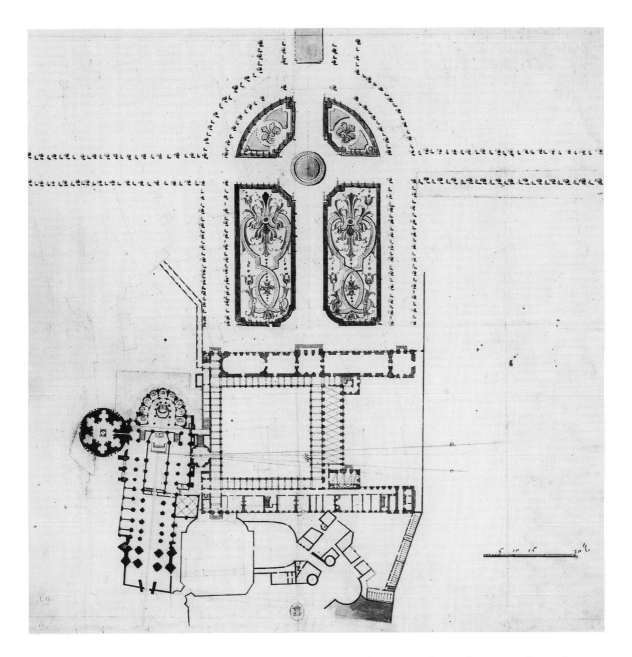

176. De Cotte's definitive project, ground floor, basilica and Abbey of Saint-Denis, 1699 (Va 93, t. 6, 69).

this time: on 26 May 1699, Dom François Quenet, supervisor of building operations at Saint-Denis, wrote to de Loo that the Architecte Ordinaire was so busy with the king's work that it was difficult to gain access to him for the pur-

pose of viewing the preliminary plans. Quenet noted that de Cotte had entrusted the preparation of some of the drawings to assistants and that he did not expect payment from the monks, although he was willing to accept a gift (see chap. 1). When Quenet pointed out inconsistencies in the elevations, de Cotte assured him that all of the details would be coordinated in the final stage of planning, at which time he would make available the construction drawings.[3]

Initially, de Cotte's plans met with opposition from the monks on the grounds that they were overly elaborate and costly. An alternative project was solicited from the architect Jacques Bayeux, who proposed retaining the old refectory and prior's lodging.[4] However, de Loo was committed to erecting a splendid new structure. He urged the archbishop of Paris, Louis-Antoine de Noailles, to arrange for an audience with Louis XIV in order to secure royal approval of de Cotte's project (for de Cotte's relationship with the Noailles brothers, see chap. 10).

A record of the meeting, which took place on 17 July 1699 in the Cabinet du Roi at Versailles, has come down to us. Upon being introduced to de Loo,

the Grand Monarch responded, "The Abbey of Saint-Denis is the first and greatest abbey of my realm, which my predecessors, the kings, have always loved very much." Father de Loo replied, "Sire, . . . we can alter nothing in the buildings without the honor of your consent, and since they are extremely dilapidated, I had a project prepared, upon which I most humbly request that Your Majesty cast an eye." "Let us see this plan," said the king, and having himself laid it across one of his desks, he examined it for over one-half hour with the assistance of Monsieur de Cotte, and in the sole presence of the archbishop of Paris, the prior, and three monks. [Louis XIV] asked several questions concerning the location of rooms, the function of the large *salles* below the dormitory, and the guest suites. Father de Loo told him that the purpose [of the *salles*] was [to provide room] for the coronation of the queens. "Add, my Father," rejoined the king, "and for the funerals of the kings." . . . Then Dom de Loo went with the archbishop to Madame de Maintenon's apartment, where she likewise examined the plan.[5]

Later that year de Loo won approval of the designs at a general chapter meeting of the Congrégation. Despite further opposition from the monks of Saint-Denis, after some debate they capitulated.[6] Although it was understood that de Cotte would oversee building operations, the monks proposed enlisting the services of Dom Guillaume de la Tremblaye, a Benedictine architect from Caen, who worked principally on Norman abbeys.[7] Even so, a note in the Necrology of Saint-Denis attests to the longstanding interest of de Cotte in the progress of the work from 1699 until his death in 1735:

To the overall design of our new building, so characteristic of [de Cotte's] good taste and noble ideas, he added his solicitude, his visits to inspect construction without allowing another architect [to take his place], and the basic design of everything architectural. The conception of the woodwork, the doors, the paneling, and generally all things within the scope of his knowledge was guided by his love of our House, which never suffered from the encumbrance of his expenses, the necessary visits, or even the illnesses of his final days. . . . Such fervor lasting over thirty-five years deserves perpetual gratitude.[8]

Work on the foundations commenced 29 April 1700 and the first stone was laid 30 May 1701.[9] The east wing (1700–1702, 1708–14) and the south wing (1714–24) were completed during de Cotte's lifetime according to his plans. Jacques V Gabriel altered the design of the west wing, begun in 1737.[10]

One of de Loo's objectives was to provide the brethren with suitable quarters. The Maurist Reform had abandoned the use of communal dormitories, preferring individual cells as an aid to meditation and study.[11] The constitution of 1646 ordained the length and width of each cell to be a minimum of nine *pieds* and maximum of eleven *pieds*.

De Loo also wished to house the king and court more suitably during ceremonial occasions. Before Louis XIV entered the period of personal rule, he had experienced the most lamentable accommodations in the abbey—"ruineux, incommodes & mal assortis" according to Félibien, during the wars of the Fronde (June 1652).[12] Louis's concerns were not solely devoted to his well-being in this life; he also sought suitable shelter for his mortal remains following his death. In the 1660s he and Colbert had invited both François Mansart and Bernini to propose designs for an immense centrally planned Bourbon funerary chapel to be constructed at the apse end of the basilica of Saint-Denis (not built). We cannot help but surmise the extent of Louis's interest in a new monastery in 1699; already in his sixty-second year, he was anticipating his final journey there. He concluded the audience with de Loo by saying, "My Father, pray to God for me while I live, and likewise after my death, when I will lie in your church."[13]

Plans

A large number of extant drawings for the new Abbey of Saint-Denis, along with scattered documents, provide a firm basis for understanding de Cotte's method of working in the instance of a major commission. It was not unusual for the Bâtiments initially to provide ground plans only, with the understanding that once these were approved, elevations would follow. At the beginning of the process he and his draftsmen designated the various buildings of the old abbey in black hatched lines on an immense site plan; he then superimposed the new building *en masse* in red along the right-hand flank of the church and rendered a new formal garden in green outline (fig. 177).[14] A typical Civitas Dei, the old monastery had been assembled in rambling fashion over several centuries. No single compositional principle served to organize the loose aggregation of structures on the south side of the church: cloister, chapter house, *parlement*, dormitory, pharmacy, brewery, bakery, and so forth. The size and shape of each depended on its individual function. In contrast, with a bold gesture characteristic of the Age of Absolutism, de Cotte deter-

mined to sweep away these irregularly grouped buildings and to draw the manifold parts together into a four-winged structure of huge size and regular outline. He preserved only one element of the old complex, the medieval two-towered Porte Suger on the southwest (figs. 176–77, lower right).

The definitive project for the ground floor appears in a colored drawing (fig. 176). Entry is gained from the west (bottom of the plan), either through a new ceremonial courtyard leading from the square in front of the basilica, or through the Porte Suger, retained as a service entrance. The chief means of passage between the

177. Plan, basilica and former abbey, Saint-Denis, with superimposed *plan-en-masse* of projected abbey (Va 438, 66).

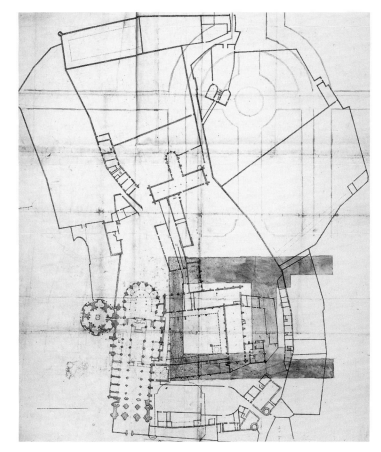

basilica and the convent is a rotunda abutting the south transept. In the center of the complex lies an immense cloister. The ground floor of the west wing is reserved for guest quarters and bureaux of the various abbatial departments. A corridor running the entire length of the wing allows circulation within this public area while skirting the cloister and other parts reserved for the monks. The Grand Appartement, laid out in the east wing facing the garden, serves alternately the monastic community and the royal family. From north to south the rooms consist of the following sequence (left to right): the double apsidal Salle Capitulaire, or chapter house, where the brethren were seated during meetings, but which became the Salle Militaire during royal funerals; the Salle du Roi, festooned with sumptuous hangings during royal visits or draped in black in honor of the dead king; the vestibule leading to the garden; the Salle des Gardes du Roi, where an empty catafalque was placed and the daily ceremony of the funerary meal occurred; and the Salle des Princes Légitimés in the southeast pavilion, intended for reception of the court.[15] In the south wing the refectory doubles as locus of the monks' daily repasts and occasional funerary and anniversary feasts. Flanking the refectory on either side are the kitchen and the great ceremonial staircase, the principal means of access to the monks' cells on the second floor.

In the scheme of the old monastery, the monks' quarters consisted of a communal dormitory located behind the *chevet* of the church. De Cotte's reconstruction plan calls for ninety-eight cells lining three corridors on the upper floor, although the number of monks barely exceeded half that figure during the eighteenth century. Since no complete plans of the second floor have survived, we are indebted to Mariette for having published de Cotte's layout (fig. 178).[16] The cells vary slightly in size, measuring roughly nine by eleven to twelve *pieds*, slightly larger than the size prescribed by the Congrégation. De Cotte's plans do not specify a location for the apartment of the *grand prieur*; it ultimately comprised three continuous cells in the northeast pavilion, near the Grand Chauffoir (fig. 178, upper right).[17] The second-floor plan also reveals the location of the library in the projecting arm of the west wing (lower left). Its prominent position is indicative of the emphasis placed by the Congrégation on scholarship and the preservation of sacred learning.

The rules concerning *bienséance* and *convenance* in architectural practice guided de Cotte in determining the form of the new abbey. Medieval monastic buildings invariably featured a quadrilateral cloister lying adjacent to the nave and south transept of the church, with various communal quarters arranged in a jumble around it. However, in the sixteenth century a new building type, the monumental palace-monastery complex, was introduced at the Escorial of Philip II (Juan de Herrera, c. 1563–84). In this structure, which also included a royal suite and mausoleum, the emphasis was on representational and hospitable areas—staircases, state apartments, and guest rooms—all arranged axially. In France a comparable palace-monastery, the Benedictine nunnery of the Val-de-Grâce, set the standard for royal abbeys. The building was the result of a vow by Anne of Austria in 1638 to rebuild an older convent in gratitude for the birth of Louis XIV after twenty years of childless marriage. François Mansart, in his preliminary (unexecuted) schemes for the new convent, respected Anne's request for a magnificent royal apartment. Realizing that the building would host court ceremonies, the designers responsible for the executed plan combined the theme of the medieval quadrilateral cloister with the grandiose symmetry of the Escorial (Gabriel Le Duc et al., 1654–65; fig. 179).[18] The layout of

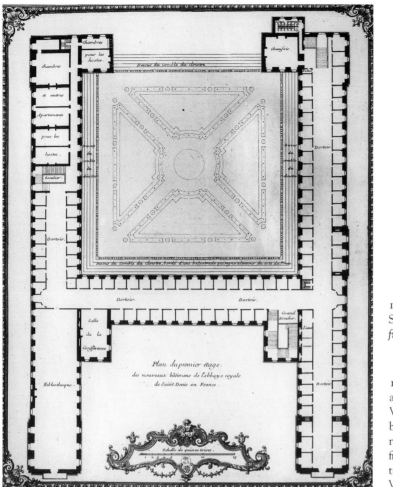

178. Plan, *premier étage*, Abbey of
Saint-Denis (Mariette, *L'architecture
française*, Va 438).

179. François Mansart et al., plan
and east elevation, church of the
Val-de-Grâce, Paris (1645–65); Gabriel Le Duc et al., Benedictine nunnery (1654–65, incorporating
fifteenth- through seventeenth-century structures) (print by Marot,
Va 258).

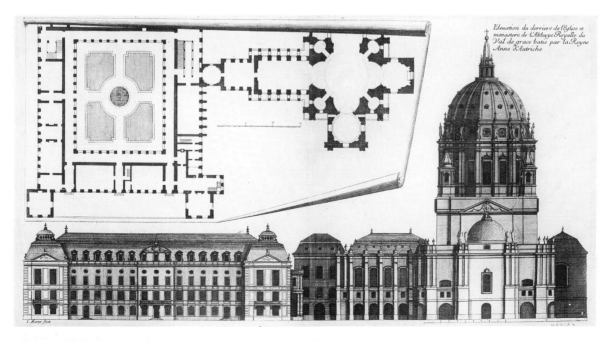

the Val-de-Grâce complex as constructed, as well as that of Mansart's unbuilt proposals, kept in the drawing collection of the Gabriel family, provided de Cotte with the essential conception of the new Saint-Denis—a large four-wing building of classical design attached to the right-hand flank of the basilica and enclosing a great cloister. De Cotte's plan also follows the example of the Val-de-Grâce in the incorporation of blocky volumes at the corners.

Elevations

Of the numerous extant elevation drawings for Saint-Denis, four representing the garden façade (east wing), serve a variety of purposes.[19] An early graphite process drawing of eight bays incorporates overlapping proposals for various details, such as the shape of the roofs, the height of the pediments, and the profile of the cornice. A colored presentation drawing offers alternative solutions for the end pavilions (fig. 180). A finished line drawing in ink shows the elevation as adopted, and finally, an enlarged detail in graphite of a single bay, with measurements for each part, was intended to guide the builders.

180. Elevation, garden façade, east wing, Abbey of Saint-Denis (Va 93, t. 6, 90).

Throughout the sequence the chief characteristics of the wing remain its low horizontality and self-contained massing, since the three pavilions break forward only slightly from the plane of the wall. A blind arcade that encompasses the entire façade animates the ground floor. For the sake of uniform repetition of the bays, many of the windows are false, as the plans reveal (see fig. 176). The presentation drawing incorporates a row of windows at mezzanine level to illuminate the high, vaulted *salles* of the Grand Appartement (see the corresponding section, fig. 181, far left). Later these windows were changed to tablets with guttae "toes"; the tablets provide a visual connective between the arcade below and the gently arched windows above (fig. 182). The classical orders appear nowhere on the façade. Ornament is restricted to vertical strips of channeled rustication and elegant console-and-shell keystones above the arcade.

De Cotte's elevation for the entry façade fronting the courtyard (west wing) is extremely simple—a span of twenty-six bays of unadorned windows yawns between two pavilions.[20] The Porte Suger and the monastic wall would largely have blocked this wall from view; the focal point was to be the left-hand pavilion, the "Entrée du Monastere" specified in the presentation draw-

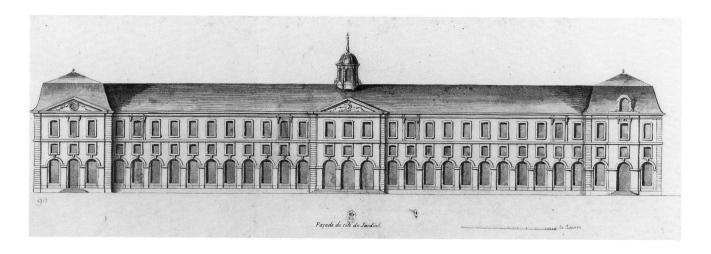

Façade du côté du Jardin.

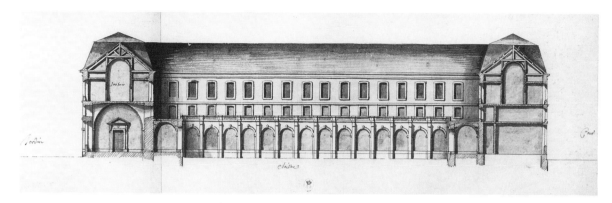

181. Elevation of south cloister wing and east-west section, Abbey of Saint-Denis (Va 93, t. 6, 89).

182. Garden façade, east wing, Abbey of Saint-Denis.

ing. In the earliest elevation of the refectory façade (south front; fig. 183) the terminal pavilions are quite plain compared to the tripartite composition ultimately used, further proof that the design went through several stages. The relatively loose execution of this sheet, with its transparent washes, freehand detailing, and idiosyncratic touches (the faintly medieval wall buttresses vary in width), suggests that de Cotte may have drawn the initial elevations himself. This possibility is corroborated by the presence here of his handwriting and such idiosyncratic details as

sketchy foliage and smoke curling from the chimney. In fact, the drafting style reflects the manner of de Cotte's Italian drawings of a decade earlier (compare figs. 14, 19–20).

An elevation of the south cloister wall also exists (fig. 181). The balustrade along the cornice and the strip buttresses subdividing the bays of the arcade impart a classical air to the cloister. However, the orders appear only within the barrel-vaulted galleries of the cloister ambulatory, where Tuscan pilasters mark the bays (fig. 184). In addition, the cloister elevation contains

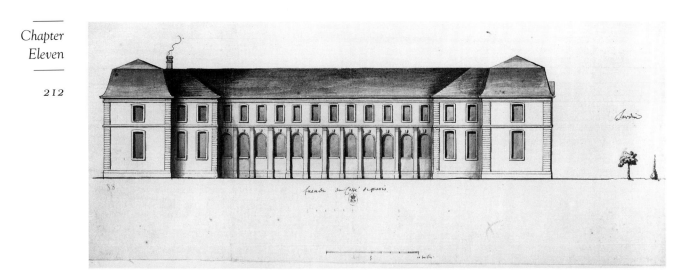

183. Elevation, project, refectory façade, south wing, Abbey of Saint Denis (Va 93, t. 6, 88).

184. Cloister, interior, Abbey of Saint-Denis.

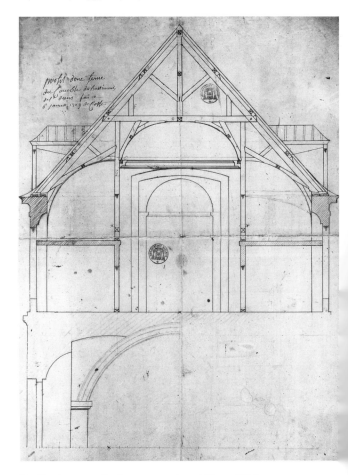

185. Section, *premier étage*, west wing, Abbey of Saint-Denis, 6 January 1709 (Ha 18, t. 1, n.n.).

cross sections of the east and west wings, revealed to be multileveled and complex. Especially noteworthy on the upper floor are the barrel-vaulted corridors giving onto monks' cells of shorter height on either side. The mezzanine level in the west wing was intended to house archives and offices (right center). The abbreviated nature of this presentation drawing is apparent when compared with more detailed drawings showing the same areas. For example, a cross section of the upper floor of the west wing contains an explicit diagram of the timber framework supporting the roof (fig. 185).[21] The drawing is signed and dated—"profil d'une ferme du comble du Bastiment de St Denis fait ce 6 janvier 1709 de Cotte"—demonstrating that the architect prepared construction drawings as needed, not necessarily as part of the early design process.

The cloister elevation says little about the decoration of the interior with the exception of one element in the Grand Appartement—the pedimented door frames cut from stone (fig. 181, left). These lend a feeling of grave nobility to the interior, especially when the whole series of portals is visible *en enfilade* (fig. 186).

Like the quadrilateral ground plan, the austere elevations derive from a tradition of monastic design that originated in the sixteenth century, when new abbeys were erected in France in an economical, stripped-down style based on that of contemporary secular buildings. Decorative features consisted principally of quoins, stringcourses, and regularly spaced windows with simple moldings (compare the Convent of the Val-de-Grâce, fig. 179). The medieval cloister acquired classical overtones when architects attached a pilaster order to the traditional round-headed arcade. In accordance with the rule of *convenance*, the austere style was held to be equivalent to the monastic principles of silence, abstinence, and obedience.

This monastic idiom is closely related to the style of institutional architecture, as exemplified by the Hôtel Royal des Invalides, Paris, whose main courtyard is composed of a simple but monumental two-story arcade (Libéral Bruant, 1671–74). The elevation of the Invalides north façade (toward the Seine), with its blind arcade along the ground story, may have been one of the sources for de Cotte's garden elevation of Saint-Denis. In addition, his mentor, Hardouin-Mansart, was a master of so-called *constructions utilitaires*, such as the Grand Commun, Versailles, an immense, sparsely articulated four-wing building providing lodgings for the royal households (designed 1679). Hardouin-Mansart's most lauded work in this vein is the Orangerie bordering the south wing of the Palace

186. Salle Capitulaire, Grand Appartement, east wing, Abbey of Saint-Denis.

of Versailles, not only for its sober exterior elevations, but particularly for the massive barrel-vaulted stone corridors within (1684–86; fig. 7). Antoine-Nicolas Dezallier d'Argenville characterized the Orangerie in 1787 as follows: "Everything here is noble, grand, and masculine, even though extremely simple, and doubtless it is this simplicity that makes [the building] meritorious."[22] That description could apply equally to de Cotte's conception of Saint-Denis. These and comparable buildings were considered to be masterpieces of stereotomy, the art of stone masonry, much discussed in theoretical writing from de l'Orme to Daviler.[23] The French claimed to have invented the craft in the Middle Ages and to have brought it to perfection in the sixteenth and seventeenth centuries. Monastic and utilitarian buildings composed of simple volumes were thought to possess a monumental effect worthy of the antique through the use of basic proportions and the fine dressing of stone, rather than dependence on the classical orders.

De Cotte's design for Saint-Denis may have influenced the work of de la Tremblaye, the architect-monk whom the brethren planned to call to supervise construction, although there is no record of his having worked there. The so-called Benedictine Norman style practiced by de la Tremblaye, which is characterized by elegant severity and the use of massive arcades for ground-floor elevations and cloisters, probably reflects de Cotte's elevations to some degree (compare de la Tremblaye's Abbaye-aux-Hommes, Caen, begun a few years after Saint-Denis in 1704 and constructed principally from 1710 to 1763).[24]

At Saint-Denis the severity of the architecture was relieved somewhat on the interior, where various decorative elements provided richness—wood paneling, paintings, some sculpture, and forged iron grills and balustrades. The majesty and quiet elegance of the abbey strongly impressed eighteenth-century observers. Wrote Brice, "The monastery newly rebuilt after the designs of de Cotte, Premier Architecte du Roi, is a building of grandeur and beauty with few equals."[25] Or, as Antoine-Nicolas Dezallier d'Argenville put it, "Its height, its length, and the grandeur of the rooms and dormitories composing it contribute greatly to its magnificence."[26] This assessment has changed little over the centuries: more recently Joan Evans in a history of post-medieval French abbeys (1956) called Saint-Denis "the most splendid *ensemble* in French monastic architecture of the classical period."[27]

Epilogue

On 26 September 1733 the duc d'Antin wrote to Nicolas Wleughels, director of the Académie de France in Rome, concerning de Cotte's failing health—he was then in his late seventies: "Monsieur de Cotte, Premier Architecte, has been very ill; even though he is old and blind, his passing would be the greatest loss that we could sustain."[1] De Cotte's condition must have improved, however, because two months later he and his son carried out an inspection of the Hôtel d'Armagnac, Paris, for the purpose of proposing repairs.[2] Moreover, he attended two meetings of the Académie d'architecture the next year and made his last appearance there in 1735. According to the Necrology of the Abbey of Saint-Denis, de Cotte was active until the end, despite "the illnesses of his final days."[3] In short, he apparently had a productive old age, as did many figures of the Grand Siècle, such as Louis XIV, who lived to the age of seventy-seven, and André Le Nostre, who died in his eighty-eighth year.

Nevertheless, late in 1734 de Cotte stepped down from the position of leadership, as the *Mercure de France* reported: "Because Monsieur de Cotte, Premier Architecte du Roi, had requested retirement on account of his infirmities, the post was conferred upon Monsieur [Jacques V] Gabriel, His Majesty's Architecte Ordinaire, Premier Architecte des Ponts et Chaussées de France, and Contrôleur des Dedans du Château de Versailles; Monsieur de Cotte retains the pen-sion of twelve thousand *livres* attached to the office of Premier Architecte du Roi."[4] This marked the transfer of power to the Gabriel dynasty.[5] Ange-Jacques Gabriel became Contrôleur of Versailles, and the following year he took de Cotte's seat in the first class of the Académie. Louis XV entrusted the two Gabriels with large-scale renovations at Versailles (1735–39) and Fontainebleau (1737). The younger Gabriel became Premier Architecte in 1742.

De Cotte passed away in 1735 and was buried at Saint-Germain-l'Auxerrois, the royal parish church of the Louvre.[6] The *Mercure de France* made the following announcement:

The Arts have just suffered a considerable loss in the person of Monsieur de Cotte, the father, . . . who died in his house at Passy, near Paris, 15 July last, in his seventy-ninth year. The genius and the superiority of his talents, which so distinguished him in society, brought him esteem, and merited the favor of Louis le Grand, during whose reign he built the peristyle of the Trianon, directed work at the Dôme des Invalides, completed the chapel of Versailles, erected the new monastery at Saint-Denis, and [designed] numerous palatial dwellings in the capital and the realm, as well as in foreign countries.[7]

As was the norm in architectural dynasties, de Cotte trained a son to be his collaborator and successor. Jules-Robert de Cotte occupied various administrative positions in the Bâtiments, including Contrôleur à Paris (1710), and often acted on his father's behalf: for example, he carried the plans of the new Buen Retiro Palace to Philip V in Madrid (1715).[8] He completed the building projects left unfinished by his father.[9] However, despite family connections and wealth, and notwithstanding the assessment of Balthasar Neumann in 1723—"His son is as capable as the father"—Jules-Robert lacked the artistic powers of his two namesakes.[10]

The most immediate impact of Robert de Cotte's work was in the area of palace design. As we have seen, his projects for Schleissheim, the Buen Retiro, and Würzburg, although themselves not executed, influenced the designs of non-French architects, especially those of Vanvitelli for the Palace of Caserta, outside Naples. In France, the younger Gabriel consulted de Cotte's palace drawings when conceiving his own Grands Projets for Versailles and Compiègne in the forties and fifties. In the instance of the *maison de plaisance*, Blondel defended the authority of his book devoted to this building type by claiming to have consulted the "grands Maîtres de l'Art," placing de Cotte at the head of his list (1737–38).[11] Various architects adopted compositional devices from de Cotte's *hôtel* designs, such as Mollet for the Hôtel d'Humières, Paris (1716–17, garden façade; compare the neighboring garden façade, Hôtel du Maine) and Courtonne for the Hôtel de Noirmoutiers, Paris (1719–23, court façade; compare the court façade, Hôtel d'Estrées).[12] And de Cotte's plans for Saint-Roch and Saint-Louis de Versailles provided motifs for the basilica designs of Mansart de Sagonne and the elder Gabriel.

De Cotte was one of several artists in the Hardouin-Mansart school whose work influenced the younger generation; thus his impact is not always easily separated from that of his colleagues Gabriel, Boffrand, and Lassurance, among others. For example, entry drawings by various architects for the Prix de Rome, consisting of projects for specific architectural types,

especially in the years 1723 (*hôtel particulier*), 1726 (church portal), 1731 (centrally planned château), and 1738 (city gate in the form of a triumphal arch), reflect the move toward lighter and more elegant surfaces and more commodious plans that typifies the early eighteenth-century reworking of the Hardouin-Mansart style.[13] Some favored elements in de Cotte's formal vocabulary continued to be developed later in the century, such as the freestanding block with symmetrical, mostly astylar elevations espoused in his *hôtel* designs. Indeed, Palladianism achieved its most rigorous expression in the Neoclassical period (e.g., A.-J. Gabriel's Petit Trianon, Versailles, 1762–68). Be that as it may, a shift in taste was evident by mid-century, when Blondel in the *Architecture françoise* (1752–56) and *Cours d'architecture* (1771–77) criticized the compositional principles and the handling of the orders not only in de Cotte's work but also in Le Vau's, François Mansart's, and Hardouin-Mansart's.[14]

On the whole de Cotte's influence was short-lived, waning considerably by 1750, when Neoclassicism was ascendant. Whereas the work of his contemporary, Boffrand, with its stark, unadorned surfaces, monumental volumes, and elements of tension, opened an avenue toward the future, de Cotte's work summed up a past tradition. His designs represent a concluding statement in the development of architectural forms from the French Renaissance through the Late Baroque. As Bricaire de la Dixmerie wrote in 1769, "The [seventeenth and eighteenth] centuries quarrel over de Cotte. He had one foot in each, and merited that both one and the other should claim him as their own."[15] Although not a great design innovator, he was a master who beautifully synthesized French and Italian principles of composition and rhetorical expression with the programmatic needs of his clients. There is little that is eccentric or idiosyncratic in his work, and admittedly, some of the exterior elevations, especially in the realm of the *hôtel,* tend toward the formulaic. But patrons sought de Cotte's expertise not because they perceived him to be a unique artistic personality, but because he represented a tradition emanating from an interconnected triad of august French institutions—the Bâtiments, the Académie, and the Crown. Moreover, it was inevitable that in many cases the rigorous system of the Bâtiments should lead toward standardization; in fact, de Cotte's role was very much like that of the principal of a large present-day firm with a geographically diversified practice requiring a high degree of delegation in the design process. Finally, the rules of *convenance* and *bienséance* precluded experimentation and required adherence to a hierarchy of accepted models. As Kalnein has put it, "In this world, drilled as it was to obey the demands of good taste, there was no room for geniuses."[16]

Nevertheless, the application of a consistent set of design principles throughout de Cotte's oeuvre implies the desire of both French and foreign patrons for a stable architectural style. Continuity was especially important in a period that was shaken by such events as the death of the Sun King, the drastic social and economic changes of the Régence, and the coming to power of the young Louis XV. Thus, with a sense of gratitude, his contemporaries paid him tribute at the moment of his death, as in the announcement published by the *Mercure de France:*

His memory will be all the more precious to posterity in that his works reflect the noble boldness and elegance, coupled with great precision and purity, of those rules bequeathed to us by the Ancients in their remaining buildings. Moreover, [his works display] that tasteful decoration and well-conceived interior planning always desirable for gracious living, for practicality, and thus for the perfection of public and private buildings.[17]

Notes

CHAPTER ONE

1. The principal short biographies of de Cotte, not always reliable, are the following: Jacques-François Blondel, *L'architecture françoise*, 4 vols. (Paris: C. A. Jombert, 1752–56; Levy, 1904), 1:231 n. a, 4:479–80; Charles-François Roland Le Virloys, *Dictionnaire d'architecture civile*, 3 vols. (Paris: Libraires associés, 1770–71), 1:429; Jean-Claude Pingeron, *Vies des architectes anciens et modernes*, 2 vols. (Paris: Jombert, 1771), 1:404–6; Jacques-François Blondel, *Cours d'architecture*, 9 vols. (Paris: Desaint, 1771–77), 6:479–80; Antoine-Nicolas Dezallier d'Argenville, *Vies des fameux architectes*, 2 vols. (Paris: Debure l'aîné, 1787), 1:412–19; Lempereur, "Dictionnaire des artistes" (manuscript), 3 vols., 1795, B.N. Est., Ya² 10, 1:291–92; Hippolyte Destailleur, *Notices sur quelques artistes français* (Paris: Rapilly, 1863), 208–20; Augustin Jal, *Dictionnaire critique de biographie et d'histoire*, 2 vols. (Paris: H. Plon, 1867), 1:433–34; Louis Etienne Dussieux, *Les artistes français à l'étranger*, 3d ed. (Paris: Lecoffre fils, 1876), 116–21 and *passim*; Charles Bauchal, *Nouveau dictionnaire biographique et critique des architectes français* (Paris: André, 1887), 158–59; Charles Lucas, "Les de Cotte ou Coste," *La grande encyclopédie*, 31 vols. (Paris: H. Lamirault, 1891), 13.2:18–19; Léopold Mar, "Robert de Cotte et son fils, biographie locale," *Bulletin de la Société historique d'Auteuil et de Passy* 4 (1901–3): 260–64; Pierre Marcel, "Robert de Cotte (1656–1735)," *L'architecte*, 1907, pp. 29–33; Louis Réau, "Robert de Cotte," *Les architectes célèbres*, 2 vols. (Paris: L. Mazenod, 1958–59), 1:98–99, 2:273; Jacques-Silvestre de Sacy, "Robert de Cotte," *Dictionnaire de biographie française*, 17 vols. to date (Paris: Letouzey, 1961), 9:834–36.

The most extensive biography of de Cotte and his family, based on unpublished documents not cited here, is by José-Luc d'Iberville-Moreau, "Robert de Cotte: His Career as an Architect and the Organisation of the Service des Bâtiments," Ph.D. diss., University of London, 1972; further information, likewise from unpublished sources, appears in Bertrand Jestaz, "Jules Hardouin-Mansart: L'oeuvre personelle, les méthodes de travail et les collaborateurs," *Positions des thèses*, Ecole des chartes, 1962, pp. 67–72.

2. *Le Mercure galant*, May 1708, p. 298. The name is variously spelled de Cotte, de Coste, or de Caute. In 1771 Pingeron described de Cotte with these words: "Cet artiste étoit doué d'une imagination très-vive, qui étoit réglée par un jugement sain, & par un travail continuel. . . . Ces belles qualités étoient relevées par la simplicité de ses moeurs, & par un extérieure modeste. Cet artiste étoit d'un caractere obligeant, & très-vertueux" (*Vies*, 1:405).

3. François Souchal, *French Sculptors of the Seventeenth and Eighteenth Centuries: The Reign of Louis XIV*, 3 vols. (Oxford: Cassirer, 1977–87), 1:211; Pierre Rosenberg et al., *Musée du Louvre, catalogue illustré des peintures*, vol. 2: *Ecole française, XVIIᵉ et XVIIIᵉ siècles* (Paris: Musées nationaux, 1974), 215. For the portraits of Robert de Cotte, see Léon Charvet, *Architectes lyonnais* (Lyon: Bernour & Cumin, 1899), 94.

4. Without suitable documentation, de Cotte's birth date remains approximate; Jean-Daniel Ludmann, *Le Palais Rohan de Strasbourg*, 2 vols. (Strasbourg: Dernières nouvelles, 1979–80), 1:31. The early biographers give the date 1657: Roland Le Virloys, *Dictionnaire* (1770–71), 429; Pingeron, *Vies* (1771), 1:404; Blondel, *Cours d'architecture* (1771–77), 6:479. The date then appears as 1656—Dezallier d'Argenville, *Vies* (1787), 1:412—the year subsequently given by most writers. Mar (1901–3), who used numerous documents for his biographical notice on de Cotte, specified the birth date as 7 January 1657, without citing a reference; "Robert de Cotte," 260. Boislisle published the date 14 January 1657, also without documentation; Louis de Rouvroy, duc de Saint-Simon, *Mémoires*, edited by Arthur de Boislisle, 41 vols. (Paris: Hachette, 1879–1930), 16:39 n. 4. The January 1657 date accords with de Cotte's age at his death (15 July 1735), reported to be "78" years in the registers of Saint-Germain-l'Auxerrois, where he was buried: Henri Herluison, *Actes d'état-civil d'artistes français* (Orléans: author, 1873), 89; see Jal, *Dictionnaire critique*, 434. Likewise, the *Mercure de France* (August 1735, pp. 1817–18) reported de Cotte on his death to be "in his seventy-ninth year," i.e., 78 years old.

5. *Explication facile et briefve des cinq ordres d'architecture* (Paris: author, 1644).

6. Jules Guiffrey, *Comptes des bâtiments du roi sous le règne de Louis XIV, 1664–1715*, 5 vols. (Paris: Imprimerie nationale, 1881–1901), 4:554. The father is traditionally identified as Charles.

7. For a genealogical chart of these intermarried families, see Allan Braham and Peter Smith, *François Mansart*, 2 vols. (London: Zwemmer, 1973), 1:190.

8. O¹ 46, fol. 32–33; Arch. nat. X¹ᴬ 8696, fol. 140–41; E 1982, fol. 386–87.

9. Henry Lemonnier, ed., *Procès-verbaux de l'Académie royale d'architecture, 1671–1793*, 10 vols. (Paris: Société de l'histoire de l'art français, 1911–29), 1:xvii, 109, 4:vii; Bruno Pons, *De Paris à Versailles 1699–1736: Les sculpteurs ornemanistes parisiens et l'art décoratif des Bâtiments du roi* (Strasbourg: Universités de Strasbourg, 1986), 113; idem, "Hôtels Robert de Cotte, Hôtels Jules-Robert de Cotte," in Bruno Pons and Anne Forray-Carlier, eds., *Le faubourg Saint-Germain: La rue de Bac* (Paris: Délégation à l'action artistique de la ville de Paris, 1990), 100.

10. Letter of 20 April 1719; letter of 1 October 1720 to Louis-Antoine de Noailles, archbishop of Paris; Hd 135a, 671; Marcel, nos. 413, 428, pp. 113, 117.

11. Letter of 15 February 1723 to the prince-bishop of Würzburg; Max H. von Freeden, *Quellen zur Geschichte des Barocks in Franken unter dem Einfluss des Hauses Schönborn* (Würzburg: Kommissionsverlag F. Schöningh, 1955), no. 1029, 1.2:787; also no. 1041, 1.2:806

12. H⁵ 3691; transcribed by Jannie Mayer-Long, "Les projets de Robert de Cotte pour les bâtiments conventuels de l'Abbaye de Saint-Denis," *BSHAF*, 1983, p. 68. On the relationship between de Launay and de Cotte, see Pons, "Hôtels Robert de Cotte," in Pons and Forray-Carlier, *Rue de Bac*, 98.

13. Marcel, nos. 734–35, p. 206; Yves Bottineau, *L'art de cour dans l'Espagne de Philippe V, 1700–1746* (Bordeaux: Féret, 1961), 279–80 n. 93.

14. Gilbert Gardes, "Le monument équestre de Louis XIV à Lyon et les monuments équestres de ce roi aux XVIIᵉ et XVIIIᵉ siècles," in *L'art baroque à Lyon*, Actes du colloque (Lyon: Institut d'histoire de l'art, 1975), 101 nn. 84–85.

15. Max Hauttmann, "Die Entwürfe Robert de Cottes für Schloss Schleissheim," *Münchner Jahrbuch* 6 (1911): 275.

16. *Mercure de France*, November 1725, p. 2682, quoted by Hubert Glasner, ed., *Kurfürst Max Emanuel: Bayern und Europa um 1700*, 2 vols. (Munich: Schloss Schleissheim, 1976), 1:264 n. 12.

17. For the Watteau, Margaret Morgan Graselli and Pierre Rosenberg, *Watteau, 1684–1724* (Washington, D.C.: National Gallery of Art, 1984), 384–86. The Boulle medal cabinets, if not made for Robert de Cotte, may have been commissioned by Jules-Robert's father-in-law, Nicolas de Launay, the royal silversmith mentioned in the Saint-Denis correspondence. However, they are not mentioned in the inventories after the death of de Launay (1727), Robert de Cotte (1735), or his widow (1740), as Gillian Wilson generously informed me. See Gillian Wilson, "Selected Acquisitions Made by the Department of Decorative Arts in 1984," *J. Paul Getty Museum Journal* 13 (1985): 67–69. The so-called Mantle Clock of Robert de Cotte (c. 1715; private collection), thought to be based on drawings by Pierre Le Pautre in the Fonds de Cotte (Ha 18, t. 2, 2076), is, perhaps, a commissioned piece arranged by the Premier Architecte for André-Charles Boulle; see Jean-Nérée Ronfort in *Vergoldete Bronzen: Die Bronzearbeiten des Spätbarock und Klassizismus*, ed. Hans Ottomeyer and Peter Pröschel, 2 vols. (Munich: Klinkhardt & Biermann, 1986), 2:488–89. Barry Shifman kindly brought these objects to my attention.

18. Letter of 28 September 1663; *Lettres, instructions et mémoires de Colbert*, ed. Pierre Clément, 8 vols. (Paris: Imprimerie impériale, 1861–82), 5:269.

19. Pierre Bourget and Georges Cattaui, *Jules Hardouin Mansart* (Paris: Vincent, Fréal, 1960); Jestaz, "Jules Hardouin-Mansart: L'oeuvre personelle."

20. De Cotte, who was involved in the decoration of the Château Neuf, had a permanent apartment there; Bruno Pons, "Le décor de l'appartement du Grand Dauphin au Château Neuf de Meudon (1709)," *GBA* 117 (1991): 60.

21. Dezallier d'Argenville, *Vies*, 1:360.

22. The appointment as Directeur of the Académie in 1699 indicates that de Cotte had worked for the Bâtiments since 1674, when he was about seventeen years old; Jeanne Lejeaux, "Robert de Cotte et la direction de l'Académie d'architecture," *BSHAF*, 1938, p. 30. The date is reiterated in the *lettres de noblesse*, with a list of sites where de Cotte had conducted work under Mansart, including Versailles, Trianon, Clagny, Marly, the Invalides, and the Places des Victoires and Vendôme (n. 8 above).

23. Jestaz, "Jules Hardouin-Mansart: L'oeuvre personelle," 70.

24. For the payments, see Guiffrey, *Comptes*, 2:222, 230–31, 285, 301, 308, 358, 365, 401, 427, 476, 544, 642, 835, 1123, 3:1688–89; Albert Laprade, *François d'Orbay, architecte de Louis XIV* (Paris: Vincent, Fréal, 1960), 216 n. 2; Jestaz, "Jules Hardouin-Mansart: L'oeuvre personelle," 71. For drawings of the church, Marly (1687–88), see Va 78a, t. 2, 2208–2209, 2244 (illustrated in Bourget and Cattaui, *Jules Hardouin Mansart*, pl. CXXVI); payments cited by Guiffrey, *Comptes*, 3:158.

25. In his unpublished paper for the Colloque Versailles, Château de Versailles, 1986, "Jules Hardouin-Mansart et ses dessinateurs," Bertrand Jestaz attributed to de Cotte certain drawings for royal projects of the 1680s.

26. Guiffrey, *Comptes*, 2:729.

27. Jestaz, "Jules Hardouin-Mansart: L'oeuvre personelle," 71. Château de Maintenon (1686–87): Va 28, t. 8, 363, 366–373, Va 430, 364–365 (363, 365 illustrated in

Franklin Hamilton Hazlehurst, *Gardens of Illusion: The Genius of André Le Nostre* [Nashville: Vanderbilt University Press, 1980], 340–41, figs. 256–57); Guiffrey, *Comptes*, 2:913, 1085, 1145, 1283–91. Château d'Ancy-le-Franc (c. 1690): Va 89, t. 1, 378–387; Bertrand Jestaz, *Le voyage d'Italie de Robert de Cotte* (Paris: E. de Boccard, 1966), 41.

28. Jules-Robert, whose rank, profession, and wealth depended on his father's position. Dezallier d'Argenville, *Vies*, 1:413.

29. Lemonnier, *Académie d'architecture*, 2:135.

30. Bertrand Jestaz, "Le Trianon de Marbre ou Louis XIV architecte," *GBA* 74 (1969): 259–86; Alfred Marie and Jeanne Marie, *Versailles au temps de Louis XIV. III⁰ partie: Mansart et Robert de Cotte* (Paris: Imprimerie nationale, 1976), chaps. 1–2; Daniel Meyer, "A propos du péristyle du Grand Trianon," *Revue de l'art*, no. 15 (1972): 79–80.

31. Archives de la Guerre, Paris, A¹ 786, pièce 63; transcribed by Jestaz, "Trianon," 269.

32. Louvois to Villacerf, Archives de la Guerre, A¹ 787, pièce 151; transcribed by Jestaz, "Trianon," 276–77.

33. *Mémoires du duc de Luynes sur la cour de Louis XV (1735–1758)*, ed. Louis-Etienne Dussieux and Eudoxe Soulié, 17 vols. (Paris: F. Didot, 1860–65), 2:279, quoted by Alfred Marie, "Trianon de Porcelaine et Grand Trianon," *BSHAF*, 1945–46, p. 90.

34. O¹ 1884¹, no. 2; Danielle Gallet-Guerne, with Christian Baulez, *Versailles: Dessins d'architecture de la direction générale des Bâtiments du roi*, vol. 1: *Le château, les jardins, le parc, Trianon* (Paris: Archives nationales, 1983), no. 2276, p. 428; undated but presumably from 1687–88; Mme Gallet kindly informed me that her original dating of 1691 is too late. Attributed to de Cotte by Jestaz, n. 25 above.

35. *Mercure de France*, August 1735, pp. 1817–18.

36. For evidence of the financial strain caused by the war, see the Mémoires des dépenses (1664–90) in Ms. fr. 7801, 1428.

37. Ms. fr. 7801, 1416–1417. For the history of the Surintendance, see Bernard Barbiche, "Henri IV et la surintendance des bâtiments," *Bulletin monumental* 142 (1984): 19–39; Roger Guillemet, *Essai sur la surintendance des Bâtiments du roi sous le règne de Louis XIV (1662–1715)* (Paris: A. Rousseau, 1912); Myra Nan Rosenfeld, "The Royal Building Administration in France from Charles V to Louis XIV," in *The Architect: Chapters in the History of the Profession*, ed. Spiro Kostof (New York: Oxford University Press, 1977), 161–79.

38. O¹ 1246, n.d. but presumably 1699.

39. Lemonnier, *Académie royale d'architecture*, 3:vii, 58–59, 62–63.

40. Guiffrey, *Comptes*, 4:554.

41. De Cotte's position as Mansart's right-hand man, his elevation to head of the Département de Paris (1699–1709), his role as Contrôleur at the Invalides (1699–1707;

both cited in Guiffrey, *Comptes*), and the subsequent title of Premier Architecte all ensured that he would play a major administrative role in the completion and decoration of the Hôtel and Dôme des Invalides; in particular, see references in O¹ 1665 for the years 1691, 1699, 1708; also Pons, *Sculpteurs ornemanistes*, 191, 198; Bertrand Jestaz, "Jules Hardouin-Mansart et l'église des Invalides," *GBA* 66 (1965): 68–69; Patrik Reuterswärd, *The Two Churches of the Hôtel des Invalides* (Stockholm: Nationalmuseum, 1965), 79–87; François Souchal, *Les frères Coustou* (Paris: E. de Boccard, 1980), 54–55, 126–29; idem, *Les Slodtz, sculpteurs et décorateurs du roi (1685–1764)* (Paris: E. de Boccard, 1967), 589, 592, 601, 608.

42. Stipulated, for example, in Ms. fr. 7801, 2540.

43. Guiffrey, *Comptes*, 4:554; de Cotte received further remuneration for attendance at the Académie and for other posts, such as Conseiller du Roy en Ses Conseils, Intendant et Ordonnateur Triennal des Bâtiments (4500 *livres*).

44. "Fonctions du Sieur de Coste dans le bureau qu'il tiendra prés de Nous sous nos ordres; Premierement Il sera chargé de la conduite du Bureau ou se feront tous les desseings pour le service du Roy qu'il fera faire sur ceux que Nous aurons reglé, gardera les originaux de tous lesdits desseings dans des portefeuilles bien en ordre et séparez pour chaque maison royale, et les enregistrera a mesure sur un registre avec la datte du jour qu'ils auront été faits, laquelle datte sera encore mise sur le desseing; sera chargé pareillement de tous les desseings qui étoient dans le bureau lors de la démission de M. de Villacerf, dont sera fait un Inventaire qu'il gardera soigneusement" (O¹ 1246). In short, as Dezallier d'Argenville states (*Vies*, 1:413), "Mansart étoit alors surintendant des bâtimens, & de Cotte son beau-frère avoit le détail de tous les édifices dont son maître donnoit les dessins."

45. Letter of Dom François Quenet to Dom Arnoult de Loo, 26 May 1699, H⁵ 3691, quoted by Mayer-Long, "Abbaye de Saint-Denis," 68.

46. O¹ 43, fol. 72, no. 246; transcribed by Lejeaux, "Académie d'architecture," 24.

47. Guiffrey, *Comptes*, 4:1022; Marcel, nos. 369–70, pp. 100–101, both of whom give the erroneous date, 1701. See Gardes, "Monument équestre," in *Art baroque à Lyon*, 101 nn. 84–85.

48. For the process of collaboration in the Bâtiments, see Fiske Kimball, *The Creation of the Rococo*, 2d ed. (New York: W. W. Norton, 1964), 36–40; Jestaz, "Jules Hardouin-Mansart: L'oeuvre personelle"; Reuterswärd, *Hôtel des Invalides*, 79–87; Pons, *Sculpteurs ornemanistes*, 29–51.

49. O¹ 1246. At this time Pierre Le Pautre entered the service of the king officially as Dessinateur, working principally at the Versailles office. See the annual payrolls in Guiffrey, *Comptes*, for employees, positions, and salaries.

50. Anatole de Montaiglon, *Procès-verbaux de l'Académie*

royale de peinture et de sculpture, 1648–1793, 11 vols. (Paris: Nobele, 1875–92), 3:254, 350, 374, 407; 4:10, 22–23, 126, 128, 185, 325, 330, 351.

51. Lemonnier, *Académie d'architecture*, 4:110, 179–81; *Mercure galant*, August 1710, pp. 156–58.

52. Lemonnier, *Académie royale d'architecture*, 2:192, 196–97.

53. Ibid., 2:257.

54. Ibid., 4:318–19.

55. The royal *brevet* appointing de Cotte, 6 June 1708, was read before the Académie on 21 January 1709 (ibid., 3:311).

56. *Mercure galant*, May 1708, pp. 298–99.

57. E.g., Guiffrey, *Comptes*, 5:296, 389, 739, 836, 925.

58. Philippe de Courcillon, marquis de Dangeau, *Abrégé des mémoires ou journal du marquis de Dangeau*, ed. Mme de Genlis, 4 vols. (Paris: Treuttel et Wurtz, 1817), 3:63. Letter of 24 February 1723 from Neumann to the prince-bishop of Würzburg; von Freeden, *Quellen*, no. 1034, 1.2:792. For de Cotte's residences on the rue de Tournelles and rue des Orties, Paris, and the house in Passy, see Guiffrey, *Comptes*, 5:218, 241–42 (1706–8); Va 227, 2385–2387; Mar, "Robert de Cotte," 262.

59. O¹ 1246, fol. 83–88; Sophie Jugie-Bertrac, "Le duc d'Antin, directeur-général des Bâtiments du roi (1708–1736)," *Positions des thèses*, Ecole des chartes, 1986, pp. 93–100; Jules Guiffrey, *Le duc d'Antin et Louis XIV. Rapports sur l'administration des Bâtiments, annotés par le roi* (Paris: Académie des bibliophiles, 1869); Guillemet, *Surintendance*, 201–21.

60. O¹ 1046, 207–8. The Surintendance was suppressed again in 1726.

61. On the system of the Bâtiments, contracts, and contractors, see Nicolas Delamare, *Traité de la police*, 4 vols., 2d ed. (Paris: J. & P. Cot, 1719–38), 4:14–121; Augustin-Charles Daviler, *Cours d'architecture*, additional material by Alexandre Le Blond, 2 vols. (Paris: J. Mariette, 1710), 2:548–49, 699, 884, for the words *devis*, *toisé*, and *marchés d'ouvrage, à la toise, la clef à la main, au rabais*; Jugie-Bertrac, *Duc d'Antin*, 97–98; Michel Gallet, *Stately Mansions: Eighteenth Century Paris Architecture* (New York: Praeger, 1972), 13–16; Christopher Tadgell, *Ange-Jacques Gabriel* (London: Zwemmer, 1978), 14–17; Pons, *Sculpteurs ornemanistes*, 45–47; Micheline Baulant, "Le salaire des ouvriers du bâtiment à Paris de 1400 à 1726," *Annales: Economies, sociétés, civilisations* 26 (1971): 463–83.

62. O¹ 1054, 23–24.

63. Letter of 8 March 1723 to the prince-bishop of Würzburg; von Freeden, *Quellen*, no. 1037, 1.2:796.

64. O¹ 1045, cited by Guillemet, *Surintendance*, 211; Marcel Marion, *Histoire financière de la France depuis 1715* (Paris: A. Rousseau, 1914).

65. See the list of posts enumerated in Ms. fr. 7801, fol. 250, n.d., but dating from de Cotte's tenure.

66. De Cotte's name appears regularly in documents for the decoration of the chapel and its vestibule (O¹ 1784). Kimball denies him any measure of creative responsibility (*Creation of the Rococo*, 79) whereas Souchal accords him a leading role (*Frères Coustou*, 65–70, 81–82). Probably at least until the mid 1720s de Cotte laid down the principal outlines of a project for Versailles verbally or in sketches; subsequently the Gabriels assumed the major administrative and creative roles there (Christian Baulez, "Versailles," in Michel Gallet and Yves Bottineau, *Les Gabriel* [Paris: Picard, 1982], 30–31, 144–54). For the other rooms, Souchal, *Frères Coustou*, 119; Alfred Marie and Jeanne Marie, *Versailles au temps de Louis XV, 1715–1745* (Paris: Imprimerie nationale, 1984), 188–203, 268–75; Pons, *Sculpteurs ornemanistes*, 141; Souchal, *French Sculptors*, 3:438–39.

67. Although historians have alternately given and denied de Cotte credit for the design (Maurice Vloberg, *Notre Dame de Paris et le voeu de Louis XIII* [Paris: author, 1926], 100–112; Kimball, *Creation of the Rococo*, 84–88), it appears that, as at Versailles, the project was collaborative in the fullest sense of the term. The underlying architectonic composition may have been de Cotte's contribution—the Gothic piers were encased in a classical shell—while the rich decoration was the invention of *ornemanistes* and sculptors like François-Antoine Vassé, favored by de Cotte for relief carving (Michel Le Moël, "Catalogue des plans et dessins d'architecture concernant Notre-Dame de Paris au XVIIᵉ et XVIIIᵉ siècles conservés aux Archives nationales et à la Bibliothèque nationale," *Mémoires de la Société d'histoire de Paris et Ile-de-France* 21 [1970]: 155–72; Souchal, *Frères Coustou*, 83–92; Pons, *Sculpteurs ornemanistes*, 38–41, 92, 96–101, 166–68, 203–5).

68. De Cotte's official duties during the Regency were largely restricted to inspection of royal sites for the purpose of determining the need for maintenance; e.g., E 1994, fol. 179 (Meudon); E 2000, fol. 384–85 (Amboise); E 2003, fol. 187–88 (royal farms).

69. For Louis XV de Cotte drew up plans of Reims Cathedral in preparation for the coronation (1723; Pons, *Sculpteurs ornemanistes*, 90 n. 242); made proposals for the Bibliothèque du roi in Paris (1720s; Marcel, nos. 199–204, pp. 50–52; Jean Babelon, *Le Cabinet du Roi ou le Salon Louis XV de la Bibliothèque nationale* [Paris and Brussels: G. Vanoest, 1927]; Pons, *Sculpteurs ornemanistes*, 137, 224–25; Jean Porcher, "Deux projets de constructions pour la Bibliothèque du Roi," *BSHAF*, 1930, pp. 100–101).

70. Letter of 22 December 1714, Hd 135, 177; Marcel, no. 623, p. 173; transcribed by John Finley Oglevee, ed., *Letters of the Archbishop-Elector Joseph Clemens of Cologne to Robert de Cotte (1712–1720)* (Bowling Green, Ohio: author, 1956), 41–42.

71. Letter of 28 February 1715, Hd 135, 177; Marcel, no.

626, p. 174; Oglevee, *Letters*, 44.

72. Undated draft of a letter from de Cotte to Carlier, January 1715 (Hd 135b, 1019; Marcel, no. 725, p. 203).

73. Catherine Grodecki, "La Résidence de Saverne sous les trois premiers cardinaux de Rohan," *Le Château de Saverne*, ed. Alphonse Wollbrett (Saverne: Société d'histoire et d'archéologie de Saverne et environs, 1969), 41.

74. Letter of 9 March 1718, Hd 135, 177; Marcel, no. 678, p. 189; Oglevee, *Letters*, 132.

75. Michel Gallet, "L'architecte Pierre de Vigny (1690–1772): Ses constructions, son esthétique," *GBA* 82 (1973): 263–86. For de Noinville, see Marcel, nos. 393–96, pp. 108–9; Yves Beauvalot, "La construction du Palais des Etats de Bourgogne et de la Place Royale à Dijon (1674–1725) de Daniel Gittard à Robert de Cotte: L'oeuvre de Jules Hardouin-Mansart," supplementary number of *Mémoires de la Commission des antiquités du département de la Côte-d'or* (Dijon: Académie des sciences, arts et belles-lettres, 1981). For Simon, Madeleine Huillet d'Istria, "L'art de François d'Orbay révélé par la Cathédrale de Montauban," *XVIIᵉ siècle* 72 (1966): 7.

76. Wend Graf Kalnein and Michael Levey, *Art and Architecture of the Eighteenth Century in France* (Harmondsworth: Penguin, 1972), 251.

77. Gallet and Bottineau, *Les Gabriel*, 21–129.

78. Michel Gallet and Jörg Garms, *Germain Boffrand, 1667–1754* (Paris and Lunéville: Délégation à l'action artistique de la ville de Paris, 1986).

79. Letter of 3 April 1723 to the prince-bishop of Würzburg; von Freeden, *Quellen*, no. 1046, 1.2:817.

80. Bibliothèque de l'Arsenal, Paris, Ms. 3054, 80–81, 96–105, 192–93, including criticism of de Cotte's urban structures.

81. Sébastien Le Clerc, *Traité d'architecture* (Paris: P. Giffart, 1714), "au lecteur"; Werner Szambien, *Symétrie, goût, caractère: Théorie et terminologie à l'âge classique 1550–1800* (Paris: Picard, 1986), 99–110.

82. Szambien, *Symétrie*, 92–98; Rémy G. Saisselin, *The Rule of Reason and the Ruses of the Heart* (Cleveland: Case Western Reserve University Press, 1970); Peter-Eckhard Knabe, *Schlüsselbegriffe des kunsttheoretischen Denkens in Frankreich von der Spätklassik bis zum Ende der Aufklärung* (Dusseldorf: Schwann, 1972); Anne Röver, *Bienséance. Die ästhetische Situation im Ancien Régime: Pariser Privatarchitektur* (Hildesheim: Georg Olms, 1977).

83. J. L. de Cordemoy, *Nouveau traité de toute l'architecture*, 2d ed. (Paris: J. B. Coignard, 1714; Farnborough: Gregg, 1966), 3, 85, 229.

84. Le Clerc, *Traité d'architecture*, 39; Richard Cleary, "Jacques-François Blondel and the Notion of Architectural Convenance," M.A. thesis, University of Wisconsin–Madison, 1977; Szambien, *Symétrie*, 167–73.

85. Michel de Frémin, *Mémoires critiques d'architecture*

(Paris: Charles Saugrain, 1702; Farnborough: Gregg, 1967), 44–45.

86. De Cordemoy, *Nouveau traité*, 236; Jean Courtonne, *Traité de la perspective pratique* (Paris: J. Vincent, 1725), 92. Also see Daviler, *Cours d'architecture*, 1:185.1.

87. Jacques-François Blondel, *De la distribution des maisons de plaisance* (Paris: C. A. Jombert, 1737; Farnborough: Gregg, 1967), 1:3–4.

CHAPTER TWO

1. Louvois to La Teulière, 29 August 1689, Archives de la Guerre, A¹ 855, fol. 360, cited by Jestaz, *Voyage*, 19.

2. Jestaz, *Voyage*, 157. De Cotte's travel diary is housed in the Bibliothèque nationale, Cabinet des manuscrits (Ms. fr. 14663–14664), while the drawings from the trip are kept separately in the Cabinet des estampes, where they are dispersed among Italian holdings in the Topographie. Jestaz, *Voyage*, has published a transcription of the journal, a catalogue of the drawings, and an analysis of the journal in terms of orthography and the use of guidebooks as sources; reviewed by Jacques Bousquet, *Bibliothèque de l'Ecole des chartes* 125 (1967): 221–30. Whereas Jestaz focuses on the architect's reaction to historical styles, from ancient to contemporary, I analyze de Cotte's responses to specific building types. Moreover, I attempt to discern relationships between the monuments viewed on the trip and de Cotte's subsequent designs.

3. Jestaz, *Voyage*, 171.

4. Ibid.

5. Ibid., 242.

6. Ibid., 170, 244.

7. Ibid., 167–68, 174.

8. Ibid., 190, 196.

9. Ibid., 226.

10. Ibid., 225.

11. Ibid., 192.

12. Ibid., 251.

13. Ibid., 162.

14. Ibid., 169.

15. Ibid., 163.

16. Leon Battista Alberti, *On the Art of Building in Ten Books*, trans. Joseph Rykwert et al. (Cambridge, Mass.: MIT Press, 1988), 294.

17. Jestaz, *Voyage*, 192.

18. Ibid., 239.

19. Susan Davis Baldino, "The Importance of Palladio's Villas for Seventeenth-Century France," *Athenor*, no. 10 (1991): 11–15, with further bibliography; Jestaz, *Voyage*, 110–17.

20. Alessandro Baldan, *Storia della riviera del Brenta*, 3 vols. (Vicenza: Moro, 1980–81), 3:221–23.

21. Jestaz, *Voyage*, 195.

22. Ibid., 171.

23. Ibid., 216.

24. Ibid., 179.

25. Ibid., 241–42.

26. Ibid., 162.

27. Ibid., 250.

28. Ibid., 216.

29. Ibid.

30. Ibid., 170–72.

31. Ibid., 174.

32. Ibid., 224.

33. Ibid.

34. Ibid., 172.

35. Ibid., 177.

36. Ibid., 163.

37. Ibid., 220.

38. Ibid., 230.

39. Ibid., 217.

40. Ibid., 231.

41. Ibid., 181.

42. Ibid., 168.

43. Ibid., 199, 203.

44. Illustrated in Robert Neuman, "Robert de Cotte and the Baroque Ecclesiastical Façade in France," *JSAH* 44 (1985): 252, fig. 2. The present discussion of Italian portals is derived from this article.

45. Jestaz, *Voyage*, 178.

46. Ibid., 177.

47. Ibid., 212.

48. Ibid., 229.

49. Ibid., 218–19.

50. Ibid., 218.

CHAPTER THREE

1. Braham and Smith, *François Mansart*, 1:173–74.

2. Pons, "Hôtels Robert de Cotte," in Pons and Forray-Carlier, *Rue de Bac*, 99.

3. At some time in the eighteenth century the collection was numbered in red in the lower left-hand corner (Ye 36). The drawings can be located by searching through the handwritten card catalogue composed by Alfred Marie, which is organized by number (Fichier de Cotte, Ye 187; a printed catalogue is in preparation). Most of the drawings are in the following series: Ha, Hd, Va, Vb, Vc, Vd. For an introduction to the collection, see Destailleur, *Notices sur quelques artistes*, 212–20; Marcel, xviii–xxx. The drawings formed the basis for exhibitions devoted to de Cotte and Hardouin-Mansart respectively: *Dessins et souvenirs de Robert de Cotte, premier architecte du roi (1656–1735)* (Paris: Hôtel des Invalides, 1937); *Hardouin-Mansart et son école* (Paris: Bibliothèque nationale, 1946).

4. Alfred Marie, "Inventaires des portefeuilles no. 1036,

1037, 1038, 1039, 1040, 1041, conservés à la Bibliothèque de l'Institut" (typescript, Paris, 1941); Monique Hébert and Jacques Thirion, *Catalogue général des cartes, plans et dessins d'architecture*, vol. 1, *Serie N. Paris et le département de la Seine* (Paris: Imprimerie nationale, 1958).

5. They are principally in Hd and Ms. fr. 7801, 9447.

6. Letter of 23 August 1715, Hd 135, 177; Marcel, no. 634, pp. 176–77; Oglevee, *Letters*, 56–57.

7. On drawing materials, techniques, and studio practices, see Christophe Ballard, *L'art de dessiner proprement les plans, porfils, elevations geometrales, & perspectives* (Paris: Ballard, 1697); Hubert Gautier, *L'art de laver* (Brussels: Foppens, 1708), chaps. 9–12; Daviler, *Cours d'architecture*, 2:532–33, 547, 578, 660, 789–90; Katharina Krause, "Zu Zeichnungen französischer Architekten um 1700," *Zeitschrift für Kunstgeschichte* 53 (1990): 59–88; Gallet-Guerne, *Versailles*, 13–14; Maya Hambly, *Drawing Instruments, 1580–1980* (London: Philip Wilson, 1988); Pons, *Sculpteurs ornemanistes*, 29–30, 35. For architectural models, usually made of wood, plaster, or wax, see Ludmann, *Palais Rohan*, 1:67; Oglevee, *Letters*, 79, 83–84.

8. Illustrated in color by Bertrand Jestaz, *L'Hôtel et l'Eglise des Invalides* (Paris: Picard, 1990), 16–17.

9. Buchotte, *Les règles du dessin et du lavis pour les plans particuliers des ouvrages et des bâtimens, et pour leurs coupes, profils, élévations & façades, tant de l'architecture militaire que civile* (Paris: C. Jombert, 1754 ed.), 34.

10. Saint-Simon, *Mémoires*, 16:39; Dezallier d'Argenville, *Vies*, 2:365, comments favorably on Mansart's drafting skills.

11. "Cet Artiste . . . composoit avec une facilité surprenante" (Roland Le Virloys, *Dictionnaire*, 1:429); "Robert de Cotte composoit avec beaucoup de facilité" (Pingeron, *Vies*, 1:405); "Il dessinoit et composoit avec facilité" (Lempereur, *Dictionnaire*, 1:291, quoted by Pons, *Sculpteurs ornemanistes*, 32).

12. Jestaz, "Jules Hardouin-Mansart: L'oeuvre personelle"; Jestaz, "Trianon," 267.

13. Kimball, *Creation of the Rococo*, 37; Laprade, *François d'Orbay*, 216–17 n. 1; Jestaz, *Voyage*, 34, 253–54.

14. Va 270a, 2754–2757; Kimball, *Creation of the Rococo*, 128–29; Pons, "Hôtels Robert de Cotte," in Pons and Forray-Carlier, *Rue de Bac*, 99–100.

15. Va 78h, t. 3, 2676 (cf. 2677); Pons, *Sculpteurs ornemanistes*, 32, 92.

16. Ha 18a, 1203, undocumented, dated by Ludmann to c. 1725, probably for Prince William VIII of Hesse-Kassel, for whom de Cotte prepared designs for Schloss Tilburg, c. 1715–17 (chap. 5); conceivably an unexecuted design for the Palais des Prinzen Wilhelm built in the first two decades of the century in the Oberneustadt, Kassel (undocumented, destroyed 1943; Wolf von Both and Hans Vogel, *Landgraf Wilhelm VIII. von Hessen-Kassel* [Berlin: Deutscher Kunst-

verlag, 1964], 177). For this and related gallery schemes, see Ludmann, *Palais Rohan*, 2:479; Jean-Daniel Ludmann and Bruno Pons, "Nouveaux documents sur la galerie de l'Hôtel de Toulouse," *BSHAF*, 1981, pp. 115–28. The rhythmical alternation of broad and narrow bays separated by slender paneled pilasters, and the form of the large cartouches in the wider bays, bordered by reversed scrolls at the top and a segmental arch at the bottom, were hallmarks of interior designs produced in de Cotte's studio.

17. The fundamental study is Pons, *Sculpteurs ornemanistes*, part 1; also 110–13, 131–32, 211–12, 216–17, and *passim*. For decorative projects produced under de Cotte, see Kimball, *Creation of the Rococo*, 37, 94–95, 104–5, 117–18, 125–29, 142–43; Ludmann, *Palais Rohan*, 2:465–84; Jean-Daniel Ludmann, "Nouveaux documents sur l'Hôtel du Doyenné du Grand Chapitre, actuel Evêché de Strasbourg," *Cahiers alsaciennes d'archéologie, d'art et d'histoire* 23 (1980): 73–88; Marie, *Versailles au temps de Louis XV*, 70–77; Jean-Luc Bordeaux, "La commande royale de 1724 pour l'Hôtel du Grand Maître à Versailles," *GBA* 104 (1984): 113–26; Pons, "Château Neuf de Meudon," 59–76; Hauttmann, "Schloss Schleissheim"; Yves Bottineau, "Philip V and the Alcázar at Madrid," *Burlington Magazine* 98 (1956): 68–75; Grodecki, "Saverne," in Wollbrett, *Saverne*, 39–59; Babelon, *Cabinet du Roi*.

Shortly after de Cotte's death, Jacques-François Blondel credited him with inventing the *cheminée à la royale*, the placing of a large mirror on the chimney breast over the mantle (*Maisons de plaisance*, 2:68), an attribution repeated by de Cotte's biographers and subsequently disproven by modern scholarship (Kimball, *Creation of the Rococo*, 52, 67–71, 143), although he may have popularized the motif (Pons, "Hôtels Robert de Cotte," in Pons and Forray-Carlier, *Rue de Bac*, 100).

18. The most gifted figure working with de Cotte was Vassé, chief designer and sculptor at the Galerie Dorée, Hôtel de Toulouse, Paris (1716–19); see Souchal, *French Sculptors*, 3:402–42. Other collaborators included René Charpentier, sculptor and designer, who assisted de Cotte on the interior decor of Saint-Roch, Paris (1720s); Laurent Le Prince and Charles Rousseau at the Château de Saverne (1721–22); André Legoupil, Pierre Taupin, and Jules Degoullons, sculptors in the Société pour les Bâtiments du roi, working at such sites as the new choir of Notre-Dame de Paris (1710–15). All are discussed by Pons, *Sculpteurs ornemanistes*.

CHAPTER FOUR

1. Louis Réau, *L'art français sur le Rhin au XVIIIᵉ siècle* (Paris: H. Champion, 1922); idem, *Histoire de l'expansion de l'art français*, 4 vols. (Paris: H. Laurens, 1924–33); idem, *L'Europe française au siècle des Lumières* (Paris: Michel,

1938); Pierre du Colombier, *L'art français dans les cours rhénanes* (Paris: La Renaissance du Livre, 1930); idem, *L'architecture française en Allemagne au XVIIIᵉ siècle*, 2 vols. (Paris: Presses universitaires, 1956); Adrien Faucheir-Magna, *The Small German Courts in the Eighteenth Century* (London: Methuen, 1958), chap. 2; Kalnein and Levey, *Art and Architecture*, 250–59; George L. Hersey, *Architecture, Poetry, and Number in the Royal Palace at Caserta* (Cambridge, Mass.: MIT Press, 1983), 45–48.

2. Letter of 8 March 1723; von Freeden, *Quellen*, no. 1037, 1.2:796.

3. Blondel, *Cours d'architecture*, 2:233–36.

4. De Cordemoy, *Nouveau traité*, 87.

5. Courtonne, *Traité*, 93.

6. Daviler, *Cours d'architecture*, 2:676, 742–43; Blondel, *Cours d'architecture*, 2:245–46.

7. *Mercure galant*, August 1719, pp. 156–58.

8. Saint-Simon, *Mémoires*, 28:163.

9. Letter of 5 November 1699 to the Duchess of Hanover; Gertrude Scott Stevenson, trans. and ed., *The Letters of Madame: The Correspondence of Elizabeth-Charlotte of Bavaria*, 2 vols. (New York: D. Appleton, 1925), 1:192; cited by Christian Baulez, "Le Grand Projet," in Gallet and Bottineau, *Les Gabriel*, 182, 301 n. 1. See also Pingeron, *Vies*, 2:348–49. On projects for expanding and ameliorating the palace, some dating from c. 1678, see Alfred Marie and Jeanne Marie, *Mansart à Versailles*, 2 vols. (Paris: J. Fréal, 1972), 2:636–43; Guy Walton, *Louis XIV's Versailles* (Chicago: University of Chicago Press, 1986), 93–95.

10. Bottineau, "Philip V"; idem, *Art de cour*; idem, "Antoine du Verger et l'Alcázar de Madrid en 1711," *GBA* 87 (1976): 178–80; Pons, *Sculpteurs ornemanistes*, 206–7, 237.

11. Jonathan Brown and J. H. Elliott, *A Palace for a King: The Buen Retiro and the Court of Philip IV* (New Haven: Yale University Press, 1980).

12. Barbara von Barghahn, *Philip IV and the "Golden House" of the Buen Retiro*, 2 vols. (New York: Garland, 1986), 1:9–10.

13. Françoise d'Aubigné, marquise de Maintenon, *Lettres inédites*, 4 vols. (Paris: Bossange, 1826), 1:270, quoted by Bottineau, *Art de cour*, 259. Plans of the Buen Retiro and environs, Ha 20, 996–1000, 1002, 1018.

14. First pair of projects (1712–13): 1000a–b, letter of de Cotte to René Carlier, 26 January 1713, Hd 135b, 1019; Marcel, no. 706, p. 198; transcribed by Bottineau, *Art de cour*, 618–19.

15. Hd 135b, 1019; Marcel, no. 728, p. 204; transcribed by Bottineau, *Art de cour*, 264. De Cotte remodeled the Hôtel de Beauvais for Orry in 1706; see chap. 7, n. 15 below.

16. Hd 135b, 1019; Marcel, no. 728, p. 204; transcribed by Réau, *Histoire de l'expansion*, vol. 1, *Le monde latin*, 361.

17. Second pair of projects (1714–15): first proposal, Hd 135b, 1003–1009, 1015; second proposal, 1010–1013,

1016–1017.

18. Hd 135b, 1019; Marcel, no. 729, p. 204; transcribed by Bottineau, *Art de cour*, 619–22.

19. Daviler, *Cours d'architecture*, 2:369–70.

20. In eighteenth-century France the imperial stair, called by Daviler the *escalier à deux rampes parallèles*, was a subcategory of the *grand escalier*, defined as the most spacious stair in a building, ushering the visitor from the vestibule to the *premier étage* only (Daviler, *Cours d'architecture*, 2:574–76, 1:324). De Cotte used the form standard in his day, a single central flight leading to a pair of flights; some precedents are composed of the reverse configuration. See Jean-Jacques Gloton, "L'escalier baroque dans l'architecture aixoise du XVIIIᵉ siècle," in *Actes du 90ᵉ congrès national des sociétés savantes* (Nice, 1965), 3 vols. (Paris: Bibliothèque nationale), 3:569–70. Robert W. Berger, Michael Rabens, and Catherine C. McCurrach generously assisted me in identifying stairs.

21. Robert W. Berger, *Antoine Le Pautre: A French Architect of the Era of Louis XIV* (New York: New York University Press, 1969), 25; also the plan of a château by Le Pautre, c. 1652–65, p. 30. Braham and Smith, *François Mansart*, 1:132 n. 24; 2: pls. 474ff., are reluctant to discuss the proposed Louvre stairs, some ambiguously drawn. For the Louvre project of Candiani, which features an imperial stair (1664), see Daniela del Pesco, *Il Louvre di Bernini nella Francia di Luigi XIV* (Naples: Fiorentino, 1984), 13–14, 25, figs. 8–9.

22. Yvan Christ, *Le Louvre et les Tuileries* (Paris: Tel, 1949), 74–75, figs. 83, 86; Daviler, *Cours d'architecture*, 1:324. François d'Orbay proposed an imperial stair for the remodeling of the royal Château de Saint-Germain, 1673; Laprade, *François d'Orbay*, pl. VII.11.A. For Le Vau's imperial stair at the Hôtel de Lionne, Paris (1662–65; interior refitted by de Cotte in 1703), see Anthony Blunt, *Art and Architecture in France, 1500–1700*, 5th ed. (Harmondsworth, 1982), 228.

23. Bertrand Jestaz, "Documents sur l'oeuvre de Jules Hardouin-Mansart à Chantilly," *Bulletin monumental* 149 (1991): 41; Berger, *Le Pautre*, 71 n. 30; Daviler, *Cours d'architecture*, 1:186.17, pl. 63R. For the unexecuted proposal for an imperial stair at Versailles, see Marie and Marie, *Mansart à Versailles*, 641, plan K.

24. The Château du Raincy (early 1640s), the remodeling of the Château de Meudon (1654–c. 1657), the Château de Vaux-le-Vicomte (1656–61), and projects for the East Front of the Louvre (1661/2–64). On the *salon à l'italienne*, see Daviler, *Cours d'architecture*, 2:847–48; Cordemoy, *Nouveau traité*, 102, 157–58; Blondel, *Maisons de plaisance*, 1:31; Claude Mignot, "Petit lexique de l'hôtel parisien," *XVIIᵉ siècle* 41, no. 162 (1989): 103–4; Berger, *Le Pautre*, 26–29; idem, "Louis Le Vau's Château du Raincy," *Architectura* 6 (1976): 40–43; Dietrich Feldmann, "Das Hôtel de La Vrillière und die Räume 'à l'italienne' bei Louis Le Vau," *Zeit-*

schrift für Kunstgeschichte 45 (1982): 410–20.

25. Hd 135b, 1019; Marcel, no. 723, p. 202; transcribed by Wend Graf Kalnein, *Das kurfürstliche Schloss Clemensruhe in Poppelsdorf* (Düsseldorf: Schwann, 1956), 175–76. For the summer apartments at the Alcázar, see Steven N. Orso, *Philip IV and the Decoration of the Alcázar of Madrid* (Princeton: Princeton University Press, 1986), 23. For theoretical discussion of the disposition of apartments with respect to the sun and the seasons, see Alberti, *De re aedificatoria*, book 5, chap. 17; Louis Savot, *L'architecture françoise des bastimens particuliers* (Paris: François Clouzier, 1673), 48; Daviler, *Cours d'architecture*, 2:378; Charles Etienne Briseux, *L'art de bâtir des maisons de campagne*, 2 vols., 2d ed. (Paris: Gibert, 1761; Farnborough: Gregg, 1966), 1:24.

26. Louis XIV dined publicly in the preceding room, the Salle du Grand Couvert; Pierre Verlet, *Le Château de Versailles* (Paris: Fayard, 1985), 210; H. Murray Baillie, "Etiquette and the Planning of the State Apartments in Baroque Palaces," *Archeologia* 101 (1967): 188 fig. 7, 190.

27. Yves Bottineau, "Aspects de la cour d'Espagne au XVIIᵉ siècle: Etiquette de la chambre du roi," *Bulletin hispanique* 74 (1972): 138–57, with further bibliography.

28. Louis XIV, *Mémoires for the Instruction of the Dauphin*, trans. Paul Sonnino (New York: Free Press, 1970), 101; different ed. cited by Baillie, "Etiquette," 183 n. 1. On the origins of the French royal *appartement*, see Bertrand Jestaz, "Etiquette et distribution intérieure dans les maisons royales de la Renaissance," *Bulletin monumental* 146 (1988): 109–20; Henri Brocher, *A la cour de Louis XIV: Le rang et l'étiquette sous l'ancien régime* (Paris: Alcan, 1934).

29. Vd 31, 990; Bottineau, "Philip V"; idem, "Verger."

30. Referring specifically to the Hymen Room (S) (Hd 135b, 1019; Marcel, no. 701, p. 195; quoted by Bottineau, "Philip V," 73). Carlier's plan of the old Buen Retiro shows the same insistent differentiation of spaces.

31. Briseux, *Maisons de campagne*, 1:116, 123; Marc Antoine Laugier, *Essai sur l'architecture* 2d ed. (Paris: Duchesne, 1755), 105. De Cordemoy, *Nouveau traité*, 92–94, was opposed to the use of the giant order on secular buildings.

32. Daviler, *Cours d'architecture*, 1:187, pl. 64A; Blondel, *Cours d'architecture*, 2:246. For the tradition of the square dome, see Ursula Reinhardt, *Die bischöflichen Residenzen von Châlons-sur-Marne, Verdun und Strasbourg. Ein Beitrag zum Werk des Ersten Königlichen Architekten Robert de Cotte (1656–1735)* (Basel: Reinhardt, 1972), 147–48. On the Versailles dome, see Marie and Marie, *Mansart à Versailles*, 2:636–43; Walton, *Louis XIV's Versailles*, 93–95. For the motif of the crown, see Berger, *Le Pautre*, 29–30.

33. Hd 135b, 1019; Marcel, no. 728, p. 204; transcribed by Réau, *Histoire de l'expansion*, vol. 1, *Le monde latin*, 361.

34. F. Lesueur, "Les dernières étapes de la construction de Chambord," *Bulletin monumental* 109 (1951): 7–40; Lemonnier, *Académie d'architecture*, 3:xviii, 22, 89.

35. Sebastiano Serlio, *On Domestic Architecture: The Sixth Book*, introduction by Myra Nan Rosenfeld (New York: Architectural History Foundation, and Cambridge, Mass.: MIT Press, 1978), 68–70; Hilary Ballon, *The Paris of Henri IV* (New York: Architectural History Foundation, and Cambridge, Mass.: MIT Press, 1991), 315 n. 54. Also, Serlio, *Seventh Book*, chaps. 3, 21.

36. Catherine Wilkinson, "The Escorial and the Invention of the Imperial Staircase," AB 57 (1975): 65–90; Lemonnier, *Académie d'architecture*, 3:179–81.

37. Hersey, *Caserta*, 104, 153–71; Alfredo Vigo Trasancos, "En torno a unos planos para el palacio del Buen Retiro y su impacto en la Reggia de Caserta," *Archivo español de arte* 59 (1986): 69–76.

38. Glasner, *Kurfürst Max Emanuel*.

39. Sabine Heym, *Henrico Zuccalli (um 1642–1724): Der kurbayerische Hofbaumeister* (Munich: Schnell & Steiner, 1984).

40. Erich Hubala, "Henrico Zuccallis Schlossbau in Schleissheim, Planung und Baugeschichte 1700–1704," *Münchner Jahrbuch der bildenden Kunst* 17 (1966): 161–200; Michael Petzet, "Unbekannte Entwürfe Zuccallis für die Schleissheimer Schlossbauten," *Münchner Jahrbuch der bildenden Kunst* 22 (1971): 179–204; Dorith Riedl, *Henrico Zuccalli: Planung und Bau des Neuen Schlosses Schleissheim* (Munich: author, 1977); Samuel J. Klingensmith, "The Utility of Splendor: Program and Plan in the Palaces of the Court of Bavaria, 1600–1800," Ph.D. diss., Cornell University, 1986, 124–26, 139–55.

41. Jörg Garms, "Boffrand," in Gallet and Garms, *Boffrand*, 59–61.

42. Letter of 4 January 1705 to Gräfin Arco, transcribed by Richard A. L. Paulus, *Der Baumeister Henrico Zuccalli am kurbayerischen Hofe zu München* (Strasbourg: J. H. E. Heitz, 1912), 262–63.

43. Klingensmith, "Utility of Splendor," 157. The drawings from Munich are in MS 1039, nos. 6–7, 23 (Schleissheim) and nos. 11, 25 (Nymphenburg); Michael Petzet, "Entwürfe für Schloss Nymphenburg," *Zeitschrift für Bayerische Landesgeschichte* 35 (1972): 205–12; and Petzet, "Schleissheimer Schlossbauten," 196–97. In the same year Pierre-Alexis Delamaire presented a portfolio of drawings to the elector in the hope of attracting his patronage.

44. Altes Schloss: Va 29, t. 1, 108. First proposal: Ha 19, 121, Va 29, t. 1, 99–102, 104, 106–107. Second proposal: plans, Vd 29, t. 1, 103, 105, 120, Ha 19, 121–122, 129–130r; elevations and sections, Ha 19, 130v, 156, 158r; chapel, Ha 19, 157–158v, 159, 161. The majority of sheets in Paris are preliminary drawings. The presentation drawing of a gallery interior, related to Ha 19, 156, may have been part of a group of finished drawings taken back to Bavaria by Max Emanuel (Kupferstichkabinet, Munich, Sammlung Halm-Maffey XIV, 27). The proposals were originally discussed in part by Hauttmann, "Schloss Schleissheim."

45. Hd 135b, 1019; Marcel, no. 728, p. 204.

46. Nathan T. Whitman, "Fontainebleau, the Luxembourg, and the French Domed Entry Pavilion," *JSAH* 46 (1987): 356–73; Braham and Smith, *François Mansart*, 2: pls. 153, 477, and *passim*. A cross section of the Buen Retiro entrance pavilion shows it domically vaulted within, but not capped by an exterior dome (Ha 18, 1009). The entrance screen is not a feature of the large ground floor plan for Schleissheim, Va 29, t. 1, 99.

47. Friedrich Carl von Moser, *Teutsches Hof-Recht*, 2 vols. (Frankfurt and Leipzig: J. B. Andrea, 1754–55), 2:275, quoted in translation by Klingensmith, "Utility of Splendor," 462. I am indebted to Christian F. Otto for permission to use material from this dissertation (in press).

48. Another early sketch of the ground plan, 104, shows clearly the entry pavilion; unlike the finished plans, it features stairs in the angles of the *cour d'honneur* (similar to Zuccalli's quadrangular plan, 1700), a major reception room (*Hauptsaal*) in the *corps-de-logis* to left of the axis, and a *grande galerie* in the north wing.

49. Ragnar Josephson, "Quelques dessins de Claude Perrault pour le Louvre," GBA 16 (1927): 175, 179–83.

50. Petzet, "Schleissheimer Schlossbauten," 191, 198, figs. 13, 20.

51. Baillie, "Etiquette," 193–96; Klingensmith, "Utility of Splendor," chaps. 4–6, for a thorough study based on primary sources.

52. Daviler, *Cours d'architecture*, 1:180, 2:377–78.

53. Maren Holst, "Robert de Cottes Entwürf für die Schleissheimer Schlosskapelle und Balthasar Neumanns Schönbornkapelle am Würzburger Dom," *Architectura* 11 (1981): 147–56.

54. Hubala, "Zuccallis Schlossbau," "Project C," 163, 168, figs. 2, 5; Luisa Hager and Gerhard Hojer, *Schleissheim: Neues Schloss und Garten* (Munich: Bayerische Verwaltung der staatlichen Schlosser, Gärten und Seen, 1973), with modern plans.

55. Runar Strandberg, "The French Formal Garden after Le Nostre," in Elisabeth Blair MacDougall, ed., *The French Formal Garden* (Washington, D.C.: Dumbarton Oaks, 1974), 43–67.

56. For an introduction to Joseph Clemens, see Oglevee, *Letters*, v–xxiv. The elector returned to Bonn in February 1715.

57. Letter of 25 June 1713 to de Cotte, Hd 135, 116; Marcel, no. 609, p. 169; Oglevee, *Letters*, 3.

58. Catalogued by Marcel, 166–95; transcribed by Oglevee, *Letters*, 1–100. In addition to their correspondence, architect and patron met in Paris during November–December 1715.

59. Letter of 7 September 1716, Hd 135, 177; Marcel, no. 657, p. 183; Oglevee, *Letters*, 81.

60. Letter of 25 June 1713, Hd 135, 116; Marcel, no. 609, p. 169; Oglevee, *Letters*, 10.

61. Hauberat's twenty-eight letters to de Cotte are transcribed by Oglevee, *Letters*, 101–54, who includes a brief biography, 164 n. 46. Pons, *Sculpteurs ornemanistes*, 73.

62. Zuccalli's building: Ha 19, 115, 147–148, 150–152. De Cotte's proposals: 115, 118–119, 1014. Final projects: 109–112, 116–117, 123–124, 126–128, 149, 153–154; interiors, 162–171, 175–176. See Edmund Renard, "Die Bauten der Kurfürsten Josef Clemens und Clemens August von Köln" (part 1), *Bonner Jahrbücher* 99 (1896): 175–99; Kalnein, *Poppelsdorf*, 47–54; Kalnein and Levey, *Art and Architecture*, 253–54; Fritz Baumgart, *Universität Bonn und Poppelsdorf* (Bonn: Scheur, 1937); Max Braubach, "Von den Schlossbauten und Sammlungen der kölnischen Kurfürsten des 18. Jahrhunderts," *Annalen des Historischen Vereins für den Niederrhein* 153–54 (1953): 106–16; Hans-Joachim Kunst, "Die Stadtresidenz der Kölner Kurfürsten," in Heinrich Lützeler, ed., *Die Bonner Universität: Bauen und Bildwerke* (Bonn: Bouvier & Röhrscheid, 1968), 9–28.

63. Letter of 25 June 1713, Hd 135, 116; Marcel, no. 609, p. 169; Oglevee, *Letters*, 7–8.

64. Baillie, "Etiquette," 193–96; Klingensmith, "Utility of Splendor," 291–92. Joseph Clemens lists the ceremonies performed in the *salle des gardes* in a letter to de Cotte, 18 December 1714, Hd 135, 177; Marcel, no. 622, p. 173; Oglevee, *Letters*, 40.

65. Letter of 8 April 1714, Hd 135, 177; Marcel, no. 615, 170–71; Oglevee, *Letters*, 17.

66. The key to the rooms marked on plan 118 is reprinted by Oglevee, *Letters*, 187–90.

67. Braham and Smith, *François Mansart*, 2: pls. 511, 513.

68. Letter of 11 June 1714, Hd 135, 177; Marcel, no. 616, p. 171; Oglevee, *Letters*, 21.

69. Originally proposed 25 June 1713, reiterated 8 April 1714, Hd 135, 116; Marcel, nos. 609, 615, pp. 169, 170–71; Oglevee, *Letters*, 8–9, 17.

70. Letter of 15 August 1714, Hd 135, 177; Marcel, no. 618, p. 172; Oglevee, *Letters*, 30–31.

71. Letter of 23 August 1715, Hd 135, 177; Marcel, no. 634, pp. 176–77; Oglevee, *Letters*, 56–57.

72. For the elector's Grand Appartement at Bonn (Ha 19, 127), see Baillie, "Etiquette," 194–96. The interior designs issuing from de Cotte's studio are discussed by Kimball, *Creation of the Rococo*, 126–27; Pons, *Sculpteurs ornemanistes*, 118–19 n. 332. Much was lost in the disastrous fire of 1777. The building now houses the University of Bonn: Gisbert Knopp and Wilfried Hansmann, *Universitätsgebäude in Bonn* (Neuss: Gesellschaft fur Buchbruckerei, 1976).

73. Letters of 20 October 1716, 4 December 1717, 27 April 1719, Hd 135, 177; Marcel, nos. 654, 675, 689, pp. 182, 188, 192; and Renard, "Bauten des Kurfürsten Joseph Clemens," 202. Plans 111–112, 128 show the imperial stair accessible from the east entry, thus shifted from its position in plans 118, 1014.

74. Letters of 21 November 1714, 23 August 1715, Hd 135, 177; Marcel, nos. 620, 634, pp. 172–73, 176–77; Oglevee, *Letters*, 35–36, 57; du Colombier, *Architecture française*, 135–37. Photograph of present state in Heym, *Henrico Zuccalli*, 67.

75. De Cotte's Würzburg drawings have been much studied, but not in the context of his earlier palace designs: Richard Sedlmaier and Rudolf Pfister, *Die fürstbischöfliche Residenz zu Würzburg*, 2 vols. (Munich: G. Müller, 1923), 1:28–35; Erich Hubala and Otto Mayer, *Die Residenz zu Würzburg* (Würzburg: Popp, 1984), 143–49; Georges Brunel, "Les contacts entre Balthasar Neumann et Robert de Cotte," *Actes du XXIIᵉ Congrès international d'histoire de l'art*, 3 vols. (Budapest: Akadémiai Kiadó, 1972), 2:115–19; Charles Edward Meyer, "The Staircase of the Episcopal Palace at Würzburg," Ph.D. diss., University of Michigan, 1967, 71–86; Pierre du Colombier, "La Résidence de Wurtzbourg: L'influence française sur l'architecture allemande au début du XVIIIᵉ siècle," *La Renaissance de l'art français*, August 1923, pp. 447–56.

76. Letter of Philipp Christoph von Erthal to Lothar Franz von Schönborn, 24 February 1720; von Freeden, no. 733, 1.2:578–79.

77. Christian F. Otto, *Space into Light: The Churches of Balthasar Neumann* (New York: Architectural History Foundation, and Cambridge, Mass.: MIT Press, 1979), 134.

78. Vd 29, 1193–1197; Kunstbibliothek, Berlin, Hdz 4682 (Eckhart Berckenhagen, *Die Französischen Zeichnungen der Kunstbibliothek Berlin* [Berlin: Hessling, 1970], 148).

79. Letter of 1 March 1723; von Freeden, *Quellen*, no. 1036, 1.2:793; see also Karl Lohmeyer, *Die Briefe Balthasar Neumanns von seiner pariser Studienreise, 1723* (Düsseldorf: L. Schwann, 1911).

80. Letter of 14 April 1723; von Freeden, *Quellen*, no. 1057, 1.2:829.

81. Letter of 12 April 1723; ibid., no. 1055, 1.2:827; similarly, nos. 1029, 1038, 1.2:787, 800. See also Neumann's comments quoted above in chap. 1.

82. Letter of 8 March 1723; ibid., no. 1037, 1.2:796.

83. For the reverse imperial stair at the Château de Saverne (c. 1666–74; architect unknown) and Balthasar Neumann's sketch plan of it, see Roger Lehni, "Le château sous les princes-évêques de Fürstenburg (1663–1704)," in Wollbrett, *Saverne*, 23, figs. 20–21.

84. Letter of 15 February 1723; von Freeden, *Quellen*, no. 1029, 1.2:785–86.

85. Braham and Smith, *François Mansart*, 2: pls. 484ff.

86. Baillie, "Etiquette," 196–97, 199.

87. Letter of 8 March 1723; von Freeden, *Quellen*, no. 1037, 1.2:796.

88. Letter of 22 March 1723; ibid., no. 1041, 1.2:805–6.

89. Letter of 12 April 1723; ibid., no. 1055, 1.2:827.

90. Letter of 3 April 1723; ibid., no. 1046, 1.2:815–16.

91. Letter of 7 April 1723; ibid., no. 1052, 1.2:822–23.

92. Letter of Anselm Freiherr von Ritter to Johann Philipp Franz, 4 April 1723; ibid., no. 1049, 1.2:819–20.

93. Although Boffrand also advocated a single stair (von Freeden, *Quellen*, no. 1046, 1.2:814), the project published in his *Livre d'architecture* ([Paris: G. Cavelier, 1745; Farnborough: Gregg, 1969], 91–95, pls. LV–LX) retains the double stair as well as the two longitudinal ovals in the side wings; see also Garms, "Boffrand," in Gallet and Garms, *Germain Boffrand*, 63–68.

94. Jean-Pierre Samoyault, "Fontainebleau," in Gallet and Bottineau, *Les Gabriel*, 34–36.

95. Plans: Va 446, 1474–1476, Va 77, t. 6, 1479–1482a; elevations: Va 77, t. 6, 1477–1478. Plans 1481 and 1482a are inscribed on the back, possibly by de Cotte, "projet pour fontainebleau 1729." The drawings have not been analyzed previously, but their existence was first acknowledged by Louis Dimier, *Les villes d'art célèbres, Fontainebleau* (Paris: Renouard, 1925), 102–3.

96. Baillie, "Etiquette," 180, 182, fig. 5; Jestaz, "Etiquette et distribution," 111–16; Yves Bottineau, "Etudes sur l'Appartement du Roi à Fontainebleau au XVIIIᵉ siècle," *Positions des thèses et mémoires de l'Ecole du Louvre*, 1945–53, pp. 43–49.

97. Tadgell, *Gabriel*, 33, 49; Baulez, "Grand Projet," in Gallet and Bottineau, *Les Gabriel*, 187.

CHAPTER FIVE

1. Blondel, *Maisons de plaisance*, 1:7.

2. Blondel, *Cours d'architecture*, 2:249–52; Jörg Garms, "La première moitié du XVIIIᵉ siècle," in Jean-Pierre Babelon, ed., *Le château en France*, 2d ed. (Paris: Berger-Levrault and CNMHS, 1988), 321–32; Dietrich von Frank, *Die 'maison de plaisance': Ihre Entwicklung in Frankreich und Rezeption in Deutschland, Dargestellt an ausgewählten Beispielen* (Munich: Scaneg, 1989).

3. Daviler, *Cours d'architecture*, 2:465, 676–77.

4. Among the numerous projects in the Fonds de Cotte for remodeling country houses, mostly undocumented, the following châteaux are represented: Ancy-le-Franc, Anet, Croissy-Beaubourg, after 1711 (Marcel, no. 359, p. 96; Runar Strandberg, "Dessins et documents inédits concernant les constructions de Jean-Baptiste Colbert, marquis de Torcy, pour son hôtel de Paris et ses Châteaux de Croissy, Sablé et Bois-Dauphin," *GBA* 99 [1982]: 137–41), Maison du marquis de Fontenay, Guermantes, in 1710–11 (Michel Borjon, "La galerie du Château de Guermantes," *BSHAF*, 1985, pp. 105–28), La Chapelle, La Muette, in 1717–19 (Marcel, nos. 319–20, p. 83), Meilhaud, in 1721–22, Saint-

Maur-les-Fossés, Thouars (Bauchal, *Dictionnaire biographique*, 158; de Sacy, "Robert de Cotte," 835), Vitry-sur-Seine, Château of Graf von Sinzendorf, imperial ambassador to France (de Sacy, "Robert de Cotte," 836; Ludmann, *Palais Rohan*, 1:33). Also, remodeling of the Château de Chanteloup for the princesse des Ursins, 1711 (MS 1038, no. 5, MS 1604, nos. 2, 51, 52; R. Edouard André, "Documents inédits sur l'histoire du château et des jardins de Chanteloup," *BSHAF*, 1935, pp. 21–39).

Undated projects in the Fonds de Cotte for new structures include the Château d'Orly (Jörg Garms, "Der Grundriss der Malgrange I von Boffrand," *Wiener Jahrbuch für Kunstgeschichte* 22 [1969]: 186, fig. 244), *maison de plaisance* of Monsieur de Vauvray, Ménagerie of the duchesse de Lorraine at Lunéville (Garms, "Boffrand," in Gallet and Garms, *Germain Boffrand*, 105); unidentified projects for pavilions (Ha 18, t. 2, 2101–2102, t. 3, 2517). See the list of country residences in *Hardouin-Mansart et son école*, 63.

5. Blondel, *Maisons de plaisance*, 1:2–3.

6. Ibid, 1:31; Briseux, *Maisons de campagne*, 1:22.

7. On the function of rooms, see Daviler, *Cours d'architecture*, 1:185.8–13; Blondel, *Maisons de plaisance*, 1:24–36; Briseux, *Maisons de campagne*, 1:21–25.

8. Jestaz, *Voyage*, 157–58.

9. Geoffrey Symcox, *Victor Amadeus II: Absolutism in the Savoyard State, 1675–1730* (Berkeley: University of California Press, 1983).

10. First project, characterized by double pavilions on the four corners and two zones of rooms along the cross axis: the pen-and-ink plan (Vb 5, 13, illustrated in Garms, "Malgrange I," fig. 246) apparently reflects Garove's conception, the shortcomings of which—cramped spaces and lack of easy circulation—were corrected in a pencil drawing by de Cotte (Vb 5, 11). The new building, whose construction was initiated by Garove, and of which the eastern (right-hand) part stands today, has the same double pavilions and is of the same scale as that represented in the first project. Second project: Vb 5, 12, 15. Site plans: 7–8, 14. For the various attributions of the drawings, see Albert Brinkmann, *Theatrum Novum Pedemontii* (Düsseldorf: Schwann, 1931), 50–51; Kalnein and Levey, *Art and Architecture*, 214; Garms, "Malgrange I," 186–87, n. 10.

11. Vb 132z, 10, 37–38; Vb 5, 39–40, 42–47. For the correspondence requesting Hardouin-Mansart's assistance in preparing new designs for the Venaria, for which there is no evidence of a response: Hd 135, 41, 48; Marcel, nos. 602–3, p. 166, transcribed by Brinkmann, *Theatrum Novum Pedemontii*, 82–89; commented on by Richard Pommer, *Eighteenth-Century Architecture in Piedmont* (New York: New York University Press, 1967), 146–49.

12. Gianfranco Gritella, *Rivoli: Genesi di una residenza Sabauda* (Modena: Panini, 1986), 82–83.

13. Monique Châtenet, *Le Château de Madrid au bois de*

Boulogne (Paris: Picard, 1987); for drawings of Madrid in the Fonds de Cotte (c. 1733–35; Va 438, 2625–2630), see pp. 43–44, 50–51; on sources in the Italian villa tradition, pp. 105–9. Also, Per Gustav Hamberg, "The Villa of Lorenzo il Magnifico at Poggio ai Caiano and the Origin of Palladianism," in Åke Bengtsson et al., *Idea and Form: Studies in the History of Art* (Stockholm: Almquist & Wiksell, 1959), 76–87.

14. Klingensmith, "Utility of Splendor," 30.

15. Garms, "Malgrange I," discusses the relationship between de Cotte's second project for Rivoli and Boffrand's plan for Malgrange I, the country house outside Nancy commissioned by the duc de Lorraine. The plan that Boffrand submitted to the Académie for approval on 22 February 1712 is that in the Fonds de Cotte bearing de Cotte's additions—columnar supports within the vestibule and three sets of stairs to the right of the longitudinal axis, intended to reconcile differences in ground level (Va 54, t. 1, 808; Lemonnier, *Académie d'architecture*, 4:4).

16. Blondel, *Maisons de plaisance*, 1:8.

17. Jestaz, *Voyage*, 253.

18. Briseux, *Maisons de campagne*, 1:116.

19. Ibid., 1:130.

20. Of Juvarra's plan for Rivoli (c. 1718), which borrowed motifs from Garove but not from de Cotte, only the great central section was built, attached to Garove's east wing.

21. Letter of 25 March 1715, Hd 135, 177; Marcel, no. 628, pp. 174–75; Oglevee, *Letters*, 47.

22. Letter of 25 April 1715, Hd 135, 177; Marcel, no. 630, p. 175; Oglevee, *Letters*, 49.

23. Vc 255, t. 2, 172; Oglevee, *Letters*, 50–53. See Pierre du Colombier, "Deux projets de Robert de Cotte pour l'électeur de Cologne," *Archives alsaciennes d'histoire de l'art* 7 (1928): 97–106.

24. Edmund Renard and Wolff Metternich, *Schloss Brühl* (Berlin: Deutscher Verein für Kunstwissenschaft, 1934), 13–14.

25. Runar Strandberg, "Le Château de Champs," GBA 61 (1963): 81–100.

26. Vc 254, 137–138; du Colombier, "Deux projets," 106–8.

27. Letter of 13 August 1704, Hd 135, 177; Marcel, no. 604, pp. 166–67; Oglevee, *Letters*, 171. My discussion is based on the exhaustive monograph by Kalnein, *Poppelsdorf*. Surviving drawings are in Vc 254, 131–135, and Landeskonservator Rheinland. For the date of the wooden model, see Ludmann, *Palais Rohan*, 2:579 n. 41. Also see Lützeler, *Bonner Universität*.

28. Letter of 24 May 1715, Hd 135, 177; Marcel, no. 631, pp. 175–76; Oglevee, *Letters*, 53.

29. For de Cotte's first project, see Kalnein, *Poppelsdorf*, 56–62, fig. 75, who hypothesizes double arcaded *loggie* encircling the court.

30. Letter of 1 September 1715, Hd 135, 177; Marcel, no. 635, p. 177; Oglevee, *Letters*, 60–61.

31. Serlio, *Sixth Book*, 27, 69, 72, 82–83, figs. 33, 43, pls. XXVIII–XXIX, LXXI; also, Seventh Book, chap. 12.

32. Formal precedents for Poppelsdorf, including the Palace of Charles V, Granada, are discussed by Kalnein, *Poppelsdorf*, 107–16; the relationship to Serlio's Sixth Book is my own observation. On the origins of the circular courtyard, see Hamberg, "Poggio ai Caiano," 86.

33. For the history of the site, see Kalnein, *Poppelsdorf*, chap. 1. Vignola's design for Caprarola was similarly dependent on the plan of the unfinished fortress by Antonio da Sangallo that it replaced; see Daviler, *Cours d'architecture*, 1:256–58.

34. Serlio, *Sixth Book*, 68–69.

35. Ragnar Josephson, *Nicodème Tessin: L'architecte de Charles XII à la cour de Louis XIV* (Paris: Van Oest, 1930), 58, 70, pl. XII; Jestaz, *Voyage*, 151.

36. Letter of 17 August 1705; transcribed by Roger-Armand Weigert and Carl Hernmarck, *Les relations artistiques entre la France et la Suède, 1693–1718* (Stockholm: Egnellska Boktryckeriet, 1964), 343. Like de Cotte, Tessin was drawn to Palladio's works on his Italian travels; Henry Ley, "Tessin's Opinions of Italian Renaissance Architecture," in *Actes du XXIIᵉ Congrès international d'histoire de l'art* (Budapest, 1969), ed. György Rózsa (Budapest: Akadémiai Kiado, 1972): 2:101–3.

37. On the attic order, see Courtonne, *Traité*, 103–4.

38. Briseux, *Maisons de campagne*, 1:115.

39. Prince William, who had visited Paris in his youth, sought to remodel the medieval castle most likely between 1715 (acquisiton of the estate) and 1717 (his marriage). The old building apparently stood until a new structure was erected in 1755. For the dating, a transcript of de Cotte's *mémoire*, reproductions of the drawings (Vc 75, 474–480), and an engraved view of the moated castle, see Annelise Rauch-Elkan, "Acht Pläne und ein Baumémoire Robert de Cottes für Schloss Tilbourg in Brabant," *Brabantia*, 2 February 1958, 43–52. Also, Both and Vogel, *Wilhelm VIII von Hessen-Kassel*, 21–22. On the connection between the Hesse-Kassel dynasty and French artists, which sprang originally from Protestant connections, see du Colombier, *Architecture française*, 1:41–45. For an undocumented project for a gallery identified as that of the Prince of Hesse-Kassel, see chap. 3 above.

40. Claude Mignot, "De la cuisine à la salle à manger, ou de quelques détours de l'art de la distribution," *XVIIᵉ siècle* 41, no. 162 (1989): 17–35.

41. Briseux, *Maisons de campagne*, 1:25; Blondel, *Maisons de plaisance*, 1:88–89.

42. For Challuau, see Wolfram Prinz and Ronald G. Kecks, *Das französische Schloss der Renaissance*, Frankfurter

Forschungen zur Kunst, vol. 12 (Berlin: Gebr. Mann, 1985), 461–64.

43. De Cordemoy, *Nouveau traité*, 101.

44. Blondel, *Maisons de plaisance*, 1:6–7. Garden designs from the de Cotte studio are of the traditional French formal type: Antoine-Joseph Dezallier d'Argenville, *La théorie et la pratique du jardinage* (Paris: J. Mariette, 1713).

45. Vc 75, 474; transcribed by Rauch-Elkan, "Schloss Tilbourg," 50.

46. Tadgell, *Gabriel*, 140–41; Jean-Marie Moulin, "Compiègne," in Gallet and Bottineau, *Les Gabriel*, 232. Old château: O¹ 1408.

47. Va 60, t. 13, 1649, Va 60, t. 14, 1648 (site plan dated 1729), 1654, 1656, Va 434, 1650–1653, 1655; the plans vary slightly in room shapes. Alfred Marie, "Quelques notes sur le Château de Compiègne avant sa transformation par Gabriel," *Bulletin de la Société historique de Compiègne* 22 (1944): 67–73; Françoise Thiveaud-Le Hénand, "Le reconstruction du Château de Compiègne au XVIIIᵉ siècle," *Positions des thèses*, Ecole des chartes, 1970, pp. 205–14.

48. Louis Hautecoeur, "Le plan en X à propos d'un projet de Boffrand," *BSHAF*, 1959, pp. 22, 166–74; Prinz and Kecks, *Französische Schloss*, 456–60.

49. The plan apparently derives from a casino project by Carlo Fontana consisting of three arms projecting from a central rotunda (1689); Allan Braham and Hellmut Hager, *Carlo Fontana: The Drawings at Windsor Castle* (London: Zwemmer, 1977), 107–9, pls. 232–37. For a useful résumé of the Franco-Italian sources of the centralized villa, including the X-shaped plan, see Pommer, *Piedmont*, 68–71. Cf. also Antoine Le Pautre's fourth design from the *Desseins de plusieurs palais* (Berger, *Le Pautre*, pls. 28–30).

50. Garms, "Boffrand," in Gallet and Garms, *Germain Boffrand*, 85–87.

51. Louis Hautecoeur, *Première moitié du XVIIIᵉ siècle*, vol. 3 of *Histoire de l'architecture classique en France* (Paris: Picard, 1950), 12–13.

52. On the emblematic character of sixteenth-century French châteaux, see Wolfram Prinz, *Schloss Chambord und die Villa Rotonda in Vicenza: Studien zur Ikonologie* (Berlin: Gebr. Mann, 1980), 55–61.

53. The Premier Architecte did not go to Saverne but acted as mediator between the patron, designers in the Bâtiments, and the assistants on the site, Charles Le Bouteux, Charles Carbonnet, Le Chevalier, and Laurent Gourlade. No essential architectural changes were made to the château, which on Armand-Gaston's arrival consisted of three wings of medieval and Renaissance construction and a late seventeenth-century garden wing erected by the bishops of Fürstenburg, together enclosing a *cour d'honneur*. Interior remodeling focused on the splendid Grand Appartement (1712/17–23) and Appartement du Cardinal (c. 1728), both in the rococo style. Exterior additions included the simple Episcopal Chapel (c. 1720) and the Nouveau Pavillon, an elegant point of entry on the garden side intended to impress visitors arriving from Strasbourg (1728–30). The large suite of drawings in the Bibliothèque nationale and the Bibliothèque de l'Institut has been studied by Catherine Grodecki, "Travaux du premier cardinal de Rohan au Château de Saverne d'après des documents inédits, 1704–1730," *Cahiers alsaciens d'archéologie, d'art et d'histoire* 11 (1967): 97–112; idem, "Résidence de Saverne," in Wollbrett, *Saverne*, 39–59. See also Marcel, nos. 551–55, pp. 148–49; Michèle Beaulieu, *Robert Le Lorrain (1666–1743)* (Neuilly-sur-Seine: Arthena, 1982), 61–63.

54. Georges Vigarello, *Concepts of Cleanliness: Changing Attitudes in France since the Middle Ages*, trans. Jeran Birrell (Cambridge: Cambridge University Press, 1988), chaps. 7–8.

55. First project: Va 67, t. 3, 1251, two unnumbered plans. Second project: 1245–1246, 1250, 1253–1254. Third project: 1242, 1244, 1248–1249, 1257; MS 1038, no. 13, MS 1042, nos. 6, 7, 8, 13, MS 1605, no. 93. The present discussion elaborates on Grodecki, "Résidence de Saverne," in Wollbrett, *Saverne*, 49–51, who does not address the bathing function.

56. Runar Strandberg, "Le Château d'Issy, la construction de Pierre Bullet," *GBA* 96 (1980): 197–208.

57. Blondel, *Maisons de plaisance*, 1:72; 2:129–33. For the *appartement des bains*, Daviler, *Cours d'architecture*, 1:352, 2:378; Hautecoeur, *Architecture classique*, 3:201–2; Gallet, *Stately Mansions*, 120–21.

58. Blondel, *Maisons de plaisance*, 1:73. The usual subsidiary furnace and drying rooms do not appear in the first project.

59. On water closets, see Hautecoeur, *Architecture classique*, 3:201–3.

60. Letter of 1 October 1730, Hd 135b, n.n.; Marcel, no. 553, p. 149, transcribed by Réau, *Art français*, 66. On the subject of *glacières* for conserving ice and snow, see Briseux, *Maisons de campagne*, 1:13–15.

61. Jean-Marie Pérouse de Montclos, *Histoire de l'architecture française: De la Renaissance à la Révolution* (Paris: Mengès, 1989), 333–35.

62. As defined by Blondel, *Cours d'architecture*, 1:413–16.

63. On this question, see Grodecki, "Résidence de Saverne," in Wollbrett, *Saverne*, 51.

CHAPTER SIX

1. Delamare, *Police*, 4:10.

2. Ibid., 1:86–87.

3. *Colbert, 1619–1683* (Paris: Hôtel de la Monnaie, 1983), 275–78.

4. Martin Lister, *A Journey to Paris in the Year 1698*, 3d ed.

(London: J. Tonson, 1699), reprint ed. by Raymond Phineas Stearns (Urbana: University of Illinois Press, 1967), 15; Joachim-Christophe Nemeitz, *Séjour de Paris* (Leiden: Jean van Abcoude, 1727), chap. 13, "Des promenades," reprinted in Alfred Franklin, ed., *La vie privée d'autrefois* (*La vie de Paris sous la Régence*, vol. 1) (Paris: Plon, 1897), 82–98; Mark Girouard, *Cities and People: A Social and Architectural History* (New Haven: Yale University Press, 1985), 166–80.

5. "Eloge de M. de la Mare," Delamare, *Police*, 4:[vii–ix]; Paul-Martin Bondois, "Le commissaire Nicolas Delamare et le *Traité de la Police*," *Revue d'histoire moderne* 10 (1935): 313–51.

6. "En effet, il est reservé à la Police de veiller sur la régularité, & sur la forme des bâtimens; de prescrire l'alignement, la construction, & la hauteur des maisons; de conserver la largeur & la liberté de la voye publique; d'empêcher les enterprises qui pourroient nuire aux passans, ou causer de la difformité; d'entretenire la propreté dans les rues par le moyen du pavé & du nettoyement; en un mot les Halles, les Marchez, les Places publiques & tout ce qui interesse, ou la décoration de la Ville, ou la commodité des habitans, se trouve du ressort de la Police" (Delamare, *Police*, 4:10). See Alan Williams, *The Police of Paris, 1718–1789* (Baton Rouge: Louisiana State University Press, 1979), xvii–xviii, 5–16. Delamare recognized that Paris, despite the density of its population, was an enjoyable place to live because its laws and building codes ensured a measurable degree of privacy, health, and well-being. Believing that laws regulating public life had descended from the ancients, he included a general history of Paris from the Gauls to the Bourbons, illustrated by a series of eight maps tracing the city's growth (e.g., my fig. 68). His treatment of such topics as market and guild regulations, lighting and cleaning of streets, and mechanics of water distribution is so comprehensive that the result is an astonishingly vivid picture of Parisian life.

7. Delamare, *Police*, 4:400–403.

8. Ibid., 4:37.

9. Ibid., 4:37, 367–68.

10. Dominique Labarre de Raillicourt, "Les Beausire, architectes du roi," *BSHAF*, 1958, pp. 83–87.

11. For an example of the bureaucratic process involving the entire hierarchy, the restoration of the Petit Pont (1718), see Delamare, *Police*, 4:361–63; Marcel, nos. 173–75, pp. 44–45. For a list of urban projects in the Fonds de Cotte, see *Hardouin-Mansart et son école*, 52–53, 62–63.

12. Edward Wright, *Some Observations Made in Travelling through France, Italy, &c., in the Years MDCCXX, MDCCXXI, and MDCCXXII*, 2d ed., 2 vols. (London: A. Millar, 1764), 1:4.

13. For a discussion of the ramparts and the Bullet-Blondel *Plan de Paris*, see Gaston Bardet, *Naissance et méconnaissance de l'urbanisme: Paris* (Paris: SABRI, 1951), 197–217.

14. Delamare, *Police*, 4:396; *Louis XIV et l'urbanisme royal parisien* (Paris: Musée de l'histoire de France, Archives nationales, 1984), 6. In the first third of the eighteenth century Paris continued to expand at a rapid pace consistent with the overall trend during the two centuries: a population of about 250,000 in 1600 more than doubled to about 550,000 inhabitants by 1800; Girouard, *Cities and People*, 212.

15. Delamare, *Police*, 1:103.

16. Va 444, 1615.

17. Delamare, *Police*, 4:396.

18. Henri Sauval, *Histoire et recherches des antiquités de la ville de Paris*, 3 vols. (Paris: C. Moette, 1724; Geneva: Minkoff, 1974), 2:287.

19. Va 278, t. 1–2, 2359, signed, "Bon áprouve par le Roy le 8ᵉ desambre 1700 Mansart." There is no evidence that the gates were constructed. Undated drawings for several small bureaux in the region west of the Tuileries are in Va 278f, t. 1–3, 2597–2604.

20. Germain Brice, *Description de la ville de Paris*, 9th ed., 4 vols. (Paris: Libraires associés, 1752; Geneva: Droz, 1971), 1:173.

21. Hd 135d, 1617 (undated); Marcel, no. 27, p. 8; *Colbert*, no. 438, p. 301. See also Marcel, nos. 25–26 (dated 1667, the first phase of activity) and nos. 28–31 (c. 1716–19), pp. 8–10; Dominique Leborgne, ed., *Les Champs Elysées et leur quartier* (Paris: Délégation à l'action artistique de la ville de Paris, 1988), 13–16.

22. Brice, *Ville de Paris*, 1:184; a drawing for the Grille de Chaillot is in Va 278, t. 1–2, 2596.

23. N I Seine 51–52. Cf. N III Seine 700¹ (22 June 1696), 30 (3 February 1719), and Arch. nat. Vers. Arch. Album no. 59, pièce 5 (early eighteenth century), all of which show the esplanade as it appeared without projects; *Louis XIV et l'urbanisme royal parisien*, nos. 22, 62, pp. 8, 18. See also Hazlehurst, *Le Nostre*, 175–77, 184 n. 15, and Runar Strandberg, "Jean-Baptiste Bullet de Chamblain, architecte du roi (1665–1726)," *BSHAF*, 1962, pp. 236–39.

24. *Gazette d'Amsterdam* (*Avec privilège de nos seigneurs les Etats de Hollande*), 79 (27 September 1700), quoted by Arthur Michel de Boislisle, "Notices historiques sur la Place des Victoires et sur la Place de Vendôme," *Mémoires de la Société de l'histoire de Paris et de l'Ile-de-France* 15 (1888): 241.

25. Va 444, 2353.

26. On obelisks, *Selected Lectures of Rudolph Wittkower: The Impact of Non-European Civilizations on the Art of the West*, ed. Donald Martin Reynolds (Cambridge: Cambridge University Press, 1989), 72–87, 114–21.

27. Hd 135e, n.n., in Marcel, no. 217, pp. 56–57; Brice, *Ville de Paris*, 1:159. Drawings for the Pont Tournant are in Va 220, 2368–2369, with contemporary prints.

28. Va 444, 2354–2356; gates bordering the moat appear on the plan Va 444, 1615 (fig. 69).

29. Jacques Hillairet, *Dictionnaire historique des rues de Paris*, 2 vols (Paris: Editions de Minuit, 1963), 2:577. For a history of Parisian city gates, see Delamare, *Police*, 1:88 and passim, 101–5.

30. Delamare, *Police*, 4:403.

31. Grille de fer: Va 278f, t. 3, 2355, Va 220, 2360e; Italianate portal, in the following sequence: Va 220, 2360d, c, a, b; tollhouse and officers' lodgings: Va 220, 2592–2593, Va 278f, t. 3, 2594, Va 440, 2590.

32. *Louis XIV et l'urbanisme royal parisien*, no. 14, p. 7.

33. Brice, *Ville de Paris*, 1:153; Hazlehurst, *Le Nostre*, 167–85.

34. Sauval, *Paris*, 2:59.

35. *Gazette d'Amsterdam* 79 (27 September 1700), quoted by de Boislisle, "Notices historiques," 241.

36. Va 220, 2370–2371, 2373–2377. There is no accompanying plan showing the intended location of these undated projects, nor evidence that they were built. A design for the large Tuileries *parterre* by Jules-Robert de Cotte was etched by Jacques-Gabriel Huquier the Younger (c. 1758–64; B.N. Est. A 17660).

37. Brice, *Ville de Paris*, 1:156–57.

38. On the problem of determining de Cotte's responsibility at the Invalides, see chap. 1, n. 41, above; Guiffrey, *Comptes*, 4:912; Hc 14, t. 2. For the Infirmary see O¹ 1665, no. 117 (27 September 1691), cited in René Baillargeat, ed., *Les Invalides, trois siècles d'histoire* (Paris: Musée de l'Armée, 1974), no. 20, p. 26, and Hc 14, t. 1, 1688–1689. For the Logement des Pères (1691), see Hc 14, t. 1, 1686–1687a. The Aisle de Cotte was the work of Jules-Robert (1747–50): Arch. nat. M.C., CXV, 567, cited in Mireille Rambaud, *Documents du Minutier central concernant l'histoire de l'art (1700–1750)*, 2 vols. (Paris: SEVPEN, 1964, 1971), 1:430; for the plan and elevation, Abbé Gabriel-Louis Calabre Pérau, *Description historique de l'Hôtel royal des Invalides* (Paris: G. Desprez, 1756; Geneva: Minkoff, 1974), pl. 18; also Baillargeat, *Trois siècles*, no. 68, p. 35. For the project for a base for the statue of Louis XIV in the Cour Royale (unexecuted), see Hc 14, t. 1, 1711, dated 1724; Marcel, nos. 62–65, pp. 15–16; François Souchal, "Les Coustou aux Invalides," GBA 83 (1974): 273–74. For Langlois's print, "Le Roi accompagné de sa cour visite l'Hôtel des Invalides . . . le 18 septembre 1706," in which Mansart, seconded by de Cotte, offers Louis XIV the key to the Dôme (*Almanach*, 1707), see Georges Dethan, *Nouvelle histoire de Paris: Paris au temps de Louis XIV, 1660–1715* (Paris: Hachette, 1990), 148.

39. Sauval, *Paris*, 1:537.

40. Hc 14, t. 1, 1716, originally drawn by Dubois c. 1717–20, later inscribed 1726 on the verso.

41. Contemporaries acknowledged the similarity of the project to the Vatican piazza: Brice, *Ville de Paris*, 4:8.

42. Although de Cordemoy, *Nouveau Traité*, 125–26, makes no specific mention of the Invalides project, he describes this type of semicircular classical surround ("portique") as appropriate to public spaces in which spectacles are held, because its form suggests an ancient theater. For the concept of the *teatro* in Baroque city planning, see Rudolph Wittkower, *Palladio and Palladianism* (New York: G. Braziller, 1974), 26–27; Richard Krautheimer, *The Rome of Alexander VII, 1655–1667* (Princeton: Princeton University Press, 1985), 3–7.

43. Archives de la Guerre, A¹ 473, pièce 150, 8 April 1676, quoted by Reuterswärd, *Hôtel des Invalides*, 15, 28.

44. Weigart and Hernmark, *Relations artistiques*, 198.

45. Va Grand Rouleau, 1670, 1672; Hc 14, t. 1, 1671. Two graphite drawings, O¹ 1665, nos. 115, 131, also likely date from the 1690s. Reuterswärd, *Hôtel des Invalides*, 28–29, 75, fig. 27, attributes them "probably" to de Cotte, although stylistically they do not resemble his hand. It should be noted that in 115 the draftsman included an alternative project for a pair of straight arms parallel to the façade of the Dôme. A project for semicircular arcades enclosing the square was conceived by Pierre Bullet; Runar Strandberg dates the extant drawings to the same time, c. 1698: "Libéral Bruand et les problèmes que soulèvent l'Eglise des Soldats et le Dôme des Invalides," *Konsthistorisk Tidskrift* 35 (1966): 15–22, figs. 14–15.

46. Pierre Bellocq, *L'Eglise des Invalides* (Paris: M. Brunet, 1702); Jean-François Félibien, *Description de la nouvelle église de l'Hôstel Royal des Invalides* (Paris: Jacques Quillau, 1706), illustrated in Pérouse de Monclos, *Architecture française*, 320, fig. 350.

47. Hc 14, t. 1, 1716 and 1719 (the latter dating from c. 1717). In a plan that shows the complex in a fairly advanced state (between 1720 and 1745) the adopted solution is a large semicircular *place* with seven tree-lined radiating avenues (Hc 14, t. 1, 1720).

48. Hd 135d, 1717–1718; Marcel, nos. 91–93, p. 20; Delamare, *Police*, 4:396.

49. Pérau, *Hôtel Royal des Invalides*, 50–51, pl. 11; Maurice Séguin, "L'Esplanade des Invalides," *Bulletin de la Société d'histoire et d'archéologie des VIIᵉ et XVᵉ arrondissements de Paris*, no. 31 (March 1930): 176–80.

50. Delamare, *Police*, 4:391, with laws pertaining to maintenance of *places royales*, 390–95. For the history of Parisian squares, see Sauval, *Paris*, 1:617–33; Delamare, *Police*, 1:97–98; Richard Cleary, *The Places Royales of Louis XIV and Louis XV* (New York: Architectural History Foundation, and Cambridge, Mass.: MIT Press, forthcoming). For early unexecuted projects from the circle of Hardouin-Mansart (not necessarily by de Cotte) that involve remodeling the Place Dauphine (1671–89) and the Place du Collège des Quatre Nations (n.d.), see Jörg Garms, "Projects for the

Pont Neuf and the Place Dauphine in the First Half of the Eighteenth Century," *JSAH* 26 (1967): 102–13; Ballon, *Paris of Henri IV*, 127–45.

51. De Boislisle, "Notices historiques"; *Place des Victoires et ses abords* (Paris: Mairie du 1er arrondissement, 1983), 14–34; Ferdinand de Saint-Simon, *Place des Victoires* (Paris: Vendôme, 1984), 288.

52. "Aresté le present dessein par sa majesté à marly ce 8 novembre 1692 pour former la rue et former la portion circulaire . . . de Cotte": Va 441, 1569; also Va 230e, 929, plan, and 930, elevation.

53. De Boislisle, "Notices historiques"; Ragnar Josephson, "Les projets pour la Place Vendôme," *L'architecture*, 1928, pp. 83–91; Pons, *Sculpteurs ornemanistes*, 113–29.

54. De Cordemoy, *Nouveau Traité*, 124, implies that an architect other than Mansart was responsible for the second (1699) design (cited by Cleary, *Places Royales*).

55. Runar Strandberg, "Les dessins d'architecture de Pierre Bullet pour la Place Vendôme et l'Hôtel Reich de Pennautier-d'Evreux," *GBA* 60 (1965): 71–72.

56. Va 441, 1806.

57. Va 234, 1804. Kimball, *Creation of the Rococo*, 37, and Kalnein and Levey, *Art and Architecture*, 206, accept the attribution to de Cotte.

58. For drawings of the Place Vendôme in the Fonds de Cotte, see Va 234, 1807, 2479, 2711–2711b; Va 441, 1493, 1805, 1808, 1810–1813.

59. Delamare, *Police*, 1:97; Girouard, *Cities and People*, 179–80.

60. Delamare, *Police*, 4:366.

61. Ibid. For a historical account of quays and docks along the Seine written by a contemporary, see Sauval, *Paris*, 1:241–48.

62. Delamare, *Police*, 4:360, 367.

63. Quoted by Adolphe Berty and Louis Tisserand, *Région du faubourg Saint-Germain*, vol. 4 of *Topographie historique du vieux Paris* (Paris: Imprimerie impériale, 1882), 387; Marcel, nos. 100–102, 119, pp. 22–25, 30.

64. Ha 18, t. 1, 2664, Va 444, 2561 (first decade, eighteenth century); Va 444, 2648 (inscribed and dated 1716, possibly by de Cotte); Ha 18, t. 1, 2663, Hc 14, t. 1, 1719 (c. 1716–17).

65. Delamare, *Police*, 4:402.

66. Va 270a, 2754–2757. Now the site of the Caisse des Dépôts et Consignations, which preserves the pedimental sculpture *Minerva Protecting Architecture*. Brice, *Ville de Paris*, 4:138–39; Pons, "Hôtels Robert de Cotte," in Pons and Forray-Carlier, *Rue de Bac*, 98–102.

67. Va 444, 1036. Robert Neuman, "Robert de Cotte, Architect of the Late Baroque," Ph.D. diss., University of Michigan, 1978, 156–59; Isabelle Derens, "Hôtel des Mousquetaires Gris," in Pons and Forray-Carlier, *Rue de Bac*, 28–

35. For the barracks of the Mousquetaires Noires in the faubourg Saint-Antoine (1699), see Neuman, ibid., 160–63.

68. Va 255d, 739–740; Delamare, *Police*, 4:366, 401–3; Brice, *Ville de Paris*, 1:173, 187; Marcel, nos. 168–69, 176–77, pp. 43–45.

69. Brice, *Ville de Paris*, 1:187.

70. Beausire's drawing is in Va 277, t. 4, 2380; Charles Duplomb, *Histoire général des ponts de Paris*, 2 vols. (Paris: J. Mersch, 1911–13), 1:99–100.

71. Delamare, *Police*, 4:400; also, Brice, *Ville de Paris*, 4:339–40; *Ile Saint-Louis* (Paris: Musée Carnavalet, 1980), 34, 95. Destroyed 1795.

72. Va 255m, 731–734; Marcel, nos. 171–72, p. 44; on wooden bridges, Jean Mesqui, *Le pont en France avant le temps des ingénieurs* (Paris: Picard, 1986), 216–24.

73. Note 11 above.

74. For the theoretical assumptions underlying water distribution in the city, see Delamare, *Police*, 4:380–81; for water resources outside Paris—eaux de Belleville, de Pre-Saint-Gervais, de Rungis, and de Cachan—and the location of public fountains, see Sauval, *Paris*, 1:210–13. A good general introduction may be found in Pierre Lavedan et al., *L'urbanisme à l'époque moderne, XVIe–XVIIIe siècles* (Geneva: Droz, 1982), 144–46.

75. The inadequacy of the water supply was a problem that evaded effective solution. Projects for canals in and around Paris had a variety of goals: to increase the availability of water, to relieve the city from the threat of floods, to cleanse the sewers, and to provide a navigable route through Paris. For the causes of flooding and proposed remedies, see Sauval, *Paris*, 1:206–10, and Delamare, *Police*, 4:295–300. In 1690 de Cotte joined a group of government officials forming a society to build the Canal Saint-Maur to bring water from Saint-Maur (Marcel, nos. 39–41, p. 12; O¹ 1595). Proposals were also made for waterways across Paris, such as a canal from the Bastille to the Savonnerie (1714–15), a second from the Arsenal to the hill of Chaillot (1723?), and a third circumscribing the city (1727; Marcel, nos. 146–52, pp. 36–42). In 1724 plans were drawn up to increase the volume of water coming from the Aqueduc d'Arcueil (Marcel, nos. 205–14, pp. 52–55). Such projects usually failed because of the funding required and technical difficulties encountered in linking different water levels. The improvement of the sewer system was a related goal. For example, in 1718 and later in 1737–40, the Egout du Marais, which ran beneath the rue Saint-Louis (rue de Tourenne), was repaired and rebuilt (Va 244g, 737; Delamare, *Police*, 4:401; Lavedan, *Urbanisme à l'époque moderne*, 146; Marcel, no. 157, pp. 40–41). For a contemporary description of the Parisian sewer system, see Sauval, *Paris*, 1:248–54. On projects for canals and other elements in the water system in the seventeenth century, see Bardet, *Nais-*

sance et méconnaissance, 176–84, and Henry Lemonnier, "Un projet de canal autour de Paris au XVIIᵉ siècle," *BSHAF*, 1912, pp. 70–73; also Ms. fr. 9447, 1442 and n.n.

76. Water vendors were described late in the century in a brief chapter by Louis-Sébastien Mercier, *Tableau de Paris*, 8 vols. (Amsterdam: n.p., 1782 ed.), 1:154: "On achete l'eau à Paris. Les fontaines publiques sont si rares & si mal entretenues, qu'on a recours à la riviere; aucune maison bourgeoise n'est pourvue d'eau assez abondamment. Vingt mille Porteurs d'eau du matin au soir, montent deux seaux pleins, depuis le premier jusqu'au septieme étage, & quelquefois par-delà: la voie d'eau coûte six liards ou deux sols. Quand le porteur d'eau est robuste, il fait environ trente voyages par jour."

77. Brice, *Ville de Paris*, 4:177–79. Twenty-one drawings are preserved in Va 224b in three groups, of which the last is the definitive project (several drawings are evidently missing): (1) 2556–2559; (2) 2560–2561; (3) 2184–2184e, 2185a, 2562, 2186. Prints were published by de Fer (1716; Va 244b) and Bernard Forest de Belidor, *Architecture hydraulique* (Paris: C. A. Jombert, 1737–39), chap. 4. The painting by Jean-Baptiste Nicolas Raguenet, *La chaussée du Pont-Neuf* (1777; Musée Carnavalet, Paris) shows the Samaritaine after the restoration by A.-J. Gabriel and Soufflot in 1769; *Pont Neuf, 1578–1978* (Paris: Musée Carnavalet, 1978), nos. 35, 52, pp. 28–29, 33.

78. François Boucher, "Un gouverneur de la Samaritaine, René Duvernay de la Vallée (1710–1766)," *Bulletin de la Société de l'histoire de Paris et de l'Ile-de-France* 60 (1933): 6; Sauval, *Paris*, 1:212–13.

79. Blondel, *Architecture françoise*, 2:13.

80. Souchal, *French Sculptors*, 1:60, 308. The inscription read "FONS HORTORUM / PUTEUS AQUARUM VIVENTIUM."

81. Blondel, *Architecture françoise*, 3:49. For further documentation on the Samaritaine, see *Pont-Neuf, 1578–1978*, nos. 32–38, pp. 27–29; N III Seine 622 (1694), N IV Seine 62/21–22 (1747), N III Seine 678 (c. 1775), 631/1–9 (late eighteenth century); O¹ 1597, 1693 (various dates).

82. Va 232b, 1748; also inscribed "approuve le 7 may 1719 Le duc d'Antin," and bearing notations on measurements in de Cotte's hand. A copy is in Nationalmuseum, Stockholm, Cronstedt 313.

83. Delamare, *Police*, 4:401. See also Brice, *Ville de Paris*, 1:266. 1 *muid* = 268 liters.

84. Plans: Va 232b, 1747–1747b, 1748 recto; elevations: 1748 recto and verso; sections: 1748 verso, 1749. Projects for the square unrelated to the 1719 design are in Va 231, 1745–1746, and Va 441, 1753. *Devis* for conduits for the reservoir are in O¹ 1595, 154 (23 August 1719). *Mercure de France*, March 1719, p. 176. Blondel, *Architecture françoise*, 3:46–50.

85. E.g., Bigant, *Château d'Eau, fontaine de la Place du Palais Royal*, n.d., in Va 232b, which also contains images of the taking of the reservoir in 1848.

86. Françoise Boudon et al., *Système de l'architecture urbaine: Le quartier des Halles à Paris* (Paris: CNRS, 1977), 325, fig. 418.

87. Souchal, *French Sculptors*, 1:138–39; idem, *Frères Coustou*, 145–46. For documents concerning the Aqueduc d'Arcueil and eaux d'Arcueil (eaux de Rungis), see n. 75 above.

88. Blondel, *Architecture françoise*, 3:49.

89. The subsequent history of the Château d'Eau is told by a large number of documents in O¹ 1578, 1596, dealing principally with the remodeling of the reservoirs, enlargement and embellishment of the Place du Palais-Royal, and proposals for a new Château d'Eau. Related plans are in N III Seine 627/1–2 (1755), 1323 (1817), 550/1–8, 570; N IV Seine 89 (1815). Some of the material is reviewed by Victor Champier and G.-Roger Sandoz, *Le Palais Royal d'après des documents inédits (1629–1900)* 2 vols. (Paris: Société de propagation des livres d'art, 1900), 1:288–91.

90. Some forty public fountains were in operation by 1700, thanks particularly to Colbert's initiative. The continuing expansion of the city required the addition of some fifteen more in the years 1700 to 1735. Beausire's official title—Directeur et Contrôleur des Edifices de la Ville de Paris, ayant charge des Eaux et Fontaines d'icelle—explains his participation in these commissions, often as designer. Labarre de Raillicourt, "Beausire," 83–84, attributes nine fountains to Beausire on the basis of documents. Regulations concerning water from public fountains are in Delamare, *Police*, 1:580–85; on the relationship between public utilities and the monarch's *gloire*, see Delamare, *Police*, 4:381.

A sketch for the Fontaine des Capucines, located on the southern side of the rue Saint-Honoré facing the entrance to the Place Vendôme, suggests de Cotte's participation in the development of that project (Va 235d, 744). Built on a square plan, the two-story structure was incorporated into the exterior wall of the Couvent des Capucines, just west of the Couvent des Feuillants (Delagrive, *Plan des fontaines de Paris*; Bretez, *Plan de Turgot*). The early sources give the date 1718, although none specifies the architect: Delamare, *Police*, 4:401, includes a list of five fountains commissioned by royal decree in 1719.

CHAPTER SEVEN

1. This chapter, a revision and expansion of my article, "French Domestic Architecture in the Early Eighteenth Century: The Town Houses of Robert de Cotte," *JSAH* 39 (1980): 128–44, treats de Cotte's major designs for new

houses of the *hôtel-entre-cour-et-jardin* type. For a broad listing of *hôtel* drawings in the Fonds de Cotte, mostly undocumented interior renovations and not necessarily projects overseen by de Cotte, see *Hardouin-Mansart et son école*, 61–64. For de Cotte's role in designing the *porte-cochère* of the Hôtel de Maisons, Paris, for François Duret (1707), see Bruno Pons, "Hôtel de Maisons," in Françoise Magny, ed., *Le faubourg Saint-Germain: Rue de l'Université* (Paris: Institut Néerlandais, 1987), 84. On the Petit Luxembourg, Paris (1709–13), for which the commission went to Boffrand but early sketches and late critiques were by de Cotte, see Garms, "Germain Boffrand," in Gallet and Garms, *Germain Boffrand*, 34–39 and errata sheet. For documents pertaining to de Cotte's design of the Hôtel de Charles Ycard, 6 Place Vendôme (1712–14), see Pons, *Sculpteurs ornemanistes*, 113, 211. For de Cotte's contribution to the Hôtels de Rohan and de Soubise, Paris, especially the project for a wing connecting the two houses (c. 1710–15; in my opinion, a synthesis of the styles of Boffrand and de Cotte), see Garms, "Germain Boffrand," 46–47, and Jean-Pierre Babelon, "Les façades sur jardin des Palais Rohan-Soubise," *Revue de l'art*, no. 4 (1969): 66–73. For the unexecuted project for the *hôtel* of the comte de Hanau, Strasbourg (1728), see Adrien Weirich, "L'Hôtel de Hanau, contribution à l'histoire de ses origines," *Cahiers alsaciens d'archéologie, d'art et d'histoire* 11 (1967): 319–32; Réau, *Art français*, 70–71. For the modest Hôtel d'Armagnac, Paris (1734), Marcel, nos. 219–22, pp. 58–59. For the Maisons de Robert de Cotte, Paris, see chap. 6 above.

2. Elinor Barber, *The Bourgeoisie in Eighteenth-Century France* (Princeton: Princeton University Press, 1955, 93–98; Charles Louandre, *La noblesse française sous l'ancienne monarchie* (Paris: G. Charpentier, 1880); Franklin L. Ford, *Robe and Sword: The Regrouping of the French Aristocracy after Louis XIV* (Cambridge, Mass.: Harvard University Press, 1953). For the impact on the fine arts, see Robert Neuman, "Watteau's *L'enseigne de Gersaint* and Baroque Emblematic Tradition," *GBA* 104 (1984): 153–64.

3. In the second major type of layout, the *corps-de-logis* was placed on the street, with the court and garden located beyond; this formula was less used in the eighteenth century.

4. Louis Audiger, *La maison réglée et l'art de diriger la maison d'un grand seigneur*, Paris: Brunet, 1692.

5. The uses of the rooms are explicitly detailed in the house-building manuals of the period. See for example Daviler, *Cours d'architecture*, 1:185.7–18; Mignot, "Petit lexique."

6. For types of *cabinets*, see Daviler, *Cours d'architecture*, 2:438–39.

7. Jean-Pierre Babelon, "Du 'Grand Ferrare' à Carnavalet: Naissance de l'hôtel classique," *Revue de l'art*, no. 40–41 (1978): 83–108.

8. Jean-Pierre Babelon, "Le passage du corps d'hôtel simple au corps double," *XVIIᵉ siècle*, 41, no. 162 (1989): 7–16. On the major *hôtel* designers of the seventeenth century, see Braham and Smith, *François Mansart*, 1:31–38, 68–79, 92–102; Berger, *Le Pautre*, 17–20, 37–46; Constance Tooth, "The Early Private Houses of Louis Le Vau," *Burlington Magazine* 109 (1967): 510–18.

9. Mignot, "De la cuisine à la salle à manger," 17–35.

10. Daviler, *Cours d'architecture*, 1:180, 2:377–78; Jean-Pierre Babelon, *Demeures parisiennes sous Henri IV et Louis XIII*, 2d ed. (Paris: Le Temps, 1977), 188–90.

11. Babelon, *Demeures parisiennes*, 133–40. See for example the elevations for an ideal residence in Daviler, *Cours d'architecture*, 1: pls. 63.A–B. As early as 1706, de Cordemoy complained that many architects mistook sculptural richness and the multiplication of pilasters and moldings as a guarantee of artistic merit: *Nouveau traité*, 64.

12. Kalnein and Levey, *Art and Architecture*, 218–28, 239–50; Hautecoeur, *Architecture classique*, 3:179–215. The ideals of *hôtel* design changed so dramatically between the editions of 1691 and 1710 of Daviler's *Cours d'architecture* that Alexandre Le Blond added new sections on updated plans, stairs, and interiors to the later edition.

13. Louis Hautecoeur, *Le règne de Louis XIV*, vol. 2 of *L'architecture classique en France* (Paris: Picard, 1948), 590–92. In 1724, de Cotte was called on by Marie-Anne de Bourbon, princesse de Conti, to remodel Mansart's Hôtel de Lorge; see Bertrand Jestaz, "L'Hôtel de Lorge et sa place dans l'oeuvre de Jules Hardouin-Mansart," *Bulletin monumental* 129 (1971): 161–81.

14. Lassurance produced five Parisian *hôtels* during the first decade alone: Hôtel de Rothelin (1700), Hôtel Desmarets (1704), and the Hôtels d'Auvergne, de Béthune, and de Maisons (1708).

15. Illustrated in Neuman, "Town Houses of Robert de Cotte," 133, figs. 2–3.

16. One of de Cotte's earliest domestic tasks was the interior remodeling of Le Vau's Hôtel de Lionne in 1703 for the Chancellor de Pontchartrain (Kimball, *Creation of the Rococo*, 94–95). It was followed by structural remodeling of Le Pautre's Hôtel de Beauvais in 1706 for Jean Orry, seigneur de Vignory and the king's representative at the Spanish court (Buen Retiro, chap. 5 above; for the *hôtel* see Berger, *Le Pautre*, 41 n. 27; Michel Le Moël, *L'architecture privée à Paris au Grand Siècle* [Paris: Bibliothèque historique de la ville de Paris, 1990], 297–310). One of de Cotte's best-known domestic commissions is the celebrated remodeling of François Mansart's Hôtel de la Vrillière, erected 1635–38. After passing through various hands, the house was purchased in January 1713 by Louis-Alexandre de Bourbon, comte de Toulouse, legitimized son of Louis XIV and Mme de Montespan. De Cotte's work (1713–19) consisted of a new system of *appartements*, a modern stair, and integration of several adjacent houses with the right wing of the *hôtel*.

For a history of the house with documentation, see Braham and Smith, *François Mansart*, 1:209–14. On the Galerie Dorée, virtually the only part of the building to survive (much altered) within the complex of the Banque de France presently occupying the site, see Kimball, *Creation of the Rococo*, 104–5, 117–19; Ludmann and Pons, "Hôtel de Toulouse," 115–28; *Place des Victoires et ses abords*, 55–68. For de Cotte's project to remodel the Hôtel de Roquelaure (1722–24), see Bruno Pons, "Hôtel de Roquelaure," in *Le faubourg Saint-Germain: La rue Saint-Dominique* (Paris: Musée Rodin, 1984), 164. Rosalys Coope discusses the Hôtel de Lesdiguières, for which de Cotte drew up unexecuted proposals for remodeling, in "John Thorpe and the Hôtel Zamet in Paris," *Burlington Magazine* 124 (1982): 671–79.

17. For Duret's entrepreneurial activities in the faubourg Saint-Germain, see Bruno Pons, "Hôtel de La Vrillière," in *Rue Saint-Dominique*, 190–91. According to a recent hypothesis, de Cotte may have provided plans for another of Duret's town houses, the Hôtel Le Vayer, located near the Hôtel du Lude; see Anne Forray, "Hôtel Le Vayer," in Magny, *Rue de l'Université*, 69.

18. The site, at present 244, boulevard Saint-Germain, is occupied by the offices of the Ministère des travaux publiques. For the documents, bibliography, numerous alterations, and information on the *hôtel*'s most illustrious owner, Joseph Bonnier de la Mosson, see Bruno Pons, "Hôtel du Lude," in *Rue Saint-Dominique*, 150–63.

19. Daviler, *Cours d'architecture*, 1:161; Blondel, *Maisons de plaisance*, 1:27.

20. Daviler, *Cours d'architecture*, 1:185.3.

21. Blondel, *Architecture française*, 1:253.

22. As was often the case, subsequent owners made extensive alterations to the building so that it might conform to their own needs. The role of the patron in determining the layout is commented on by Frémin, *Mémoires critiques*, 54; Daviler, *Cours d'architecture*, 1:185.1; Gallet, *Stately Mansions*, 29–34.

23. Located at 79, rue de Grenelle, housing the embassy of the former Soviet Union since 1864. The site was purchased 1 July 1711; construction contracts have not been located. The building is dated 1713 by Brice, *Ville de Paris*, 3:485. For a description of the *hôtel* see Blondel, *Architecture française*, 1:231–33, pls. 40–43. For a discussion of the inhabitants and known documents, see Françoise de Catheu, "Le développement du faubourg Saint-Germain du XVIᵉ au XVIIIᵉ siècles; 2. L'Hôtel d'Estrées," *Bulletin de la Société de l'histoire de Paris et de l'Ile-de-France* 82–83 (1955–56): 31–39, and H. Rault, "Le Grand et le Petit Hôtel d'Estrées," in *Le faubourg Saint-Germain: La rue de Grenelle* (Paris: Galerie de la SEITA, 1980), 32–34. See also Yvan Christ et al., *Le faubourg Saint-Germain* (Paris: Deux Mondes, 1966), 240–43, for photographs of the interior in its present state. The Fonds de Cotte includes drawings for the *hôtel*, some of which may postdate construction and were intended for reproduction by Mariette (Va 270d, 2115b–c, e–f). A few of de Cotte's initial drawings are extant (Va 270d, 2115a, d, 2116a).

24. The Hôtel Salé (Jean Bouillier, 1656–60) was the first to have paired concavities on either side of the street portal; Jean-Pierre Babelon, "La maison du bourgeois gentilhomme: L'Hôtel Salé," *Revue de l'art*, no. 68 (1985): 7–34.

25. Illustrated in Blunt, *Art and Architecture*, 228, fig. 186.

26. Garms, "Boffrand," in Gallet and Garms, *Germain Boffrand*, 28–30.

27. Hôtel de Torcy, Va 273e, 305–313; unidentified hôtel, Ha 18, t. 1, 435–436; Maison pour le maréchal de Montesquiou, Va 444, 296, Ha 18, t. 1, 297–304; Hôtel de Chatillon, Va 270a, 703–709; Hôtel, rue de Richelieu, Ha 18, t. 3, 2522–2524.

28. At 78, rue de Lille, now the Hôtel de Beauharnais (German Embassy), after the patron responsible for the famous Neo-Egyptian portal and interior renovations in the early nineteenth century. Boffrand's designs were published by Blondel, *Architecture française*, 1:280–82. See Karl Hammer, "Hôtel de Torcy," in *La rue de Lille, l'Hôtel de Salm* (Paris: Institut néerlandais and Musée national de la Légion d'honneur, 1983), 44–52; idem, *Hôtel Beauharnais, Paris* (Munich: Artemis, 1983), 9–44; Garms, "Boffrand," in Gallet and Garms, *Germain Boffrand*, 53–57.

29. Documents indicate that Boffrand erected the *hôtel* on a speculative basis and sold it to the marquis de Torcy in 1716 (see also Brice, *Ville de Paris*, 4:139–40; Blondel, *Architecture française*, 1:280). This information is not necessarily at variance with the evidence of the drawings. As a leading minister at the court of Louis XIV and a member of so powerful a family, Torcy would have preferred the more ample accommodations provided by Boffrand for his library and collections. After I published the Fonds de Cotte drawings in 1980, Runar Strandberg discovered duplicates in the Torcy archives at the Château de Bois-Dauphin, identified as pp. 4, 8, 10 ("Marquis de Torcy," 134). He makes numerous errors in analyzing the drawings, failing to realize, for example, that the court elevation of de Cotte's project rises two stories while the garden front rises three. A second project for the Hôtel de Torcy in the same collection, drawn in a similar hand, is thus probably not by Hardouin-Mansart but conceivably represents de Cotte's alternative for a larger building—it measures twenty-two *toises* in width (Bois-Dauphin, pp. 3, 6–7, 9, 11). Two further drawings (Bois-Dauphin, pp. 1–2) are for the Château de Sablé, not the Hôtel de Torcy. De Cotte produced drawings for the marquis as early as 1711.

30. Strandberg, "Château de Champs."

31. Blondel, *Architecture française*, 1:232, criticized the street pavilions of the Hôtel d'Estrées as too simple in

design.

32. Pierre de Montesquiou, comte d'Artagnan (1645–1725), maréchal de France (1709) and governor of Brittany; *Nouvelle biographie générale*, 46 vols. (Paris: F. Didot frères, 1855–66), 36:192–93.

33. The project was abandoned when the comte de Châtillon purchased the Hôtel de Neuchâtel in 1719 (Bruno Pons, "Hôtel de Neuchâtel," in *Rue Saint-Dominique*, 68–71).

34. On the articulation of façades through the use of pavilions, orders, and sculpture—for which the good taste of the architect formed the standard—see the lengthy discussion in Briseux, *Maisons de campagne*, 2:115–52, postdating de Cotte's activity but strongly influenced by Parisian designs of the early eighteenth century.

35. Courtonne, *Traité*, 97.

36. For the new type of flushing toilet, which replaced the close-stool, see Daviler, *Cours d'architecture*, 1:185.9–10, 2:369–70.

37. Briseux, *Maisons de campagne*, 1:115–17.

38. A.-J. Dezallier d'Argenville, *Jardinage*, 3.

39. Le Moël, *Architecture privée*, 220–35.

40. Formerly located on the present site of 12, rue des Capucines; destroyed after 1859. Blondel, *Architecture française*, 3:111–13, pls. 405–8, gives the date 1713 and a description of the house before its alteration in 1749 for Pierre de Meulan. Early sketches: Va 235, 2652bis, 2653a–d; presentation drawings: Va 235, 2652a–c, 2654, 2655a–b. See also Brice, *Ville de Paris*, 1:455; Hillairet, *Dictionnaire*, 1:267, for the subsequent history of the house. On the neighboring *hôtels*, see Jörg Garms, "Ein Pariser Hôtel particulier auf Dreieckigem Grundstück," in *Orient und Okzident im Spiegel der Kunst*, Günter Brucher et al., eds. (Graz: Akademische Druck und Verlagsanstalt, 1986), 125–38.

41. At present the Conservatoire de musique Darius Milhaud. Jean Boyer, "Une oeuvre inédite de Robert de Cotte à Aix-en-Provence: L'Hôtel de Caumont," *BSHAF*, 1964, pp. 55–67; Jean-Jacques Gloton, *Renaissance et baroque à Aix-en-Provence*, 2 vols. (Rome: Ecole française de Rome, 1979), 2:357–60; Va 13, t. 2, 878–885.

42. At present 82–84, rue de Lille; destroyed after 1838. The pedimental sculpture of the garden façade survives, installed at the Hôtel Pontalba, Paris (U.S. Embassy). Blondel, *Architecture française*, 1:276–79, pls. 113–17; Françoise de Catheu, "La décoration des Hôtels du Maine au faubourg Saint-Germain," *BSHAF*, 1945–46, pp. 101–4; Rambaud, *Minutier central*, 1:405; B. Gournay, "Hôtel du Maine," in *Rue de Lille*, 59–63, who is unaware of the Institut drawings.

43. J. H. Shennan, *Philippe, Duke of Orléans* (London: Thames & Hudson, 1979), 28–31, 43–44; W. H. Lewis, *The Sunset of the Splendid Century* (London: Eyre & Spottiswoode, 1955), chaps. 12–14.

44. MS 1037, nos. 22, 31, with the inscription "Hôtel de Conti" in the pediment of the street portal. Chevotet drawings: Musée Carnavalet, Paris, Estampes, P.C. 117F; Ecole des beaux-arts, Paris, coll. Lesoufaché nos. 1898–1899. On Mollet, see Kalnein and Levey, *Art and Architecture*, 242–44.

45. On window balconies, see Daviler, *Cours d'architecture*, 1: pl. 51a.

46. Va 272, 1020–1022. The site appears in several plans of the developing faubourg Saint-Germain in the Fonds de Cotte: Va 444, 1615, 2648, 2651; Ha 18a, 2664.

47. Va 444, 1023, is most closely associated with the *hôtel* type. Three-wing plan: Va 444, 1025, 1026, 1028; Va 272, 1021. Square plan: Va 444, 1024, 1029. Elevations: Va 272, 2496–2498.

48. Cf. the U-shaped court bordered by double columns in the unexecuted plan A for the Hôtel de Hanau, 1728; Weirich, "Hôtel de Hanau," 323–24.

49. For the subsequent history, see Françoise Magny, "Palais Bourbon," in *Le faubourg Saint-Germain: Palais Bourbon, sa place* (Paris: Institut néerlandais, 1987), 18–24.

50. Fried Lübbecke, *Das Palais Thurn und Taxis in Frankfurt am Main* (Frankfurt am Main: W. Kramer, 1955); du Colombier, *Architecture française*, 1:144–46.

51. Lübbecke, *Palais Thurn und Taxis*, 152–53; Marcel, no. 651, p. 181. Wooden model, c. 1730, Fürst Thurn und Taxis Zentralarchiv, Regensburg: Martin Dallmeier, ed., *500 Jahre Post, Thurn und Taxis* (Regensburg: Fürst Thurn und Taxis Zentralarchiv, 1990), B.IV.b.9, p. 98.

52. Process drawings: Ha 19, 155, Vc 325, 1198–1199; final project, Ha 18, t. 1, 1201, Vc 325, 1200–1200a; FZA, Plansammlung B 2 (Lübbecke, *Palais Thurn und Taxis*, 84–86, 122, 166, figs. 41, 62, 83; Dallmeier, *500 Jahre Post*, B.IV.b.7, p. 98).

53. Hd 135b, 1202 (Marcel, nos. 738–39, pp. 207–8; abridged transcription in modern French without de Cotte's handwritten addenda in Réau, *Art français*, 87–90); FZA, Frankfurt-Akten 10, fol. 21–24 (Dallmeier, *500 Jahre Post*, B.IV.b.4, p. 96).

54. Compare a plan of c. 1790 showing that on the whole de Cotte's original scheme was maintained (FZA, Plansammlung A 1 r; Dallmeier, *500 Jahre Post*, B.IV.b.8, p. 98; illustrated in Lübbecke, *Palais Thurn und Taxis*, 169, fig. 82).

CHAPTER EIGHT

1. Louis Trenard, "Les villes françaises de 1650 à 1780," *L'information historique* 46, no. 3 (1984): 125–36; Cleary, *Places Royales*, especially on the role played by the *intendants*. For de Cotte's work in completing Hardouin-Mansart's ensemble at Dijon (1709–11), see Yves Beauvalot, "La construction du Palais des Etats de Bourgogne et de

la Place Royale à Dijon (1674–1725) de Daniel Gittard à Robert de Cotte: L'oeuvre de Jules Hardouin-Mansart," supplementary number of *Mémoires de la Commission des antiquités du département de la Côte-d'or* (Dijon: Académie des sciences, arts et belles-lettres, 1981); Marcel, nos. 393–96, pp. 108–9. For the pedestal of the *Equestrian Louis XIV* at Montpellier (1717), see Bernard Sournia, Ghislaine Fabre, and Marie-Sylvie Grandjouan, *Projets et dessins pour la Place Royal du Peyrou à Montpellier* (Montpellier: Secrétariat régional de l'inventaire général, 1980), 26–27; Souchal, *French Sculptors*, 2:171–72; Marcel, nos. 476–77, p. 129. Sketches for the Porte du Jaar, Châlons-sur-Marne (1719–20?) are in Va 51, t. 3, 656–60.

2. Gardes, "Monument équestre," in *Art baroque à Lyon*, 79–161; François Souchal, "Les Coustou à Lyon," in *Art baroque à Lyon*, 59–78. In addition, de Cotte presented Hardouin-Mansart's plans for the restoration of the mid seventeenth-century Hôtel de Ville, which had been ravaged by fire in 1674; Tony Desjardins, *Monographie de l'Hôtel de Ville de Lyon* (Paris: Morel, 1867); Marcel, nos. 369–70, pp. 100–101. For an accessible illustrated survey of urbanism in Lyon, see Gilbert Gardes, *Lyon, l'art et la ville*, 2 vols. (Paris: CNRS, 1988).

3. Gilbert Gardes, "La décoration de la Place Royale de Louis le Grand (Place Bellecour) à Lyon, 1686–1793," *Bulletin des musées et monuments lyonnais* 5, no. 3 (1974–75): 48–52, fig. 1. Gardes's thorough study of the square should be read alongside the shorter study by Jean-Daniel Ludmann, "Projets de Robert de Cotte et de l'agence des Bâtiments du roi pour la ville de Lyon," in *Art baroque à Lyon*, 375–94.

4. Va 436, 593 without flap; Va 69, t. 6, 601, 603.

5. Va 436, 590; Va 69, t. 6, 600.

6. Cf. Va 436, 594; Va 69, t. 6, 599.

7. Va 69, t. 6, 598.

8. Va 436, 591; Va 69, t. 6, 596. Gardes, "Place Bellecour," 64, figs. 6–7.

9. Va 69, t. 6, 597.

10. Va 69, t. 6, 595; Va 436, 592.

11. Gardes, "Place Bellecour," 63, 66, 74, fig. 11, assigns the undated elevation in Archives municipales de Lyon, 1.S.167 to 1700 as a fragment of a lost project by Mansart; more likely it is by de Cotte, dating 1711–13, corresponding to the plan Va 69, t. 6, 598. On the colony of Italian businessmen and bankers, see A. Kleinclausz, *Histoire de Lyon*, 3 vols. (Lyon: Pierre Masson, 1939–52).

12. Va 69, t. 6, 604a–c, 605, related to the plan Va 69, t. 6, 597 without flap, reproduced by Ludmann, "Ville de Lyon," in *Art baroque à Lyon*, 393, fig. 125; also Arch. mun. Lyon, 2.S.292, approved 1 May 1714.

13. Jestaz, *Voyage d'Italie*, 192.

14. Va 69, t. 6, 606; Arch. mun. Lyon, 2.S.392, 3.S.698 (a late copy of 1812).

15. For the history of the Loge au Change, see Daniel Ternois, "La Loge du Change," in *L'oeuvre de Soufflot à Lyon: Etudes et documents* (Lyon: Presses universitaires à Lyon, 1982), 77–97; Ludmann, "Ville de Lyon," in *Art baroque à Lyon*, 383–87; Serlio, *Sixth Book*, 25. For the building type of the *bourse*, see Paul Roudié, "L'ancienne Bourse des Marchands de Bordeaux au XVIe siècle," *Revue de l'art*, no. 20 (1973): 78–87.

16. Va 69, t. 11, 622–623, 628–631; Hd 135a, 636. Marcel, nos. 378–80, p. 104.

17. First project: Va 69, t. 11, 620–621, 624–625; Hd 135a, 636. Second project: 626–627. Third project: Va 69, t. 11, 619, 632–632a.

18. The third project might also date from the late teens or the twenties, when the merchants sought to counteract the attractions of the new quartier de Bellecour, which was luring business away from the Place du Change.

19. Paul Courteault, *La Place Royale de Bordeaux* (Paris: A. Colin, 1922); Tadgell, *Gabriel*, 167–71; Jean-Paul Avisseau, "La Place Royale de Bordeaux," in Gallet and Bottineau, *Les Gabriel*, 104–11; Cleary, *Places Royales*.

20. Va 431, 1317, without flap.

21. Jean-Paul Avisseau, "La Place Royale de Bordeaux, sa fonction maritime," *Monuments historiques de la France*, no. 120 (1981): 16–23.

22. See Courteault, *Place Royale*, pl. 1.

23. Letter of 4 May 1728, Hd 135c, 1319; Marcel, no. 547, p. 147; transcribed in part by Courteault, *Place Royale*, 31.

24. Letter of 13 June 1728, Hd 135c, 1319; Marcel, no. 548, p. 147; transcribed by Courteault, *Place Royale*, 32–33.

25. De Cotte's project is in Va 431, 1317, with flap; 1318. Hd 135c, 1319; Marcel, no. 550, p. 147; transcribed by Courteault, *Place Royale*, 33–36.

26. Ibid.

27. Jean-Pierre Bardet, *Rouen aux XVIIe et XVIIIe siècles: Les mutations d'un espace social*, 2 vols. (Paris: SEDES, 1983). I am indebted to Marie-Françoise Rose and François Gay for research assistance in Rouen.

28. Henri Wallon, *Une page d'histoire locale: La Bourse Découverte et les quais de Rouen* (Rouen: Lestringant, 1897), 84–85. Hautecoeur, *Architecture classique*, 3:546, and Souchal, *Frères Coustou*, 153, give the building to a certain Cuillier or Cuiller, a Parisian architect, but I am unaware of the source of this attribution, not mentioned in the literature published by local historians.

29. Va 76, t. 15, 2437–2442. A nineteenth-century print of the Douane as built (Bibliothèque municipale de Rouen, 4835) shows the same elevation as in the drawings.

30. For the attribution, Souchal, *Frères Coustou*, 152–54.

31. The Douane and the gates were destroyed in 1826–27 during rebuilding of the quay; Nicétas Périaux, *Histoire sommaire et chronologie de la ville de Rouen* (Brionne: Le Portulan, 1874), 357, 534. A larger Hôtel des Douanes was

erected on the quay in 1836 (Bibl. mun. Rouen, 4819–4821).

32. Project with oval vestibule: Va 449, 2429–2432. Project with double stair: 2433–2436. For the background, see Wallon, *Bourse découverte*.

33. Jeanne Lejeaux, "Jean-François Blondel, architecte," *L'architecture* 40 (1927): 398–99; Jacques Delécluse, *Les consuls de Rouen* (Rouen: Edit. du P'tit Normand, 1985).

34. Va 76, t. 21, 2445–2448, 2450–2464, 2466; Va 449, 2449, 2465 (many sheets within the sequence are missing). The only date on the drawings, 11 March 1713, probably the terminus a quo, appears on a cross section of the quay indicating the river's height (2446).

35. Construction proceeded from 1713 to 1715, was suspended during the regency, and resumed 1723–29: *arrêt* of 5 February 1723 requiring de Cotte and de Gasville to facilitate completion of the Grenier à Sel (E 2046, fol. 311–12); Pierre Chirol, *Un siècle de vandalisme: Rouen disparu* (Rouen: Defontaine, 1929), pl. LXXX. City plans by Nicolas de Fer (1724) and de Beaurain (1750) show the Grenier à Sel partially built, beginning on the western side. The building appears fully constructed in a plan of Rouen in Va 76, t. 21 (n.d., after mid-century). The disposition of *dépôts* in a plan of the Grenier in Bibl. mun. Rouen, 4738 (1761) is somewhat different from that in the Fonds de Cotte drawings. To accommodate the need to garrison soldiers in Rouen, the Grenier was altered in 1773–76 to provide a barracks, the Caserne de Saint-Sever (Périaux, *Histoire sommaire*, 523; Bardet, *Rouen*, 1:143; Lattré plan, 1784).

36. Daniel Rabreau, "Royale ou commerciale, la place à l'époque des Lumières," *Monuments historiques de la France*, no. 120 (1982): 31–37.

CHAPTER NINE

1. Françoise Hamon, "Les églises parisiennes du XVIIIe siècle," *Revue de l'art*, no. 32 (1976): 7–14. The present chapter incorporates material from my articles, "Baroque Ecclesiastical Façade," and "Projects by Robert de Cotte for the Church of Saint-Louis de Versailles in the Parc-aux-Cerfs," *Eighteenth-Century Life* 17 (1993): 182–93. For further ecclesiastical projects in the Fonds de Cotte, see *Hardouin-Mansart et son école*, 47–50; Marcel, no. 412, pp. 112–13; Renard, "Die Bauten der Kurfürsten Joseph Clemens," 208–10; Oglevee, *Letters*, 70, 72; Pons, *Sculpteurs ornemanistes*, 163. For Saint-Charles, Sedan, Abbé Joseph Gillet, *Charles-Maurice Le Tellier, archevêque-duc de Reims* (Paris: Hachette, 1881), 128–29.

2. Va 78a, t. 2, 2208–2209, 2244.

3. Huillet d'Istria, "Cathédrale de Montauban."

4. Va 408, t. 1, 278–283, Va 432, 277, Hd 135, 284. For a full account, see Georges Chenesseau, *Sainte-Croix d'Orléans*, 3 vols. (Paris: Champion, 1921), 1:236–47; Michel

Gallet, "Gabriel à Orléans et à Blois," in Gallet and Bottineau, *Les Gabriel*, 48–51. The documents suggest that de Cotte had drawn up an elevation for the Sainte-Croix portal early in 1709, but the well-known surviving elevation is in Hénault's hand (277). On de Cotte's contribution to the restoration of the Gothic royal church of Saint-Louis de Poissy, see Marcel, nos. 287–317, pp. 75–82; Alain Erlande-Brandenburg, "La priorale Saint-Louis de Poissy," *Bulletin monumental* 129 (1971): 95–100. On de Cotte's attitude toward Gothic style, see Jestaz, *Voyage d'Italie*, 65–80.

5. Correspondence concerning the church of Notre-Dame de Bonne-Nouvelle, Orléans, substantiates the assumption that de Cotte improved on Hénault's designs for Sainte-Croix: Georges Chenesseau, "Un essai d'alliance du 'gothique' et de 'l'antique' par un architecte orléanais au XVIIIe siècle," *Bulletin de la Société archéologique et historique de l'Orléanais* 23 (1936): 140–43.

6. For a history of the site, see Paul and Marie-Louise Biver, *Abbayes, monastères, couvents de femmes à Paris des origines à la fin du XVIIIe siècle* (Paris: Presses universitaires, 1975), 291–98; L. Lambeau, "Les dames de Saint-Michel," *Procès-verbaux de la Commission municipale du vieux Paris* 9 (1906): 110. Attempts to catalogue parts of the large number of surviving drawings were made by Hébert and Thirion, *Catalogue général*, 124; Braham and Smith, *François Mansart*, 1:200–202. Jules Hardouin-Mansart and Jacques V Gabriel were evidently involved earlier in renovation of the convent.

7. First, Va 258d, 848, N III Seine 124, 244/1, 245; second, Va 258d, 855, N III Seine 244/2, illustrated with flap by Hamon, "Eglises parisiennes," 8 fig. 3; and third, Va 443, 854, Va 258d, 856–860, N II Seine 89. A date of 1715 on the third project suggests that this proposal was conceived or reconsidered a few years later. It is tempting to surmise that a group of drawings in the Fonds de Cotte for an unidentified domed church with a choir on the cross axis might represent an early project for the Visitation, but the width of the site, thirty-five *toises*, precludes this hypothesis (Ha 18, t. 1–3, 2228–2234, 2236).

8. Braham and Smith, *François Mansart*, 1:27, 2: pls. 109–17.

9. On centralizing plans in French ecclesiastical architecture, see Reuterswärd, *Hôtel des Invalides*, 39–69; Marie and Marie, *Mansart à Versailles*, 1:531–35; Braham and Smith, *François Mansart*, 1:28. Mansart's church influenced Pierre Bullet's design of a Visitandine foundation in 1681: Runar Strandberg, "Sainte-Marie de Chaillot d'après des documents inédits," *BSHAF*, 1972, pp. 189–201.

10. Nathan T. Whitman, "Roman Tradition and the Aedicular Façade," *JSAH* 29 (1970): 108–23.

11. Jörg Garms, "Boffrand à l'église de la Merci," *BSHAF*, 1964, pp. 184–87.

12. Howard Hibbard, *Carlo Maderno and Roman Architec-*

ture, 1580–1630 (London: Zwemmer, 1971), 40–41. De Cotte did not comment on S. Susanna in his Italian journal, but he recorded the plan; Jestaz, *Voyage d'Italie*, 268.

13. Va 21, t. 4, 267, erroneously identified as the church of Saint-Jean, Dijon, on the sheet; Marcel, no. 406, p. 111. The accompanying *mémoire* is undated (Hd 135, 271) but a terminus ad quem is established by the accepted project of Martin de Noinville, 21 September 1718, for which see *Dijon, capitale provinciale au XVIIIᵉ siècle* (Dijon: Musée de Dijon, 1959), no. 187; Bib. nat. Est. H 117266.

14. The drawings and documents are in Va 408, t. 1, 285, 287–294; Va 432, 286; Hd 135, 295 (Marcel, nos. 386–92, pp. 106–8). For Hénault's projects and a transcription of Hénault's letters to de Cotte and the duc d'Antin, see Chenesseau, "Essai d'alliance," summarized in Georges Chenesseau, "Notre-Dame de Bonne-Nouvelle," *Bulletin des antiquités de France*, 1936, pp. 197–98. No new construction was undertaken by the Benedictines until the 1730s (Chenesseau, "Essai d'alliance," 134). The monastery suffered alteration and destruction in the nineteenth century.

15. Vb 50, 1158, illustrated in Neuman, "Baroque Ecclesiastical Façade," 252, fig. 2. De Cotte wrote, "J'allé voir l'église de Lorette qui est assez grande et réculier, le portaille a esté fait soub le pontificat de Grégoir 13 et de Sixte Cinq. Cette ouvrage est d'asez bon goust, en ayant pris les deseins et le plan de l'églisse" (Jestaz, *Voyage d'Italie*, 215, 258).

16. For the development of the Parc-aux-Cerfs, see Alfred Marie, "L'église Saint-Louis de Versailles," *Histoire et archéologie dans les Yvelines* no. 5 (1979): 17–18, reprinted in Marie and Marie, *Versailles au temps de Louis XV*, 88–91. An early eighteenth-century plan (undated) in the Fonds de Cotte, Va 78h, t. 2, 1635, shows the extreme regularization of the sector, based on a grid pattern, and the space allotted in the northwest corner for the new basilica, bordered by the rues de Satory, des Tournelles, Saint-Honoré, and d'Anjou.

17. For the dating see Abbé Gallet, *Eglise Saint-Louis de Versailles* (Versailles: Lebon, 1897), 4–6.

18. When Versailles was designated a bishopric in 1791, the Lazarists departed from their parishes in the town. Saint-Louis was consecrated as a cathedral in 1843. For the ecclesiastical background, see Gallet, *Saint-Louis de Versailles*, 1–68; Jacques Levron, *La cathédrale Saint-Louis de Versailles* (Lyon: Lescuyer, 1967), 3–14.

19. Marie, "Eglise Saint-Louis de Versailles," 21–26.

20. Marie, "Eglise Saint-Louis de Versailles," 20, was cognizant of the ground plans only, since the elevations are incorrectly catalogued with Notre-Dame de Versailles. Two drawings bear inscriptions on the verso (Va 421, 1450b, 1451): "Plan projetté pour la nouvelle paroisse dans le parc au cerf a versailles fait par M. De Cotte en lannée 1724."

21. Gallet, *Saint-Louis de Versailles*, 14. For a description of the Logement des Pères, see Marie, "Eglise Saint-Louis de Versailles," 18–21.

22. Va 421, 1450, signed "Bon Louis," "bon ce 8 d avril 1724 le duc dantin," and "ce projet [the basilica] a ete parellemen approuve par SAS le meme jour." The ground plan of the Logement des Pères appears throughout the sequence of proposals with only minor variations in detail: Va 421, 1448–1450, 1450b, 1451, 1453; Va 448f, 1446. The second and third story plans, originally attached to the large site plans, are now mounted on separate sheets: Va 421, 1449a, 1450a, 1450c. The definitive layout of the Logement as built is recorded in two identical series of plans independent of the projected basilica; these are not part of the Fonds de Cotte. The inscription "PLAN DE LA PAROISSE ST. LOUIS DE VERSAILLES" indicates that they were drafted between 1730, when the chapel was elevated to parish status, and 1742, when construction began on the basilica: Archives des Yvelines, A 236; and Va 421, H 186407. The latter is illustrated by Marie, "Eglise Saint-Louis de Versailles," 19. I am indebted to S. Roudière, Conservateur of the Arch. Yvelines, for archival assistance at Versailles.

23. Interior and exterior views of the Logement: Va 78h, t. 3, 1457 recto and verso; Va 78h, t. 2, 1456; Ha 18, t. 3, 2245. My article, "Saint-Louis de Versailles," illustrates some drawings not included here.

24. Chap. 3 above, nn. 16–17. Projects for the decoration of the Chapelle Provisoire de Saint-Louis are discussed by Pons, *Sculpteurs ornemanistes*, 217–18.

25. Marcel Léry, "Une visite à l'église Notre-Dame de Versailles," *Revue de l'histoire de Versailles et de Seine-et-Oise* 14 (1912): 216–31; Marie and Marie, *Mansart à Versailles*, 1:160–68.

26. Braham and Smith, *François Mansart*, 1:58–62.

27. The stalls are shown on the plan of the choir reproduced by Marie and Marie, *Mansart à Versailles*, 1:163.

28. Françoise Hamon, "La Chapelle de la Vierge en l'église Saint-Roch à Paris," *Bulletin monumental* 129 (1970): 229–37.

29. Va 421, 1450, 1450b.

30. Va 448f, 1446–1447 recto and verso, 1454; Va 421, 1449.

31. Jestaz, *Voyage d'Italie*, 128, 268.

32. Pierre Moisy, "Deux cathédrales françaises: La Rochelle et Versailles," GBA 39 (1952): 101–2.

33. Some of the similarities have been discussed by Marie, "Eglise Saint-Louis de Versailles," 21–22.

34. D'Orbay's façade and the early eighteenth-century remodeled façade (destroyed 1806) are illustrated by François Souchal, "Le portail de l'église des Capucins à Paris," GBA 73 (1969): 195, 200, figs. 2, 5.

35. Ha 18, 2612, first identified by Ludmann, *Palais Rohan*, 2:432–33; this was the basis for two further drawings, Va 236, 1353–1354. For the arguments concerning the rela-

tive degree of impact on the final design by either Slodtz or de Cotte, see Souchal, "Eglise des Capucines," 196–202, and Neuman, "Baroque Ecclesiastical Façade," 260–61, especially nn. 38–39.

36. J. Duval, "Le 'couvent et hôpital' de la Charité de Paris (1602–1794)," *Positions des thèses,* Ecole des chartes, 1941, p. 51. For the eighteenth-century sources, which differ on the matter of attribution and dating, see Neuman, "Baroque Ecclesiastical Façade," 261 n. 40.

37. MS 1604, no. 42.

38. With the suppression of the religious order in 1790, the church was divided into two stories for use as a hospital ward. In 1798 the façade was altered by Nicolas-Marie Clavareau, leaving only a remnant of the Doric order.

39. For the history of the church, see Jean-Pierre Babelon, *L'église Saint-Roch à Paris* (Paris: J. Lanore, 1972), 16–63.

40. No elevations are extant, but Hardouin-Mansart's façade appears on several plans: N III Seine 665 (dated 24 January 1706), Va 441, 2567 (without the flap added later by de Cotte); see also Nationalmuseum, Stockholm, CTH 7972, 8020; Hamon, "Chapelle de la Vierge," 229–35, figs. 1–4, incorrectly captioned.

41. Nationalmuseum, Stockholm, CTH 8058, 7973; see Strandberg, "Bullet de Chamblain," 240–45, figs. 8–9; and J.-P. Babelon, *Saint-Roch,* 31.

42. Pons, *Sculpteurs ornemanistes,* 41, 163, 169.

43. Va 233, 2568. For the dating and the tower's appearance before demolition in 1878 to accommodate enlargement of the rue des Pyramides, see J.-P. Babelon, *Saint-Roch,* 33–34, 63, fig. 67.

44. Construction of the façade began 1 March 1736: Jean Aymar Piganiol de la Force, *Description historique de la ville de Paris,* 8 vols. (Paris: Theodore Legras, 1742), 2:338. It was probably complete by 1738, the date given on Blanzy's print of 1740. The church was finally consecrated 10 July 1740: Maurice Dumolin and Georges Outardel, *Les églises de France. Paris et la Seine* (Paris: Letouzey, 1936), 161.

45. Three stages as follows: (1) plan, Va 441, 2567 with flap, elevation, Va 441, 2569 (the two differ in some details); (2) plan and elevation, Va 441, 2570, verso and recto (*Louis XV: Un moment de perfection de l'art français* [Paris: Hôtel de la Monnaie, 1974], no. 20, pp. 37–38); (3) elevation as built, reflecting changes presumably made by Jules-Robert de Cotte, MS 1604, no. 41, incorrectly identified as Saint-Thomas d'Aquin, Paris (illustrated in Neuman, "Baroque Ecclesiastical Façade," 264, fig. 17).

46. Blondel, *Architecture française,* 3:48, 120–23; see also the criticisms expressed by Jacques-François Blondel and Jean-François Bastide, *L'homme du monde éclairé par les arts,* 2 vols. (Amsterdam: Bastide, 1774) 1:96–97, cited by Richard Cleary, "Romancing the Tome; or an Academician's Pursuit of a Popular Audience in Eighteenth-Century France," *JSAH* 48 (1989): 146–47. But compare the evaluation of Piganiol de la Force, *Ville de Paris,* 2:338: "Au reste tous les Connoisseurs admirent l'élégance de ce Portail, les graces du dessein, & la fécondité du génie de M. de Cotte qui a sçu vaincre toutes les difficultés d'un terrain ingrat, & ils regardent ce Portail comme un des plus réguliers, & des plus beaux qu'il y ait à Paris"; Brice, *Ville de Paris,* 1:ix–x: "Les Connoisseurs regardent ce morceau d'Architecture comme un des plus beaux qu'il y ait à Paris"; Antoine Martial Lefèvre, *Description des curiosités des églises de Paris* (Paris: C. P. Gueffier, 1759), 338: "Le portail de l'Eglise de Saint Roch, est d'une fort belle architecture, & fort estimé des Connoisseurs." For the decorative sculpture on the façade, see J.-P. Babelon, *Saint-Roch,* 33.

47. *Dictionnaire des églises de France, Belgique, Luxembourg, Suisse,* 5 vols. (Paris: Laffont, 1966–71), 4.C: 110–11.

CHAPTER TEN

1. For further projects see *Hardouin-Mansart et son école,* 54. For the attribution of the *évêché,* Reims (1690), Henri Jadart, *Le Palais Archiépiscopal de Reims au point de vue de l'art et de l'histoire, du XIIIᵉ au XXᵉ siècle* (Reims: L. Michaud, 1908), 18–20. For the *évêché* of Notre-Dame de Paris (n.d.), Va 253h, 540–545.

2. Blondel, *Cours d'architecture,* 2:329; Daviler, *Cours d'architecture,* 2:582. For a brief survey of the type, see Hautecoeur, *Architecture classique,* 3:53–54, 74–79.

3. Blondel, *Cours d'architecture,* 2:329.

4. Letter of 8 April 1692 to Jean-Nicolas Colbert, archbishop of Rouen; *Correspondence de Fénelon, archevêque de Cambrai,* Augustin Caron, ed., 11 vols. (Paris: Ferra jeune, 1827), 5:543.

5. Quoted without citation by Maxime Souplet, *Le Palais Episcopal de Verdun: Art et histoire* (Verdun: Huguet, 1970), 26.

6. Louis Grignon, *Topographie historique de la ville de Châlons-sur-Marne* (Châlons-sur-Marne: Martin frères, 1889), reprint edited by Jean-Marie Arnoult and Jean-Pierre Ravaux (Châlons-sur-Marne: Association des amis de la Bibliothèque enfantine, 1976), 74.

7. Marcel, nos. 413–52, pp. 113–21. The letters and drawings are discussed by Reinhardt, *Bischöflichen Residenzen,* 23–46. Models by François Roumier for the interior of the new Palais Episcopal are discussed by Pons, *Sculpteurs ornemanistes,* 159, 257–58.

8. Marcel, nos. 178–97, pp. 46–50.

9. De Cotte to M. Perrier, *intendant* of Cardinal de Noailles, 30 June 1721, Hd 135a, 671; Marcel, nos. 429–30, p. 118; transcribed by Reinhardt, *Bischöflichen Residenzen,* 24, 32. Plan, neighborhood, Va 51, t. 3, 661; ecclesiastical proj-

ects, 662–665; Porte du Jaar, 656–660; remodeling, Couvent des Filles de Sainte-Marie, 666–670.

10. Letter of 30 April 1719, Hd 135a, 671; Marcel, no. 415, p. 114; Reinhardt, *Bischöflichen Residenzen*, 25, n. 10.

11. Grignon, *Topographie historique*, 75; Reinhardt, *Bischöflichen Residenzen*, 28.

12. Old Palais Episcopal: Va 443, 637–638, Va 51, t. 3, 639–643. First project, 649–650; second project, first variant, Va 443, 644, Va 51, t. 3, 648, second variant, Va 443, 646, Va 51, t. 3, 647, 651–655.

13. No elevation remains of the street façade giving onto the *parvis* of the cathedral, save two summary sketches on the plans (647, 649). Both show a simple three-bay composition with rusticated quoins framing a tall central door.

14. Marcel, nos. 478–541, pp. 129–45; Reinhardt, *Bischöflichen Residenzen*, 46–81.

15. Letter of 26 May 1724, Ms. fr. 7801, 424–35, Hd 135c, 1550; Marcel, no. 480, p. 130; Reinhardt, *Bischöflichen Residenzen*, 49. On the condition of the old *évêché* see Archives de l'Hospice de Verdun, I.B. 94, 95, 97–99.

16. Letter of 17 July 1725, Hd 135c, 1550; Marcel, no. 498, p. 136; Reinhardt, *Bischöflichen Residenzen*, 50.

17. Letter of 19 June 1725, Hd 135c, 1550; Marcel, no. 496, pp. 135–36; Reinhardt, *Bischöflichen Residenzen*, 49, n. 58.

18. Letter of 30 September 1724, Hd 135c, 1550; Marcel, no. 488, pp. 133–34; Reinhardt, *Bischöflichen Residenzen*, 58.

19. See the plan as built, Souplet, *Palais Episcopal*, 23.

20. Former *évêché*, Va 55, t. 5, 1525–1528; first project, 1535; second project (three variations), 1529–1530, 1534, Va 443, 1531–1533; third project, Va 55, t. 5, 1536; chapel, 1541, 1543, 1546, 1548; exterior elevations, 1544–1545 (do not match extant plans); sections of wings, 1547–1549; 1542.

21. Berger, *Le Pautre*, pls. 28–30; Blunt, *Art and Architecture*, 327–29, with further bibliography; Garms, "Boffrand," in Gallet and Garms, *Germain Boffrand*, 78–82.

22. Jestaz, *Voyage*, 203, cited by Reinhardt, *Bischöflichen Residenzen*, 124.

23. To Jossenay, 24 May 1725, Hd 135c, 1550; Marcel, no. 495, p. 135; Reinhardt, *Bischöflichen Residenzen*, 74.

24. Letter of 15 June 1724; Marcel, no. 481, p. 131.

25. To de Cotte, 29 September 1724, Hd 135c, 1550; Marcel, no. 487, p. 133; Reinhardt, *Bischöflichen Residenzen*, 75.

26. Letter of 30 August 1724, Hd 135c, 1550; Marcel, no. 485, pp. 132–33; Reinhardt, *Bischöflichen Residenzen*, 158.

27. Patron, designers, and building history are the subject of an exhaustive monograph by Ludmann, *Palais Rohan*; also see Reinhardt, *Bischöflichen Residenzen*, 81–108 and passim.

28. De Cotte was also consulted on the design of the new Hôtel du Grand-Doyenné (1721–31) and the remodeling of the choir of the Cathedral of Notre-Dame (1730): Marcel, nos. 556–82, pp. 150–58; Jean-Daniel Ludmann, "Nouveaux documents sur l'Hôtel du Doyenné du Grand Chapitre, actuel Evêché de Strasbourg," *Cahiers alsaciens d'archéologie, d'art, et d'histoire* 23 (1980): 73–88.

29. See chap. 7, n. 1. On Massol's career, see Ludmann, *Palais Rohan*, 1:37–40.

30. Former *évêché*: Va 67, 1214; Archives départementales du Bas-Rhin, Strasbourg, G 6541.4. Palais Rohan: first project, MS 1605, no. 100; second project, E 2085, fol. 517–518; third project, MS 1605, no. 102, MS 1606, nos. 9–10, MS 1040, no. 9; fourth project, Va 67, 1214, 1216, Va 435, 1215; fifth project, construction drawings by Massol, Archives municipales, Strasbourg B. 4914–4915, 4919, 4921; street elevation, Musée des arts décoratifs, Strasbourg.

31. Garms, "Boffrand," in Gallet and Garms, *Germain Boffrand*, 70–78, 104–5.

32. Beaulieu, *Robert Le Lorrain*, 64–71.

33. Ludmann, *Palais Rohan*, 1:10; Saint-Simon, *Mémoires*, 5:288–91, 7:81–86.

34. Jean-Daniel Ludmann, "Fêtes et cérémonies royales à Strasbourg sous l'ancien régime," *Saisons d'Alsace*, no. 75 (1981): 138–62.

CHAPTER ELEVEN

1. For the royal ceremonies, see Frère Jacques Doublet, *Histoire de l'Abbaye de S. Denys en France* (Paris: M. Soly, 1625); Dom Michel Félibien, *Histoire de l'Abbaye royale de Saint-Denys en France* (Paris: F. Leonard, 1706), book 8; Félicie d'Ayzac, *Histoire de l'Abbaye de Saint-Denis* (Paris: Imprimerie impériale, 1860–61), 1:105–43.

2. Hautecoeur, *Architecture classique*, 3:851.

3. Letter of Dom François Quenet to de Loo, 26 May 1699, H⁵ 3691; transcribed in part by Mayer-Long, "Abbaye de Saint-Denis," 68. I am indebted to Dom Yves Chaussy for informing me of the documents in the Archives nationales series H, LL, and the "Nécrologe de l'Abbaye de Saint-Denis" in the Bibliothèque nationale.

4. H⁵ 3691; Mayer-Long, "Abbaye de Saint-Denis," 67 n. 7, identifies Jacques Bayeux.

5. "Nécrologe de l'Abbaye," Ms. fr. 8600, 2:111–12, transcribed in part by Mayer-Long, "Abbaye de Saint-Denis," 69. For Quenet, see the "Nécrologe de l'Abbaye," 1:92.

6. Dom Edmond Martène, *Histoire de la Congrégation de Saint-Maur (1612–1747)*, 9 vols. (Paris: A. Picard, 1928–43), 7:213–14.

7. H⁵ 3691.

8. "Nécrologe de l'Abbaye," Ms. fr. 8600, 2:36; transcribed by Mayer-Long, "Abbaye de Saint-Denis," 67 n. 18.

9. "Nécrologe de l'Abbaye," Ms. fr. 8600, 2:112. A chronology accompanying the drawings in the Fonds de Cotte gives an outline of early construction (Va 93, t. 6, n.n.; predates 1735). Progress of the work is apparent from abbatial payment records (Archives communales de Saint-Denis, GG 193; Arch. nat. H⁵ 4273, L 834, LL 1223, cited by Mayer-Long, "Abbaye de Saint-Denis," 67, nn. 14, 17).

10. On the changes made to de Cotte's project after his death, see the "Instruction pour le Bâtiment de l'abbaye Royalle de St. Denis," and correspondence of J.-B. de Bourneuf (5 July 1737) and Gabriel (8 June 1740), in H⁵ 3691. Deconsecrated during the Revolution, the building became one of three Maisons d'Education de la Légion d'Honneur by Napoleonic decree 25 March 1809, the function it still serves. For the older literature, which should be consulted with caution: Paul Jarry and Paul Vitry, "La Maison de la Légion d'Honneur à Saint-Denis," *Procès-verbaux de la Commission municipale du vieux Paris* 29 (1926): 72–76; Gaston Brière and Paul Vitry, *L'Abbaye de Saint-Denis* (Paris: H. Laurens, 1948); Yvan Christ, "Ce Saint-Denis méconnu: Un chef d'oeuvre du classicism français," *Jardin des arts*, no. 134 (January 1966): 12–23.

11. On Benedictine monastic life and architecture, see Joan Evans, *Monastic Architecture in France from the Renaissance to the Revolution* (Cambridge: Cambridge University Press, 1964), chap. 1.

12. Félibien, *Saint-Denys*, 491–92.

13. "Nécrologe de l'Abbaye," Ms. fr. 8600, 2:111–12, transcribed by Mayer-Long, "Abbaye de Saint-Denis," 69.

14. Plans: Va 438, 66–68, 70–72, 74–77, Va 93, t. 6, 69, 78 (see also Va 416), N II Seine 214/1ᴬ⁻ᴮ–2 (illustrated in Michel Le Moël, *L'Abbaye royale de Saint-Denis, Maison d'Education de la Légion d'Honneur* [Paris: La Tourelle-Maloine, 1980], 23, fig. 28; Mayer-Long, "Abbaye de Saint-Denis," 62, fig. 4). I am grateful to Mme Conédic, surintendante, who allowed me free run of the building, and M. Pilliard, contre-maître of the restoration, who gave me blueprints of the abbey in its present state. For an accessible discussion of the old abbey, see Jules Formige, *L'Abbaye royale de Saint-Denis, recherches nouvelles* (Paris: Presses universitaires de France, 1960).

15. For a reconstruction of the rooms and their functions, see d'Ayzac, *Saint-Denis*, 2:351–446.

16. Jean Mariette, *L'architecture françoise*, 5 vols. (Paris: author, 1727–38), 1: pls. 20–26.

17. D'Ayzac, *Saint-Denis*, 2:422–23.

18. Braham and Smith, *François Mansart*, 1:62–64. See Pérouse de Montclos, *Architecture française*, 359–62, on the building type of the monastery.

19. Elevations: Va 93, t. 6, 80–91.

20. Illustrated in Mayer-Long, "Abbaye de Saint-Denis," 66, fig. 19. Two years after de Cotte's death, his successor Jacques V Gabriel rejected the concept of separate ceremonial and service courts. In new plans for the west wing, whose elevation derived from that of the east wing, he introduced a projecting entrance pavilion and octagonal vestibule on the main axis, and called for demolition of the Porte Suger (Va 438, n.n., dated 8 July 1737; N III Seine 215/1–2, 8, illustrated in Le Moël, *Saint-Denis*, 26, fig. 33). The wing was erected rapidly (Va 438, n.n., "Plan de l'Abbaye de Saint-Denis 1740"). A single-story hemicycle enclosing the courtyard followed, providing a service wing with a classical portal on axis. It went through several stages of design before construction: François Franque, 1774 (Va 438); Samson-Nicolas Le Noir Le Romain, 1775 (Va 438, N III Seine 166/1–2); Charles de Wailly, 1778 (N III Seine 167/1–5).

21. Sections: Ha 18, t. 1, n.n.; Va 438, 79.

22. A.-N. Dezallier d'Argenville, *Vies*, 1:358.

23. Daviler, *Cours d'architecture*, 1:236–44; Jean-Marie Pérouse de Montclos, *Architecture à la française: XVIᵉ, XVIIᵉ, XVIIIᵉ siècles* (Paris: Picard, 1982), 79–102.

24. Pierre Gouhier, *L'Abbaye aux Hommes, Saint-Etienne de Caen* (Paris: CEFAG, 1960). On de la Tremblaye and the Norman style, see Evans, *Monastic Architecture*, 33–36, 48.

25. Brice, *Ville de Paris*, 4:348.

26. Antoine-Nicolas Dezallier d'Argenville, *Voyage pittoresque des environs de Paris* (Paris: de Bure, 1757; Geneva: Minkoff, 1972), 349. See Laugier, *Essai*, 128, who preferred the style and craftsmanship of the medieval Abbey of Saint-Denis.

27. Evans, *Monastic Architecture*, 49.

EPILOGUE

1. *Correspondance des Directeurs de l'Académie de France à Rome*, Anatole de Montaiglon and Jules Guiffrey, eds., 17 vols. (Paris: 1887–1908), 9:9. De Cotte's poor health was mentioned in correspondence with Michel Robert Le Peletier des Forts in September 1730: Marcel, no. 349, p. 93.

2. Marcel, nos. 219–22, pp. 58–59, cited by Ludmann, *Palais Rohan*, 1:174 n. 71.

3. See chap. 11, n. 8.

4. *Mercure de France*, December 1734, p. 2944.

5. Brevet de P.ᵉʳ architecte du Roy en faveur du S. Gabriel, 20 December 1734 (O¹ 78, fol. 292–93); Christian Baulez, "Versailles," in Gallet and Bottineau, *Les Gabriel*, 31, 144–48; Pons, *Sculpteurs ornemanistes*, 141.

6. On the death of de Cotte, and the taking of his body from Passy to Saint-Germain-l'Auxerrois, see Herluison, *Actes d'état-civil*, 89; Jal, *Dictionnaire critique*, 1:434; Mar, "Robert de Cotte," 263.

7. *Mercure de France*, August 1735, pp. 1817–18.

8. For de Cotte's descendants and Jules-Robert's positions in the Bâtiments, see Herluison, *Actes d'état-civil*, 89; Brice, *Ville de Paris*, 1:171; Jal, *Dictionnaire critique*, 1:434;

Mar, "Robert de Cotte," 263–64; Lemonnier, *Procès-verbaux*, 4:xxxvii; Guiffrey, *Comptes*, 4:1236, 5:566; Montaiglon, *Académie de peinture*, 4:98–99. Numerous documents in the O¹ series attest to the activities of the younger de Cotte (Curzon Fichier, 50³/2).

9. Jules-Robert has been credited chiefly with erecting the façade of Saint-Roch, Paris (1736–38), largely in accordance with his father's designs; the north wing of the Bibliothèque du Roi, Paris (now Bibliothèque nationale; he succeeded his father there in 1735; work was completed after 1741; J.-L. Pascal reconstructed the wing in the late nineteenth century); and the Esplanade and Aisle de Cotte at the Hôtel des Invalides (1747–50): Blondel, *Architecture françoise*, 3:48; Brice, *Ville de Paris*, 1:ix; J.-P. Babelon, *Saint-Roch*, 31; A.-N. Dezallier d'Argenville, *Vies*, 419; Bauchal, *Dictionnaire biographique*, 159–60; J. Babelon, *Cabinet du Roi*, 12–13; Gallet, *Stately Mansions*, 152. For the Invalides, see chap. 6 above.

10. Letter of 15 February 1723 to the prince-bishop of Würzburg; von Freeden, *Quellen*, no. 1029, 1.2:785.

11. Blondel, *Maisons de plaisance*, 2:ii.

12. Blondel, *Architecture françoise*, 1: 235–36, 273–76, pls. 56, 112.

13. Jean-Marie Pérouse de Montclos, *Les Prix de Rome* (Paris: Berger-Levrault; Ecole nationale supérieure des beaux-arts, 1984), 33–37, 39–40, 43–44. Compare, respectively, de Cotte's designs for the Hôtel du Maine, Paris; Saint-Louis de Versailles; Schloss Poppelsdorf, Bonn; Porte de la Conférence, Paris.

14. On Blondel's criticisms see Antoine Picon, *Architectes et ingénieurs au siècle des Lumières* (Marseilles: Parenthèses, 1988), 65–74. But compare his overall assessment of de Cotte: "Son style d'Architecture ëtoit correct; il avoit une imagination brillante: après les Mansards & les Perrault, auxquels il ne faut comparer personne, il peut être regardé comme un des meilleurs Architectes François" (*Cours*, 6:480).

15. Nicolas Bricaire de la Dixmerie, *Les deux âges du goût et du génie français* (Paris: Lacombe, 1769): 159.

16. Kalnein and Levey, *Art and Architecture*, 238.

17. *Mercure de France*, August 1735, pp. 1817–18, cited by Kalnein and Levey, *Art and Architecture*, 259.

Selected Bibliography

Alberti, Leon Battista. *On the Art of Building in Ten Books*. Translated by Joseph Rykwert et al. Cambridge, Mass.: MIT Press, 1988.

L'art baroque à Lyon. Actes du colloque, 1972. Lyon: Institut d'histoire de l'art, 1975.

Babelon, Jean. *Le Cabinet du Roi ou le Salon Louis XV de la Bibliothèque nationale*. Paris and Brussels: G. Vanoest, 1927.

Babelon, Jean-Pierre. *L'église Saint-Roch à Paris*. Paris: J. Lanore, 1972.

Baillargeat, René, ed. *Les Invalides: Trois siècles d'histoire*. Paris: Musée de l'Armée, 1974.

Baillie, H. Murray. "Etiquette and the Planning of the State Apartments in Baroque Palaces." *Archeologia* 101 (1967): 169–99.

Bauchal, Charles. *Nouveau dictionnaire biographique et critique des architectes français*. Paris: André, 1887.

Berger, Robert W. *Antoine Le Pautre*. New York: New York University Press, 1969.

Blondel, Jacques-François. *L'architecture françoise*. 4 vols. Paris: C. A. Jombert, 1752–56; Levy, 1904.

———. *Cours d'architecture*. 9 vols. Paris: Desaint, 1771–77.

———. *De le distribution des maisons de plaisance*. 2 vols. Paris: C. A. Jombert, 1737–38; Farnborough: Gregg, 1967.

Blunt, Anthony. *Art and Architecture in France, 1500–1700*. 5th ed. Harmondsworth: Penguin, 1982.

Boislisle, Arthur Michel de. "Notices historiques sur la Place des Victoires et sur la Place de Vendôme." *Mémoires de la Société de l'histoire de Paris et de l'Ile-de-France* 15 (1888): 1–272.

Bottineau, Yves. "Antoine du Verger et l'Alcázar de Madrid en 1711." *GBA* 87 (1976): 178–80.

———. *L'art de cour dans l'Espagne de Philippe V, 1700–1746*. Bordeaux: Féret, 1961.

———. "Philip V and the Alcázar at Madrid." *Burlington Magazine* 98 (1956): 68–75.

Bourget, Pierre, and Georges Cattaui. *Jules Hardouin Mansart*. Paris: Vincent, Fréal, 1960.

Boyer, Jean. "Une oeuvre inédite de Robert de Cotte à Aix-en-Provence: L'Hôtel de Caumont." *BSHAF*, 1964, pp. 55–67.

Braham, Allan, and Peter Smith. *François Mansart*. 2 vols. London: Zwemmer, 1973.

Brice, Germain. *Description de la ville de Paris*. 9th ed. 4 vols. Paris: Libraires associés, 1752; Geneva: Droz, 1971.

Briseux, Charles-Etienne. *L'art de bâtir des maisons de campagne*. 2 vols. Paris: Prault père, 1743; J. B. Gibert, 1761; Farnborough: Gregg, 1966.

Catheu, Françoise de. "La décoration des Hôtels du Maine au faubourg Saint-Germain." *BSHAF*, 1945–46, pp. 100–108.

———. "Le développement du faubourg Saint-Germain du XVIᵉ au XVIIIᵉ siècles; 2. L'Hôtel d'Estrées." *Bulletin de la Société de l'histoire de Paris et de l'Ile-de-France* 82–83 (1955–56): 31–39.

Chenesseau, Georges. "Un essai d'alliance du 'gothique' et de 'l'antique' par un architecte orléanais au XVIIIᵉ siècle." *Bulletin de la Société archéologique et historique de l'Orléanais* 23 (1936): 132–44.

———. *Sainte-Croix d'Orléans*. 3 vols. Paris: Champion, 1921.

Cleary, Richard. *The Places Royales of Louis XIV and Louis XV.* New York: Architectural History Foundation, and Cambridge, Mass.: MIT Press, forthcoming.

Colombier, Pierre du. *L'architecture française en Allemagne au XVIIIᵉ siècle.* 2 vols. Paris: Presses universitaires de France, 1956.

———. "Deux projets de Robert de Cotte pour l'électeur de Cologne." *Archives alsaciennes d'histoire de l'art* 7 (1928): 97–108.

———. "La Résidence de Wurtzbourg: L'influence française sur l'architecture allemande au début du XVIIIᵉ siècle." *La Renaissance de l'art français,* August 1923, pp. 447–56.

Cordemoy, J. L. de. *Nouveau traité de toute l'architecture.* 2d ed. Paris: J. B. Coignard, 1714; Farnborough: Gregg, 1966.

Cotte, Fremin de. *Explication facile et briefve des cinq ordres d'architecture.* Paris: author, 1644.

Courteault, Paul. *La Place Royale de Bordeaux.* Paris: A. Colin, 1922.

Courtonne, Jean. *Traité de la perspective pratique.* Paris: J. Vincent, 1725.

Daviler, Augustin-Charles. *Cours d'architecture.* 2 vols. Paris: N. Langlois, 1691; J. Mariette, 1710 (Alexandre Le Blond, ed.); Pierre-Jean Mariette, 1756.

Delamare, Nicolas. *Traité de la police.* 4 vols. Vol. 4 completed by Anne-Louis Le Cler du Brillet. 2d ed. Paris: J. & P. Cot, 1719–38.

Deroy, Léon. "L'Hôtel de Belle-Isle et de Robert de Cotte." *Bulletin de la Société d'histoire et d'archéologie des XVIIᵉ et XVᵉ arrondissements,* no. 36 (1937): 77–87.

Dessins et souvenirs de Robert de Cotte, premier architecte du roi (1656–1735). Paris: Hôtel des Invalides, 1937.

Dezallier d'Argenville, Antoine-Joseph. *La théorie et la pratique du jardinage.* Paris: J. Mariette, 1713.

Dezallier d'Argenville, Antoine-Nicolas. *Vies des fameux architectes.* 2 vols. Paris: Debure l'aîné, 1787; Geneva: Minkoff, 1972.

———. *Voyage pittoresque de Paris.* Paris: De Bure, 1778.

Du Cerceau, Jacques Androuet. *Les trois livres d'architecture.* 3 vols. Paris: Prevost, 1559; Wechel, 1561; author, 1582; Ridgewood, N.J.: Gregg, 1965.

Le faubourg Saint-Germain: La rue de Grenelle. Paris: Galerie de la SEITA, 1980.

Le faubourg Saint-Germain: La rue de Varenne. Paris: Musée Rodin, 1981.

Le faubourg Saint-Germain: La rue Saint-Dominique. Paris: Musée Rodin, 1984.

Freeden, Max H. von. *Quellen zur Geschichte des Barocks in Franken unter dem Einfluss des Hauses Schönborn.* Vol. 1, part 2. Würzburg: Kommissionsverlag F. Schöningh, 1955.

Frémin, Michel de. *Mémoires critiques d'architecture.* Paris: Charles Saugrain, 1702; Farnborough: Gregg, 1967.

Gallet, Michel. *Stately Mansions: Eighteenth Century Paris Architecture.* New York: Praeger, 1972.

Gallet, Michel, and Yves Bottineau. *Les Gabriel.* Paris: Picard, 1982.

Gallet, Michel, and Jörg Garms. *Germain Boffrand, 1667–1754.* Paris and Lunéville: Délégation à l'action artistique de la ville de Paris, 1986.

Gallet-Guerne, Danielle, with Christian Baulez. *Versailles: Dessins d'architecture de la direction générale des Bâtiments du roi.* Vol. 1, *Le château, les jardins, le parc, Trianon.* Paris: Archives nationales, 1983.

Gardes, Gilbert. "La décoration de la Place Royale de Louis le Grand (Place Bellecour) à Lyon, 1686–1793." *Bulletin des musées et monuments lyonnais* 5 (1974–75), nos. 1–2, pp. 185–207, 219–29, nos. 3–4, pp. 37–97, 261–90.

Garms, Jörg. "Der Grundriss der Malgrange I von Boffrand." *Wiener Jahrbuch für Kunstgeschichte* 22 (1969): 184–88.

Glasner, Hubert, ed. *Kurfürst Max Emanuel: Bayern und Europa um 1700.* 2 vols. Munich: Schloss Schleissheim, 1976.

Gloton, Jean-Jacques. *Renaissance et baroque à Aix-en-Provence.* 2 vols. Rome: Ecole française de Rome, 1979.

Guiffrey, Jules. *Comptes des bâtiments du roi sous le règne de Louis XIV, 1664–1715.* 5 vols. Paris: Imprimerie nationale, 1881–1901.

———. *Le duc d'Antin et Louis XIV. Rapports sur l'administration des Bâtiments, annotés par le roi.* Paris: Académie des bibliophïles, 1869.

Guillemet, Roger. *Essai sur la surintendance des Bâtiments du roi sous le règne de Louis XIV (1662–1715).* Paris: A. Rousseau, 1912.

Hardouin-Mansart et son école. Paris: Bibliothèque nationale, 1946.

Hautecoeur, Louis. *Histoire de l'architecture classique en France.* Vols. 1–3. Paris: Picard, 1943–50. Rev. ed. of vol. 1, 1963–66.

Hauttmann, Max. "Die Entwürfe Robert de Cottes für Schloss Schleissheim." *Münchner Jahrbuch* 6 (1911): 256–76.

Hébert, Monique, and Jacques Thirion. *Catalogue général des cartes, plans et dessins d'architecture.* Vol. 1. *Serie N. Paris et le département de la Seine.* Paris: Imprimerie national, 1958.

Herluisson, Henri. *Actes d'état-civil d'artistes français.* Orléans: author, 1873; Geneva: Slatkine, 1972.

Huillet d'Istria, Madeleine. "L'art de François d'Orbay révélé par la Cathédrale de Montauban." *XVIIᵉ siècle* 72 (1966): 1–69.

Iberville-Moreau, José-Luc d'. "Robert de Cotte: His Career as an Architect and the Organisation of the Service des Bâtiments." Ph.D. diss., University of London, 1972.

Jal, Augustin. *Dictionnaire critique de biographie et d'histoire.* 2 vols. Paris: H. Plon, 1867.

Jestaz, Bertrand. "Jules Hardouin-Mansart et l'église des Invalides." *GBA* 66 (1965): 59–74.

———. "Jules Hardouin-Mansart: L'oeuvre personelle, les méthodes de travail et les collaborateurs." *Positions des thèses.* Ecole des chartes, 1962, pp. 67–72.

———. "Le Trianon de Marbre ou Louis XIV architecte." *GBA* 74 (1969): 259–86.

———. *Le voyage d'Italie de Robert de Cotte.* Paris: E. de Boccard, 1966.

Jugie-Bertrac, Sophie. "Le duc d'Antin, directeur-général des Bâtiments du roi (1708–1736)." *Positions des thèses,* Ecole des chartes, 1986, pp. 93–100.

Kalnein, Wend Graf. *Das kurfürstliche Schloss Clemensruhe in Poppelsdorf.* Düsseldorf: Schwann, 1956.

Kalnein, Wend Graf, and Michael Levey. *Art and Architecture of the Eighteenth Century in France.* Harmondsworth: Penguin, 1972.

Kimball, Fiske. *The Creation of the Rococo.* 2d ed. New York: W. W. Norton, 1964.

Laprade, Albert. *François d'Orbay, architecte de Louis XIV.* Paris: Vincent, Fréal, 1960.

Le Clerc, Sébastien. *Traité d'architecture.* Paris: P. Giffart, 1714.

Lefèvre, Antoine Martial. *Description des curiosités des églises de Paris.* Paris: C. P. Gueffier, 1759.

Lejeaux, Jeanne. "Robert de Cotte et la direction de l'Académie d'architecture." *BSHAF,* 1938, pp. 22–32.

Lemonnier, Henry, ed. *Procès-verbaux de l'Académie royale d'architecture, 1671–1793.* 10 vols. Paris: Société de l'histoire de l'art français, 1911–29.

Lübbecke, Fried. *Das Palais Thurn und Taxis in Frankfurt am Main.* Frankfurt am Main: W. Kramer, 1955.

Lucas, Charles. "Les de Cotte ou Coste." In *La grande encyclopédie,* vol. 13, part 2, 18–19. 31 vols. Paris: H. Lamirault, 1891.

Ludmann, Jean-Daniel. *Le Palais Rohan de Strasbourg.* 2 vols. Strasbourg: Dernières nouvelles, 1979–80.

Ludmann, Jean-Daniel, and Bruno Pons. "Nouveaux documents sur la galerie de l'Hôtel de Toulouse." *BSHAF,* 1981, pp. 115–28.

Magny, Françoise, ed. *Le faubourg Saint-Germain: Palais Bourbon, sa place.* Paris: Institut néerlandais, 1987.

———, ed. *Le faubourg Saint-Germain: Rue de l'Université.* Paris: Institut néerlandais, 1987.

Mar, Léopold. "Robert de Cotte et son fils, biographie locale." *Bulletin de la Société historique d'Auteuil et de Passy* 4 (1901–3): 260–64.

Marcel, Pierre. *Inventaire des papiers manuscrits du*

cabinet de Robert de Cotte. Paris: Champion, 1906.

———. "Robert de Cotte (1656–1735)." *L'architecte,* 2d year (1907): 29–33.

Marie, Alfred. "Le Château de Compiègne avant sa transformation par Gabriel." *Bulletin de la Société historique de Compiègne* 22 (1944): 67–73.

———. "L'église Saint-Louis de Versailles." *Histoire et archéologie dans les Yveslines,* no. 5 (1979): 17–26.

Marie, Alfred, and Jeanne Marie. *Mansart à Versailles.* 2 vols. Paris: J. Fréal, 1972.

———. *Versailles au temps de Louis XIV. IIIᵉ partie: Mansart et Robert de Cotte.* Paris: Imprimerie nationale, 1976.

———. *Versailles au temps de Louis XV, 1715–1745.* Paris: Imprimerie nationale, 1984.

Mayer-Long, Jannie. "Les projets de Robert de Cotte pour les bâtiments conventuels de l'Abbaye de Saint-Denis." *BSHAF,* 1983, pp. 59–69.

Mignot, Claude. "Petit lexique de l'hôtel parisien," *XVIIᵉ siècle* 41, no. 162 (1989): 101–9.

———. "De la cuisine à la salle à manger, ou de quelques détours de l'art de la distribution." *XVIIᵉ siècle* 41, no. 162 (1989): 17–35.

Montaiglon, Anatole de. *Procès-verbaux de l'Académie royale de peinture et de sculpture, 1648–1793.* 11 vols. Paris: Nobele, 1875–92.

Neuman, Robert. "Robert de Cotte and the Baroque Ecclesiastical Façade in France." *JSAH* 44 (1985): 250–65.

———. "Robert de Cotte, Architect of the Late Baroque." Ph.D. diss., University of Michigan, 1978.

———. "French Domestic Architecture in the Early Eighteenth Century: The Town Houses of Robert de Cotte." *JSAH* 39 (1980): 128–44.

———. "Projects by Robert de Cotte for the Church of Saint-Louis de Versailles in the Parc-aux-Cerfs," *Eighteenth-Century Life* 17 (1993): 182–93.

———. "Watteau's *L'enseigne de Gersaint* and Baroque Emblematic Tradition." *GBA* 104 (1984): 153–64.

Oglevee, John Finley, ed. *Letters of the Archbishop-Elector Joseph Clemens of Cologne to Robert de Cotte (1712–1720).* Bowling Green, Ohio: author, 1956.

Pérouse de Montclos, Jean-Marie. *Histoire de l'architecture française: De la Renaissance à la Révolution.* Paris: Mengès, 1989.

Piganiol de la Force, Jean Aymer. *Description historique de la ville de Paris.* 8 vols. Paris: Legras, 1742; 10 vols. Paris: Deprez, 1765.

Pingeron, Jean-Claude. *Vies des architectes anciens et modernes.* 2 vols. Paris: Jombert, 1771; Geneva: Minkoff, 1973.

Pons, Bruno. *De Paris à Versailles 1699–1736: Les sculpteurs ornemanistes parisiens et l'art décoratif des Bâtiments du roi.* Strasbourg: Universités de Strasbourg, 1986.

Pons, Bruno, and Anne Forray-Carlier, eds. *Le faubourg Saint-Germain: La rue de Bac.* Paris: Délégation à l'action artistique de la ville de Paris, 1990.

Ponsonailhe, Charles. "La Maison de Robert de Cotte." *Réunion des sociétés des beaux-arts des départements* 25 (1901): 508–16.

Rauch-Elkan, Annelise. "Acht Pläne und ein Baumémoire Robert de Cottes für Schloss Tilbourg in Brabant." *Brabantia,* 2 February 1958, pp. 43–52.

Réau, Louis. *L'art français sur le Rhin au XVIIIᵉ siècle.* Paris: H. Champion, 1922.

———. *L'Europe française au siècle des Lumières.* Paris: Michel, 1938.

———. *Histoire de l'expansion de l'art français.* 4 vols. Paris: H. Laurens, 1924–33.

———. "Robert de Cotte." In *Les architectes célèbres,* 1:98–99, 2:273. Edited by Pierre Francastel. 2 vols. Paris: L. Mazenod, 1958–59.

Reinhardt, Ursula. *Die bischöflichen Residenzen von Châlons-sur-Marne, Verdun und Strasbourg.* Basel: F. Reinhardt, 1972.

Renard, Edmund. "Die Bauten der Kurfürsten Joseph Clemens und Clemens August von Köln" (part 1). *Bonner Jahrbücher* 99 (1896): 164–240.

Reuterswärd, Patrik. *The Two Churches of the Hôtel des Invalides*. Stockholm: Nationalmuseum, 1965.

Roland Le Virloys, Charles-François. *Dictionnaire d'architecture civile*. 3 vols. Paris: Libraires associés, 1770–71.

La rue de Lille, l'Hôtel de Salm. Paris: Institut néerlandais and Musée national de la Légion d'honneur, 1983.

Sacy, Jacques-Silvestre de. "Robert de Cotte." In *Dictionnaire de biographie française*, 9:834–36. 17 vols. Paris: Letouzey, 1961.

Saint-Simon, Louis de Rouvroy, duc de. *Mémoires*. Edited by Arthur de Boislisle. 41 vols. Paris: Hachette, 1879–1930.

Sauval, Henri. *Histoire et recherches des antiquités de la ville de Paris*. 3 vols. Paris: C. Moette, 1724; Geneva: Minkoff, 1974.

Serlio, Sebastiano. *On Domestic Architecture: The Sixth Book*. Introduction by Myra Nan Rosenfeld. New York: Architectural History Foundation, and Cambridge, Mass.: MIT Press, 1978.

———. *I sette libri dell'architettura*. Venice: Francesco de' Franceschi Senese, 1584; Sala Bolognese: A. Forni, 1987.

Souchal, François. *French Sculptors of the Seventeenth and Eighteenth Centuries: The Reign of Louis XIV*. 3 vols. Oxford: Cassirer, 1977–87.

———. "Le portail de l'église des Capucines à Paris." *GBA* 73 (1969): 193–206.

Strandberg, Runar. "Dessins et documents inédits concernant les constructions de Jean-Baptiste Colbert, marquis de Torcy, pour son hôtel de Paris et ses Châteaux de Croissy, Sablé et Bois-Dauphin." *GBA* 99 (1982): 130–46.

———. "Le Château de Champs." *GBA* 61 (1963): 81–100.

———. "Jean-Baptiste Bullet de Chamblain, architecte du roi (1665–1726)." *BSHAF*, 1962, pp. 193–255.

Szambien, Werner. *Symétrie, goût, caractère: Théorie et terminologie à l'âge classique 1550–1800*. Paris: Picard, 1986.

Tadgell, Christopher. *Ange-Jacques Gabriel*. London: Zwemmer, 1978.

Thiveaud-Le Hénand, Françoise. "Le reconstruction du Château de Compiègne au XVIIIᵉ siècle." *Positions des thèses*. Ecole des chartes, 1970, pp. 205–14.

Vloberg, Maurice. *Notre-Dame de Paris et le voeu de Louis XIII*. Paris: author, 1926.

Walton, Guy. *Louis XIV's Versailles*. Chicago: University of Chicago Press, 1986.

Weigert, Roger-Armand, and Carl Hernmarck. *Les relations artistiques entre la France et la Suède, 1693–1718*. Stockholm: Egnellska Boktryckeriet, 1964.

Weirich, Adrien. "L'Hôtel de Hanau, contribution à l'histoire de ses origines." *Cahiers alsaciens d'archéologie, d'art et d'histoire* 11 (1967): 319–32.

Wollbrett, Alphonse, ed. *Le Château de Saverne*. Saverne: Société d'histoire et d'archéologie de Saverne et environs, 1969.

Illustration Acknowledgments

Alinari/Art Resource, N.Y., 21
Archives Nationales, 13, 143
Avery Library of Columbia University, 33, 55
Bibliothèque de l'Institut, 113, 114, 159
Phot. Bibl. Nat. Paris, 4, 5, 9, 14, 15, 17, 18, 19,
    20, 22, 23, 24, 25, 26, 27, 28, 29, 30, 31, 32,
    34, 35, 36, 37, 38, 39, 40, 41, 42, 43, 44, 45,
    47, 48, 49, 50, 51, 52, 53, 54, 58, 59, 60, 61,
    62, 63, 64, 65, 66, 67, 69, 70, 71, 72, 73, 74,
    75, 76, 77, 78, 79, 80, 81, 82, 83, 84, 85, 86,
    87, 89, 90, 91, 92, 94, 95, 96, 97, 98, 99, 100,
    101, 102, 103, 104, 105, 106, 107, 108, 109,
    110, 111, 115, 116, 117, 118, 119, 120, 123,
    126, 127, 128, 129, 130, 131, 132, 133, 134,
    135, 136, 137, 138, 139, 140, 141, 142, 144,
    145, 146, 147, 148, 149, 150, 151, 152, 153,
    154, 155, 156, 157, 158, 161, 162, 163, 165,
    166, 168, 169, 171, 176, 177, 178, 179, 180,
    181, 183, 185
Sheila S. Blair, 167
Civici musei veneziani d'arte e di storia, 16
The Conway Library of the Courtauld Institute
of Art, 66
Fürst Thurn und Taxis Zentralarchiv, Museale
    Gegenstände, Foto: Atelier Wagmüller, Re-
    gensburg, 121
The Frick Collection, New York, 1
Girardon/Art Resource, N.Y., 3
Landeskonservator Rheinland, 56
Library of Congress, 11
Marburg/Art Resource, N.Y., 124, 125
Musée Carnavalet, Paris (Cliché: Musées de la
    ville de Paris © by ARS, New York/SPADEM,
    Paris 1992), 88
Robert Neuman, 6, 7, 8, 10, 12, 160, 164, 175,
    182, 184, 186
Presseamt Stadt Bonn, F. Schulz, 57
Réunion des musées nationaux, 2
Roger-Viollet, 93
Ute Schendel, 122, 170, 172, 173, 174
Staatliche Museen zu Berlin, Kunstbibliotek, 46
Suzanne Sutton, 112
Widener Library, Harvard University, 68

Index

Page references to illustrations are printed in boldface type.